Islamic Architecture Today and Tomorrow

Islamic Architecture Today and Tomorrow
(Re)defining the Field

Edited by Mohammad Gharipour and Daniel E. Coslett

Bristol, UK / Chicago, USA

Islamic Architecture Today and Tomorrow: (Re)defining the Field is the eighth book in the Critical Studies in Architecture of the Middle East series. The series is edited by Mohammad Gharipour (Morgan State University, Baltimore) and Christiane Gruber (University of Michigan, Ann Arbor). Critical Studies in Architecture of the Middle East is devoted to the most recent scholarship concerning historic and contemporary architecture, landscape and urban design of the Middle East and of regions shaped by diasporic communities more globally. We invite interdisciplinary studies from diverse perspectives that address the visual characteristics of the built environment, ranging from architectural case studies to urban analysis.

First published in the UK in 2022 by
Intellect, The Mill, Parnall Road, Fishponds, Bristol, BS16 3JG, UK

First published in the USA in 2022 by
Intellect, The University of Chicago Press, 1427 E. 60th Street,
Chicago, IL 60637, USA

Copyright © 2022 Intellect Ltd

All rights reserved. No part of this publication may be reproduced, stored in a retrieval system or transmitted, in any form or by any means, electronic, mechanical, photocopying, recording or otherwise, without written permission.

A catalogue record for this book is available from the British Library.

Cover designer: Aleksandra Szumlas
Cover image: Angelo Candalepas and Associates Pty Limited, The Mosque for the Australian Islamic Mission © Brett Boardman Photography.
Production editor: Laura Christopher
Series: Critical Studies in Architecture of the Middle East
Series editors: Mohammad Gharipour and Christiane Gruber
Typesetting: NewgenKnowledge Works

Print ISBN: 978-1-78938-604-2
ePDF ISBN: 978-1-78938-605-9
ePUB ISBN: 978-1-78938-606-6
Series ISSN: 2059- 3562

Printed and bound by CPI Group (UK) Ltd, Croydon, CR0 4YY

To the designers, planners, builders, artisans, conservators, historians, curators, and teachers whose efforts have generated, sustained, and made known the built environments of the Islamic world for past, present, and future generations.

To His Highness the Aga Khan, for his generosity and inspiring dedication to the field of Islamic architecture.

Contents

List of Figures		xi
Acknowledgements		xvii
Introduction.	The Changed and Changing Field of 'Islamic Architecture' *Mohammad Gharipour and Daniel E. Coslett*	1

Part 1. Research and Scholarship   9

Chapter 1.	The Study of Islamic Architecture: Reflections on an Expanding Field *Sheila S. Blair and Jonathan M. Bloom*	11
Chapter 2.	Widening the Horizons for the Study of Islamic Architecture *Bernard O'Kane*	29
Chapter 3.	Modern Architecture and Colonialism in the Islamic World *Brian L. McLaren*	43

Part 2. Scope and Scale   55

Chapter 4.	From Garden to Landscape: Lessons from the Taj and the Alhambra *D. Fairchild Ruggles*	57
Chapter 5.	Invisible Geographies in the Study of Islamic Architecture *Abidin Kusno*	69
Chapter 6.	Silencing Palestinian Architectural History in Israel: Reflections on Scholarship and Activism *Alona Nitzan-Shiftan*	79

| Chapter 7. | Islamic Architecture in the Americas: Advancing a Transregional and Hemispheric Approach
Caroline 'Olivia' M. Wolf | 93 |

Part 3. Historiography and Context   113

Chapter 8.	Cultural Encounters, Local Practice, and Historical Process in the Ancient Middle East *Dell Upton*	115
Chapter 9.	Neo-Eurocentrism and Science: Implications for the Historiography of Islamic Art and Architecture *Samer Akkach*	125
Chapter 10.	Carving an Epistemological Space for Southeast Asia: Historiographical and Critical Engagements *Imran bin Tajudeen*	141

Part 4. Fieldwork and Documentation   159

Chapter 11.	A Field without Fieldwork: Sustaining the Study of Islamic Architecture in the Twenty-First Century *Nancy Um*	161
Chapter 12.	Architectural History in Turkey: Between Fieldwork and Archival Research *Patricia Blessing*	175
Chapter 13.	Documenting Islamic Architecture: Objectives and Outcomes in a Time of War *Sharon C. Smith*	189

Part 5. Education and Pedagogy   203

| Chapter 14. | Reorienting Perspectives: Why I Do Not Teach a Course Titled 'Islamic Architecture'
Jelena Bogdanović | 205 |
| Chapter 15. | Decolonizing Architectural Knowledge: Situating Middle Eastern Pedagogies in a Globalizing World
Ashraf M. Salama | 221 |

| Chapter 16. | Educating the Public about Islamic Art and Architecture through Museums
Sheila R. Canby | 233 |

Part 6. Curation and Publication — 245

Chapter 17.	Displaying Islamic Arts in Global Cities *Jorge Correia*	247
Chapter 18.	Curating the 'Islamic': The Personal and the Political *Leslee Katrina Michelsen*	259
Chapter 19.	Islamic Architecture on the Move: Publishing Architectural History in the Digital Age *Nancy Micklewright*	271
Chapter 20.	Illustrating Islamic Architecture: On Visual Presentation and Scholarship *Lorenz Korn*	285

Part 7. Globalization and Change — 309

Chapter 21.	Uneven Geographies and Neoliberal Urban Transformation in Arab Cities *Rami F. Daher*	311
Chapter 22.	Affection for *Nouvel* Architecture: On Contemporary (Islamic) Architecture and Affect *Şebnem Yücel*	325
Chapter 23.	The 'Islamic-Modern' Project in this Age of Uncertainty *Vikramaditya Prakash*	339

Part 8. Experience and Use — 353

| Chapter 24. | The Tourist Gaze, Visiting Mosques, and the Folds of Architecture
Elif Kalaycıoğlu and Waleed Hazbun | 355 |
| Chapter 25. | Decolonizing the Conservation of Islamic Built Heritage in Egypt
Hossam Mahdy | 371 |

Chapter 26.	(Dis)placement and Placemaking: Reconsidering Islamic Architecture through Refugee Agency *Kıvanç Kılınç and Bülent Batuman*	387

Part 9. Practice and Profession — 399

Chapter 27.	'Islamic Architecture' and the Profession *Nasser Rabbat*	401
Chapter 28.	A Trinity of Values in Architecture for Muslim Societies *Rasem Badran*	409
Chapter 29.	Relevance, Tradition, and Practice in Islamic Architecture *Kamil Khan Mumtaz*	421
Chapter 30.	Architectural Competitions: Creating Dialogues and Promoting Excellence *Hasan-Uddin Khan*	435

Contributor Biographies	453
Index	461

Figures

1.1:	An ice-house in Abarquh, Iran, photographed in 1999.	15
1.2:	An interior view of the Dome of the Rock, Jerusalem, photographed in 1977.	18
1.3:	The entrance to the Qing-period Hongshuiquan Mosque on the upper reaches of the Yellow River in Qinghai, China, photographed in 2014.	19
1.4:	I. M. Pei's Museum of Islamic Art, Doha (opened 2008), photographed in 2008.	20
1.5:	An isometric reconstruction of the rock-cut ruins at Viar, Iran, drawn in 2009.	21
1.6:	The Qasba of the Wadayas, Rabat, photographed in 1993.	23
2.1:	Petronas Towers, Kuala Lumpur, and Burj Khalifa, Dubai.	33
2.2:	Abraj al-Bait, Mecca.	35
2.3:	Anonymous tomb before and after restoration at Shah-i Zinda, Samarqand.	36
2.4:	Üç Şerefeli Mosque, Edirne, before and after restoration.	37
3.1:	Mosque of Ahmad al-Karamanli, Tripoli, 1736-1737. View of tile restoration.	50
3.2:	Florestano Di Fausto, Artisanal Quarter, Suq al Mushir, Tripoli, 1935. View of courtyard.	51
4.1:	Taj Mahal, 1632-1643, Agra.	61
4.2:	Pasha 'Abd al-Kari (also known as the Dar al-Aman), 1860, Fez.	61
4.3:	Taj Mahal plan.	62
4.4:	Mahtab Bagh, 1632-1643, Agra.	64
4.5:	Patio de la Acequia at the Generalife Palace, 1302-1308, Granada.	66
5.1:	A *musholla* in the middle of a *kampung* near housing complexes in West Jakarta.	72
5.2:	A plan for building a *musholla* in Jakarta.	73
6.1:	General view of Nazareth, 1948.	82
6.2:	'White City' advertisement for Tel Aviv Municipality (2004).	84
6.3:	View toward the Anis Srouji Family Villa.	85
6.4:	Garden Mansions – general view (rendering).	86
6.5:	Housing for refugees by Eylon Meromi.	87
7.1:	Example of an *artesonado* ceiling, Palacio de Dávalos, Guadalajara, La Mancha, Spain.	97
7.2:	New York City Central Synagogue, New York.	99
7.3:	Palacete Rosa, Ipiranga, São Paulo.	101
7.4:	Brazil Mosque, São Paulo.	104
7.5:	Islamic Center of Washington, Washington, DC.	106

8.1:	Temple of Bel (*c.*first–second centuries CE), Palmyra (Tadmor), Syria. Reconstructed portion of *peribolos* wall (sacred enclosure) with interior colonnade.	118
8.2:	Temple of Bel. Note *merlon*s (stepped pyramidal ornaments) above colonnade at right.	119
8.3:	Temple of Bel. Reassembled corner *merlon* (stepped pyramidal ornament).	120
8.4:	Temple of Bel. *Cella* (inner chamber) and south *thalamus* (raised, stage-like shrine).	121
9.1:	The Auburn Gallipoli Mosque, Sydney, Australia.	134
9.2:	The Australia Islamic Centre and Mosque, Newport, Victoria, Australia, by Pritzker Prize-winning Australian architect Glenn Murcutt with Hakan Elevli Associates (2016).	135
10.1:	The Telok Manok Mosque, at Narathiwat, in the former Malay state of Patani in today's southern Thailand.	146
10.2:	Remaining structures and ventilation towers connected to underwater tunnels at the ruins of Taman Sari, the eighteenth-century royal water gardens of Yogyakarta, Central Java, Indonesia.	147
10.3:	The third gateway along the *qibla* axis of Kudus Mosque, in Central Java, Indonesia.	148
10.4:	The 65-metre-high Limo Kaum Mosque in the Minangkabau highlands of West Sumatra, Indonesia.	149
10.5:	One of numerous stone roundels at Mantingan Mosque, north coast Central Java, Indonesia.	152
10.6:	Mosque of Kampung Hulu, Melaka, Malaysia.	153
11.1:	View of Mocha, with Bayt Sidi Nunu in the foreground and the Mosque of al-Shadhili in the background, in 1996.	164
11.2:	View of Mocha, screenshot from Google Earth VR, 2019.	165
11.3:	Dissertations related to Islamic art from 1992 to 2018, drawn from CAA's dissertation rosters.	169
11.4:	Dissertations related to Islamic art by institution from 1992 to 2018, drawn from CAA's dissertation rosters.	170
12.1:	Migrating storks in Sarıyer, in the northern section of Istanbul's European side, photographed in March 2015.	179
12.2:	The interior of the Mahmud Pasha Hammam (1462), Istanbul, photographed in 2016.	181
12.3:	Stencilled graffiti celebrating the election of Istanbul mayor Ekrem İmamoğlu in June 2019, photographed in Istanbul in July 2019.	182
12.4:	The Gök Medrese (1271) in Sivas, photographed in 2008.	183
13.1:	The original login page for Archnet, *c.*2003.	193
13.2:	The Archnet home page, *c.*2014.	194
13.3:	The triumphal arch in Palmyra, *c.*1980s–1990s.	195
13.4:	Palmyra's triumphal arch recreated in Trafalgar Square, London, in 2016.	196
13.5:	A street in Aleppo, Syria, 2016.	198

Figures

13.6:	The work of András Riedlmayer presented as a permanent collection on Archnet.	199
14.1:	Zlatko Ugljen's Šerefudin White Mosque in Visoko, Bosnia and Herzegovina, 1969-1979.	208
14.2:	Adrian Smith and Bill Baker's Burj Khalifa (known as the Burj Dubai until 2010) in Dubai, 2010.	211
14.3:	*Mashrabiya 2.0-3D-Printed Ceramic Evaporative Façade*, by Leslie Forehand with Shelby Doyle, Erin Hunt, and Nick Senske.	213
14.4:	I. M. Pei's Museum of Islamic Art in Doha, 2008, and the Mosque of Ibn Tulun in Cairo, 879 and later.	215
15.1:	A representation of the inherited models of architectural education.	225
16.1:	Bowl with Arabic Inscription. Iran, Nishapur, from the tenth century.	238
16.2:	View of two *mashrabiya* screens in gallery 453 at the Metropolitan Museum of Art, New York.	239
17.1:	A street in Dubai, photographed in 2015.	251
17.2:	John Beasley Greene, view of Houses in Cairo, 1854-1855.	252
17.3:	The Museum of Islamic Art in Doha, photographed in 2017.	253
18.1:	The Shangri La Museum of Islamic Art, Culture & Design in Honolulu, Hawai'i.	262
18.2:	Anne Samat, *Varada, The Goddess of Love*, and *Abhaya*, 2017, yarns, PVC, paper, and plastic.	263
18.3:	Bahia Shehab, *My People*, 2018, acrylic and latex on wood.	268
19.1:	Felix Bonfils, *Damascus Fountain*, c.1850.	274
19.2:	The Istanbul panoramas as presented in *JSAH*.	276
19.3:	Zhenrou Zhou's Pagoda SketchUp model animation that illustrates the alignment of the structure's interiors and its icons, in addition to the path one takes in ascending the tower.	278
19.4:	Screenshot image of fieldwork underway in an Islamic cemetery by members of the Maldives Heritage Survey team.	280
20.1:	The Maydan and palace area in Isfahan in bird's-eye view.	289
20.2:	View of the canal with bridges in Cairo and plans of various mosques.	290
20.3:	The Madrasa of Shah Sultan Husayn at Isfahan.	292
20.4:	The upper section of the façade of the Mausoleum of Mu'mina Khatun in Nakhchivan, Azerbaijan.	294
20.5:	The Mausoleum of Yusuf ibn Kuthayr and the Mausoleum of Mu'mina Khatun Khatun in Nakhchivan, Azerbaijan.	295
20.6:	The dome hall and minaret of the Great Mosque at Barsiyan.	297
20.7:	The layout of a double page in the *Survey of Persian Art*, depicting the Gunbad-i Qabus.	298
20.8:	Reconstruction of the dome hall of the Great Mosque of Burujird, in its supposed original appearance as a 'mosquée kiosque', according to the ideas of André Godard.	300
20.9:	Schematic drawings illustrating 'the concept of dome'.	301

20.10:	Details of masonry and schematic views of exterior corners of the south dome of the Great (Friday) Mosque of Isfahan.	302
20.11:	North dome of the Great (Friday) Mosque of Isfahan.	303
20.12:	The *qibla* iwan and dome hall of the Great Mosque of Burujird.	304
21.1:	The Abdali development under construction in Amman, Jordan (2015).	315
21.2:	*Living Well*, by Emad Hajjaj (known as Abu Mahjoub).	316
21.3:	Neoliberal developments in Amman, Jordan (2013).	317
22.1:	Concept renderings of Jean Nouvel's resort at Sharaan, Saudi Arabia.	332
23.1:	Exterior views of the Mughal Sheraton Hotel, Agra, by ARCOP Design Group/ Ramesh Khosla, Ranjit Sabikhi, Ajoy Choudhury, and Ray Affleck (1976).	344
23.2:	The façade of Jean Nouvel's Institut du monde arabe in Paris, France (1987).	346
23.3:	Paul Klee's *Twittering Machine* (1922).	349
23.4:	Arata Isozaki, integration of Tange's and Kahn's proposals, Abbas Abad Master Plan, Tehran (1974).	351
24.1:	Photographs of the al-Azhar Mosque courtyard, Cairo, 1867, by Maison Bonfils and the interior of the Grand Mosque, Bursa (now Turkey), 1894, by Sébah and Joaillier.	361
24.2:	Visitors in the garden of the courtyard of La Grande Mosquée de Paris, Paris.	363
24.3:	People gather to perform Friday prayer in Hagia Sophia, Istanbul, on July 24, 2020.	367
25.1:	Mahmoud Mukhtar, *Nahdet Masr* (The Renaissance of Egypt), Cairo, 1928.	376
25.2:	Sabil-Kuttab Nafisa al-Bayda, Cairo.	378
25.3:	The al-Azhar Mosque, Cairo.	380
25.4:	The Ibn Tulun Mosque, Cairo.	383
26.1:	Refugee shelter (Tempohome) on Alte Jakobstraße in Kreuzberg, Berlin (photographed July 29, 2021).	391
26.2:	An apartment building in Ayn-el-Mreisseh, Beirut, inhabited by refugees and migrant workers (2019).	393
27.1:	The Museum of Islamic Art, Doha, by I. M. Pei, 2008, seen from the entrance bridge.	405
28.1:	Justice Palace and Grand Mosque, Riyadh, by Rasem Badran/Dar Al-Omran (1985-1992).	414
28.2:	Interior of the Grand Mosque, Riyadh, by Rasem Badran/Dar Al-Omran (1985-1992).	415
28.3:	Bujairi Quarter, Diriyah, Saudi Arabia, by Rasem Badran/Dar Al-Omran (2000-2015).	416
28.4:	Bujairi Quarter, Diriyah, Saudi Arabia, by Rasem Badran/Dar Al-Omran (2000-2015).	417
28.5:	King Abdul Aziz Historical Center, Riyadh, by Rasem Badran/Dar Al-Omran (1996-1999).	418
28.6:	King Abdul Aziz Historical Center, Riyadh, by Rasem Badran/Dar Al-Omran (1996-1999).	419

Figures

29.1:	Pak Wigah Mosque, Kiranwala Sayidan, near Mandi Bahauddin, Gujrat, by Kamil Khan Mumtaz Architects.	428
29.2:	Tomb of Baba Hassan Deen and Hafiz Iqbal, Gujjarpura, near the Tomb of Madhu Lal Hussain and the Shalamar Garden, Lahore, by Kamil Khan Mumtaz Architects, 2000–2009.	429
29.3:	Tomb of Baba Hassan Deen and Hafiz Iqbal, Gujjarpura, near the Tomb of Madhu Lal Hussain and the Shalamar Garden, Lahore, by Kamil Khan Mumtaz Architects, 2000–2009.	430
29.4:	Sally Town Mosque, Harbanspura Road, Lahore, by Kamil Khan Mumtaz Architects, 2006.	432
29.5:	Sally Town Mosque, Harbanspura Road, Lahore, by Kamil Khan Mumtaz Architects, 2006.	433
30.1:	The Bibliotheca Alexandrina, Alexandria, by Snøhetta (2001).	440
30.2:	The mausoleum or *mazaar* of Pakistan's founder, Qaid-e-Azam by Yahya Merchant.	443
30.3:	The very first Steering Committee of the Aga Khan Award for Architecture, which developed the award program in 1977–1980.	444
30.4:	The Sancaklar Mosque, near Istanbul, by Emre Arolat Architecture (2012).	446
30.5:	A rendering of the 2019 winning entry design for the KFAS Headquarters and Conference Center in Kuwait by the Swiss-German firm Topotek 1.	448

Acknowledgements

First and foremost, we thank the many contributors whose works constitute this edited volume, which we hope readers will find both comprehensive and compelling. Authors have spent considerable time and effort writing these chapters, many during the ongoing pandemic, and we are particularly grateful for their perseverance, patience, and generosity. It has been a pleasure thinking, writing, and discussing this material with each and every one of them at all stages of this project during this challenging time. Putting this volume together has been a wonderful learning experience in many ways.

Many of the chapters included here began as commentary essays published in the *International Journal of Islamic Architecture*. We appreciate the efforts of the entire editorial team at the journal, the dedicated members of which facilitated their original publication during the past few years, including Kivanç Kilinç, Heather Ferguson, Patricia Blessing, and Henry Johnson in particular. We also thank Amy Rollason, Tim Mitchell, Faith Newcombe, Laura Christopher, and Helen Gannon at Intellect for their work with both the journal and this volume.

Thanks are owed as well to our many colleagues, friends, and family members, whose support has meant more than words can say.

Mohammad Gharipour and Daniel E. Coslett

Introduction

The Changed and Changing Field of 'Islamic Architecture'

Mohammad Gharipour and Daniel E. Coslett

The architecture – historic and contemporary – of the Islamic world has attracted increasingly significant attention in non-specialist circles during recent decades. Indeed, as the eyes of the world have focused on the Middle East and North Africa – whether in the aftermath of 9/11, lured by stunning Persian Gulf 'starchitecture', or amidst the excitement of the so-called 'Arab Spring' – questions regarding what constitutes Islamic identity and architecture have surfaced again and again. Many minds immediately turn to mosques in Mecca and medieval Egypt, and perhaps to Ottoman Turkey, but there is of course so much more. 'Islamic architecture' appears in the United States, Brazil, France, Australia, and elsewhere far from the traditional epicentres of historic Islam. Depending on one's definition, it includes both sacred and secular built environments, as well as those with long histories and those that may be brand new. Skyscrapers, hotels, schools, cultural centres, boulevards, and even whole cities might be considered 'Islamic' by today's scholars and practitioners of design.

Since its establishment as a specialist field by art historians in nineteenth-century Europe, Islamic art (and architecture) has captured the attention of visual and cultural historians, urbanists, designers, preservationists, tourism professionals, and others. Initially deeply saturated with dominant orientalist and colonialist perspectives, the field has changed quite a bit as it has become more inclusive, diverse, and geographically diffused.[1] Indeed, many scholars have wrestled with the meaning of 'Islamic architecture', acknowledging the inadequacy of traditional conceptions that – despite significant changes – remain tied to orientalist notions of 'the other' and fail to capture the diversity of Islamic contexts in our increasingly interconnected world.[2] When considering the critical areas of authenticity, identity, symbolism, style, agency, and function, one is struck by the field's breadth, potential flexibility, complexity, and relevance, both in assessing its past and plotting its future as a living, changing arena. Adding to the dynamism of architecture and the global Islamic context today is the movement toward historiographic critique on the part of scholars who define the field and educate future researchers, teachers, and designers. Calls for revisions to global histories, along with increased awareness of the entangled nature of the postcolonial world, further complicate assumptions about a field that was once envisioned quite narrowly as exclusively medieval, sacred, and Middle Eastern.[3]

Defining 'Islamic Architecture'

While some readers may be expertly acquainted with Islamic art and architecture, many will be unsure of the field's nature, likely recognizing some imprecision in the meaning of 'Islamic architecture'. What constitutes 'Islamic' built environments? From where and what time do they come? Are they exclusively sacred? These remain in many ways open questions and most attempts to define the terminology related to the field still end up retaining some degree of ambiguity or flexibility. Indeed, as Nasser Rabbat has noted, the idea that 'Islamic architecture' is the 'formal expression of Islam' – despite the absence of a consensus on what that really means and a durable denial of Islam's heterogeneity – remains 'the background of every major debate within the field, or in the larger discipline of art history as it tries to accommodate its structure and epistemological contours to the age of postcolonial criticism and globalization'.[4] While traditional interpretations of the field have been seriously challenged since the publication of Edward Said's seminal *Orientalism* in 1978, the legacies of orientalism, periodization based on ruling dynasties, and longstanding emphases on religion have remained inexorable and some regions are still often overlooked.[5] In the words of Sheila Blair and Jonathan Bloom, 'Islamic architecture' persists as an 'unwieldy field' encompassing 'much, if not most, of the art produced over fourteen centuries in the "Islamic lands"'.[6] Hasan-Uddin Khan, mindful of geographic and temporal limitations and assumptions carried by the 'Islamic' label when referring to the culture and religion of Muslims, considers 'Islam as a civilization, encompassing the secular and the religious', and thus prefers the term 'arts of Islam' in an effort to be as inclusive as possible.[7] In search of a fully decolonized art history, Wendy Shaw urges scholars to think beyond the enduring Hegelian structure of art history that views objects through the lenses of construction and content, and to consider sensorial experience in what she calls 'perceptual culture' while prioritizing 'reception over production'.[8]

As we have done in our capacities as editorial team members at the *International Journal of Islamic Architecture* (*IJIA*), in this volume we aim to expand readers' ideas about built environments in the Islamic world by inviting them to go beyond the conventional boundaries of 'Islamic' architecture and by exploring architecture through an interdisciplinary lens in relation to a wide range of factors (e.g., social and cultural histories, geography, politics, aesthetics, technology, and conservation). Using this transdisciplinary framework reveals new perspectives within the field and acknowledges and engages experts from disciplines outside of architecture, thereby expanding understandings of Islamic architecture today. It also encourages new ways of thinking about lived and experienced spaces rather than museumified objects in isolation. As noted above, this work has been going on for some time. The volume thus reflects and extends some of the 'new approaches, greater crossdisciplinarity, and an increasingly sophisticated engagement with theory and criticism [that] are repositioning Islamic architecture in a more reflective place', described by Rabbat, despite growing political and social hostility to Islam in some parts of the world.[9]

This emphasis on transdisciplinary collaborations has led to some interesting outcomes, as can be seen in the pages of *IJIA*, where we have worked with contributors from diverse academic disciplines, including art history, urban planning, landscape design, sociology, anthropology, and archaeology. These partnerships can be challenging, since disciplinary barriers can make us sensitive to criticism and resistant to alternative viewpoints on the subjects we study, but they have produced some refreshingly original essays. We admire and appreciate the bravery of scholars who welcome such opportunities, sharing their expertise and knowledge while tearing down disciplinary barriers. Many of the authors here have undertaken this type of inspiring work in *IJIA* and elsewhere. Indeed, this collection, in its totality, may be read as an endorsement for even more collaborative transdisciplinary research, teaching, publication, and design work.

Ultimately, we therefore advance a comprehensive definition of 'Islamic architecture' that embraces different historical and contemporary contexts, geographies, scales, functions, and meanings. It recognizes the inseparable nature of the secular and sacred and the significance of experience and perception in studying, understanding, and designing built environments within the Islamic world and beyond. Like the world it describes, the term's definition is changing.

Re-envisioning the Field

Reconceptualizing terminology is of course but one step. In order to change – to expand, diversify, globalize, decolonize – one must first know (what one can) of the existing field. The future of Islamic architecture should be transdisciplinary, inclusive, responsive to contemporary events, historically cognizant, and future-oriented. Significant progress has been made, but there is ample room to expand and diversify the field.

Any paradigm shift would require bold collaborations and stepping outside academic and intellectual comfort zones. We need to redefine the notion of research and scholarship, to go beyond our conventions, admit and appreciate diversity in scholarship, and to encourage critical thinking by engaging new platforms and venues. This may be quite challenging in a strained academic world dealing with budgetary restrictions and driven by tenure criteria that afford insufficient value to publishing in newspapers, magazines, and encyclopaedias, and for documenting endangered sites, conducting creative pedagogical projects, and promoting innovative study-abroad programs. It is obvious that we need to become more entrepreneurial and inclusive in order to maintain our position as contributors to important scholarship and critical thinking. While expertise remains vitally important, there is so much to learn from scholars in other fields and with different backgrounds and experiences. Our biggest achievement – the research framework within which we operate – has been shaped throughout decades and even centuries; however, longstanding practices and systems of inquiry become substantial liabilities when they impose limitations on creative thinking and the productive use of holistic and global approaches.

The relegation of Islamic architecture to the past – the denial of its contemporaneity – is merely one such limitation. Related to this historicizing tendency is the separation of architectural history/theory and the practice/experience of architecture in the Islamic world today.[10]

How can architectural research inform and educate the professional audience across the Islamic world while raising consciousness about creativity, good design, global vision, and meaningful preservation in the Islamic world and beyond? How might the consideration of contemporary design processes help historians better understand the past, and vice versa? Much of the architecture in the Islamic world is indeed a living, changing practice that is deeply rooted in history. Whether architects today embrace or reject that past (or some understanding thereof), it remains relevant. 'Local versus learned' knowledge matters.[11] An emphasis on the importance of transhistorical connections – architectural, material, spiritual, experiential, or otherwise – might open new avenues for creativity and deeper understandings of today's built environments, both historic and new.

This Volume

Here we present a selection of short critical reflections on the field of Islamic architecture by scholars and practitioners, many of whom have helped define its contours over the past several decades. Many of the essays contained in this volume first appeared in *IJIA*'s tenth anniversary issue, the theme of which was '"Islamic Architecture": Reflections on the Field'.[12] Several others included here are revised versions of thematic commentaries previously published in *IJIA*. The remainder have been commissioned specifically for this volume, drafted to fill gaps and further explore certain critical areas. This collected set of commentaries ultimately explores issues of pressing scholarly and professional concern for the wider field of Islamic architectural studies, including the related arenas of art, architectural history, design, urbanism, preservation or conservation, historiography, and education. The volume reviews past efforts and responds to new trends and innovations in both scholarship and practice. It explores changing methodologies, identifies new challenges, introduces creative approaches to old questions, asks new questions, and addresses contemporary issues and on-going controversies relevant to the field and, arguably, to the broader public as well.

The volume's 30 essays are grouped into nine sections that cover the realm of architecture in the Islamic world, from its study and publication to its preservation, creation, and use. These are not mutually exclusive categories and inevitably some degree of overlap exists between them. While some essays are more specifically place- or context-focused, their insights offer avenues for the exploration of other related areas and issues, leaving the reader to explore connections through comparison and extension. Authors have written their chapters in a manner intended to be accessible to both specialist and student alike.

Contributors address research and scholarship in the first section, exploring the nature of Islamic architecture as a changing intellectual field of inquiry. The next section, on scope and scale, includes essays that advocate for the expansion of that field through the consideration of both overlooked spaces and geographies. The writing of architectural histories on this material is considered in the following section on historiography and context. Authors then consider the state of fieldwork, archives, and documentation in today's complicated world wherein conflict and technology can bring challenging instability. Education and pedagogy are the themes for the next section. There authors consider both classrooms and museum galleries as spaces of learning for students and members of the public, for whom some of the scholarly developments in recent decades may be less known. Museums and written works are considered next in a section on curation and publication that explores how visitors and readers interact with information and visuals. Authors then explore neo-liberalism and preservation in a section on globalization and change in Islamic cities and at tourism sites. Demonstrating that architecture provides a setting for activity and is a vector of agency rather than just an object to be studied, authors in the subsequent section on experience and use address heritage management and displacement. Finally, chapters on professional practice consider the wider field of design today, and close attention is paid to the personal experiences and identity of architects.

No single volume can capture the full complexity of the field, nor can one answer all the existing questions regarding its past and future. However, this one does consider much of the current state of affairs in terms of research, publication, teaching, and design across the wider Islamic world. The assembled collection thus indexes the field of Islamic architecture and offers suggestions from scholars – established and emerging – on where it might be headed, highlighting the messiness and widening inclusivity of a once-narrow field. Rather than a definitive conclusion, it is therefore both a snapshot and an invitation for continued dialogue and expansive thinking.

Notes

1 Orientalism remains influential in the field of architectural history. See, for example, Nasser Rabbat, 'The Hidden Hand: Edward Said's Orientalism and Architectural History', *Journal of the Society of Architectural Historians* 77.4 (2018): 388–96.

2 Sheila S. Blair and Jonathan M. Bloom, 'The Mirage of Islamic Art: Reflections on the Study of an Unwieldy Field', *Art Bulletin* 85.1 (2003): 152–84; Nasser Rabbat, 'Islamic Architecture as a Field of Historical Inquiry', *Architectural Design* 74.6 (2004): 18–23; Finbarr Barry Flood, 'From the Prophet to Postmodernism? New World Orders and the End of Islamic Art', in *Making Art History: A Changing Discipline and Its Institutions*, ed. Elizabeth C. Mansfield (London: Routledge, 2007), 31–53; Nasser Rabbat, 'What Is Islamic Architecture Anyway?', *Journal of Art Historiography* 6 (2012): 1–15, https://arthistoriography.files.wordpress.com/2012/05/rabbat1.pdf; Heghnar Z. Watenpaugh, "Resonance and Circulation: The Category 'Islamic Art and Architecture,'" in *A Companion to Islamic Art & Architecture*, ed. Finbarr Barry Flood and Gülru Necipoğlu (New York: Wiley, 2017), 1123–44; Wendy M. K. Shaw, *What is 'Islamic' Art?* (Cambridge: Cambridge University Press, 2019), 1–29. For an earlier discussion of 'Islamic' cities from western and 'non-western' perspectives, see Anthony King, 'Terminologies and Types: Making Sense of Some Types of Dwellings and Cities', in *Ordering Space, Types in Architecture and Design*, ed. Karen A. Franck and Lynda H. Schneekloth (New York: Van

Nostrand Reinhold, 1994), 127–46. Several chapters in the present volume include more substantial literature reviews that detail the wider development of scholarship on Islamic art and architecture.
3. Vikramaditya Prakash, 'The "Islamic" from a Global Historiographical Perspective', *International Journal of Islamic Architecture* 6.1 (2017): 17–24.
4. Rabbat, 'What Is Islamic Architecture Anyway?', 2.
5. Ibid., 12; Rabbat, 'Islamic Architecture as a Field', 19–21; Shaw, *What Is 'Islamic' Art?*, 3–20. The latest edition of Robert Hillenbrand, *Islamic Art and Architecture* (London: Thames and Hudson, 2021) is illustrative; though it includes a welcomed new chapter on the eighteenth and nineteenth centuries, South Asia and sub-Saharan Africa are absent.
6. Blair and Bloom, 'The Mirage', 152.
7. Hasan-Uddin Khan, 'Editorial: Towards a New Paradigm for the Architecture and Arts of Islam', *International Journal of Islamic Architecture* 1.1 (2012): 6.
8. Shaw, *What Is 'Islamic' Art?*, 27.
9. Nasser Rabbat, 'Continuity and Rupture in Islamic Architecture', *International Journal of Islamic Architecture* 10.1 (2021): 47.
10. This assumption rests on the notions that 'Islamic architecture' is exclusively religious in nature and therefore incompatible with today's allegedly secular society. Both premises are faulty.
11. Rabbat, 'Continuity and Rupture', 49.
12. Mohammad Gharipour and Daniel E. Coslett, eds, '"Islamic Architecture": Reflections on the Field', special issue, *International Journal of Islamic Architecture* 10.1 (2021).

Part 1

Research and Scholarship

Chapter 1

The Study of Islamic Architecture: Reflections on an Expanding Field

Sheila S. Blair and Jonathan M. Bloom

In 2001, partly as a response to the events of September 11, *The Art Bulletin* asked us to write an article on the state of the field of Islamic art and architecture suitable for a general audience.[1] Since its publication in 2003, a few scholars in the field have criticized some of what we wrote, but many others have found it useful.[2] To judge from the Academia.edu alerts we get at the beginning of every semester, it remains a staple of introductory courses about Islamic art. In the article, we reflected on the enormous changes that had taken place over the 25 years since we had begun studying the subject. Now, almost two decades later, for this volume on the state of the field of Islamic architecture in 2020, we have been asked to reflect similarly on how the study of Islamic architecture has changed over the course of our careers. This invitation came at a particularly opportune moment, as we recently retired from positions teaching the subject at Boston College and Virginia Commonwealth University, nearly 40 years after earning our Ph.D.s in the history of Islamic art and architecture. Over the years we have written or edited, singly or jointly, over twenty books and hundreds of articles on virtually all aspects of the subject – ranging from the Dome of the Rock to contemporary Islamic art – but architecture, particularly in the medieval Iranian world and the Islamic west, has always remained at the core of our interests.

One of the biggest changes we have seen has been the incorporation of Islamic architecture (and art) into the world history of architecture (and art). In addition to the chapters in such classic surveys by Janson, Gardner, Kostoff, and the like, whose original treatment has often been expanded by experts in the field, Islamic architecture has been given a prominent place in major multi-author surveys.[3] We ourselves were deeply involved in the commissioning and editing of the articles on Islamic architecture for the 34-volume *Dictionary of Art,* which has 130 double-column pages devoted specifically to Islamic architecture,[4] as well as its transformation into the *Grove Encyclopedia of Islamic Art and Architecture.*[5] The ill-fated *Cambridge World History of Religious Architecture*, which was never published, was planned to have two out of its nine volumes devoted to Islamic architecture. (The 48 chapters on Islamic architecture written by 38 contributors – on various thematic and geographical/chronological topics from the rise of Islam to the twenty-first century – are now scheduled to be published separately by Brepols.) The most recent addition to the field is the new two-volume 21st edition of *Sir Banister Fletcher's Global History of Architecture,* which has ten chapters out of 102 written by experts on specific periods and regions of the Islamic world.[6] Earlier editions of the work had considered 'Saracen' architecture one of the 'ahistorical' styles, making this is a noteworthy improvement. Clearly the study of Islamic architecture has come of age. Considering how vast the changes have been over these decades, here we can only touch on five of what we consider the most important topics illustrated by a few representative examples, taken from a particularly American perspective.

Typology

Although the phrase 'Islamic architecture' immediately suggests mosques, madrasas, minarets, shrines, and other religious buildings, almost all scholars have also included palaces, caravanserais, and other types of historic buildings constructed in the lands where Islam has been an important, if not the most important, religion. This is not the place to question whether there should be such a subject as 'Islamic architecture', which puts the Dome of the Rock, the Alhambra, and the Taj Mahal, not to mention the Islamic Center in Washington, DC, and the Louvre Abu Dhabi, in the same intellectual basket. If that flawed basket did not exist, however, these buildings would be relegated to the peripheries of much mainstream scholarship. The Great Mosque of Córdoba and the Alhambra, for example, would hardly get much coverage in most courses or books on European (i.e., Christian) architecture, although they are as much in Europe as Paris's Notre-Dame or Rome's Villa Farnese. However one chooses to define 'Islamic architecture', most of the 'important' buildings were constructed by rulers and other significant individuals, but the study of anonymous vernacular architecture is newer and has expanded to consider distinctive forms found in the region, from the wind-towers and ice-houses of Iran to the mud-brick *ksar*s of the Sahara [Figure 1.1].[7]

The study of gardens and landscape is another area that has broadened enormously, both geographically and methodologically. There are now serious studies on gardens from Morocco and Islamic Spain to India and beyond.[8] New scientific techniques in combination with the study of literary sources have helped scholars to remove the trappings of Victorian-era gardeners and reveal some of the earlier aspects of Islamic garden design.

Geography

The study of Islamic architecture has also ballooned geographically. When we started studying in the 1970s, college-level courses were generally limited to the traditional heartlands of Islam, from Spain to Central Asia – what has been dubbed the 'rug belt'.[9] Of course, nobody could deny the importance of the Quwwat al-Islam Mosque or the Taj Mahal, but India was often treated as a distant cousin. Robert Hillenbrand's magisterial *Islamic Architecture* (1994) followed the traditional framework in limiting coverage between Spain and Afghanistan from 700 to 1700 and included only a few buildings from the subcontinent.[10] Our volume for the *Pelican History of Art* (1994) devoted a chapter and a half to Sultanate and Mughal Indian architecture, although we did not have much room for the Deccan, which has become of increased

Figure 1.1: An ice-house in Abarquh, Iran, photographed in 1999. Source: Jonathan Bloom and Sheila Blair.

interest.[11] In recent years scholars have expanded the focus with many monographs on individual buildings and larger surveys.[12]

One of the reasons for this increased interest in India may have been that Iran became largely inaccessible – especially to Americans – after the Islamic Revolution in 1979. Scholars who wanted to maintain their interest in the architecture of the Persianate world turned their attention not only to India but also to Anatolia and Central Asia, which became somewhat more open, particularly after the collapse of the Soviet Union in 1991.[13] Afghanistan, which had enjoyed a brief period of peace before the revolution of 1978, also became off-limits to scholars, especially after the Soviet invasion the following year.[14]

In contrast, the relief following the death of Francisco Franco in 1975 and the promulgation of religious freedom laws in Spain encouraged interest in the Islamic architectural heritage of the Iberian Peninsula. The Alhambra has become the most popular tourist monument in Spain, attracting some two million visitors annually, and its popularity has spawned a field that might be dubbed 'Alhambrology', with a seemingly inexhaustible supply of guidebooks, general introductions, and scholarly studies.[15] Similarly, Córdoba's fabulous mosque, which goes from being called a 'mosque' to a 'cathedral' depending on the vagaries of the local religious authorities, attracts hordes of tourists and has generated its own extensive literature.[16] No other Iberian mosques survive in such glory, but recently all the remains have been catalogued meticulously.[17] The palace city of Madinat al-Zahra outside Córdoba has also benefitted from extensive archaeological investigation presented as guidebooks, videos, and scholarly studies, and scholars have similarly investigated neighbouring country estates.[18]

In comparison to research on Spain, the nearby region of North Africa – from Libya to Morocco – has received less attention, particularly following the end of French colonial rule in the 1960s, although the legacies of colonialism itself, not only in the lands of Islam, has recently become a subject of interest.[19] Notable exceptions are studies on the origins and development of Almohad mosques as well as on palaces in the western Mediterranean.[20] Specific buildings, types of buildings, and cities have also received some attention.[21] There are, however, few synthetic overviews like the great studies of Henri Terrasse and Georges Marçais; Jonathan's *Architecture of the Islamic West*, which was published in June 2020, is designed to fill this void and encourage others to pursue specific topics in this fascinating region.[22]

In the 1970s, as students of Islamic architecture, we felt we could go virtually anywhere and be welcomed warmly. The intrepid Sheila hitchhiked to Chisht in Afghanistan, and only hepatitis kept her from reaching the minaret of Jam.[23] Since then, however, wars, civil wars, and various upheavals have limited travel in many countries in the region, including Algeria, Libya, Yemen, Syria, Palestine, Iraq, Afghanistan, Pakistan, etc. While countries such as Morocco and Tunisia have always been accessible, their religious architecture is largely off-limits to non-Muslims, which hinders scholarship and often narrows the perspective to modern national boundaries. When we were students, we entered and photographed in the Dome of the Rock with the permission of the Supreme Muslim Council; when we returned in 2014, the Israeli authorities prevented us from entering the Haram, although our Palestinian counterparts were waiting to greet us [Figure 1.2]. It is a sad commentary on how the world has changed.

One of the few positive results of the restricted access in the traditional heartlands of Islam is the welcome expansion of attention to regions once considered peripheral, including west and East Africa, Southeast Asia, and China [Figure 1.3]. Recent issues of the *International Journal of Islamic Architecture* have included articles on hitherto-unexplored places ranging from A (Albania) to Z (Zanzibar). As in the rest of the world, the situation can change almost daily. In 2013 Nancy Steinhardt invited us to accompany her on a trip through the Chinese provinces of Ningxia, Gansu, and Inner Mongolia in preparation for her book on China's early mosques.[24] We spent an extraordinary two weeks covering 2500 kilometres along back roads to visit thirteen cities and dozens of mosques and shrines. It is unlikely that the Chinese authorities would allow anyone to make that trip today. All this interest in new areas has not meant that the old subjects have been ignored. Many scholars have re-examined some of the canonical masterpieces of Islamic architecture to present new interpretations and reveal new meanings.[25]

Chronology

When we started in this field, most people considered that the Safavids were 'late', Ottoman architecture went downhill after Sinan, and Islamic architecture in Egypt ended with the Mamluks. How things have changed! In our lifetimes scholarship has expanded not only into the seventeenth and eighteenth centuries, but also into the nineteenth, twentieth, and even the twenty-first. Studies of North African urbanism under French colonial rule, the Ottoman Baroque, and the architecture of the Qajars are but a few examples of how the field has grown.[26] At the same time, other scholars are re-examining what we thought we knew about early Islamic architecture.[27] Another welcome change is that scholars are beginning to study not only the creation of buildings but also their afterlives, charting their histories over time into the colonial and postcolonial periods and even within the sphere of modern tourism.[28] Buildings – particularly venerated ones – tend to survive over the centuries, but they are repeatedly repaired, restored, and sometimes repurposed. The histories of the Dome of the Rock – as well as of the entire Haram al-Sharif – can be traced through the series of books and articles on Ayyubid, Mamluk, and Ottoman Jerusalem.[29] A recent monograph on the Quwwat al-Islam Mosque takes the building from its construction with the spolia of Hindu temples up to the present day.[30] We need more such studies.

The expansion into the contemporary world raises its own problems of what exactly makes architecture 'Islamic'. Does it have to be situated in the traditional lands of Islam? Does it have to serve a Muslim (i.e., religious) purpose? Does it have to be designed by a Muslim? Are I. M. Pei's Museum of Islamic Art in Doha [Figure 1.4], Jean Nouvel's Louvre Abu Dhabi, and Fumihiko Maki's Aga Khan Museum in Toronto (with landscaping by Vladimir Djurović) works of Islamic architecture? Contemporary Islamic architecture has become its own field. The creation of the Aga Khan Award in the 1970s has undoubtedly played a central role in

Figure 1.2: An interior view of the Dome of the Rock, Jerusalem, photographed in 1977. Source: Jonathan Bloom and Sheila Blair.

Figure 1.3: The entrance to the Qing-period Hongshuiquan Mosque on the upper reaches of the Yellow River in Qinghai, China, photographed in 2014. Source: Jonathan Bloom and Sheila Blair.

this development, and their publication of the awards exposes readers to a whole range of new buildings, as well the restoration and revitalization of buildings and their settings.[31] Similarly, UNESCO's designation of World Heritage Sites has brought attention to some of the great examples of Islamic architecture and urban entities, ranging from the historic centre of Córdoba to the State Historic and Cultural Park 'Ancient Merv'.[32] Such designations come with their own costs, however, as renovation may take precedence over sensitive restoration and tourists can overwhelm the sites.

Technology

Perhaps the biggest change in scholarship everywhere since we began in the 1970s has been the results of the introduction of the personal computer and the Internet. We wrote our dissertations on a manual typewriter and splurged on an electric typewriter to type the final copies ourselves. Five years later, we bought our first personal computer (an IBM XT) and never looked back, although we did shift to Macs in the 2000s, particularly because of their versatility in dealing with images.

Figure 1.4: I. M. Pei's Museum of Islamic Art, Doha (opened 2008), photographed in 2008. Source: Jonathan Bloom and Sheila Blair.

In order to do serious research in the 1970s and 1980s, one had to have access to a first-rate scholarly library, because many books and journals were not available elsewhere. The digital revolution has changed all that, and it is much easier to do research from any place with an Internet connection. For example, when Jonathan began researching the architecture of North Africa, many of the obscure journals were only available in the darkest reaches of a fine university library. Today, most of them can be found online with a few clicks of a mouse.

In the past, one started research with K. A. C. Creswell's massive bibliography and its supplements, along with the volumes of *Index Islamicus* and its own supplements, including a special two-volume bibliography on Islamic art and architecture published in 2012 as a supplement to *Index Islamicus*.[33] It all seems so out-of-date now with Google searches and Academia.edu, where authors post their articles – often to the chagrin of publishers – so that they are available to anyone. While it is wonderful to be able to find an article on some obscure building to download as a PDF, like anything on the Web, it may be hard for students to judge the quality of what they read, especially without the context of knowing for what purpose it was written and to what audience it was addressed.

In much the same way, finding pictures of remote sites used to be a nightmare – you either had to go there or beg for an image from a friend or colleague who had one. When we started using digital images in the early 2000s, we needed to scan them all ourselves, and preparing a lecture was an all-day affair. Today, a Google search will bring up thousands of images almost instantaneously. Some are on proprietary and curated databases, such as Artstor, ARCHNET (the Aga Khan Program in Islamic Architecture at MIT), or SAHARA (available to members of the Society of Architectural Historians), while others can be downloaded for free. That said, the study of Islamic architecture still suffers from a lack of good plans, let alone sections and elevations [Figure 1.5]. Robert Hillenbrand amassed a huge collection for his book, but most are so tiny as to be unusable for teaching, as they are not good enough to scan. Many of the plans we use regularly were drawn decades ago and do not reflect the current state of knowledge. From our experience, many students still grapple with how to read a plan.

When we started teaching in the 1980s, the two-carousel slide lecture was the norm, and the teacher was locked into the comparison of two images. You could show only slides that you

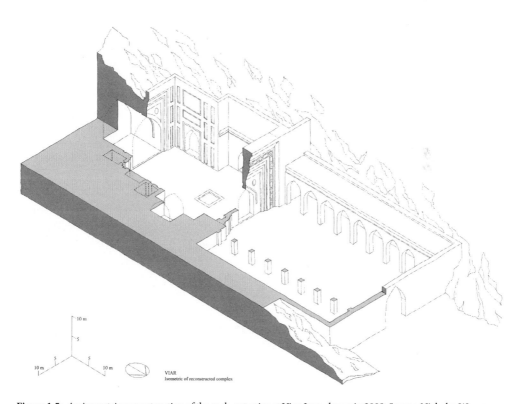

Figure 1.5: An isometric reconstruction of the rock-cut ruins at Viar, Iran, drawn in 2009. Source: Nicholas Warner.

or your slide library had. If you wanted to show a plan of a building as well as views of it, you had to keep the plan on one side and change the other unless you made multiple copies of the plan (which could take days and meant planning ahead). The advent of digital images, KeyNote, and PowerPoint changed all that, as one can easily repeat, enlarge, minimize, crop, distort, recolour, and otherwise manipulate images. Even the slide lecture format with its comparison of static images can give way to videos and virtual reality tours of buildings and sites. One of the reasons we chose to retire when we did was that we felt that we could no longer keep up with the speed of technological change, as so much material is now available online and in new formats.

Methodology

The major methodological shift we have seen in our lifetimes is a move from a purely (or largely) descriptive approach to a more interpretative one. It is no longer acceptable to simply describe a building to students and readers. One needs to interpret it, even if that interpretation may reflect as much about the interpreter as the building being studied.

In the case of archaeology, for example, the quest to simply amass material has given way to broader analyses of cultural contexts. This has been of particular importance in the study of early Islamic architecture and its setting, although the political situation in the region where Islam arose and initially spread often makes archaeological study difficult, if not impossible. There has also been a welcome movement to revisit old archaeological material and sites with new techniques.[34]

This interest in interpretation has led to an increased interest in the ways that buildings interact with their environments. One might begin with the work of Oleg Grabar and his team at Qasr al-Hayr al-Sharqi, which began by examining what had been thought to be an early Islamic palace and turned out to be an environmental study of the site and its region over time.[35] Studies of urbanism have flourished, from the historical work of scholars such as André Raymond on Cairo to multi-faceted volumes looking at the Islamic city as a living organism.[36] In the middle are specific studies on particular cities such as Fez, Rabat, Tunis, Aleppo, and Istanbul, to name just a few that come readily to mind [Figure 1.6].[37]

In the effort to interpret the meaning of Islamic architecture, rather than just describe it, the expansion of the field has made huge quantities of textual and visual information readily available, and the Internet has only increased this process. People often unwittingly assume that everyone in the past had the same access to all this information, so that they might explain the simultaneous appearance of some architectural feature or type as the result of 'influence' without bothering to consider how ideas could have been transmitted in past times when there were no photographs and few, if any, plans. Furthermore, we unwittingly assume that builders – or any artisans – shared a complete knowledge of contemporary literary culture. Sometimes we need to just sit back and reflect.

Figure 1.6: The Qasba of the Wadayas, Rabat, photographed in 1993. Source: Jonathan Bloom and Sheila Blair.

Conclusion

Many of these topics we have sketched out come together in a particularly pointed way as an inadvertent by-product of current US foreign policy, which has in our lifetimes transformed the United States from a benign presence to an occupying force in much of the region. It is increasingly difficult, if not impossible, for students and scholars from the Muslim world to come to the United States, even for scholarly conferences, and often equally difficult, if not equally impossible, for American scholars to travel to – let alone work in – the lands they wish to study. Despite the wonders of the Internet, scholars are often unaware of each other's work, and exchanging books is often a challenge, both financially and logistically. Meanwhile, publishing books, particularly monographs, has become increasingly difficult, as presses – both university and commercial – attempt to cope with the digital revolution. Print runs are minuscule, and prices are high. University libraries are reluctant to buy – or are unable to afford – specialized monographs, so publishers are less willing to print them. At the same time, journals – on virtually any imaginable subject, including Islamic architecture – proliferate, but even here subscriptions are expensive, making it increasingly difficult for students and scholars to keep up with the field. Furthermore, the academic world ultimately depends on the support of the broader population it serves, and as scholarship becomes increasingly self-referential and jargon-laden, it becomes increasingly irrelevant to that larger world. Many of these issues presuppose that one even has a university affiliation, but as two scholars who spent thirteen years freelancing before we got permanent positions, we know well how difficult it can be to do serious scholarship and be accepted without one. And, of course, architecture has to be seen and experienced to be studied, so all these obstacles impede the study of Islamic architecture, whatever it might be. It is no surprise, therefore, that younger scholars often turn away from architecture to study historiography or objects collected in museums and libraries. We only hope things will change.

Notes

This chapter was previously published as Sheila S. Blair and Jonathan M. Bloom, 'The Study of Islamic Architecture: Reflections on an Expanding Field', *International Journal of Islamic Architecture* 10.1 (2021): 57–73. The text has been updated for this publication.

1. Due to the limitations of space, we have largely limited our citations to published books. Sheila S. Blair and Jonathan M. Bloom, 'The Mirage of Islamic Art: Reflections on the Study of an Unwieldy Field', *Art Bulletin* 85.1 (2003): 152–84.
2. Moya Carey and Margaret S. Graves, eds, 'Islamic Art Historiography', *Journal of Art Historiography* 6 (2012), https://arthistoriography.wordpress.com/number-6-june-2012-2/.
3. Penelope J. E. Davies et al., *Janson's History of Art: The Western Tradition*, 8th ed. (New York: Pearson, 2010); Fred S. Kleiner, *Gardner's Art Through the Ages: A Global History*, 16th ed. (Boston: Cengage, 2020); Spiro Kostof, *A History of Architecture*, 2nd ed. (New York: Oxford University Press, 2010).
4. Jane Turner, ed., *The Dictionary of Art* (London: Macmillan, 1996), 16: 140–271.
5. Jonathan M. Bloom and Sheila S. Blair, eds, *The Grove Encyclopedia of Islamic Art and Architecture* (New York: Oxford University Press, 2009).
6. Murray Fraser, ed., *Sir Banister Fletcher's Global History of Architecture* (London: Bloomsbury, 2019).
7. Elisabeth Beazley and Michael Harverson, *Living with the Desert: Working Buildings on the Iranian Plateau* (Bangkok: Orchid Press, 2002); Hemming Jorgensen, *Ice Houses of Iran: Where – How – Why* (Costa Mesa, CA: Mazda, 2012); Mounia Chekhab-Abudaya, *Le Qṣar, type d'implantation humaine au Sahara: Architecture du sud algérien* (Oxford: Archaeopress, 2016).
8. James L. Wescoat and Joachim Wolschke-Bulmahn, eds, *Mughal Gardens: Sources, Places, Representations, and Prospects* (Washington, DC: Dumbarton Oaks Research Library and Collection, 1996); Scott Redford, *Landscape and the State in Medieval Anatolia: Seljuk Gardens and Pavilions of Alanya, Turkey* (Oxford: Archaeopress, 2000); Michel Conan, ed., *Middle East Garden Traditions: Unity and Diversity* (Washington, DC: Dumbarton Oaks Research

Library and Collection, 2007); D. Fairchild Ruggles, *Islamic Gardens and Landscapes* (Philadelphia: University of Pennsylvania Press, 2008); Mohammad Gharipour, ed., *Gardens of Renaissance Europe and the Islamic Empires: Encounters and Confluences* (State College: Pennsylvania State University Press, 2017); Julio Navarro, Fidel Garrido, and Iñigo Almela, 'The Agdal of Marrakesh (Twelfth to Twentieth Centuries): An Agricultural Space for Caliphs and Sultans. Part I: History', *Muqarnas* 34 (2017): 23–42; Julio Navarro, Fidel Garrido, and Iñigo Almela, 'The Agdal of Marrakesh (Twelfth to Twentieth Centuries): An Agricultural Space for Caliphs and Sultans. Part II: Hydraulics, Architecture, and Agriculture', *Muqarnas* 35 (2018): 1–64.

9 Walter B. Denny, *How to Read Islamic Carpets* (New York: Metropolitan Museum of Art, 2014).

10 Robert Hillenbrand, *Islamic Architecture: Form, Function and Meaning* (Edinburgh: Edinburgh University Press, 1994).

11 Sheila S. Blair and Jonathan M. Bloom, *The Art and Architecture of Islam, 1250–1800* (London: Yale University Press, 1994).

12 Michael Brand and Glenn D. Lowry, eds, *Fatehpur-Sikri* (Bombay: Marg, 1987); Catherine B. Asher, *Architecture of Mughal India* (Cambridge: Cambridge University Press, 1992); George Michell and Mark Zebrowski, *Architecture and Art of the Deccan Sultanates* (Cambridge: Cambridge University Press, 1999); Ebba Koch, *The Complete Taj Mahal and the Riverfront Gardens of Agra* (London: Thames & Hudson, 2006); Richard M. Eaton and Phillip B. Wagoner, *Power, Memory, Architecture: Contested Sites on India's Deccan Plateau, 1300–1600* (New Delhi: Oxford University Press, 2014); Holly Edwards, *Of Brick and Myth: The Genesis of Islamic Architecture in the Indus Valley* (Karachi: Oxford University Press, 2015); Keelan Overton, ed., *Iran and the Deccan: Persianate Art, Culture and Talent in Circulation, 1400–1700* (Bloomington: Indiana University Press, 2020).

13 Patricia Blessing, *Rebuilding Anatolia After the Mongol Conquest: Islamic Architecture in the Lands of Rum, 1240–1330* (Farnham, Surrey: Ashgate, 2014); Margaret Morton, *Cities of the Dead: The Ancestral Cemeteries of Kyrgyzstan* (Seattle: University of Washington Press, 2014); Richard P. McClary, *Rum Seljuq Architecture, 1170–1220: The Patronage of Sultans* (Edinburgh: Edinburgh University Press, 2017).

14 Warwick Ball, *The Monuments of Afghanistan: History, Archaeology and Architecture* (London: I. B. Tauris, 2008).

15 Oleg Grabar, *The Alhambra* (Cambridge, MA: Harvard University Press, 1978); Antonio Fernandez-Puertas, *La fachada del Palacio de Comares/The facade of the Palace of Comares* (Granada: Patronato de la Alhambra, 1980); Antonio Fernandez-Puertas, *The Alhambra* (London: Saqi Books, 1997); Michael Jacobs, *Alhambra* (New York: Rizzoli, 2000); Robert Irwin, *The Alhambra* (London: Profile Books, 2004); Jesús Bermúdez López et al., *The Alhambra and the Generalife: Official Guide* (Madrid: TF, 2010); Olga Bush, *Reframing the Alhambra: Architecture, Poetry, Textiles, and Court Ceremonial* (Edinburgh: Edinburgh University Press, 2018).

16 Heather Ecker, 'The Great Mosque of Córdoba in the Twelfth and Thirteenth Centuries', *Muqarnas* 20 (2003): 113–42; Pedro Marfil Ruiz, *La Puerta de los Visires de la Mezquita Omeya de Córdoba* (Cordoba: Lulu, 2009); Felix Arnold, 'Mathematics and the Islamic Architecture of Córdoba', *Arts* 7.3 (2018): 1–15; David A. King, 'The Enigmatic Orientation of the Great Mosque of Córdoba', *Suhayl* 16–17 (2018–19): 33–111.

17 Susana Calvo Capilla, *Las mezquitas de al-Andalus*, Estudios Andalusies (Almería: Fundación Ibn Tufayl des estudios árabes, 2014).
18 Antonio Vallejo Triano, *Madinat al-Zahra: Official Guide to the Archeological Complex* (Córdoba: Junta de Andalucia, 2005); Antonio Vallejo Triano, dir., *Madinat al-Zahra: La Ciudad Brillante*, DVD (Córdoba: Museo de Madinat al-Zahra, 2010); Antonio Vallejo Triano, *La Ciudad califal de Madīnat al-Zahrā': Arqueología de su arquitectura* (Córdoba: Almuzara, 2010); Glaire D. Anderson, *The Islamic Villa in Early Medieval Iberia: Architecture and Court Culture in Umayyad Córdoba* (Farnham, Surrey: Ashgate, 2013).
19 See, for example, chapters in Daniel E. Coslett, ed., *Neocolonialism and Built Heritage: Echoes of Empire in Africa, Asia, and Europe* (New York: Routledge, 2020).
20 Christian Ewert and Jens-Peter Wisshak, *Forschungen zur almohadischen Moschee. I. Vorstufen. Hierarchichische Gliederungen westislamischer Betsäle des i. bis 11. Jahrhunderts: Die Hauptmoscheen von Kairouan und Córdoba und ihr Bannkreis*, Madrider Beiträge (Mainz am Rhein: Philipp von Zabern, 1981); Christian Ewert and Jens-Peter Wisshak, *Forschungen zur almohadischen Moschee. II: Die Moschee von Tinmal*, Madrider Beiträge (Mainz am Rhein: Philipp von Zabern, 1984); Christian Ewert and Jens-Peter Wisshak, 'Forschungen zur almohadischen Moschee: III, Die Qaṣba-Moschee in Marrakesch', *Madrider Mitteilungen* 28 (1987): 179–210; Christian Ewert and Jens-Peter Wisshak, *Forschungen zur almohadischen Moschee: IV: Die Kapitelle der Kutubīya-Moschee in Marrakesch und der Moschee von Tinmal* (Mainz: Von Zabern, 1991); Lamia Hadda, *L'architettura palaziale tra Africa del Nord e Sicilia normanna (Secoli X-XII)* (Naples: Liguori, 2015); Felix Arnold, *Islamic Palace Architecture in the Western Mediterranean: A History* (New York: Oxford University Press, 2017).
21 Janet L. Abu-Lughod, *Rabat: Urban Apartheid in Morocco* (Princeton: Princeton University Press, 1980); Jacques Revault, *Palais et demeures de Tunis, I (XVIe-XVIIe S.)* (Paris: Editions C.N.R.S., 1967); Jacques Revault, *Palais et demeures de Tunis, II (XVIIIe-XIXe S.)* (Paris: Editions C.N.R.S., 1971); Jacques Revault, *Palais et résidences d'été de la région de Tunis (XVIe-XIXe s.)* (Paris: Editions de C.N.R.S., 1974); Jacques Revault, *Palais, demeures et maisons de plaisance à Tunis et ses environs (du XVIe au XIXe siècle)* (Aix-en-Provence: Edisud, 1984); Jacques Revault, Lucien Golvin, and Ali Amahan, *Palais et demeures de Fès, I: Époques mérinide et saadienne (XIV-XVIIe siècles)* (Paris: Editions du CNRS, 1985); Ahmed Saadaoui, *Tunis, ville ottomane: Trois siècles d'urbanisme et d'architecture* (Tunis: Centre de Publication Universitaire, 2001).
22 Henri Terrasse, *L'art hispano-mauresque des origines au XIIIe siècle*, Publications de l'Institut des Hautes Études Marocaines (Paris: G. van Oest, 1932); Georges Marçais, *L'architecture musulmane d'occident* (Paris: Arts et Metiers Graphiques, 1954); Jonathan M. Bloom, *Architecture of the Islamic West: Islamic Architecture in North Africa and the Iberian Peninsula 700–1800* (New Haven: Yale University Press, 2020).
23 Janine Sourdel-Thomine, *Le minaret ghouride de Jām: Un chef d'œuvre du xiieme siècle* (Paris: Diffusion de Boccard, 2004); Finbarr Barry Flood, 'Janine Sourdel-Thomine. Le Minaret Gouride de Jām: Un Chef d'Oeuvre Du XIIe Siècle', *Art Bulletin* 87.3 (2005): 536–43; Finbarr B. Flood, *Objects of Translation: Material Culture and Medieval 'Hindu-Muslim' Encounter* (Princeton: Princeton University Press, 2009).

24 Nancy Shatzman Steinhardt, *China's Early Mosques* (Edinburgh: Edinburgh University Press, 2015).
25 Yasser Tabbaa, *Constructions of Power and Piety in Medieval Aleppo* (University Park: Pennsylvania State University Press, 1997); Finbarr B. Flood, *The Great Mosque of Damascus: Studies on the Makings of an Umayyad Visual Culture* (Leiden: Brill, 2001); Gülru Necipoğlu, *The Age of Sinan: Architectural Culture in the Ottoman Empire* (Princeton: Princeton University Press, 2005); Doris Behrens-Abouseif, *Cairo of the Mamluks: A History of the Architecture and Its Culture* (London: I. B. Tauris, 2007); Abdallah Kahil, *The Sultan Hasan Complex in Cairo, 1357–1364: A Case Study in the Formation of Mamluk Style* (Wurzburg: Ergon in Kommission, 2008); Bernard O'Kane, *The Mosques of Egypt* (Cairo: American University in Cairo Press, 2016).
26 Nelly Hanna, *An Urban History of Būlāq in the Mamluk and Ottoman Periods* (Cairo: Institut français d'archéologie orientale, 1983); Zeynep Çelik, *Urban Forms and Colonial Confrontations: Algiers Under French Rule* (Berkeley: University of California Press, 1997); Renata Holod and Hasan-Uddin Khan, *The Contemporary Mosque: Architects, Clients and Designs Since the 1950s* (New York: Rizzoli, 1997); Markus Ritter, *Moscheen und Madrasabauten in Iran 1785–1848, Architektur zwischen Rückgriff und Neuerung* (Leiden: Brill, 2006); Stefan Weber, *Damascus Ottoman Modernity and Urban Transformation (1808–1918)* (Aarhus: Aarhus University Press, 2009); Doğan Kuban, *Ottoman Architecture*, trans. Adair Mill (Woodbridge, Suffolk: Antique Collectors' Club, 2010); Mohammad al-Asad, *Contemporary Architecture and Urbanism in the Middle East* (Gainesville: University Press of Florida, 2012); Azra Akšamija, *Mosque Manifesto: Propositions for Spaces of Coexistence* (Berlin: Revolver Publishing, 2015); Kishwar Rizvi, *The Transnational Mosque: Architecture and Historical Memory in the Contemporary Middle East* (Chapel Hill: University of North Carolina Press, 2015).
27 Mattia Giudetti, *In the Shadow of the Church: The Building of Mosques in Early Medieval Syria* (Leiden: Brill, 2016); Markus Ritter, *Der Umayyadische Palast des 8. Jahrhunderts in Hirbat al-Minya am See von Tiberias: Bau und Baudekor*, Studien zur islamischen Kunst und Archäologie (Wiesbaden: Reichert Verlag, 2017).
28 In addition to the works of Coslett and Çelik cited above, on Cairo see Nezar AlSayyad, Irene A. Bierman, and Nasser Rabbat, eds, *Making Cairo Medieval* (Lanham: Lexington Books, 2005); Diane Singerman and Paul Amar, eds, *Cairo Cosmopolitan: Politics, Culture, and Urban Space in the New Globalized Middle East* (Cairo: American University in Cairo Press, 2006); Paula Sanders, *Creating Medieval Cairo: Empire, Religion, and Architectural Preservation in Nineteenth-Century Egypt* (Cairo: American University in Cairo Press, 2008). For an example of a study of a single building over time, see Simon O'Meara, *The Kaʿba Orientations: Readings in Islam's Ancient House* (Edinburgh: Edinburgh University Press, 2020).
29 Michael Hamilton Burgoyne, *Mamluk Jerusalem, an Architectural Study* (London: World of Islam Festival Trust, 1987); Sylvia Auld and Robert Hillenbrand, eds, *Ottoman Jerusalem, the Living City: 1517–1917* (London: British School of Archaeology in Jerusalem/Administration of Auqaf and Islamic Affairs, Jerusalem/Altajir World of Islam Trust, 2000); Gülru Necipoğlu, 'The Dome of the Rock as Palimpsest: ʿAbd al-Malik's Grand Narrative and Sultan Suleyman's Glosses', *Muqarnas* 25 (2008): 17–105; Robert Hillenbrand and Sylvia Auld, *Ayyubid Jerusalem*

(London: Al Taljir Trust, 2009); Marcus Milwright, *The Dome of the Rock and Its Umayyad Mosaic Inscriptions* (Edinburgh: Edinburgh University Press, 2016); Lawrence Nees, *Perspectives on Early Islamic Art in Jerusalem* (Leiden: Brill, 2016).

30 Catherine B. Asher, *Delhi's Qutb Complex: The Minar, Mosque and Mehrauli* (Mumbai: Marg, 2017).

31 Sherban Cantacuzeno, ed., *Architecture in Continuity: Building in the Islamic World Today, the Aga Khan Award for Architecture* (New York: Aperture, 1985); Cynthia C. Davidson, ed., *Legacies for the Future: Contemporary Architecture in Islamic Societies* (London: Thames & Hudson, 1998); Kenneth Frampton, Charles Correa, and David Robson, eds, *Modernity and Community: Architecture in the Islamic World* (London: Thames & Hudson, 2001); *Architecture and Polyphony: Building in the Islamic World Today* (London: Thames & Hudson, 2004).

32 For a list of UNESCO World Heritage Sites, see 'World Heritage List', United Nations Education, Scientific, and Cultural Organization, accessed January 27, 2020, https://whc.unesco.org/en/list/.

33 Susan Sinclair, ed., *Bibliography of Art and Architecture in the Islamic World* (Leiden: Brill, 2012).

34 Garth Fowden, *Quṣayr ʿAmra: Art and the Umayyad Elite in Late Antique Syria* (Berkeley: University of California, 2004); Alastair Northedge, *The Historical Topography of Samarra* (London: British School of Archaeology in Iraq/Fondation Max van Berchem, 2005); Rocco Rante and Annabelle Collinet, eds, *Nishapur Revisited: Stratigraphy and Ceramics of the Qohandez* (Oxford: Oxbow Books, 2013).

35 Oleg Grabar et al., *City in the Desert: Qasr al-Hayr East* (Cambridge, MA: Harvard University Press, 1978); Christiane Gruber and Michelle Al-Ferzly, *City in the Desert, Revisited: Oleg Grabar at Qasr al-Hayr al-Sharqi, 1964–71* (Ann Arbor, MI: Kelsey Museum, 2021), https://lsa.umich.edu/kelsey/publications/all-publications/city-in-the-desert--revisited--oleg-grabar-at-qasr-al-hayr-al-sh.html.

36 André Raymond, *Artisans et commerçants au Caire au XVIIIe siècle* (Damascus: Institut français de Damas, 1973–74); Eugen Wirth, *Die Orientalische Stadt im islamischen Vorderasien und Nordafrika: städtische Bausubstanz un räumlich Ordnung, Wirtschaftsleben und soziale Organisation* (Mainz: Philipp von Zabern, 2000); Salma K. Jayyusi et al., eds, *The City in the Islamic World*, sect. 1 (Boston: Brill, 2008).

37 Simon O'Meara, *Space and Muslim Urban Life: At the Limits of the Labyrinth of Fez* (Abingdon: Routledge, 2007); Heinz Gaube and Eugen Wirth, *Aleppo: Historische und geographische Beiträge zur baulichen Gestaltung, zur sozialen Organisation und zur wirtschaftlichen Dynamik einer vorderasiatischen Fernhandelsmetropole*, Beihefte der Tübiger Atlas des Vorderen Orients, Reihe B, Geisteswissenschaften (Wiesbaden: Ludwig Reichert Verlag, 1984); Zeynep Çelik, *The Remaking of Istanbul: Portrait of an Ottoman City in the Nineteenth Century* (Seattle: University of Washington Press, 1986); Saadaoui, *Tunis*; Julia Gonnella, Wahid Khayyata, and Kay Kohlmeyer, *Die Zitadelle von Aleppo under der Tempel des Wettergottes, neue Forschungen und Entdeckungen* (Münster: Rhema, 2005).

Chapter 2

Widening the Horizons for the Study of Islamic Architecture

Bernard O'Kane

Four major reviews of the field of Islamic art and architecture have been made in the past fifty years: one by Oleg Grabar in 1976,[1] a second by Robert Hillenbrand in 2003,[2] a third in the same year by Sheila Blair and Jonathan Bloom,[3] and the fourth by Gülru Necipoğlu in 2012.[4] While it is a little early for self-congratulation, it is surprising in the relatively short span of time since the latter how much progress has been made on many of the matters of earlier concern. I will deal first with what I consider to be the elephant in the room, i.e., the study of western architecture,[5] and then move to the topic of geographical and temporal expansions within the study of Islamic architecture.

Without

A late concern of western architectural historians has been the divorce of art and architectural history, a feature apparent since the methodological upheavals of art history in the 1960s and 1970s.[6] A recent study of this phenomenon makes a cogent plea for the re-integration of the disciplines.[7] Fortunately, this divorce never seems to have been threatened in Islamic art, where, as Grabar put it, 'architecture is *the* particularly characteristic genre of Islamic art'.[8] A new generation of Islamic art historians continues to incorporate the study of architecture, painting, and decorative arts in their publications.[9]

The biggest challenge now, as previously, is to expand the horizons of those teaching and learning western architectural history so as to include non-western subjects. There has been progress as of late. In 2004, the US National Architectural Accreditation Board (NAAB) raised the standard of comprehension to understanding the parallel and divergent canons and traditions of architecture and urban design in the non-western world, i.e., to a level comparable to that of western architectural traditions. The publication of *A Global History of Architecture* by Ching, Jarzombek, and Prakash followed shortly thereafter;[10] its timeliness is shown by the recent (2017) appearance of a third edition. Perhaps even more importantly, it has led, through the initiative of two of its authors, to the foundation of the Global Architectural History Teaching Collaborative (GAHTC), which provides a library offering more than two hundred lectures on its free teacher-to-teacher platform. It benefits from continuing funding from the Mellon Foundation.[11]

Just as importantly, the publication of non-western material in the field has surged. Arguably the most prestigious academic periodical for architectural historians is the *Journal of the Society of Architectural Historians*. In the first two decades of the twenty-first century it published twenty-three articles directly related to Islamic architectural history. The Islamic architectural historian Zeynep Çelik articulated the journal's changes in policy in her 'Editor's Concluding Notes'; in her three-year editorship, she had specifically targeted the inclusion of more non-western topics, as well as articles on a topic of implicit interest to everyone in the field: the teaching of architectural history in the context of studio architecture.[12]

The very existence of the *International Journal of Islamic Architecture* is evidence of the broadening of the field, as is the appearance, for example, of *Archnet-IJAR: International Journal of Architectural Research*, which in its review of its first ten years of publication showed that contributors from Malaysia, Turkey, Egypt, and Qatar alone considerably outnumbered those from the US and Europe.[13]

However, a quick survey of the architectural books listed on the websites of the major publishing houses of universities with both architecture and art history schools still revealed huge imbalances in 2020. For instance, only 6 out of 423 books in Yale University Press's online heading of architecture were on Islamic topics, and another 10 on non-western ones. I thought, this being the first one I had looked at, that this poor showing might have been affected by the numerous titles in their series on *The Buildings of England* (and more recently those of Ireland and Scotland), but lists on architecture from presses at Princeton, Harvard, and MIT were equally or even more disappointing.[14] The figures from MIT (only two Islamic and another three non-western out of a total of 733), whose publications seem to address a greater proportion of architects to architectural historians than the other presses, were particularly indicative of the still-remaining gap between good intentions and realities in the field.

Within

The *International Journal of Islamic Architecture* (and this volume), although focusing on urban design and planning, architecture, and landscape design in the historic Islamic world, has a special commitment to contemporary architecture and urban design. This is a refreshing development, for only recently has architecture from the nineteenth century onwards been getting the attention it deserved within our field. Perhaps one should not be too surprised; the British Society of Architectural Historians, founded in 1956 as a chapter of the American Society of Architectural Historians, was initially uninterested in modern architecture.[15]

In 1994, it was still possible for the major textbook covering the second half of Islamic art and architectural history to stop at 1800.[16] Even then, this might not have been exclusively the authors' bias; when writing my own *Treasures of Islam: Artistic Glories of the Muslim World* (2007),[17] it was only over the strenuous objections of the publisher that I was able to incorporate a photograph of the Petronas Towers [Figure 2.1].

That building was one of the recipients of the Aga Khan Award for Architecture, an institution that has done much to widen everyone's idea of what Islamic architecture can and should be.[18] Its continuing strength is a matter for celebration, even if at times the jury's choices reveal

Widening the Horizons for the Study of Islamic Architecture

Figure 2.1: Petronas Towers, Kuala Lumpur (left) and Burj Khalifa, Dubai (right). Source: Bernard O'Kane.

some surprising omissions.[19] The single largest category of premiated building types is community development and improvement. Is the lower ranking of mosques a deliberate retreat from this category or a measure of their recent architectural conservatism?[20]

One of the unfortunate developments in contemporary mosque design, and in the use of older mosques in modern times, is a reduction in the sense of spaciousness, namely the frequent division of the interior into gender-separated areas. Was this initiated – or just accentuated – by Salafi ideology promoted by so many Saudi-funded mosques outside of the Arabian Peninsula?[21] Marion Katz has studied the historical background of women in mosques,[22] but its architectural manifestations, with their associated ideological underpinnings, unfortunately have yet to be the subject of any detailed study. This also raises the subject of gender studies, now long researched in western architecture,[23] but which, in addition to the initial efforts that have been thoroughly chronicled by Heghnar Watenpaugh,[24] deserves more attention from within our field.

In 2003 Hillenbrand mentioned the difficulty in doing fieldwork in some countries, including Algeria, Libya, Iraq, Iran, and Afghanistan.[25] Nearly twenty years on, and it is again possible to work in Algeria and Iran, although Libya, Iraq, and Afghanistan remain out of bounds, as do Syria and Yemen now too. The political turmoil has been accompanied by destruction of architectural heritage, savagely, as in the case of Aleppo, and heartbreakingly, as in the case of the deliberate destruction wrought by ISIS in Iraq, from the earliest dated *muqarnas* dome at Imam Dur to the monuments of Mosul.[26] The roots of the Salafist's scorn for heritage echo the Saudi government's policy of destruction of earlier buildings around the Meccan haram – bad enough in itself, even without their grotesque replacement, the Abraj al-Bait [Figure 2.2].[27] A different ideology, but just as destructive, has been manifested recently by the Chinese government's obliteration of Uighur heritage.[28]

Almost as much a cause for concern is the restoration policies in many countries. The over-restoration mentioned by Hillenbrand in Uzbekistan has continued with the lamentable work at the Shah-i Zinda [Figure 2.3], and even a formerly reputable state, such as Turkey (which has the finest cohort of architectural historians of any Islamic country), has a mixed record, combining revelatory uncovering of original paintings behind later layers of plaster[29] with deadening over-painting[30] or even removal of original work [Figure 2.4].[31]

2017 saw the publication of the most recent survey of Islamic Art, *A Companion to Islamic Art and Architecture*;[32] two of its eight-part chronological divisions were on the periods 1700–1950, and one on 1950 to the present. In the same year, the editors of the 1994 survey held a conference on *Islamic Art: Past, Present, Future*,[33] acknowledging how much in the meantime thinking has changed on the importance of bringing research in the field up to the present time. The premier journal in the field, *Muqarnas*, has indeed, in accordance with its editor's policies, increased its chronological and geographical range,[34] although surprisingly twentieth- and twenty-first-century architecture seems to have been almost completely immune from this expansion.[35] Four panels out of nine at the 2018 Historians of Islamic Art Association were also related to subjects after 1800, including one on the use of digital technologies.

Figure 2.2: Abraj al-Bait, Mecca. Source: Wikimedia Commons/King Eliot.

Figure 2.3: Anonymous tomb, before (left) and after (right) restoration at Shah-i Zinda, Samarqand. Source: Bernard O'Kane.

Digital technologies have indeed transformed our field, like so many others, in the period since the 2003 surveys. Not that the Internet did not exist before then, but the availability of material on the web, including museum collections,[36] archives of books, journals, and photographs,[37] databases of various kinds,[38] publishers' websites, and repositories of scholars' articles,[39] has grown at an astonishing rate. No longer, on trips to Europe or North America, need I spend a day or two at the copying machine in libraries with obscure periodicals, thanks to digital document delivery.[40] One consequence of this is that English, for better or worse, has become even more dominant in publications, even by German and Italian authors.[41] This is even more of a problem for scholars writing in Arabic, Turkish, Persian, Udru, and Malay who wish to reach an international audience – although architectural historians will be expected to read the languages of the areas in which they specialize, this can hardly be expected to apply to international architects.

This growth has been matched by that of positions for scholars. The foundation of the Historians of Islamic Art Association reflects an unprecedented expansion in the last two decades of teaching and museum positions, as does the success of its biennial symposiums. Publications have increased accordingly,[42] covering sub-fields from mosques in the European diaspora[43] to those in China,[44] although some of those on more ostensibly mainstream topics, such as architecture in the Gulf, suffer from their highlighting of projects in development that are unlikely to be realized.[45]

Widening the Horizons for the Study of Islamic Architecture

Figure 2.4: Üç Şerefeli Mosque, Edirne, before (top) and after (bottom) restoration. Source: Bernard O'Kane.

The Future

What of the future? The imminent and eagerly anticipated publication of Finbarr Barry Flood's *Islam and Image: Beyond Aniconism and Iconoclasm* perhaps shows the danger of predicting it, given the earlier opinion of Grabar on the surfeit of publications on the subject.[46] It can hardly be doubted that by now most scholars, no matter from which background, are sufficiently woke to be aware of orientalist tropes,[47] a topic that, forty years on from Edward Said's exposé, has become a publishing industry in its own right.[48] The physical expansion of the field, mentioned above, is paralleled by its methodological expansion, which means that we can look forward not only to the exploration of formerly little-known areas of the field, but also to viewing better-known subjects through an unfamiliar lens. So in terms of breadth, depth, and methodological variety, there is much to be celebrated in current scholarship, even if on the ground in many Islamic countries the quality of most modern architecture leaves much to be desired.[49] The extent to which we are able to influence this is limited, but that need not stop us from trying.[50]

Notes

This chapter was previously published as Bernard O'Kane, 'Widening the Horizons for the Study of Islamic Architecture', *International Journal of Islamic Architecture* 10.1 (2021): 75–87. The text has been updated for this publication.

1. Oleg Grabar, 'Islamic Art and Archaeology', in *The Study of the Middle East: Research and Scholarship in the Humanities and the Social Sciences*, ed. Leonard Binder (New York: Wiley, 1975), 229–63.
2. Robert Hillenbrand, 'Studying Islamic Architecture: Challenges and Perspectives', *Architectural History* 46 (2003): 1–18.
3. Sheila Blair and Jonathan Bloom, 'The Mirage of Islamic Art: Reflections on the Study of an Unwieldy Field', *Art Bulletin* 85 (2003): 152–84.
4. Gülru Necipoğlu, 'The Concept of Islamic Art: Inherited Discourses and New Approaches', *Journal of Art Historiography* 6 (2012): 1–26. See also Mohammad Gharipour and Daniel E. Coslett, eds, '"Islamic Architecture": Reflections on the Field', special issue, *International Journal of Islamic Architecture* 10.1 (2021), within which this essay was originally published.
5. To isolate it may in itself be seen as perpetuating the privilege that the 'western canon' has exerted over the field since its inception, but in practice the categorization seems unlikely to be replaced any time soon. See Zeynep Çelik, 'Editor's Concluding Notes', *Journal of the Society of Architectural Historians* 62.1 (2003): 121–24; Sibel Bozdoğan, 'Architectural History in Professional Education: Reflections on Postcolonial Challenges to the Modern Survey', *Journal of Architectural Education* 52.4 (1984): 207–15; Joe Nasr and Mercedes Volait, 'Still on the Margin', *ABE Journal* 1 (2012), http://journals.openedition.org/abe/304.

32 Finbarr Barry Flood and Gülru Necipoğlu, eds, *Companion to Islamic Art and Architecture* (Oxford: Wiley, 2017), 2. vols. Unfortunately, at a price of ('just' – according to the Wiley website in 2020) $410.75, it is beyond the reach of most students.
33 Jonathan Bloom and Sheila Blair, eds, *Islamic Art: Past, Present, Future* (New Haven: Yale University Press, 2019).
34 See Gülru Necipoğlu, 'Reflections on Thirty Years of *Muqarnas*', *Muqarnas* 30 (2013): 1–12. The journal is also a showcase for the expansion of methodological approaches mentioned by her earlier. See Necipoğlu, 'The Concept of Islamic Art'.
35 With the exception of some articles in the special issue on 'History and Ideology: Architectural Heritage of the "Lands of Rum"', *Muqarnas* 24 (2007), and an article on the new Great Mosque of Granada, a building that is self-effacing to the point of the anodyne. See Olga Bush, 'Entangled Gazes: The Polysemy of the New Great Mosque of Granada', *Muqarnas* 32 (2015): 97–133.
36 Such collections often contain architectural material. The recent redesign of galleries of Islamic art and architecture in major institutions has been an opportunity to update museological practices, none more successfully than at the British Museum; major new museums of Islamic art, such as that of Qatar and the Aga Khan in Toronto have also opened in the meantime.
37 Jstor.org, available through many institutions, and Hathitrust.org are prime examples. The Bibliothèque Nationale in Paris has been assiduous in making its out-of-copyright holdings available (see www.gallica.bnf.fr). The Creswell archive at the Ashmolean, now online and running again after a period of inaccessibility, and a Barakat Trust-funded initiative supervised by Omniya Abdel Barr and exploring ways to integrate Creswell material in various collections with a view to a searchable database. See 'K. A. C. Creswell's photographs of the Middle East', Victoria and Albert Museum, accessed January 27, 2020, https://www.vam.ac.uk/articles/creswells-egypt-syria-and-palestine-photographs.
38 Archnet (archnet.org), the usual first resource for our field, has greatly expanded recently, as has the *Thesaurus d'Épigraphie Islamique* (www. epigraphie-islamique.org). Other recently appeared databases related to architectural epigraphy include *The Monumental Inscriptions of Historic Cairo* (islamicinscriptions.cultnat.org) and the *Database for Ottoman Inscriptions* (ottomaninscriptions.com).
39 Academia.edu and Researchgate.net are the best known. Both are venture capital funded, and have been criticized for monetizing their content, but an announced profit-free alternative (ScholarlyHub) has yet to materialize. See Jefferson Pooley, 'Metrics Mania: The Case Against Academia.edu', *Chronicle of Higher Education*, January 7, 2018, https://www.chronicle.com/article/The-Case-Against-Academiaedu/242141.
40 For those without the backup of an institution's interlibrary loan service, an appeal to colleagues on the relevant scholarly Facebook page often produces results.
41 This is a little less so when it comes to Spanish and French scholars (with Yves Porter being a notable exception).
42 The recent donation of the CAA Charles Rufus Morey Award to Kishwar Rizvi, *The Transnational Mosque: Architecture and Historical Memory in the Contemporary Middle East* (Chapel Hill: University of North Carolina Press, 2015) is a welcome recognition from the broader field.

43 Ergün Erkoçu and Cihan Buğdacı, *The Mosque: Political, Architectural and Social Transformations* (Rotterdam: NAI Publishers, 2009); Azra Akšamija, *Mosque Manifesto* (Berlin: Revolver Publishing, 2015); Christian Welzbacher, *Europas Moscheen: Islamische Architektur im Aufbruch* (Munich: Deutscher Kunstverlag, 2017); Shahed Saleem, *The British Mosque: An Architectural and Social History* (Swindon: Historic England, 2018).

44 Nancy Shatzman Steinhardt, *China's Early Mosques* (Edinburgh: Edinburgh University Press, 2015); Qing Chen, 'Mosques of the Maritime Muslim Community of China: A Study of Mosques in the South and Southeast Coastal Regions of China' (Ph.D. diss., SOAS, University of London, 2015); George Lane, ed., *The Phoenix Mosque and the Persians of Medieval Hangzhou* (London: Gingko, 2018).

45 E. G. Gesa Schönberg and Philip Jodidio, *Architecture in the Emirates* (Cologne: Taschen, 2007); E. G. Gesa Schönberg and Philip Jodidio, *Contemporary Architecture in Arabia* (Berlin: GBP Architekten, 2008). The work of even one of the most respected figures in the field, Mohammad al-Asad, *Contemporary Architecture and Urbanism in the Middle East* (Tallahassee: University of Florida, 2012), is not immune to this stricture.

46 Ibid., 254.

47 Although whether these scholars would agree that Said's work 'had the effect of reifying a category of modern discourse that masked deeper structures of what might be called non-Orientalist Orientalism' is another matter. See Wael B. Hallaq, *Restating Orientalism: A Critique of Modern Knowledge* (New York: Columbia University Press, 2018), 269–70. For a thoughtful analysis of how the field has developed in response see Zeynep Çelik, 'Reflections on Architectural History Forty Years after Edward Said's *Orientalism*', *Journal of the Society of Architectural Historians* 77.4 (2018): 381–87.

48 For example, see Edmund Burke III and David Prochaska, eds, *Genealogies of Orientalism: History, Theory, Politics* (Lincoln: University of Nebraska Press, 2008); Tugrul Keskin, ed., *Middle East Studies after September 11: Neo-orientalism, American Hegemony and Academia* (Leiden: Brill, 2018); Susannah Heschel and Umar Ryad, eds, *The Muslim Reception of European Orientalism: Reversing the Gaze* (Abingdon: Routledge, 2019).

49 This is the case worldwide, of course. The outside forces that dictate much modern mosque design are analysed in Rizvi, *Transnational Mosque*. With eleven winners of the Aga Khan Award for Architecture, Turkey heads the country list – perhaps a reflection of the extent to which the discipline is nourished there. Does the lamentable state of modern architecture in my adopted country of Egypt reflect the concomitant lack of pay and prestige of our profession within the governmental sectors of universities and museums?

50 This is the aim of Hassan Radoine, *Architecture in Context: Designing in the Middle East* (Chichester: Wiley, 2017).

Chapter 3

Modern Architecture and Colonialism in the Islamic World

Brian L. McLaren

In order to reflect on the historiography of modern architecture in the Islamic world, it is important to examine contemporary approaches in light of where this scholarship has been through the course of the last several decades, and especially how it has responded to recent directions in the broader field of historical scholarship. In the case of this essay, which examines works of architecture impacted by a particular set of political considerations – those initiated by western colonialism in its various forms – as well as in relation to a specific regional, cultural, and temporal frame – the Middle East and North Africa during the interwar period – these reflections are all the more specific and, given a recent history of considerable political turmoil, increasingly pressing.[1] In examining this area of scholarship, it is also crucial to acknowledge that it is part of an emerging tendency in the study of the architecture of the Islamic world during the modern period. Indeed, the study of colonialism and its modern built environments has become progressively more common, and in so doing it has brought scholars from a wide range of backgrounds and expertise into the discussion.

In examining the historiography of modern Islamic architecture under the aegis of colonialism, this essay begins with some of the earliest developments that followed from the emergence of postcolonial studies as a mature field of study in the 1990s, and then proceeds through a second wave of scholarship that began in the early 2000s, to discuss some of the themes and trends of our present day. In this effort, it will describe the emergence and growth of a new area of scholarly inquiry whose impact on the broader field of the architecture of the Islamic world has yet to be adequately studied. It is also important to recognize that this area of scholarship has resulted in an extension of the boundaries of both modern and Islamic architecture, while initiating a much-needed reflection on issues of identity, heritage, and local culture that continue to be important today.

Initial Developments: Orientalism and After[2]

Increased attention to the architecture of the Islamic world during the period of western colonialism came at the same time as revisionist histories of modern architecture began to expand the canon – though initially this scholarship failed to account for this architecture's western perspective. Examples of this early research include Mary McLeod's seminal essay, 'Le Corbusier and Algiers', which was published in the highly influential journal *Oppositions* in 1980.[3] The first wave of critical scholarship on the architecture and urban planning of the colonial era did not happen until more than a decade later, with the publication of works such as in Zeynep Çelik's essay, 'Le Corbusier, Orientalism, Colonialism', which examined this French architect's modern proposals for Algiers in the context of the longer history of French intervention in the Maghrib region as well as their specifically orientalist implications.[4] The profound shift in perspective between this essay's examination of proposals by Le Corbusier in Algeria and that advanced earlier by McLeod is indicative of an emerging perspective that would lead to a complete re-examination of colonialism's modern architectural legacy.

This body of research was impacted by postcolonial theory – itself a subfield of cultural studies – and especially the arguments of late literary and cultural critic Edward Said from his 1978 book, *Orientalism*.[5] Under the influence of Michel Foucault's writings, such as *The Archaeology of Knowledge* and *Discipline and Punish*, as well as the cultural and political theory of Antonio Gramsci, Said offered a forceful analysis of just how deeply imbricated the west has been in not only defining but also maintaining the identity of the non-west.[6] Indeed, in Said's own terms, orientalism was not merely a field of academic inquiry, it was 'a style of thought based upon an ontological and epistemological distinction made between "the Orient" and [...] "the Occident"', as well as being a discursive field through which 'European culture was able to manage – and even produce – the Orient'.[7] This oppositional and critical framework, which focuses on theories of difference and discourses of power and identity and the emerging influence of the postcolonial situation on a now unequivocally global context, had a profound impact on the historiography of colonial architecture and urbanism.

Notably, there were a number of broader developments in the field of Islamic architecture that took place around the time of the publication of Said's *Orientalism* – such as the initiation of the Aga Khan Award for Architecture and the Aga Khan Program for Islamic Architecture at Harvard and MIT in 1977 and the founding of the journal *Mimar: Architecture in Development* (1981–92). Just slightly later, the establishment of the International Association for the Study of Traditional Environments (IASTE) at the First International Symposium on Traditional Dwellings and Settlements at the University of California at Berkeley in 1988 and beginning in 1989 the related publication of the same name, provided an important outlet for research on the architecture of western colonialism.

This new approach to research into the architecture of the Islamic world was concretized with the publication of Nezar AlSayyad's 1992 edited collection, *Forms of Dominance: On the Architecture and Urbanism of the Colonial Enterprise*, which includes essays on a wide range of topics and geographies – such as the French and Italian colonies in North Africa and the British in India.[8] This work was impacted by parallel researches by scholars from other disciplines, such as Timothy Mitchell's *Colonising Egypt* (1989), which examines representations of Egypt at nineteenth-century world's fairs through a Foucauldian interpretation of discourses of power.[9] Early works by architectural historians include Zeynep Çelik's *Displaying the Orient: Architecture of Islam at Nineteenth Century World's Fairs* (1992), which shows a parallel concern for World's Fairs as crucial sites of exchange between west and east. Another important early study is Mark Crinson's *Empire Building: Orientalism and Victorian Architecture* (1996), which situates stylistic and architectural developments in the architecture of western colonialism within the broader history of orientalism – even pointing out distinct phases in its development.[10]

During this time the broader discourse on postcolonial theory in Islamic architecture was largely shaped by the activities of the Aga Khan Trust for Culture – whose interest in preservation of traditional environments and contemporary architecture in the Islamic world tended to raise the same issues that were evident during the colonial era – including the conflicted relationship between modernity and tradition.[11] Despite the considerable expansion of scholarship on colonial architecture and urbanism related to issues of power and identity, these early examinations were largely concerned with how the relationship between the colonizer and colonized found in the colonial system was reified in the architecture and planning of colonial cities. However, not unlike the arguments advanced in Said's *Orientalism*, which were taken to task for operating within the canon of western humanist literature, this first generation of research on the architecture of colonialism is sometimes said to inadvertently re-inscribe the very hierarchies of western power that it was seeking to critically examine and destabilize.[12] Among the issues that surfaced from this critique is the lack of attention to the heterogeneity of colonial discourses in architecture and their various forms of resistance among the local populations.

A Second Wave: Colonial Modernities

This foundational work was quickly followed by a considerable expansion of the scholarship on the architecture and urban planning of the colonial era. This new scholarship was coincident with the emergence of a wide range of approaches, many of which attempted in various ways to address the historical and historiographic lacunae of prior scholarship. These responses began in the early 2000s, with one of the most prominent directions being extending the temporal and physical boundaries of colonialism. One such example is Mark Crinson's *Modern Architecture and the End of Empire* (2003), which examines how 'modernism and other aspects of modern architecture are refracted through the prism of British imperialism and its dissolution and aftermath'.[13] Despite its debt to postcolonial theory, it avoids simple connections between architecture and power by examining the intersection of modern architecture and empire at the time of its disappearance, and taking on less conventionally architectural subjects such as the education of architects. Other tendencies in more recent scholarship include efforts to reframe the architecture of colonialism as modern, such as in Tom Avermaete, Serhat Karakayali, and Marion von Osten's edited collection *Colonial Modern: Aesthetics of the Past, Rebellions for the Future* (2010), which offers an interesting contrast to the AlSayyad volume in providing an impressive range of geographies, methodologies, and time periods – yet all under the category of Modern architecture.[14]

A number of these approaches were outlined in a 2006 essay by Jean-Louis Cohen entitled 'Architectural History and the Colonial Question: Casablanca, Algiers and Beyond', where he also traced the trajectory of the scholarship to that moment. One of the central and fundamental questions that he poses in this essay was: 'Does research into "colonial" architecture constitute a separate branch within architectural history?'[15] In answering this question, Cohen offers a critique of what he calls 'the illusion of an overpowering State', while also acknowledging the need for broad knowledge of the related pre-colonial, colonial, and metropolitan societies. He also enumerates a number of other concerns – such as the view that the colonies were merely a laboratory for experimentation that could later be implemented in Europe. In this regard, Cohen ultimately concludes that colonial modernity was a form of modernity in its own right, stating that it 'can no longer be thought of exclusively as the product of a process of diffusion, but equally as one of an almost simultaneous dynamic of the emergence of new concepts and forms'.[16]

Other authors have sought less conventional objects of study, such as my own work on the architecture of tourism in Italian colonial Libya, to interrogate the impact of more elusive, and arguably more powerful, mechanisms for the intermingling of colonial modernity with the local culture.[17] This and other related scholarship explore the profound ambivalence of modernity in the colonial context – which was marked by its encounter with both vernacular building forms and techniques and historical works of Islamic architecture – and thereby challenge conventional assumptions about the nature of modern architecture in the Islamic world. A final example from the early 2000s, Zeynep Çelik's *Empire, Architecture, and the City: French-Ottoman Encounters, 1830–1914* (2008), offers a compelling model to extend the impact of postcolonial studies into the realm of architecture and urban planning in ways that address some of its initial limitations.[18] Indeed, in examining the complex relationship between two extremely influential imperial regimes – French and Ottoman – the book takes as one of its central premises to subvert the idea that imperial power (and modernity) emanates from the west. The explicitly transnational (and transactional) nature of the cultural exchange between Ottoman and French empires described by Çelik provides a productive reference point for current historiography on the architecture of modern colonial empires in Africa and the Middle East.[19]

Conclusion: Current Challenges

In considering the historiography of the architecture of colonialism in North Africa and the Middle East during the interwar period, it is immediately apparent that the scholarship produced in this area over the course of the last 30 years has initiated a series of challenges to historians of Islamic architecture. These challenges are tied to the need to both incorporate the architecture of colonialism in the history of Islamic architecture and to account for its impact on that history. Indeed, incorporating works conceived and executed by western architects under the aegis of colonial occupation and governance means inserting this work into a diachronic history that, in most cases, includes pre-Ottoman and Ottoman developments as well as the architecture of the post-independence period. Among the questions that emerge, some of the most challenging are: What is the difference between the already existing modernizing tendencies in the Middle East and North Africa and those brought by British, French, and Italian colonialism? How did these conflicting modernities exist during the colonial period? What formulation of the modern emerged with independence from colonialism? The issue of what happened in Islamic architecture after colonialism is especially challenging, as this period produced complex and infinite combinations of continuities, discontinuities, and refractions of modern western forms and Islamic heritage. Without question, the challenges related to incorporating colonial architecture into the history of Islamic architecture have, to this point, been only partially addressed and demand serious attention.

Beyond the issue of carefully attending to the impact of these multiple and conflicting modernities on the history of modern Islamic architecture, the architecture of the colonial period initiated an equally complex and perhaps even more deeply troubling challenge related to what exactly constitutes Islamic heritage. In my own research on Libya during the period of Italian colonization, I was particularly concerned with the 'indigenous politics' that reached their highest level of development under the governorship of Italo Balbo (1934–40). This effort was aimed at improving the negative reputation of Italy in the Muslim world through carefully orchestrated gestures of reconciliation with the local populations.[20] Notably, while the Libyans were allowed within the confines of their religion and their family life to live according to their traditions, larger forms of social and political organization were established by the standards and expectations of the colonial authorities. These same principles applied to the Italian preservation of Muslim religious monuments, such as the Mosque of Ahmad al-Karamanli in Tripoli (1736–37) – the largest and most well known religious monument in the city [Figure 3.1]. Completed in 1934, this restoration project was conducted according to the most advanced standards available at the time, the aim being to remove layers of recent additions so as to return this building to its original state.[21] Naturally, this 'original state' was one that foregrounded references to Italian traditions and in that sense one might rightly understand this Islamic monument as a product of colonial discourse rather than as an example of an inviolate tradition.

In a final reflection on the issue of local culture in Libya during the period of Italian colonization, I would like to discuss an even more explicit example of the production of heritage, which in this case is related to the Italian intervention in the local artisanal industries. This was an area of particular importance during the Balbo era, when it was conceived as central to the economic and cultural development of the colony – with attention to 'prevent the disappearance of the arts and protect their conservation against the spread of imitation products'.[22] With the 1934 appointment of Sardinian ceramic artist Melkiorre Melis as head of the Muslim School of Arts and Crafts in Tripoli, the Italian intervention in these industries took a more radical direction. In response to what he saw as a scarcity of local ceramics production and an unfortunate reliance on importing majolica tiles from Tunisia (which at that time was occupied by France), Melis sought to invent a new Libyan tradition, creating a form of instruction that reflects a modern vernacular approach. This quality is evident in the design of the Artisanal Quarter at the Suq al Mushir in Tripoli, which was constructed in the Spanish bastion of the castle, just inside one of the major gates into the old city [Figure 3.2].

Figure 3.1: Mosque of Ahmad al-Karamanli, Tripoli, 1736–1737. View of tile restoration. Source: *L'Italie pour les populations islamiques de l'Afrique italienne* (Rome: Soc. Ed. 'Novissima', 1940), 22.

Figure 3.2: Florestano Di Fausto, Artisanal Quarter, Suq al Mushir, Tripoli, 1935. View of courtyard. Source: Ministry of Foreign Affairs Archive, Rome – Documents of the Ministry of Italian Africa, Volume III, Pacco 56, Fascicolo 35.

The complex was organized around an exterior courtyard lined by a series of workshops of indigenous artisans where the products of local crafts were both produced and put up for sale. However, the impact of Melis on the Artisanal Quarter was not only in his input in its decorative elaboration; this facility also included a ceramics workshop where he taught a renewed version of indigenous crafts. As a vocational training center that was intended to signal the rebirth of Libyan ceramic artisanry, there is an apparent conflict between the program of training indigenous workers to return to more traditional patterns and Melis's role as an interpreter of those traditions.

Just like the Italian activities related to the preservation of Muslim religious monuments in Libya, their intervention in the local artisanal industries poses a challenge to any effort to extricate Islamic traditions from the impact of western colonialism. Indeed, using the case of Libya, these traditions were not so much revived as they were invented in service of maintaining the colonial order. The question of Islamic heritage is related to the manner in which colonialism's intervention in the cultural arena disrupted any normative reading of local traditions. The challenge to historians of modern architecture in the Islamic world is thus to acknowledge that, just like the buildings produced during the colonial era, the traditional built environment in these regions was, under the auspices of preservation and heritage conservation, equally marked by the impact of colonialism.

Notes

This chapter was previously published as Brian L. McLaren, 'Modern Architecture and Colonialism in the Islamic World', *International Journal of Islamic Architecture* 10.1 (2021): 193–202. The text has been updated for this publication.

1 A note on colonial history: in North Africa, the French established a colony in Algeria (1830–1962) and protectorates in Tunisia (1881–1956) and Morocco (1912–56) and Italy colonized Libya (1911–42); in the Middle East, the French established mandates in Syria and Lebanon (1923–46) and the British established protectorates in Egypt (1914–22) and Transjordan (1921–46) and mandates in Palestine (1920–48) and Iraq (1920–32).
2 The title 'Orientalism and After' is drawn from the essay by the same name by Aijaz Ahmad, which offers a critique of the internal conflict in Said's orientalism between its purportedly western humanist liberalism and anti-humanist Foucauldian views. See Aijaz Ahmad, 'Orientalism and After: Ambivalence and Cosmopolitan Location in the Work of Edward Saïd', *Economic and Political Weekly* 27.30 (July 25, 1992): PE 98–PE 116.
3 Mary McLeod, 'Le Corbusier and Algiers', *Oppositions* 19/20 (1980): 54–85.
4 Zeynep Çelik, 'Le Corbusier, Orientalism, Colonialism', *Assemblage* 17 (April 1992): 58–77. The arguments in this essay were much expanded in Zeynep Çelik, *Urban Forms and Colonial Confrontations: Algiers under French Rule* (Berkeley: University of California Press, 1997). As Çclik notes, these arguments were preceded by Sibel Bozdoğan in her 'Journey to the East: Ways of Looking at the Orient and the Question of Representation', *Journal of Architectural Education* 41.4 (1988): 38–45.
5 Edward Said, *Orientalism* (New York: Pantheon Books, 1978). For a discussion of postcolonial theory in relation to cultural studies, see Delores B. Phillips, 'Postcolonial Theory', in *The Encyclopedia of Postcolonial Studies,* ed. Sangeeta Ray and Henry Schwartz (New York: John Wiley, 2016), accessed January 26, 2020, https://doi.org/10.1002/9781119076506.wbeps300.
6 Michel Foucault, *The Archaeology of Knowledge* (1969), trans. A. M. Sheridan Smith (New York: Pantheon, 1972); and *Discipline and Punish: The Birth of the Prison*, trans. Alan Sheridan (New York: Vintage Books, 1979).
7 Said, *Orientalism*, 2–3.
8 Nezar AlSayyad, ed., *Forms of Dominance: On the Architecture and Urbanism of the Colonial Enterprise* (Aldershot: Avebury, 1992). Beyond AlSayyad, the scholars in this volume include Jyoti Hosagrahar, Paul Rabinow, Mia Fuller, and Shirine Hamadeh.
9 Timothy Mitchell, *Colonising Egypt* (Berkeley: University of California Press, 1988). See also Paul Rabinow, *French Modern: Norms and Forms of the Social Environment* (Cambridge, MA: MIT Press, 1989).
10 Zeynep Çelik, *Displaying the Orient: Architecture of Islam at Nineteenth Century World's Fairs* (Berkeley: University of California Press, 1992); and Mark Crinson, *Empire*

Building: Orientalism and Victorian Architecture (New York: Routledge, 1996). An earlier contribution by an architectural historian is François Béguin, *Arabisances: Décor architectural et tracé urbain en Afrique du Nord, 1830–1950* (Paris: Dunod: 1983).

11 The Aga Khan Trust for Culture was founded in Geneva Switzerland in 1988.
12 For a thorough critique of this aspect of Said, see Ahmad, 'Orientalism and After', PE 98–PE 116. The emerging critiques of Said are succinctly stated by Nima Naghibi, in 'Colonial Discourse', *Encyclopedia of Postcolonial Studies*, ed. John C. Hawley (Westport, CT: Greenwood Press, 2001), 103–04.
13 Mark Crinson, *Modern Architecture and the End of Empire* (Burlington, VT: Ashgate, 2003), xii.
14 Tom Avermaete, Serhat Karakayali, and Marion von Osten, eds, *Colonial Modern: Aesthetics of the Past, Rebellions for the Future* (London: Black Dog Architecture, 2010). Another notable contribution to the redefinition of the modern during this time is: Jyoti Hosagrahar, *Indigenous Modernities: Negotiating Architecture and Urbanisms* (New York: Routledge, 2005).
15 Jean-Louis Cohen, 'Architectural History and the Colonial Question: Casablanca, Algiers and Beyond', *Architectural History* 49 (2006): 354.
16 Ibid., 367.
17 Brian L. McLaren, *Architecture and Tourism in Italian Colonial Libya: An Ambivalent Modernism* (Seattle: University of Washington Press, 2006). A more recent example of this approach is the focus on Tropical Architecture as described in Jiat-Hwee Chang, *A Genealogy of Tropical Architecture: Colonial Networks, Nature and Technoscience* (New York: Routledge, 2016).
18 Zeynep Çelik, *Empire, Architecture, and the City: French-Ottoman Encounters, 1830–1914* (Seattle: University of Washington Press, 2008).
19 Parallel researches in other historical disciplines especially focus on the period of decolonization, such as in Els Bogaerts and Remco Raben, eds, *Beyond Empire and Nation: The Decolonization of African and Asian Societies, 1930s–1960s* (Leiden: KITLV Press, 2012); Ruth Craggs and Claire Wintle, eds, *Cultures of Decolonisation: Transnational Productions and Practices, 1945–70* (Manchester: Manchester University Press, 2016); and Paul A. Silverstein, *Postcolonial France: Race, Islam, and the Future of the Republic* (London: Pluto Press, 2018).
20 See Italo Balbo, 'La politica sociale fascista verso gli arabi della Libia', in Reale Accademia d'Italia, Fondazione Alessandro Volta, *Convegno di scienze morali e storiche. 4–11 ottobre 1938-XVI. Tema: l'Africa. Volume I* (Roma: Reale Accademia d'Italia, 1939), 733–49.
21 Turba, Luigi. 'La Moschea dei Caramanli a Tripoli', *Le Vie d'Italia* 40.8 (August 1934): 583–91.
22 Guglielmo Quadrotta, 'Sviluppo e realizzazioni dell'artigianato in Libia', *Rassegna Economica dell'Africa Italiana* 25.7 (July 1937): 952.

Part 2

Scope and Scale

Chapter 4

From Garden to Landscape: Lessons from the Taj and the Alhambra

D. Fairchild Ruggles

The field of architectural history took several conceptual turns in the late twentieth century, with significant impacts on the way that we define the built environment of the Islamic world and its makers. The changes had a dramatic effect on the study of gardens and landscape.

The first turn was away from largely formalist interests to more social considerations, so that as scholars examined the built work, they also inquired into its impact on human communities. While a building might still be evaluated in terms of its construction material, structure, style, and ornament, the question of what the building did for the people who built and used it became increasingly important. In this way architectural history paralleled similar developments in history. The social history perspective was a profoundly humanistic change that recognized that a mosque is more than a set of walls; it provides a place for worship, for the dissemination of political news, for education, a spacious courtyard in an otherwise dense urban neighbourhood, and a quiet place for the elderly to nap. It has meaning.

One of the key proponents of this more expansive way of understanding Islamic architecture was Oleg Grabar (1929–2011). In 1976, in his 'Art of the Object', he wrote about the 'requirement of a context' to supply meaning.[1] Grabar, and those who followed him, recognized that art objects and works of architecture are acts of communication that occur in society. This led architectural historians to pay more attention to the meaning of buildings in the time and place where they were built, a meaning sometimes expressed literally via the texts inscribed on the walls of palaces, city gates, mosques, tombs, and fortifications, or at other times expressed in descriptive accounts, such as the exhaustive survey of buildings and places in Cairo written by al-Maqrizi between the years 1417 and 1438–39.[2] These approaches also drove us to think more reflectively about our own respective cultural formations, acknowledging that a larger world stage of political investments and imbalances of power have shaped the way we have written about Islamic architectural history. With respect to both the history and historiography of Islamic architecture, the social context of the building and the social context of the historian contribute to meaning.

A second, related, and perhaps more challenging turn followed this. The social history model had emphasized contemporary context, so that the participants – architect, patron, community – were regarded as contemporary stakeholders in the production of meaning, and meaning was understood to emerge from the building's relation to its surrounding physical and political context (object:context mirroring figure:ground). As the French school of theory began to impact the humanities in North America in the 1970s and 1980s, however, some scholars began to embrace a model of a visual field that acknowledged the role of the viewer in creating meaning. This new viewer did not emerge as a consequence of critical social context, but rather as a subject who read the object or building as a semiotic sign and participated in the making of the sign. Accordingly, the building was still understood to be a form of communication, but instead of it possessing a fixed and discoverable meaning deposited by the architect (and which could be found by examining its historical context), it was regarded as partaking in an unending chain of connotative references. The object and its viewer were understood to stand in relation to each other and, moreover, to have constituted each other.[3]

This theoretical model proved to be especially useful in the field of landscape history, where the landscape is endless and thus does not exist as a discrete object. It can only be objectified by virtue of having been framed, in the literal sense of seeing it through a camera lens or a window, or conceptually through the mapping of political boundaries or ecological territories. In either kind of frame, the viewer is necessary for the view to be consummated. In the (related) methodologies of art history and visual studies, the landscape emerged through the architectural frame as an object to be seen, and as the frame created the object, it also created the viewing subject.[4]

This framed landscape was markedly different from the Islamic garden as conceptualized by earlier scholars. The Islamic garden had typically been defined as a cross-axial or quadrilateral *chahar bagh*, ignoring the other types of courtyard gardens and orchards that were not laid out in a quadripartite plan. Moreover, the origins of the *chahar bagh* had traditionally been attributed to Qur'an verses referring to four running rivers of water, milk, honey, and wine (see 2:25 and 47:15 among others), while at the same time traced to pre-Islamic sources in Iran.[5] The inherent contradiction went unnoticed. Scholars explained the garden as having one unchanging symbolic meaning – the earthly foretaste of the paradise promised to the faithful.[6] They spoke reductively of 'the Islamic garden', thereby flattening differences in time and place, as though the garden of the Taj Mahal (1632–43, Agra) [Figure 4.1] was indistinguishable from the courtyard in the Palace of Pasha 'Abd al-Kari (1860, Fez) [Figure 4.2] in its form and symbolism. But when the scale of inquiry expanded to incorporate the landscape, a variety of formal configurations – from the *chahar bagh* to the residential enclosed courtyard with pool, stepped terrace gardens, and mosque courtyards – had to be considered together with land management technologies such as aqueducts and *qanat*s (underground channels), and together they required a more complex and capacious explanation of meaning. The regional perspective was a strategy of both geography and environmental studies. Focusing on landscape rather than garden, it proved a useful strategy for sidestepping long-standing assertions that had characterized the Islamic garden as a single form and explained its meaning exclusively in terms of religious symbolism.

In the twenty-first century, with profound anxiety about the effects of climate change on the earth, the environmental perspective is especially valuable because it encourages us to see gardens, landscapes, and environments on a continuous scale. It recognizes the agency of the human subject in the visual and spatial field, yet identifies the object (meaning, the landscape) not exclusively as that subject's creation but as something far more complex. The field of

From Garden to Landscape

Figure 4.1: Taj Mahal, 1632–1643, Agra. Source: Wikimedia Commons/Yann Forget.

Figure 4.2: Pasha ʿAbd al-Kari (also known as the Dar al-Aman), 1860, Fez. Source: D. Fairchild Ruggles.

study is not limited to the designed thing or building, and instead has escaped the formal and disciplinary frame. The built work that a landscape historian studies may be a free-standing structure, or it may be a plaza, a garden fountain, a road, or a ploughed plot of land; at the same time, those built works may depend upon natural systems such as rainfall or seasonal changes. The environmental approach demands that the garden and landscape historian consider topography, climate, water systems, botany, and traditional practice in describing and/or assessing a site.

The Taj Mahal as Landscape

The study of the gardens of the Taj Mahal reflects this shift. The enormous Taj Mahal tomb stands in an enclosed *chahar bagh* with its dominant axis running north-south and a second axis running east-west [Figure 4.3]. The north-south axis begins in the outer courtyard and runs through the grand multi-story portal, and through the vast garden until it reaches the tomb on its raised platform, marking the north end of the site where it abuts the Yamuna River.

Thus, instead of occupying a central position within the garden, as was common in earlier tombs such as the Tomb of Humayun (1565 or 1569, Delhi), the Taj tomb is pulled back to the far end, so that the viewer sees it from afar as a distant majestic vision. This position echoes the organization of many of the pleasure gardens in Agra, wherein the pavilion stood not in the centre but on a raised terrace along the riverfront.[7]

With regard to architectural formalism, the Taj belongs to a genealogy in which the double-shell dome, rising from the *hasht behesht* ('eight paradises', referring to its division into eight

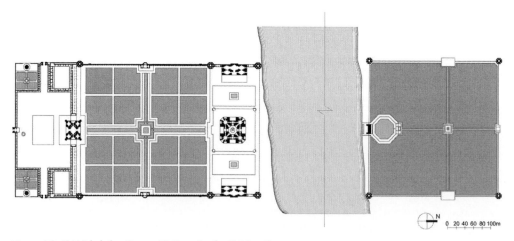

Figure 4.3: Taj Mahal plan. Source: M. Gurgain after E. Moynihan.

units) architectural plan and set within a quadripartite garden, can be traced to the Tomb of Humayun and even earlier Persian precedents. The white marble of the tomb and its sarcophagi had been used at the tomb of Salam al-Din Chisti in Fatehpur-Sikri (1571), and the floral ornament and inlay of coloured stone can be seen in the Tomb of Itmad al-Dawla (1622–28, Agra). Because of its position at the garden's perimeter, the tomb looks directly across the Yamuna River to the Mahtab Bagh (1632–43), a garden of slightly later date with an elevated platform bearing the foundations of an octagonal structure along its riverine edge.

These are formal attributes that, when accepted without historical contextualization, seem to speak for themselves. One curious outcome of this was the rise of the myth of the 'Black Taj'. The Black Taj was supposedly a twin structure that, if built, would have stood opposite the Taj, connected via a bridge across the river. Superficially, the vestiges of the Mahtab Bagh offered evidence to support the myth: its elevated platform seemed to match that of the Taj; the *chhatri* towers marking the ends of the riverfront façade seemed to respond to similar ones at the Taj; and the placement of the octagonal shape (a pool) corresponded to the placement of the Taj's central dome. In the Black Taj scenario, the two tombs – the black version mirroring the white version on the opposite bank – provided a story for the emperor Shah Jahan and his empress Mumtaz Mahal that portrayed them as a loving couple, thereby satisfying the western expectation of a monogamous marital union. However, Begley's study of the Taj's architectural inscriptions showed that, far from being a loving memorial to a deceased queen, the tomb was a fiery statement of power that demanded submission to God.[8] Neither the Mahtab Bagh's remains, when studied archaeologically, nor the texts inscribed on the Taj offered support for the idea of a Black Taj.

When a team led by Elizabeth Moynihan conducted a study of the Mahtab Bagh and published a text, dated 1652, that described its partial erasure by the river's turbulence soon after its construction, a more accurate spatial and historical context for the site was established.[9] The team's excavations and mapping of the Mahtab Bagh showed clearly that it was a garden and that its dimensions and plan had echoed that of the Taj, with the result that, when the Taj, the river, and the Mahtab Bagh were considered as an ensemble, the plan of the Taj took on a different organization. Instead of the great tomb terminating one end of its garden's central axis, it now marked the centre, with its north-south axis continuing across the river and through the garden on the other side. Such an insight is only possible when the Taj is seen in its larger spatial context and from a landscape perspective that includes the river and opposite bank [Figure 4.4].

But the scale of analysis thus far is still that of a site with clear boundaries. To place the Taj on a truly environmental scale would be to inquire into the river itself, not as a barrier traversed by the tomb garden's central axis, but as a conduit that brings water into Agra and supplies its many riparian garden sites. The Yamuna begins in the Himalaya as snowfall that melts and flows onto the IndoGangetic Plain, passing through Agra before joining the Ganges at Allahabad. The river does not simply flow past the Taj; it is the source of the water that filled its pools and irrigated its gardens. Unlike other areas of the Islamic world where water from high sources travelled to its destination via carefully engineered surface canals and aqueducts,

Figure 4.4: Mahtab Bagh, 1632–1643, Agra. Source: D. Fairchild Ruggles.

the water in Agra was raised from the river in buckets attached to chains propelled by waterwheels. At the Taj, this operation was hidden inside a *chhatri-*capped water tower, through which the water was lifted before being transported into the side area of the tomb precinct for storage before release into the Taj gardens, channels, and pools.[10] The environmental methodology also requires recognition that the desire for such elaborate waterworks, despite the naturally arid climate of the area around Agra, comes from the Mughal experience of building pleasure gardens far north in Kashmir, where the mountainous topography and storage of water in snowy peaks allowed for vigorous, copious water flows, dynamically performed by *chadar*s (textured water panels) and cascades pouring over *chini khana* (literally 'China cabinet', referring to the array of shelf-like niches) panels. If Kashmiri gardens inspired the Taj garden, and if the Yamuna carries water from the peaks above Kashmir across the plain to Agra, then the Taj might be understood to operate within an environment that measures well more than a thousand kilometres from edge to edge. But to position the architectural object against its environmental context in such a way would be to divide things that are in fact inextricable. From the environmental perspective, there is no moment when the Himalayan snow and the

Taj's channels and pools become separate entities because it is the same water that flows from one place to the other.

The monument's implacable fixity as an object is challenged by this way of seeing it not as a stationary object within an equally stationary spatial field, but as one element in a spectacular performance – sometimes with disastrous results, such as when the river overran its banks soon after the Taj's construction in 1643, but more often with delightful results, such as when the water flows through the channels and into the garden beds, irrigating plants and trees. This perspective introduces a more nuanced perspective, because it asks us to consider the monument as a working system that is connected to the river and to all the other waterfront pavilions that depended on the river for water.

The Alhambra as Landscape

The Taj Mahal is not the only site where a geographical perspective changes the way we see and understand a building and its gardens. The Alhambra and the nearby Generalife Palace, built by the sultans of Granada in the period 1232–1492 on the remains of earlier fortifications on the Sabika Hill, had numerous formal gardens and orchards with fountains and large pools that suggest that the site was amply endowed with water. But, in fact, all of these were watered by a system of canals called *acequias*. The hydraulic network was begun in 1238 when Sultan Muhammad I ordered the construction of the Acequia Real (Royal Canal), and it was expanded with secondary canals as the demand for water increased.[11] The canals drew from a dam site upstream along the Darro River, from where water from melting snows high in the Sierra flowed down through the ravine that forms one side of the Sabika Hill.[12] Although the hilltop palaces seem self-contained, encircled by massive walls, the site has no springs or natural water of its own and is utterly dependent on the water from mountain sources.

The geographical context of the Alhambra is easy to overlook when one gazes at the large body of water in the Court of the Myrtles and the spectacular fountain in the Court of the Lions, because the display in both courtyards was intended to convince the viewer that the Alhambra's patrons enjoyed an abundance of water. Thanks to expert engineering, in some sense they did. But if we look 'back stage' we can find the *acequias* that thread across the contours of the surrounding landscape and discover the large reservoirs that stored water for periods when the canals ran dry. We can then recognize the Alhambra not simply as a cluster of magnificent buildings but as a landscape with an extraordinary infrastructure. Each of the Alhambra's fountains and cultivated gardens owed its existence to water that came from elsewhere, and the same was true for the ordinary households and farms of Granada.

The emphasis on the environment can also introduce a new perspective on social systems. Whereas the methodology of architectural history focuses more sharply on the designer and patron than the lowly stonemason or digger of canals, the environmental model de-emphasizes the concept of authorship. Even where an architect or patron existed, the designed garden – once planted – was released into a temporal cycle of growth and decay, ranging from periods of a day to a season or decades, which the designer may have predicted but cannot control. The designer *inaugurates* a garden, initiating the system of cultivation, irrigation, reaping, and replanting that will inevitably be carried out by gardeners, rather than designers. Indeed, most gardens in history were not made by trained designers at all, but were the work of ordinary and anonymous gardeners or farmers. Illiterate, perhaps, but with extensive practical knowledge.

Conclusion

The journey from the designed object to human society and to the viewing subject leads us – or at least me – ultimately to the environment where, as the scale has expanded, the degree of individual human agency has diminished. We like to think of building complexes like the Taj and the Alhambra as great works of architecture and gardens, but they could not exist without the introduction of natural resources from far away, and this changes our understanding of how such sites are made – from an architect's design of a singular monument to the managed

Figure 4.5: Patio de la Acequia at the Generalife Palace, 1302–1308, Granada. Source: Jeffrey Schrader.

development of infrastructure on a large scale. In the latter, the changes are often incremental, the result of adaptations to the environment made through time, as prompted by community needs. As humans recede from the role of designers and architects, they become more present as inhabitants whose lives are profoundly affected by forces that may be beyond their individual control. Therefore, rather than thinking of architecture and landscape as the product of a few key individuals, we can ask: What is the effect of design on the people who lived (or live) at those sites? How do interventions in the land – such as dams, managed river flows, or canal systems – impact entire communities? The historical precedents of the Taj and the Alhambra may prompt us to consider contemporary implications of the same questions, although now with a greater sense of urgency and despair in view of our global leaders' failure to recognize their critical role as environmental stewards. If we have learned anything in the past decade, it is that a truly environmental approach to the land on which we live will require collective rather than individual commitments.

Notes

This chapter was previously published as D. Fairchild Ruggles, 'From Garden to Landscape: Lessons from the Taj and the Alhambra', *International Journal of Islamic Architecture* 10.1 (2021): 89–98.

1. Oleg Grabar, 'An Art of the Object', *Art Forum* 14 (1976): 36–43.
2. For an example of a study of inscriptions, see Sheila Blair, *Islamic Inscriptions* (New York: New York University Press, 1998); Maqrīzī, Kitāb al-sulūk li-maʿrifat duwal al-mulūk, 4 vols. in 12 parts (Cairo, 1934), trans. R. J. C. Broadhurst, *A History of the Ayyubid Sultans of Egypt* (Boston: Twayne Publishers, 1980).
3. Some key sources on vision, visuality, and semiotics in art and architecture are: Norman Bryson, *Vision and Painting: The Logic of the Gaze* (New Haven: Yale University Press, 1983); Hal Foster, ed., *Vision and Visuality* (Seattle: Bay Press, 1988); and Keith Moxey, 'Motivating History', *Art Bulletin* 77 (1995): 392–401.
4. A key theorist in landscape studies was Denis Cosgrove, *Social Formation and Symbolic Landscape* (Madison: University of Wisconsin Press, 1998). I have made my own contributions: D. Fairchild Ruggles, *Gardens, Landscape and Vision in the Palaces of Islamic Spain* (University Park: Pennsylvania State University Press, 2000), 107–09; and D. Fairchild Ruggles, 'Making Vision Manifest: Frame, Screen, and View in Islamic Culture', in *Sites Unseen: Landscape and Vision*, ed. D.S. Harris and D.F. Ruggles (Pittsburgh: University of Pittsburgh Press, 2007), 145–46.
5. John Brookes wrote that the Qur'an's description of four rivers of paradise 'is the origin of the quartered garden, known in Persian as the *chahar bagh*', but at the same time writes that the garden comes from 'early Persian origins'. John Brooks, *Gardens of Paradise* (New Amsterdam, NY: Meredith Press, 1987), 17–19, 28. Georges Marçais wrote: 'The part played by gardens in the past and present life of the Muslim peoples appears to stem from the conception of Paradise'.

Naficy Said, Georges Marçais, and A. S. Bazmee Ansari, 'Būstān', in *Encyclopaedia of Islam*, ed. P. Bearman, Th. Bianquis, C. E. Bosworth, E. van Donzel, W. P. Heinrichs (Leiden: Brill, 2012), accessed February 20, 2020, http://dx.doi.org/10.1163/1573-3912_islam_COM_0131.

6   I explored the different ways that a form such as the *chahar bagh* and its meaning(s) developed, in D. Fairchild Ruggles, 'The Rang Vilas Garden: An Unusual Rajput Chaharbagh at Bundi', in *Bundi Fort: A Rajput World*, ed. Milo Beach (Bombay: Marg Foundation, 2016), 130–43.

7   Ebba Koch, 'The Mughal Waterfront Garden', in *Gardens in the Time of the Great Muslim Empires*, ed. Attilio Petruccioli (Leiden: Brill, 1997), 140–60.

8   Wayne Begley, 'The Myth of the Taj Mahal and a New Theory of Its Symbolic Meaning', *Art Bulletin* 61.1 (1979): 7–37.

9   Elizabeth Moynihan, ed., *The Moonlight Garden: New Discoveries at the Taj Mahal* (Washington, DC: Smithsonian Institution, 2000), with chapters by Moynihan, David Lentz, James L. Wescoat, Jr., John Fritz, and George Michell. The 1652 document, a letter from Aurangzeb to his father (the emperor Shah Jahan), was translated by Wheeler Thackston in ibid., 28.

10 The water intake tower stands just south of the mosque, to the west of the great tomb. Ebba Koch, *The Complete Taj Mahal and the Riverfront Gardens of Agra* (London: Thames and Hudson, 2006), 208.

11 Ibn Idhari, *al-Bayan al-Mugrib*, trans. Ambrosio Huici Miranda (Tetuan: Editora Marroqui, 1954), 125.

12 The historic water systems serving the Alhambra have been thoroughly studied by Luis José García-Pulido, *El territorio de la Alhambra* (Granada: Patronato de la Alhambra y Generalife, 2013).

Chapter 5

Invisible Geographies in the Study of Islamic Architecture

Abidin Kusno

The notion of 'invisible geographies' refers to domains that cannot be easily identified in the conventional ways of studying Islamic architecture. It gestures toward the general failure of 'Islamic architecture' to capture domains that may not fall comfortably under the scope of the discourse. This essay suggests that the standard geography of Islamic architecture must be disrupted by the intrusion, insertion, and inclusion of localized, specific, and overlooked 'absent' geographies in order to open up its conventional rubrics.

Islamic architecture has long been associated with the monumental. Its presence registers an identity often of a supra-local scale. Its patrons are almost always the state or the powerful council of a religious institution. The study of Islamic architecture is therefore also a study of powerful places or sites imbued with privilege. The major sacred monuments of Islam also prescribe a particular geography to its visibility. Given that the study of Islamic architecture is tied to the construction of place (and time) and to the geography of monuments, the notion of 'invisible geographies' frames a potent challenge, as it refers to spaces that speak to no pre-given horizons. It problematizes the modernist legacy and its global ambition that has made the specificity of the local less important; it indicates blind spots in the obsessive attention given to monuments; it points to our contemporary time where Islamic identity and identification have gone virtual; it highlights the significance of contingency that carries moments of openness, of movement, and of undecidability into the struggle over power, space, and history. The following notes discuss some of these points and identify a few invisible geographies based on discursive materials and observations of a place with which I am deeply familiar.

Musholla in Alleyways

Invisible geographies might mean the geography of everyday life, which is often overlooked because of its presumed banality and polysemy, defined, as it frequently is, by the quality of possessing 'a bit of this and a bit of that'. It might also mean a marginalized neighbourhood that 'unnoticeably' exists at the periphery of any urban centre. It is not, however, existentially marginal, for it is part of the everyday-scape of everyone living in the city. It is just a geography of 'who cares'? I have perhaps seen too many of these geographies in the major cities of Islamic Indonesia, such as the alleyway neighbourhood, or *kampung*, which is a densely populated urban neighbourhood that is not cognitively or socially marginal. It is an elementary urban form in Indonesia that continues to dominate the urbanscape of most Indonesian

Figure 5.1: A *musholla* in the middle of a *kampung* near housing complexes in West Jakarta. Source: Abidin Kusno.

cities, including the capital, 'global' city of Jakarta. These neighbourhoods are characterized by irregular and unregulated settlements and zigzag alleyways. They exist in various parts of the city, often behind high-rise condominiums and luxurious shopping malls or between new housing complexes. Situated on land dominated by the informal market, the alleyway neighbourhood is precarious and filled with uncertainty as the city continues to renew itself by gentrifying the *kampung* areas [Figure 5.1].

Yet while uncertainty serves as the condition of *kampung*, many *mushollas* (small places of worship, either freestanding or attached to public buildings) continue to be built in the alleyway neighbourhoods. The scattered *mushollas*, with diverse architectural styles, are everywhere in the *kampung*. They are built rather democratically (or better, discursively), either by wealthy religious elites or by the neighbourhood community, often through *waqf* (charitable endowment) and other donations without any monitoring from, or coordination with, the government or any formal religious institution. They exist outside the gaze of the state. One could say that they are 'informal'. But does such distance from authoritative bodies give the alleyway

Figure 5.2: A plan for building a *musholla* in Jakarta. The text reads, 'Help us build Musholla Nurul Amal'. Source: Abidin Kusno.

*musholla*s a power to keep eviction or gentrification of the *kampung* at bay? Or should we say that they are built to provide a sense of certainty or to render vulnerability liveable? The *musholla*s are built, in contrast to the surrounding dwellings, in a manner that would remind one of power, prosperity, and permanence. They are in proximity with each other (some only 50 metres apart), and every one of them of course has a story or history of its own. They seem to compete with each other for influence, but they continue to co-exist with, or without regard for, each other. Is it because there are so many of them that the repetitive form eludes attention [Figure 5.2]?

The geography of *musholla*s seems to move with the *kampung*, whose territoriality is always being redrawn following urban renewal. Their geographies could be said to be invisible, as most of them are not on the official map. Mapping the *musholla* is thus as challenging as knowing the hidden sociocultural order of things, the political economy, and power relations behind their creation. Questions emerge about style, expression, and the semiotics of signs, as well as each of their roles in the *kampung*. How do we account for the emergence of a *musholla* in the context of current (self-)displacement of *kampung* dwellers who are moving out after selling off their (newly certified) lands to individual owners and property developers? What is the relation between the continuing construction of *musholla* and the displacement of *kampung*? This contradiction between erasure of *kampung* over time and the continuous production of *musholla*s is part of the unseen changes that are central to a consideration of invisible geographies of Islamic architecture. Certainly, the whole enterprise of 'Islamic architecture' would have to be shifted from the usual analysis of mosque as a state-sponsored monument to the analysis of civil societal politics and the political economies of urban transformation.

Hidden Intertwined Histories

'Invisible geographies' also refers to forgotten influences of places and cultures in the formation of ideas for *musholla* architecture. This is particularly the case when primary attention is given to the construction of the architectural image of global Islam. 'Invisible geographies' invites us to think about the relational process behind the idea of Islamic architecture and the local cosmopolitanism of religious building. Such relationality goes against the idea of a break separating the other(s) from Islam and the old from the new. The region of Indonesia is a crossroads of different cultures. Influences from Europe and the Middle East were long mediated by other geographies of great traditions emanating from India and China. The presence of Islam since the thirteenth century brought elements of different cultures, which in turn have enriched the processes of the localization of Islam in the region. Prior to western colonialism, mosques and *musholla*s took the form of hybrid Hindu-Buddhist-Chinese-Javanese local expressions, and such admixtures of different geographical styles never produced any standardized form of 'Islamic architecture' in the region. Instead, these forms draw attention to the irreducible significance of the space in between the place of origin and the place of destiny. They point to the importance of networking, reception, and retransmission in the formation of Islamic architecture. In a way, one could consider 'Islamic architecture' as an architecture-in-the-making, a process of continuing adaptation, absorption, and localization in a different place and time. How does this semiotics of hybridity carry over into the neologism of global Islamic architecture?

While the expression of Islamic architecture (in Indonesia) owes much to mediations beyond the common signifier of Islam, it is undeniable that the discourses of 'othering' Islam (under the influence of western colonialism) brought into architecture a unique appearance of distance. The early twentieth-century modernist discourses that detached Islam from Java (in part influenced by the colonial state and the increasing influence of Middle Eastern Islam among young Indonesians) has contributed much to the ongoing efforts to construct a unique identity for an Islamic architecture. In this enterprise, bringing Islam closer to the region presupposes a detachment from the local as a demarcation of the self. The effort to overcome distance between the Middle East and Southeast Asia, for instance, presupposes a separation from other localized cultures, a discourse that contributes to the invisibility of these cultures in Islamic architecture.

Yet, that which is 'absent' never fully disappears. Far from it; the unregulated processes of *musholla* buildings in the urban alleyway neighbourhood (discussed earlier) offer self-expressions that show hybridity to be continually at work. While some imagine Islamic architecture in terms of the global signifier of *kubah* (dome), others seek to re-connect with the local to make present the otherwise invisible geographies of Islamic architecture.

Moving Geography

A *musholla* is a place where inhabitants gather to pray, study, or rest. One could also add, for the 'back' alleyway *mushollas*, that it can also be a place for critical discussions on social and political issues. A designated sacred space is by no means a requirement, as daily prayers can take place anywhere. The spirit of 'anywhere' is essential for it frees one from any attachment to a place. This detachment, however, does not mean inattention to orientation (to *ka'ba*) or to the geographical imagination of Mecca as the 'centre'. It simply means that the geography of praying can be mobile and thus invisible. There is a strong sense of mobility enacted here, which makes Islamic practices both everywhere and nowhere. Can this mobility be an expression of invisible geographies (despite all the attempts to geographize Islam)?

Contemporary Indonesia offers just such an example of mobility. Aryo Danusari, an Indonesian anthropologist and film-maker, has identified a phenomenon that he called 'urban circularity', wherein the lower-middle class Islamic youth use motorbikes to move around the city's roadways so as to register both their presence and the religious practice of Islam that goes with them in urban spaces.[1] They regularly take over streets, parks, and other public spaces attached to commercial and public buildings and congregate there to discuss religious and social issues that interest them. Such 'performance' at once makes geography and architecture a matter of theatre, and it is this circulation in urban space that creates a condition of both the individuality and collectivity of the group. Furthermore, behind this performance, as Danusari points out, is a sense of marginalization among the lower-middle class youth in the city they call home. Some of these young people work during weekdays in formal establishments such as offices and shopping malls as lower-level service staff, others are freelancers working for their own informal enterprises. They perform on Saturday evenings (the secular time for hanging out) to register their own sense of religiosity against the Saturday-night scenes of the city. Members of the Tariqa Alawiya Youth Movement, as it is called, make themselves visible not through any particular geography associated with Islam. Their circulation around the city and the temporary occupation of different spaces across it depend not on the monumentality of well-known religious structures, but rather on their mobility through the urbanscape (via motorbikes). 'Islamic architecture' has become slightly irrelevant. Geography still matters (as they choose mostly public sites, not just anywhere), but only so that the performance can *take place*. They do not, however, intend to practice 'place-making', as they disappear after the performance. What is left over when the urban spaces come undone? Perhaps only impressions, memories and reminiscences of something happening, but not a permanent trace of them being here or there. Can we say that they contribute to invisible geographies of Islamic practices?

The Tariqa Alawiyas, who are followers of Arab Hadrami Sayyid descent, have another way to render visible the Islamic foundation of the city. Another performance, as Danusari also points out, in contrast to the mobility of motorbikes, *is* centred on place-making. Geography matters, for this example, in the context of absent geographies. But this is not any geography, but rather the geography of the dead, the sacred tombs of Islamic saints, which were retrieved to register the presence of historical memory of a place. The city of Jakarta is no doubt built on top of countless tombs and burial grounds, but the Tariqa Alawiyas lay claim to it as their heritage site. In 2010, the Tariqa Alawiyas clashed with public order officers who sought to remove what the Alawiyas believed to be the tombs of Hadrami saints. The event caught the attention of the masses and national media, which forced the state to grant the status of a 'national heritage' site even though it is not acknowledged by the Indonesian Council of Muslim Scholars (the Majelis Ulama Indonesia or MUI), who believe the tombs were a fraud. The Tariqa Alawiyas' claim nevertheless represents an instance of rendering visible the geographies of Islamic influence on a city that is increasingly subsumed by the geography of capital.

Conclusion

What seems to connect the Tariqa Alawiyas' movements and the proliferation of *mushollas* in the *kampung* alleyway is the profound fragmentation of the city, which is increasingly divided by the movement of capital. The Tariqa Alawiyas' youth movement seeks to connect the divided city temporarily by moving around it, covering important public spaces and jamming traffic with motorbikes. Its other movement tries to register the power of place by anchoring the sense of belonging with the geography of the dead. Similarly, the *mushollas* are expressions of fragments that nevertheless seek to speak, through an invisible network across the divided city, about the existence of the increasingly marginalized *kampung*. All these illustrative materials point to yet another 'invisible' force, that of capital, which is transforming space and yet giving context to the appearances of invisible geographies of Islamic practices in the Indonesian city. This essay suggests that there is an absence inside the field of Islamic architecture, and that we must take into account these absences as avenues to investigate various continuities, connections, and contexts outside the traditional, monumental, and sacred geography of Islam. The proximity of the absence, or the nearness of the invisible, is such that we can no longer be confident about identifying what is considered to be a part of the study of Islamic architecture. The '*mushollas* in the alleyway', the 'hidden intertwined histories', and the 'geography on the move' amplify the study of Islamic architecture and slightly displace the identity of 'Islam' and 'architecture', for these examples show the limit of architectural discourse to render visible the multiplicity of Islamic geographies. If 'invisible geographies' represent a desire to break out of the framework in which the study of 'Islamic architecture' is confined, then the question becomes about broadening the field from architecture to urbanism, from religion to geography, and from the global to the multiplicity of the local.

Acknowledgement

I would like to thank Mohammad Gharipour, without whom this essay would have been impossible, and also Shahrzad Shirvani and Nancy Um for their helpful comments on an earlier version. In particular, thanks to Shahrzad for suggesting the notion of 'invisible geographies', and Nancy for helping me to clarify the issues. I am of course responsible for any mistakes or shortcomings in the essay.

Note

> This chapter was previously published as Abidin Kusno, 'Invisible Geographies in the Study of Islamic Architecture', *International Journal of Islamic Architecture* 5.1 (2016): 29–35.

1   I am grateful to Aryo Danusari for sharing his research about the Tariqa Alawiya Youth Movement. See Aryo Danusari, 'Performing Crowds: The Circulative Urban Forms of the Tariqa Alawiya Youth Movement in Contemporary Indonesia' in *Global Prayers: Contemporary Manifestations of the Religious in the City*, ed. Jochen Becker, Katrin Klingan, Stephan Lanz, and Kathrin Wildner (Zurcih: Lars Mueller Publishers, 2013), 338–51.

Chapter 6

Silencing Palestinian Architectural History in Israel: Reflections on Scholarship and Activism

Alona Nitzan-Shiftan

During a class on the politics of architecture in Israel, a graduate student approached me with a personal inquiry, asking how to locate her family home in the history of architecture in Israel. She learned during her professional training to distinguish between different architectural modernisms – the inter-war modernism that won Tel Aviv its international fame, the bare, efficient, and repetitive modernism of the post-war era, the sleek and elegant high modernism of public buildings, and the blunt Brutalism alongside the revisionist regionalism of younger rebels. She was also familiar with the Ottoman architecture that won Acre, for example, a UNESCO declaration, and was well acquainted with the Palestinian vernacular that was ambivalently admired by Israeli architects for capturing 'the genetic code of the place'.[1] But she grew up in Nazareth, and although she could identify its Old City with the Ottoman vernacular, the house she grew up in, outside the city centre, was clearly modern [Figure 6.1]. It was built during the 1960s by a prominent architect, and its architecture fell into none of the familiar categories she learned. How can we call this architecture, she asked. Is there an Arab modernism in Israel?

This simple question testifies to an entrenched lacuna in the architectural historiography of Israel/Palestine – the architecture of Palestinians with Israeli citizenship who constitute 20 per cent of the Israeli population. But this conspicuous absence pertains to a much larger predicament of writing the architectural histories of societies that suffer intense political conflicts. Much of the scholarship on the Middle East, and on Islamic societies elsewhere, is entangled in such dynamics – national struggles and repeated outbreaks of violence. The question is how eruptions of strife shape architectural and urban histories. And reciprocally, can, or should, the history of architecture as a cultural production intervene in the predicament of conflict? When working in such sites, we often engage in an intellectual labour towards a cause. How can we judge the histories we produce as a result? Can we evaluate them as scholarly research or, rather, as activism? And why, if at all, do such qualifications matter? In this short piece I approach the absence of Palestinian architectural history in Israel as a testing ground for contemplating the broader relationship of architectural history to the political logic of nationalism and its discontents, especially when both are intimidated by conflict.

I suggest looking at the absence of Palestinian architectural history from three conflict-interrelated perspectives – the power to silence, the limits of access, and the reciprocity between activism and the writing of history.

Figure 6.1: General View of Nazareth, 1948. Source: Government Press Office (Israel).

The Power to Silence

The first and most obvious attribute of the aforementioned lacuna is the power of a dominant regime to silence the history of the subaltern. This is clearly the case in the context of the entrenched national conflict between Israel and Palestine, where the ownership over history is instrumentally translated into the right to possess the land. One does not need to dig deep in order to find the ample ways in which Israel sought to terminate Palestinian self-definition.[2] Until 1966 areas populated with so-called 'Arab Israelis' were put under military rule that restricted the mobility of Palestinians and prevented their integration into the Israeli civic body.[3] This policy emanated from the Israeli identification of its Palestinian citizens with the menacing Arab world and eventually would develop into what Oren Yiftachel describes as *ethnocracy* – democracy that provides equal rights only to the dominant ethnic group.[4] This ethnic prerogative includes the means to produce historical knowledge.

The lingering effects of ethnocracy have consistently silenced Palestinian (architectural) history, a process that according to Michel-Rolph Trouillot enters the process of historical production in four crucial moments of transforming 'facts' into knowledge: the making of sources, their assembly into archives, their retrieval into narrative, and their retrospective significance which is the 'making of history in the final instance'.[5] The silencing of Palestinian history was, indeed, inherent to the Zionist/Israeli nation-building project, and the histories that its professional and academic institutions produced. Since the early 1930s, the Jewish population in Palestine adopted modernism as a form of Zionist national expression, and prided itself on its rural settlement. For architectural professionals, the modernist path rendered 'the Arab Village' as neither a good precedent, nor a bad one. To them it was simply irrelevant to the rationalist logic producing the Zionist landscape.[6]

Breaking away from their predecessors, Sabra (Israeli-born) architects, who started to practice in the late 1950s, admired the Palestinian vernacular and carefully studied the formal attributes of 'the Arab village'. Their conviction that it was the most authentic expression of 'the place' reflected their critique of the state's rampant modernization, but it remained largely oblivious to the actual Palestinians whose culture it was. This was therefore a symptom of colonial ambivalence – Israelis desired the culture of the occupied in order to define their own architectural culture as rooted, wishfully native.[7] In so doing they reduced (or in their mind elevated) the Arab village to the zero degree of a natural phenomenon, a natural extension of the place, beyond time and therefore beyond historical narration. If anything, it was incorporated into the biblical-archaeological narrative that reaffirmed the Jewish proprietorship of the land, and cast Palestinians as its mere custodians.[8]

This enthusiasm declined after 1987, when the protest of the Palestinian intifadas decisively and forcefully asserted the Palestinian claim over this 'local architecture'. The historiographical outburst that followed focused on the history of the modern movement in Israel that provided a pacifying and righteous history. It marked the rise of an Israeli architectural historiography that hardly existed before. In 1994, when the International Style was being celebrated in the largest cultural halls,[9] my own generation of younger scholars gathered in the basement, armed with critical tools we acquired in schools overseas. We criticized the political underpinnings of celebrating the 'whitening' of Tel Aviv in the upper halls, but remained silent about the Palestinian architecture that was built at the same time [Figure 6.2].[10] This on-going relative silence that coincides with the development of critical scholarship in architecture is particularly surprising.

Many contemporary scholars in the field are unapologetically political and openly critical of the grand Zionist narratives and of Israeli violations of human rights. Many of them do write about Palestinian architecture, but mostly about its violation, destruction, and appropriation.[11] When it comes to a disciplinary history of modernism, for example, politically conscious scholars hesitate to speak on behalf of Palestinians, whom, they think, should have the liberty of writing their own history.[12] This is exactly where the challenge of conflict becomes apparent – in the implicit assumption that architecture is a national possession that can and should only be narrated by its rightful owners. Thus, the critics of the national logic that dispossessed Palestinians of their history foster the very same logic they oppose as a template for historiographic production. Moreover, the privilege of writing history is contingent on the existence of archives, language skills, state institutions, and research funds, all of which are scarce among Palestinians. As a result, whether you are part of the silencing regime or its uncompromising critic, the result is similar – Palestinian architectural history is silenced.

Figure 6.2: 'White City' advertisement for Tel Aviv Municipality (2004). 'The people of Tel Aviv are walking around with their heads held high… Now the whole world knows why!'. Source: Yehoshua/TBWA.

The Limits of Access

The visibility of this absence has recently grown together with the exponential growth in the number of Palestinians who have access to higher education in Israel. In recent years, the incoming architecture classes at the Technion, where I teach, have been roughly 40 per cent Palestinian. Faculty members, however, are overwhelmingly Israeli Jews. Thus, in our field the number of students who are Palestinian citizens of Israel has almost doubled their relative share in the general population, but are still without senior Palestinian role models.[13]

This brings me to my second point, the challenges facing scholars who wish to create a Palestinian architectural history that is not necessarily defined by its opposition to the dominant Zionist state, but rather can stand and excel on its own right. The accessibility to the historical sources they wish to study is a major obstacle. In the first half of the twentieth century, for example, borders in the region were open. Under the late Ottoman Empire and the British Mandate, the Levant functioned as an active frontier for the exchange of modern resources and ideas between the colonies and the European metropole.[14] But this frontier had different networks along which modernist knowledge had disseminated. The South African founder of Israeli modernist historiography, the late Gilbert Herbert, has highlighted the direct impact of

(Central) European modernism on Palestine, particularly because leading European architects were 'transplanted' in Palestine after they fled Fascism.[15] But, once we started to work on Palestinian modernism, we discovered that modernist knowledge circulated in the Middle East independently from Zionist networks and that Arab architects working in Palestine, trained in Arab countries, were responsible for the great impact on local Palestinian architecture during and long after the mandatory era.

Let me share some examples of research conducted by graduate students whose theses and dissertations I advised in recent years. These students work in unexplored terrains, and therefore challenge received views and tend to break new ground. We discovered, for example, that the Nazareth house that we mentioned above was part of a characteristic Arab modernist style only after visiting Ramallah, which required an illegal trip to the Palestinian Territories [Figure 6.3]. Crossing the border to Lebanon, where the architect Anis Srouji was trained, was impossible.[16] Haifa, a city that was evenly shared by Palestinians and Jews until 1948, opened a wider view onto this network. When we turn to study Antoine Tabet, a student of August Perret, one of the pioneers of modernism in Lebanon and an important advocate of the modern movement in Greater Syria, we realized that any attempt to decipher the unusual housing complex, the Garden Mansions, that he built in the late 1930s in downtown Haifa was contingent

Figure 6.3: View toward the Anis Srouji Family Villa. Source: Mira Saba Deeb, 'A Search for Arab Architectural Modernism in Palestine Space in the 1950s and 1960s' (M.Sc. thesis, Technion, 2015), 91.

Figure 6.4: Garden Mansions – general view (rendering). Source: Adeeb Daoud Naccache, 'Levantine Modernism: Antoine Tabet of Beirut, Raja Rais of Haifa and the Production of a New Architectural Style in the Garden Mansions, Haifa 1936–1945' (M.Sc. thesis, Technion, 2019), 163.

on alternatives to the praxis of archival work, such as activation of family connections overseas and informal correspondence with holders of different collections [Figure 6.4]. Indeed, how can one conduct a research that brings together a Palestinian entrepreneur, a Lebanese architect, as well as Iraqi and British funding and clients in a region riveted by numerous hermetic, sometimes volatile borders?[17] Even more demanding is the study of Palestinian cultural production under early Israel occupation (1967–82) that must resort to creative methods. Gaza is inaccessible, its historical players are largely in exile, and the state of emergency and violence in the Strip further limits the availability of cultural documents. This predicament does not allow even for the first moment of historical production that Trouillot describes, that is, the identification of facts – in our case plans and buildings – as worthy of scholarly attention [Figure 6.5]. This researcher had to search for materials through informal networks of exiled Palestinians and comb through numerous private collections in order to overcome the defining initial moment of silencing – with establishing data from scarce resources as a basis for a legitimate historical study.[18]

Activism and the Writing of History

This legitimization brings us to the third and most challenging reason for the absence of Palestinian architectural historiography in Israel, which is the seam, or the convergence, between the historian and the activist. In a 2017 conference on 'histories in conflict'[19] that I organized with Panayiota Pyla and several colleagues to mark the fiftieth anniversary of the 1967 occupation of East Jerusalem, hosted by the European Architectural History Network (EAHN) in

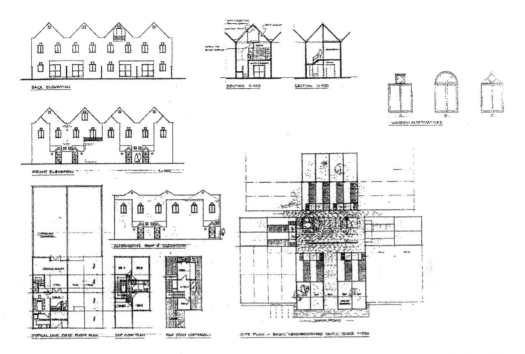

Figure 6.5: Housing for refugees by Eylon Meromi. Source: Fatina Abreek-Zubiedat, 'Architecture in Conflict beyond the Green Line Gaza and Yamit Cities 1967–1982' (Ph.D. diss., Technion, 2018), 227.

Jerusalem, we identified this historian-activist interface as the site 'where architecture/history/heritage are negotiated, contested and pulled apart'.[20] We asked whether we could conceive of history as a platform for negotiating urban justice and democracy? And if so, who is posing the rules of the game that requires we hyphenate the *historian-activist*? And where does one's primary agency reside – in scholarship, or in political action?

In areas of conflict, and in Israel/Palestine in particular, where human rights are often violated, the urgency of these questions increases. They pertain to the heart of the moment of making the sources and the archives of historical inquiry that Trouillot describes. Every historical inquiry starts in the present, in the time, space, culture, and power position from which the historian operates. Yet, how can we define the methodological difference between the activist and the historian in the way a historical question is formed? What are its implications towards the sources that we identify as worthy of field or archival work that can be qualified as research data? Activism starts with a critical analysis of a present situation that it wishes to amend. Is this *a priori* goal similarly valid as the engine of historical inquiry?

Clearly, as critical scholars we should strive to conduct the intellectual labour that would advance the public good. But perhaps we should also ask ourselves what are we compromising in the craft of the historian when this results in turning history into activism? In the context of

Israel/Palestine, architectural history is haunted by the looming presence of the Nakba and the prolonged Israeli occupation. Yet, commitment to resistance carries its own risks. According to Christopher Harker, it stereotyped the Palestinian geography 'as a place of violence and suffering, and, in this process, Palestinians themselves can become discursively erased as active subjects'.[21] To put it more bluntly, the commitment to resistance repeatedly constitutes Palestinians as victims, rather than stressing their agency as cultural producers. Scholars started amending this predicament by offering alternative historical vocabularies to analyse historical processes that extend beyond the dynamics and evolution of the Arab–Zionist conflict. We can see it in ethnographies and micro-histories of class, literature, economy, and development, to mention only a few.[22] We are yet to see this challenge significantly addressed in our own discipline.

Conclusion

According to Michel-Rolph Trouillot, 'History is the fruit of power, but power itself is never so transparent that its analysis becomes superfluous. The ultimate mark of power may be its invisibility; the ultimate challenge, the exposition of its roots'.[23] Power, as we have seen in the case of Palestinian citizens of Israel, is inclined to silence the architectural history of the subaltern. But what are the particularities of this process in sites of conflicts? We have seen that both the regime in power and its critics consider the Palestinian–Israeli conflict as the primary axis along which the vortex of historical change occurs. Since this axis is the one perpetuating inequality in the region, the knowledge it generates also perpetuates the position of the subaltern, or, in our case, the occupied victim. Following Trouillot, maybe this implicit consequence demands of us, architectural and cultural historians, to seek after the invisible roots of power in the historical modality that we pursue.

This reflexivity about writing histories in the predicament of conflict is particularly important after September 11 and the new dimensions of xenophobic sentiments that it generated towards Islam and its people and cultures. This latest wave of global violence took its toll on the politics of knowledge. It seems as if the division of power between a knowing 'West' and objectified 'Orient' that Edward Said famously theorized exploded onto a globalized world. Recently, a heated debate ensued about the potential entanglement of 'global history writing, humanitarianism, and the global heritage industry'[24] when '840 Iraqi refugees and internally displaced families were removed from the Erbil Citadel in Iraqi Kurdistan in order to transform the walled town into a heritage site'.[25] In this event, we are warned, both scholarship and humanitarian aid became trapped in the logic of the market and its implicit entitlement to erase the concrete specificity of human lives. Perhaps we should exercise similar caution regarding the scholarship we produce in order to resist oppressive regimes.

In his call for 'critical historiography', Mark Jarzombek proposes to move 'through a multitude of disciplines *in* history – while simultaneously thinking of the constrains *of* history'. This, he argues, would 'widen the indeterminate zone […] between the historian as "professional" and the historian as a possible "messenger" of repressed historicity'.[26] Can the professional historian and the political activist work mutually without losing sight of 'the cracks and fissures that one encounters', at once recognizing the lack of 'correspondence between a discipline and the unruly practices that sustain it?'[27] Especially in regions where much of our historical knowledge is generated by historians dedicated to producing the intellectual labour necessary to resist violence and combat the infringement of human rights, it may be urgent to constantly reflect on the 'constrains of history' in order to transcend the confines of official politics and seek venues to understand the dynamics of empowering and silencing multiple histories.

Acknowledgements

I am grateful to Fatina Abreek-Zubiedat, Adeeb Daoud Naccache, and Mira Saba Deeb, whose work I discuss and cherish, although this essay reflects my own position as an educator. Thanks to Uri Ram and Andrew Herscher for their insightful comments.

Notes

This chapter was previously published as Alona Nitzan-Shiftan, 'Silencing Palestinian Architectural History in Israel: Reflections on Scholarship and Activism', *International Journal of Islamic Architecture* 10.1 (2021): 233–43. The text has been updated for this publication.

1. Moshe Safdie, *Beyond Habitat* (Montreal: Tundra Books, 1973), 243.
2. See, for example, Uri Ram, 'Ways of Forgetting and the Obliterated Memory of the Palestinian Nakba', *Journal of Historical Sociology* 22.3 (2009): 366–95.
3. Shira Robinson, *Citizen Strangers: Palestinians and the Birth of Israel's Liberal Settler State* (Stanford: Stanford University Press, 2013).
4. Oren Yiftachel, *Ethnocracy: Land and Identity Politics in Israel/Palestine* (Philadelphia: University of Pennsylvania Press, 2006).
5. Michel-Rolph Trouillot, *Silencing the Past: Power and the Production of History* (Boston: Beacon Press, 2015), xxiii.
6. Julius Posener, 'Villages in Palestine (in Hebrew)', *HaBinyan – Magazine of Architecture and Town Planning* 3 (1938): 1–2.
7. See, for example, Alona Nitzan-Shiftan, 'Seizing Locality in Jerusalem', in *The End of Tranditon*, ed. Nezar AlSayyad (New York: Routledge, 2004), 231–55; Haim Yacobi and Hadas Shadar, 'The Arab Village: A Genealogy of (Post)Colonial Imagination', *Journal of Architecture* 19.6 (2014): 975–97; and Gil Eyal, 'The Discursive Origins of Israeli Separatism: The Case of the Arab Village', *Theory and Society* 25.3 (1996): 389–429.
8. Arye Dvir, 'Overall Plan for the Jerusalem National Park', in *The Jerusalem Committee, Proceedings of the First Meeting, June 30 – July 4, 1969*, ed. Julian J. Landau (Jerusalem: The Committee,

1969); Yizhar Hirschfeld, 'Traditional Dwellings in the Hebron Hills', in *The Palestinian Dwelling in the Roman-Byzantine Period* (Jerusalem: Franciscan Printing Press, 1995), 17.

9 'International Style Architecture', conference organized by the Municipality of Tel Aviv-Yafo, the Tel Aviv Foundation, and UNESCO, Tel Aviv, May 22–27, 1994.

10 For the canonic text on the modern architecture of Tel Aviv, see Judith Turner and Michael Levin, eds, *White City: International Style Architecture in Israel, A Portrait of an Era* (Tel-Aviv: Tel Aviv Museum, 1994). For critical texts, see Alona Nitzan-Shiftan, 'Whitened Houses (in Hebrew)', *Theory and Criticism* 16 (2000): 227–32; Mark LeVine, *Overthrowing Geography: Jaffa, Tel Aviv, and the Struggle for Palestine, 1880–1948* (California: University of California Press, 2005); Sharon Rotbard and Orit Gat, *White City, Black City: Architecture and War in Tel Aviv and Jaffa* (Cambridge, MA: MIT Press, 2015). The exception to the exclusion of Palestinian modernism is Shmuel Yavin and Charlotte Halle, eds, *Bauhaus in Jaffa: Modern Architecture in an Ancient City*, trans. Eliezer Erez and Natasha Dornberg (Tel Aviv: Bauhaus Center, 2006).

11 See, for example, Eyal Weizman, *Hollow Land: Israel's Architecture of Occupation* (London: Verso Books, 2007); Haim Yacobi, 'Architecture, Orientalism, and Identity: The Politics of the Israeli-Built Environment', *Israel Studies* 13.1 (2008): 94–118.

12 This is the reasoning, for example, for excluding the architecture of Palestinian citizens of Israel from the monumental exhibition and catalogue, *The Israeli Project*. See Zvi Efrat, *The Israeli Project: Building and Architecture 1948–1973* (in Hebrew) (Tel Aviv: Tel Aviv Museum of Art, 2004). Its recent English edition, *The Object of Zionism: The Architecture of Israel* (Liepzig: Spector Books, 2019), expands the research but nevertheless holds to the same position regarding Palestinian architectural production.

13 To the best of my knowledge the only Palestinian faculty member, to date, in an accredited Israeli architectural program is the practising architect Senan Abdelqader (Bezalel), and in an Israeli planning program, Yosef Jabareen (Technion).

14 Jacob Norris, *Land of Progress: Palestine in the Age of Colonial Development, 1905–1948* (Oxford: Oxford University Press, 2013); Leila Tarazi Farwaz and C. A. Bayly, eds, *Modernity and Culture: From the Mediterranean to the Indian Ocean* (New York: Columbia University Press, 2002); Abigail Jacobson, *From Empire to Empire: Jerusalem Between Ottoman and British Rule* (Syracuse, NY: Syracuse University Press, 2011).

15 Gilbert Herbert, *The Search for Synthesis: Selected Writings on Architecture and Planning* (Haifa: Architectural Heritage Research Centre, Faculty of Architecture and Town Planning, Technion, Israel Institute of Technology, 1997).

16 Mira Saba Deeb, 'A Search for Arab Architectural Modernism in Palestine Space in the 1950s and 1960s' (M.Sc. thesis, Technion, 2015).

17 Naccache Adeeb, 'Levantine Modernism: Antoine Tabet of Beirut, Raja Rais of Haifa and the Production of a New Architectural Style in the Garden Mansions, Haifa 1936–1945' (M.Sc. thesis, Technion, 2019).

18 Fatina Abreek-Zubiedat, 'Architecture in Conflict beyond the Green Line Gaza and Yamit Cities 1967–1982' (Ph.D. diss., Technion, 2018).

19 'Histories in Conflict: Cities – Buildings – Landscapes', *EAHN Third Thematic Conference*, Jerusalem, June 13–15, 2017. The event program is available at 'Histories in Conflict: Cities

| Buildings | Landscapes', European Architectural History Network, accessed May 1, 2020, https://eahn2017.com/.
20 'Histories in Conflict', European Architectural History Network, accessed May 1, 2020, https://eahn.org/social/groups/histories-in-conflict/.
21 Christopher Harker, 'Geopolitics and Family in Palestine', *Geoforum* 42.3 (2011): 307.
22 On history see Norris, *Land of Progress*; Jacobson, *From Empire to Empire*; Salim Tamari, *The Great War and the Remaking of Palestine* (Oakland: University of California Press, 2017); Beshara B. Doumani, *Family Life in the Ottoman Mediterranean: A Social History* (Cambridge: Cambridge University Press, 2017); Sherene Seikaly, *Men of Capital: Scarcity and Economy in Mandate Palestine* (Stanford: Stanford University Press, 2015); Shira N. Robinson, *Citizen Strangers: Palestinians and the Birth of Israel's Liberal Settler State* (Stanford: Stanford University Press, 2013); May Seikaly, *Haifa, Transformation of a Palestinian Arab Society, 1918–1939* (London: I. B. Tauris, 1995). On ethnography see Filip De Boeck and Sammy Baloji, 'Positing the Polis: Topography as a Way to De-Centre Urban Thinking', *Urbanisation* 2.2 (2017): 142–54; Harker, 'Geopolitics and Family in Palestine'.
23 Trouillot, *Silencing the Past*, xxiii.
24 Zeynep Çelik Alexander et al., 'Introduction: A Discussion on the Global and Universal', *Grey Room* 61 (2015): 68.
25 Daniel B. Monk and Andrew Herscher, 'The New Universalism: Refuges and Refugees Between Global History and Voucher Humanitarianism', *Grey Room* 61 (2015): 71.
26 Mark Jarzombek, 'A Prolegomena to Critical Historiography', *Journal of Architectural Education* 52.4 (1999): 203 (emphasis original).
27 Ibid.

Chapter 7

Islamic Architecture in the Americas: Advancing a Transregional and Hemispheric Approach

Caroline 'Olivia' M. Wolf

While recent decades have seen a significant expansion in the study of Islamic architecture from a global perspective, a key region in this field beckons further exploration – the Americas. As Bernard O'Kane has noted, the study of Islamic architecture located in the west remains an academic 'elephant in the room' within the field of art and architectural history.[1] The lack of scholarly literature surrounding Islamic architecture situated from Canada to the southern cone of Latin America – clearly a major component of the west – highlights the need for the rigorous development of the discipline from a hemispheric and transcultural perspective. While recent scholarly contributions, such as those of Akel Kahera and Tammy Gaber, have shed important light on contemporary mosques in the United States and Canada, respectively, and recent work by Holly Edwards and others has contributed to complex readings of orientalism in North America, the considerable legacy of Islamic architecture in the Americas still remains largely understudied due to its geographic and academic positioning beyond the constructed boundaries of the traditional Islamic world.[2] Recent examinations also tend to emphasize North American case studies and generally remain only loosely interwoven with narratives of global architectural history beneath the weighty 'Islamic architecture' label, despite there being various attributes uniquely shared among these structures across the Americas.[3] Work on Islamic architecture in Latin America remains sparse, although key studies on American mudejar architecture of the colonial period and on modern Revivalist styles have laid an important foundation for expanding research in this direction.[4] Nonetheless, the plethora of diverse examples – from Spanish mission mudejar, to the orientalist elements of Shriner Temples and contemporary Islamic religious cultural centres across the northern to southernmost regions of the hemisphere – all testify to the complex, localized legacy of Islamic architecture as an integral component of the built environment of the Americas.

This essay advocates for the rigorous expansion of the study of Islamic architecture across the Americas – from north to south – in a manner that emphasizes diasporic forms, frameworks, and networks that traverse and punctuate its built environment in a transregional fashion. Such an approach offers the opportunity to establish uniquely productive American regional or hemispheric readings of Islamic architecture that highlight specific connections within the broader narrative of global case studies. It also allows us to move beyond firmly entrenched orientalist frameworks of inquiry and isolated notions of architecture across the continents. By taking a transcontinental approach, the fresh juxtaposition of critical historiography, construction techniques, and ethnic and gendered dimensions, as well as the visual legacy of migration associated with Islamic traditions in the Americas, promises to bring forth fruitful insights.

While the field is poised for a rigorous examination of Middle Eastern architectural forms in the Americas, from colonial to contemporary times, such an endeavour is not without challenges. One of the first hurdles is the disparate character of published research on Islam-associated architecture across the northern to southern reaches of these continents to date, which tends to be insulated by period and constructed within modern national boundaries. Significantly missing are scholarly publications that address Islamic architectural forms between North and Latin America comparatively.

Foundations for Inquiry

A brief overview of the literature and key case studies associated with this topic from a temporal and geographic standpoint highlights benchmarks and persistent lacunae in the field. Beginning temporally, the study of the complex phenomenon known today as 'American mudejar' responds to a plethora of seventeenth-century colonial Latin American sites, as well as Spanish Mission structures in North America.[5] Scholars tracing the historiography of *mudéjar* have noted the term was first coined and used to describe the art and architectural phenomena associated with the craftmanship of Muslim subjects under Christian rule after the Reconquista by José Amador de los Rios in 1859.[6] Its study was popularized with the publication of texts by Spanish nationalist authors such as Marcelino Menéndes y Pelayo, as well as architect and architectural historians Fernando Chueca Goitia and Manuel Toussaint.[7] As Thomas Cummings and María Judith Feliciano have observed, Toussaint's text was both pioneering – particularly due to the scope of its survey and analysis of wooden *artesonado* ceilings – as well as problematic, as it reflected an orientalist mindset that essentially interpreted mudejar in the Americas as simply an 'Islamic' derivative and a foreign element in Ibero-America [Figure 7.1].[8] Research on construction techniques and the role of architectural treatises brought from Europe to New Spain have shed light on modes of transatlantic transmission, as well as the powerful contributions of indigenous artisans, as the study of mudejar in Latin America continued to expand into the twentieth century.[9]

Art historian María J. Feliciano and literary scholar Leyla Rouhi provided key frameworks for consideration of American mudejarismo, while calling for renewed scholarly scrutiny of the phenomenon.[10] Emphasizing mudejar in the region as particularly American, they argue its historiography and architectural afterlives must be carefully and critically re-examined, especially with respect to its ties to the nationalist and orientalist perspectives infused within the field since its onset. This call to new methodological and theoretical explorations of American mudejar has witnessed a fruitful response via new frameworks of transculturality posited by art historians such as Ila Nicole Sheren.[11] These recent approaches have broadened critical considerations of the phenomenon that unpack American mudejar's culturally palimpsest nature, which was shaped by diverse artisans of Spanish as well as indigenous and African heritage.

Figure 7.1: Example of an *artesonado* ceiling, Palacio de Dávalos, Guadalajara, La Mancha, Spain. Source: Flickr/Biblioteca Pública del Estado de Guadalajara.

Building out the context and the transnational scope of mudejarismo's visual legacy in the Americas, Spanish Mission architecture in the United States provides an important point of continuity and comparison to its Latin American parallel. Of course, American mudejar is just one of myriad architectural facets associated with the built environment of New Spain, along with other transcultured styles that merged the visual forms of indigenous and/or colonial Spanish traditions. This is embodied by styles like Plateresque and Tequitqui, elements of which are particularly known for their mixed cultural associations. These provide key case studies of American mudejar.[12] Leading architectural historians have crossed the modern border between the United States and Mexico to examine mudejarismo in New Spain's northernmost outposts in what is today Texas, New Mexico, Arizona, and California. The work of art historian George Kubler and later studies developed in the 1990s by T. B. Irving, Jacinto Quirarte, Clara Bargellini, and Michael Komanecky have expanded research in this area.[13]

In the 2000s, James Early – trained as a historian of American civilization and professor emeritus of English at Southern Methodist University, where he also taught courses on colonial architecture and cities – provided a comprehensive survey of Spanish architecture in North America, drawing on three decades of scholarship.[14] A study by Gloria Fraser Gifford, an art historian and retablo expert, on religious art and architecture in northern New Spain – the area spanning northern Mexico (northern Zacatecas and San Luis Potosí) and the Southwestern United States (Texas, New Mexico, Arizona, and California) – has also contributed to this area of study.[15] Gifford's overview of styles and construction, as well as the builders, with emphasis on guilds and women artisans, provides an exciting path forward for future comparative hemispheric studies. By taking this border-crossing approach to the study of American mudejar, parallels in construction techniques, as well as frameworks of transcultural and gendered forms of knowledge, are highlighted. This invites a broader contemplation of race, representation, and gender in the so-called 'New World'.

As this distilled overview reveals, a major challenge faced in this line of inquiry is the diversity and ambiguity of nomenclature surrounding the built forms associated with Middle Eastern traditions in the Americas. An array of divergent terms, from 'Hispano-Moorish' to 'American mudejar', carry hefty historiographic connotations that add complexity and resist categorization under current architectural taxonomies. This issue has contributed to the various disconnected approaches to architectural analysis of the stylistic phenomenon in the Americas.

The challenge of nomenclature is not limited to research of the colonial era, but it is also visible in nineteenth-century Revivalist variations, with terminology ranging from 'Neo-Moorish', 'Neo-Arab', 'Neo-Andalusian', and 'Neo-mudéjar' again creating historiographic challenges for modern studies. Here again, these ambiguous labels rife in the literature still demand a rigorous unpacking of their nationalist and orientalist underpinnings as popularly aestheticized styles with deep roots in romantic imaginaries. Examples are embodied by a panoply of miniature adaptations of the Alhambra and the iconic tower of the Giralda.[16] As Zeynep Çelik noted, world's fairs played a key role in circulating orientalist architectural styles in the west during this era,[17] while American authors like Washington Irving fanned the public's imagination for the 'exotic'.[18] Pattern books popularized by Owen Jones helped to circulate the Alhambra's stucco designs, plans, and polychrome ornament while inspiring the desire to craft constructions mimicking the site across the Americas, reflecting broader trends also seen in Europe.[19]

Omar Khalidi and Holly Edwards have demonstrated how spiritual and secular echoes of Islamic architectural forms can be encountered via orientalist styles across the northern hemisphere of the continent.[20] The style found favour in domestic architecture as a selective choice for elite residences and even large-scale residential developments, as seen in the striking example of Opa Locka in Florida.[21] Opulent commercial ventures, such as theatres, storefronts, and bazaars, similarly opted for orientalist forms.

Yet architectural evocations of the Middle East in the modern United States also went beyond these exoticizing and capitalist associations to be employed in buildings for religious and fraternal use. Synagogues in North America and beyond adopted Moorish Revivalism largely due to the influence of Gottfried Semper, who advocated for the style's use at sites of Jewish worship due to perceived shared origins in the Middle East and association with the Golden Age of Judaism in Al-Andalus.[22] New York City's Central Synagogue, designed by Henry Fernbach in 1872, provides an excellent example, with its prominent horseshoe arches and onion domes [Figure 7.2]. The style also provided a distinct aesthetic alternative to the

Islamic Architecture in the Americas

Figure 7.2: New York City Central Synagogue, New York. Source: Flickr/Wally Gobetz.

Gothic Revival style sweeping the country on Christian church façades at that time, making it particularly appealing for the Jewish community in the United States and Europe.[23]

Benevolent societies and fraternal orders, such as the Shriners – officially named the 'Ancient Arabic Order of the Nobles of the Mystic Shrine for North America' – also drew heavily on an orientalist architectural idiom. The Medinah Temple built in Chicago in 1912, as well as the Tripoli Temple in Milwaukee in 1926, opted for the Moorish Revival style, complete with lavish onion domes and vibrant polychrome accents.[24] These sites often eclectically embrace diverse regional elements. In the case of the Tripoli Temple, architectural elements associated with Moghul India, as well as Ottoman-style minarets and a turquoise-tinted Persian motif, were incorporated.[25] Of course, these sites represent just a few case studies of a countless number of such structures.

A parallel use of the Moorish Revival style flourished in modern Latin America, which shared its northern counterpart's orientalist fascination with Near and Middle Eastern architecture. From Central America to the southern cone, nineteenth-century structures inspired by the Alhambra emerged across the built environment. Here, elements of Middle Eastern architecture were also incorporated into residences, commercial ventures, and sites of leisure, faith, and fraternity in a fashion parallel to North American patronage. *Alhambras: Arquitectura NeoArabe en Latinoamerica*, edited by Rafael López Guzman and Rodrigo Gutiérrez Viñuales and published in 2016, is one of the few books dedicated to the topic. While the volume provides an exciting overview of structures, it shies away from a critical reflection on some of the more problematic aspects of the study of Revivalist styles, such as the classification of these structures as 'Neo-Arab' without interrogating the transnational dimensions suggested by this term.

While many of these examples still engage with orientalism, some also highlight the strategic use of Middle Eastern styles to underscore notions of ethnic and transnational identity through the architectural patronage of immigrants to the Americas. This is particularly true for patrons with ties to the large waves of immigration from the Levant – particularly Lebanon, Syria, and Palestine – to Latin America at the beginning of the mid-nineteenth century. São Paolo, Brazil, provides us with just one example of a key nexus for modern Middle Eastern diasporic architecture in Latin America. There, the powerful mark of the successful Syrian immigrant family – the Jafets – sponsored villas with strong orientalist elements, such as the building known today as the Palacete Rosa [Figure 7.3].[26] The lavish residence features structural horseshoe arches as well as panoramic landscapes of the Middle East rendered in the form of interior murals.

At the same time, the first continuously used mosque in all of Latin America – the 'Brazil Mosque' of São Paolo – was also collectively sponsored and designed by Syrian and Lebanese immigrants, who employed an eclectic mix of Neo-Mamluk and Ottoman Islamic architectural forms.[27] Construction efforts for the mosque began with the Muslim Mutual Aid Society (*Sociedade Beneficente Muçulmana*) in 1929, while the primary phase of construction of the purpose-built mosque appears to have taken place from 1946 to 1960.[28] Similarly, the Syrian-Lebanese club of the same city – a lively social hub for the Middle Eastern immigrant

Figure 7.3: Palacete Rosa, Ipiranga, São Paulo. Source: Caroline 'Olivia' M. Wolf.

community since the twentieth century that continues to function as such today – also employs arabesque ornament within its interior, specifically within its auditorium. The manners in which these structures engage with Middle Eastern architectural traditions – at times reflecting constructs of the orientalist imagination, or alternately crafting architectural representations of identity – highlights the transnational aspects of the patronage of these buildings.

As Oleg Grabar concluded in his landmark essay, 'Roots and Others', images associated with the so-called East 'answer deep psychological and social needs'.[29] While orientalist forms in modern architecture appear in both North and South America, shifts in immigration patterns reflective of more stringent policies in the north reveal a more prominent use of Middle Eastern architectural styles by diaspora communities in Latin America as a proud marker of ethnic identity.

From Historicist Approaches to Contemporary Designs

Building upon the powerful examples of diasporic patronage via the sites mentioned above, modern and contemporary religious structures in the Americas also tend to make strategic allusions to Middle Eastern architectural forms. Case studies of Muslim religious architectural patronage in North America serve as dialectical hemispheric counterpoints that promise fresh transnational insights in the rapidly diversifying field of Islamic architectural history.

The late 1980s and 1990s witnessed growth in the literature on Islam and Muslims in the United States, as well as the development of major mosques and religious complexes across North America. During these decades, Gulzar Haider designed such quintessential structures as the Islamic Society of North America in Plainfield, Indiana, and the Bai'tul Islam Mosque of Toronto, while publishing various germinal texts on mosques in the 'West' from the 1980s through the 1990s.[30] Haider's essay, 'Muslim Space and the Practice of Architecture: A Personal Odyssey', observes that particular Middle Eastern architectural styles in the Americas are paradoxically drawn upon as both a stereotypical setting for structures of leisure (i.e., casinos and theatres) for a general secular public, while also serving as a symbolic referent of religious space for various Muslim communities in diaspora.[31] Omar Khalidi's overview of mosques in the United States and Canada followed shortly thereafter, furthering research that helped established key case studies in the northern hemisphere.[32]

Jerrilynn D. Dodds and Edward Grazda's *New York Masjid: The Mosques of New York*, which highlighted the diverse Islamic religious architecture and communities of the city, was published in 2002. The work places a strong focus on African-American storefront mosques and religious centres with a strong immigrant, indigenous, and convert contingent, which includes a growing Latino Muslim community.[33] Enriching the discussion of mosques in the United States, Akel Ismail Kahera's research on North American mosques emphasizes the heterogeneity of Muslim religious spaces across the country, from New York to New Mexico. In the introduction to his landmark work, *Deconstructing the American Mosque: Space, Gender and Aesthetics*, Kahera laments the historical lack of literature on mosques in North America and takes on the task of defining the 'American mosque' as a new building type infused with a 'syncretic aesthetic language'.[34] Over the course of his research, Kahera has also closely examined gender debates at play in the design of North American mosques and in Muslim discourse, as well as the politics of Muslim space in the United States in the post-9/11 era.[35] Although Kahera's observations are currently contained within the geographic boundaries of the United States, his work provides a critical steppingstone for hemispheric research dialogues.

North American examinations through the lens of gender have already begun to be established transnationally. Tammy Gaber's expansive work on gendered space in Canadian mosques extends this dialogue further north, examining a range of architectural styles and regional adaptations across the country.[36] Further building on the Canadian front, Andrea Lorenz and Nadia Kurd have highlighted sites such as the Al-Rashid Mosque of Fort Edmonton and Toronto's Bai'tul Islam Mosque.[37] This research, too, provides fertile ground for further hemispheric considerations, as the parallel incorporation of orientalist forms in Muslim religious architecture in Canada invites promising analysis via comparative studies with the United States and Latin America.

Research that examines mosques from an international and global perspective, such as Renata Holod and Hasan-Uddin Khan's *The Mosque and the Modern World: Architects, Patrons and Designers since the 1950s*, and Martin Frishman and Hasan-Uddin Khan's *The Mosque: History, Architectural Development and Regional Diversity*, has played an important role in expanding the field in terms of geographic horizons and methodology.[38] Although North America is predominantly featured in these volumes, an important albeit concise case study featuring the Al-Ibrahim Mosque in Caracas, Venezuela, opened the door for further regional studies.[39] The forthcoming *The Religious Architecture of Islam*, edited by Kathryn Moore and Hasan-Uddin Khan, also offers a rigorous global perspective, and will include respective sections on the Americas in its volume dedicated to Islamic architecture in the west.[40] While it focuses on key mosques in the Middle East, Kishwar Risvi's text *The Transnational Mosque: Architecture and Historical Memory in the Contemporary Middle East* provides a critical perspective regarding the paradigms of transnational patronage in the field that can be productively applied to a hemispheric analysis of case studies in the Americas.[41]

Comparative Case Study: The Brazil Mosque of São Paulo and Islamic Center of Washington

A closer look at the Brazil Mosque of São Paulo reveals the potential for future insights via comparative analysis with mosques and Islamic centres in the United States, as it demonstrates remarkable parallels in terms of patronage, temporal development, and aesthetic choices. With its rooftop crenelations, ornate polylobe windows, and colourful arabesque interior adornment, the eclectic mix of Neo-Mamluk and Ottoman Islamic styles infused upon the Brazil Mosque visually highlights transnational styles linked to traditional Islamic architectural forms, yet are applied in an eclectic, ahistorical fashion [Figure 7.4]. Although the

Figure 7.4: Brazil Mosque, São Paulo. Source: Caroline 'Olivia' M. Wolf.

combination of historicizing elements that decorate its façade and interiors allows the building to be misread as an informed pastiche, the structure instead reflects the palimpsest identities and intentional design choices of its immigrant patrons. The building itself was designed by Paulo Camasmie, an architect of Syrian-Lebanese heritage active in São Paulo.[42] While visual evocations of Islam emanate nostalgically from the building's Egyptianizing decorative motifs and expansive interior colonnades, the plan also carefully accounts for modular spatial units of prayer, demonstrating an awareness of Muslim prayer practices. Thus, a complex interplay of architectural elements associated with Muslim identity are syncretically and strategically combined with a religiously informed use of space.

This Brazilian Latin American case study opens the door for comparative analysis with the orientalist elements incorporated into North American sites described by Khalidi as embodiments of 'faith, fantasy, and fraternity', as well as reflections regarding the syncretic architectural evocation of the past introduced by Kahera in his study of mosques and Islamic centres across the United States. Khalidi points out the allure of architectural traditions associated with the Middle East to a broader western public eager to engage with orientalist forms for their exotic appeal. Khalidi at the same time notes the role of 'imported design' for diverse diasporic religious communities in the construction of religious space, including Jewish communities.[43] Similarly, one of the earliest monumental mosques in North America, the Islamic Center of Washington, DC, designed by Cairo-based Italian architect Mario Rossi and constructed in 1957, took an 'imported design' approach that focused on re-creating historical architectural elements '"blending" old and new'.[44] Adopting a neo-Mamluk style, the centre's adornment strongly features historicizing exterior elements, such as rooftop crenelations, Fatimid-inspired keel arch windows, and a towering central minaret [Figure 7.5]. The interior is richly decorated with vibrantly painted ornamental designs, evocative of the pattern books of Owen Jones. The monumental structure – the largest mosque in the western hemisphere at the time of its construction[45] – was also fitted with cascading muqarnas and polylobed arches. Like the Brazil Mosque, the Islamic Center reflects the support of multinational religious networks, with wall tiles donated from Turkey, chandeliers from Egypt, and rugs imported from Iran.[46]

In carefully considering these two sites from a transnational and transregional perspective, what emerges is a shared place-making endeavour to establish Muslim space via an architecturally eclectic and nostalgic design strategy. Notably, both the Brazil Mosque and the Washington Islamic Center were conceived, constructed, and completed at approximately the same time. The design process for the current iteration of the Brazil Mosque was initiated around 1946, although the structure was completed much later in 1960. Similarly, the designing of the Islamic Center of Washington began in November 1944, and construction was completed in 1957.[47] This temporal comparison reveals that both structures took well over a decade to complete, pointing to the difficulties faced by minority religious immigrant communities to construct Muslim religious spaces in the Americas.

Kahera's analysis of the Islamic Center in Washington allows us to identify similar syncretic architectural elements to those employed in the Brazil Mosque. In fact, both sites adopt a specifically neo-Mamluk aesthetic.[48] This intentional choice suggests an interest in evoking

Figure 7.5: Islamic Center of Washington, Washington, DC. Source: The Carol M. Highsmith Archive, Library of Congress, Prints and Photographs Division.

an 'authentic' image of Islam that looks to the past in modes that navigate between – and problematically draw from – constructs of Muslim identity and the orientalist architecture forms already familiar with Western audiences. Kahera astutely notes in his analysis of the Islamic Center that the adoption of a sentimental historicizing aesthetic by its Palestinian Muslim patron had the additional function of fomenting collective identity in foreign North American environs.[49] The Brazil Mosque, sponsored by Muslim immigrant patrons from Syria and Lebanon, can be seen as sharing this sentimental search for a nostalgic architectural aesthetic capable of fomenting a sense of religious collectivity in diaspora.

Both religious sites also embody palimpsest spaces of diverse Islamic identities over time, as they have come to serve indigenous converts in addition to new and continuing generations of Muslim immigrant communities in the Americas. For example, Washington, DC, would become an important centre for North America's growing African-American Muslim community, while mosques across Brazil would attract a strong Afro-Latino contingent of believers attracted by Black religious and cultural revival associated with emancipation and social justice movements in both North and South America.[50] The parallel diversity of the faith-based communities associated with these case studies thereby highlights the multi-ethnic, multi-racial legacy of Islam in the Americas.

Conclusion: Hemispheric Insights and Possibilities

This reflection on the state of the field demonstrates how a comparative hemispheric approach to the legacy of Islamic architecture across the Americas could unpack new transregional insights. From colonial to contemporary eras, parallel construction techniques, styles, and materials, as well as issues of race, ethnicity, and gender associated with Islamic architecture in the region, all invite more rigorous engagement that would benefit from this comparative lens. As noted, nomenclature with roots steeped in orientalism, from which the fields of art and architectural history emerged, still awaits further critical analysis. The term 'Neo-Arab', for example, continues to evade decolonial analysis. Additionally, a comparative hemispheric reflection on contemporary mosques in the Americas advances knowledge of the unique diasporic experiences and architectural forms of diverse communities. The emphasis placed on both secular and religious spaces in this essay – from social clubs to mosques and synagogues – underscores the symbolic value of Islamic architectural forms as part of a larger discourse on diasporic cultural patrimony and frameworks of identity meaningful to Muslim-minority communities in the Americas.

Such an inquiry will bridge the discursive gap in scholarship surrounding the rich visual manifestation of Middle Eastern architecture from a global and hemispheric perspective, fostering new perspectives that expand upon traditional geographical frameworks in the field. As revealed by the examples in this essay, ample avenues call for further exploration via this proposed regional lens. A new research approach in this direction also promises to shed light on the importance of diverse diasporic agents, adaptations, and identities associated with the legacy of Islamic architecture across the Americas.

Notes

1 Bernard O'Kane, 'Widening Horizons for the Study of Islamic Architecture', *International Journal of Islamic Architecture* 10.1 (2021): 75. This essay is reproduced in the present volume.
2 Akel Ismail Kahera, *Deconstructing the American Mosque: Space, Gender and Aesthetics* (Austin: University of Texas Press, 2002); Tammy Gaber, 'Gendered Mosque Spaces: Cultural, Religious, or Accessibility Issue?', *Faith and Form* 48.1 (n.d.), accessed February 16, 2021, https://faithandform.com/feature/gendered-mosque-spaces/; Holly Edwards, *Noble Dreams, Wicked Pleasures: Orientalism in America, 1870–1930* (Princeton: Princeton University Press, 2000).

3   Key discussions of Islamic architecture as an 'unwieldy field' include Oleg Grabar, 'Reflections on the Study of Islamic Art', *Muqarnas* 1 (1983): 1–14; Sheila Blair and Jonathan Bloom, 'The Mirage of Islamic Art: Reflections on the Study of an Unwieldy Field', *Art Bulletin* 85.1 (2003): 152; as well as several essays in the present volume. Other leading scholars who have addressed the limitations of this field of study include Robert Hillenbrand, Dogan Kuban, and Hasan-Uddin Khan.

4   For Revivalist styles in Latin America, see Raphael López Guzmán, Rodrigo Gutiérrez Viñuales et al., *Alhambras: Arquitectura Neoarabe en Latinoamerica* (Granada: Almed Editores, 2016); Raphael López Guzmán, Rodrigo Gutiérrez Viñuales et al., 'The Alhambras of Latin America', *Aramco World* (January–February 2021), 12–21, https://www.aramcoworld.com/Articles/January-2021/The-Alhambras-of-Latin-America.

5   María Judith Feliciano and Leyla Rouhi, 'Introduction: Interrogating Iberian Frontiers', in *Medieval Encounters: Jewish Christian and Muslim Culture in Confluence and Dialogue* (Leiden: Brill, 2006), 317–28. The authors advocate for the non-accented spelling of the term in the context of the Americas as a mode of highlighting the style's indigenous aspects in the region and to establish the term as an English descriptor.

6   María Judith Felicano provides an overview of the popularization and circulation of the term 'mudéjar' in 'The Invention of Mudejar Art and the Viceregal Aesthetic Paradox: Notes on the Reception of Iberian Ornament in New Spain', in *Histories of Ornament: From Global to Local*, ed. Gülru Necipoğlu and Alina Payne (Princeton: Princeton University Press, 2016), 358n1. For the original source inaugurating the term's use, see José Amador de los Rios, 'El estilo mudéjar en la arquitectura', speech given at the Real Academia de las Bellas Artes de San Femando (Madrid) in 1859. See also José Amador de los Rios, *El estilo mudéjar en la arquitectura* (Madrid: Imprenta de Manuel Tello, 1872).

7   For the original texts, see Fernando Chueca Goitia, *Invariantes castizos de la arquitectura española* (Madrid: Dossat, 1947); Manuel Toussaint, *Arte mudéjar in América* (Mexico City: Editorial Porrúa, 1946). This was quickly followed in 1948 by George Kubler, *Mexican Architecture of the Sixteenth Century* (New Haven: Yale University Press, 1948). For a bibliographic essay on the historiography of mudéjar, see Jerrilynn D. Dodds, María Rosa Menocal, and Abigail Krasner Balbale, *The Arts of Intimacy: Christians, Jews and Muslims in the Making of Castilian Culture* (New Haven: Yale University Press, 2008). Feliciano and Rouhi have advocated for the use of the term without an accent to refer to its appearance in the Americas (i.e., American mudejar), while the term with the accent refers to its appearance in Spain and Portugal, or the Iberian peninsula, due to distinct contexts.

8   Thomas Cummins and Maria Feliciano, 'Mudejar Americano: Iberian Aesthetic Transmission in the New World', in *A Companion to Islamic Art and Architecture*, ed. Barry Finbarr Flood and Gülru Necipoğlu (Oxford: Wiley Blackwell, 2017), 1025.

9   Ibid. Architectural treatises are also cited in John F. Moffitt, *The Islamic Design Module in Latin America: Proportionality and the Techniques of Neo-Mudéjar Architecture* (Jefferson, NC: McFarland, 2004). A plethora of studies published circa the 1992 500-year anniversary of the 'discovery of the New World' and Reconquista of Granada led to the publication of further studies on American mudejar. See Rafael López Guzman et al., *Arquitectura y carpintería mudéjar en Nueva España* (Mexico: Grupo Azabache, 1992); I. Henares Cuéllar, *El mudéjar*

iberoamericano: Del Islam al Nuevo Mundo (Granada: El Legado Andalus, 1995); I. Henares Cuéllar and R. López Guzmán, *Mudéjar iberoamericano: Una expresión cultural de dos mundos* (Granada: Universidad de Granada, 1993); G. M. Borrás Gualis et al., *El Arte Mudéjar* (Zaragoza: UNESCO, 1995).

10 Feliciano and Rouhi, 'Introduction', 326. The authors note the many studies published around the time of the quincentenary of Columbus's arrival in the 'New World' and Reconquista of Granada (1992) led to the publication of further studies on American mudejar. See Rafael López Guzman et al., *Arquitectura y carpintería mudéjar en Nueva España* (Mexico: Grupo Azabache, 1992); I. Henares Cuéllar, *El mudéjar iberoamericano: Del Islam al Nuevo Mundo* (Granada: El Legado Andalus, 1995); Cuéllar and Guzman, *Mudéjar iberoamericano*.

11 Ila Nicole Sheren, 'Transcultured Architecture: Mudéjar's Epic Journey Reinterpreted', *Contemporaneity: Historical Presence in Visual Culture* 1 (2011): 137–51.

12 For an overview of these colonial-era architectural styles in the Americas, see Gloria Fraser Gifford, *Sanctuaries of Earth, Stone, and Light: The Churches of Northern New Spain, 1530–1821* (Tucson: University of Arizona Press, 2007).

13 See George Kubler, *Religious Architecture of New Mexico* (Chicago: Rio Grande Press, 1962); George Kubler, *The Religious Architecture of New Mexico: In the Colonial Period and since the American Occupation* (Albuquerque: University of New Mexico Press, [1940] 1973). Kubler also notably published on Ibero-American architecture across central and southern New Spain. See also George Kubler and Martín Soria, *Art and Architecture in Spain and Portugal and their American Dominions* (Harmondsworth: Penguin Books, 1959), 76–77; Thomas B. Irving, *Mudejar Crafts in the Americas with Illustrations and Maps* (Cedar Rapids: Mother Mosque Foundation, 1991); Clara Bargellini, *La Arquitectura de la Plata: Iglesias Monumentales del Centro-Norte de México, 1640–1750* (Mexico City: Universidad Nacional Autónoma de México, 1991), 111–12; Jacinto Quirarte in *Cambios: The Spirit of Transformation in Spanish Colonial Art*, ed. Gabriela Palmer and Donna Pierce (Albuquerque: University of New Mexico Press, 1992), 10–12. More recent publications include Clara Bargellini and Michael K. Komanecky, *The Arts of the Missions of Northern New Spain, 1600–1821* (Mexico City: Antiguo Colegio de San Ildefonso, 2009).

14 James Early, *Presidio, Mission, and Pueblo: Spanish Architecture and Urbanism in the United States* (Dallas: Southern Methodist University Press, 2004). On criticisms, see the review by Kenneth Hafertepe, *Winterthur Portfolio* 40.1 (2005): 79–81.

15 Gifford, *Sanctuaries of Earth, Stone, and Light*. This region's architecture has also been explored in Bargellini, *La Arquitectura de la Plata*, 111–12; Quirarte, *Cambios*, 10–12.

16 Francisco Javier Recio, 'La Giralda en la Arquitectura Americana: Réplicas, imitaciones e influencias', in *Alhambras: Arquitectura Neoárabe en Latinoamérica*, ed. Rafael López Guzmán and Rodrigo Gutiérrez Viñuales (Granada: Almed Ediciones, 2016), 121–27.

17 Zeynep Çelik, *Displaying the Orient: Architecture of Islam at Nineteenth Century World's Fairs* (Berkley: University of California Press, 1992).

18 Washington Irving's romantic texts, *Conquest of Granada* (1829) and *The Alhambra* (1832) are particularly credited for having fueled this orientalist phenomenon in literary spheres. For more on orientalism, see John Sweetman, *The Oriental Obsession: Islamic Inspiration in British and American Art and Architecture, 1500–1920* (New York: Cambridge University Press, 1988).

19 Owen Jones, *A Handbook to the Alhambra Court* (London: Crystal Palace Library, 1854).
20 Omar Khalidi, 'Fantasy, Faith and Fraternity: American Architecture of Moorish Inspiration', ARCHNET, 2004, https://archnet.org/authorities/2736/publications/4742. It was later published in *Muslims and American Popular Cultures*, vol. 2, ed. Iraj Omidyar and Ann R. Richards (Santa Barbara, CA: Praeger, 2014), 295–303. Akel Kahera also briefly discusses Opa Locka in his 'American Mosque Architecture', in *The Oxford Handbook of American Islam*, ed. Yvonne Yazbeck Haddad and Jane I. Smith (New York: Oxford University Press, 2015), 416. On orientalism, see Holly Edwards, 'A Million and One Nights: Orientalism in America, 1870–1930', in *Noble Dreams, Wicked Pleasures: Orientalism in America, 1870–1930*, ed. Holly Edwards (Princeton: Princeton University Press, 2000), 11–75.
21 Emily Neumeier has recently examined the Opa Locka site in detail. See Emily Neumeier, 'Constructing Orientalism in Interwar Florida', in *Expanding Dialogues of Diaspora: Manifestations of Middle Eastern Architecture in the Americas*, ed. Caroline 'Olivia' Wolf (Bristol: Intellect, forthcoming 2023).
22 For more on the use of Moorish Revival in synagogues in the United States and beyond, see Ivan Davidson Kalmar, 'Moorish Style: Orientalism, the Jews, and Synagogue Architecture', *Jewish Social Studies* 7.3 (2001): 68–100; Carol H. Krinsky, *Synagogues of Europe: Architecture, History, Meaning* (Cambridge, MA: MIT Press, 1985).
23 Khalidi, 'Fantasy, Faith and Fraternity'.
24 Ibid. Phil Pasquini has also published a comprehensive photographic essay documenting 'Islamic-inspired' buildings in North America in 2012. Phil Pasquini, *Domes, Arches and Minarets: A History of Islamic-inspired Buildings in America* (Novato, CA: Flypaper Press, 2012).
25 Khalidi, 'Fantasy, Faith and Fraternity'.
26 For more on the patronage of the Middle Eastern immigrant community in São Paolo, see Caroline 'Olivia' M. Wolf, 'Migrant Monuments, Monumental Migrants: São Paulo's Sculptural Homage to Syrian-Lebanese Friendship and the Crafting of Transnational Identity in Centennial Brazil', *TAREA* 4.4 (2017): 120–52.
27 Caroline 'Olivia' M. Wolf, 'Modern and Contemporary Mosques in Latin America: Tracing Local and Transnational Dimensions through Temporal and Geographic Frames', in *The Religious Architecture of Islam*, vol. 2, ed. Kathryn Moore and Hasan-Uddin Khan (Turnhout: Brepols, 2022).
28 Paulo Gabriel Hilu da Rocha Pinto, 'Muslim Identities in Brazil: Engaging Local and Transnational Spheres', in *The Middle East and Brazil: Perspectives on the New Global South*, ed. Paul Amar (Bloomington: Indiana University Press, 2014), 241–56. Da Rocha Pinto states the society was established in the city in 1929, with construction taking place from 1946 to 1960, yet the mosque's own web publications cite the construction as having taking place in 1929. See 'Mesquita Brasil', Facebook, accessed May 21, 2021, https://www.facebook.com/mesquitadobrasil.sbm/.
29 Oleg Grabar, 'Roots and Others', in *Noble Dreams and Wicked Pleasures: Orientalism in America, 1870–1930*, ed. Holly Edwards (Princeton: Princeton University Press, 2000), 3–10.
30 Works on Islamic architecture in North America by Haider include Gulzar Haider, 'Islamic Architecture in Non-Islamic Environments', in *Places of Public Gathering in Islam: Proceedings of Seminar Five, The Aga Khan Award for Architecture, Held in Amman, Jordan, 4–7 May 1980*

(Philadelphia: Smith-Edwards-Dunlap, 1980), 123–25; Gulzar Haider, 'Brother in Islam, Please Draw Us a Mosque: Muslims in the West: A Personal Account', in *Expressions of Islam in the Buildings of Islam: Proceedings of an International Seminar Sponsored by the Aga Khan Award for Architecture, Held in Jakarta and Yogyakarta, Indonesia*, October 1990, ed. Hyat Salam (Aga Khan Trust for Cultures, 1990), 155–66; Gulzar Haidar, 'Faith Is the Architect: Reflections on the Mosque', *Architecture and Comportment* 3–4 (1995): 67–73.

31 Gulzar Haider, 'Muslim Space and the Practice of Architecture: A Personal Odyssey', in *Making Muslim Space in North America and Europe*, ed. Barbara Metcalf (Berkeley: University of California Press, 1996), 31–45. Metcalf's volume examining Islamic architecture through a transnational lens in the so-called 'West' also includes an essay by Susan Slyomovics on storefront mosques in New York City, along with Metcalf's own chapter on Tablighi Jama'at in the United States and Canada. The volume set an important foundation for examining Islamic religious architecture in North America.

32 Omar Khalidi, the well-known and prolifically published Aga Khan librarian at MIT's Rotch Library, produced various texts on North American mosques and Moorish Revival architecture. For key examples, see Omar Khalidi, 'Approaches to Mosque Design in North America', in *Muslims on the Americanization Path?*, ed. Yvonne Yazbeck Haddad and John L. Esposito (Oxford: Oxford University Press, 2000), 317–34; Omar Khalidi, *Mosques in the United States of America and Canada* (Berlin: US Embassy Germany, 2006?); Omar Khalidi, 'Import, Adapt, Innovate, Mosque Design in North America', *Saudi Aramco World* (November-December 2001), 24–33; Khalidi, 'Fantasy, Faith and Fraternity'. Khalidi's 'Mosques in the United States and Canada' collection is now accessible online on ARCHNET via its 'Regional Surveys, Projects' resources at 'Mosques in North America: A Tribute to Dr. Omar Khalidi', ARCHNET, November 2014, https://archnet.org/collections/813.

33 Jerrilynn D. Dodds and Edward Grazda, *New York Masjid: The Mosques of New York* (New York: PowerHouse Books, 2002).

34 Kahera, *Deconstructing the American Mosque*, 1–2. Drawing on parallels in linguistics as well as notions of deconstruction established by the classical philosopher Ibn 'Arabi, Kahera establishes Muslim religious architecture in the United States as operating within a new American idiom still deeply engaged with Islamic theological constructs of beauty (*jamal*).

35 Akel Kahera, 'Muslim Spaces and Mosque Architecture', in *The Cambridge Companion to American Islam*, ed. Juliane Hammer and Omid Safi (Cambridge: Cambridge University Press, 2013), 228–45.

36 For an exploration of mosques across Canada, see Tammy Gaber, *Beyond the Divide: A Century of Canadian Mosque Design and Gender Allocation* (Montreal: McGill-Queen's University Press, 2022); Gaber, 'Gendered Mosque Spaces'.

37 Andrea Lorenz, 'Canada's Pioneer Mosque', *Saudi Aramco World* 49.4 (July-August 1998): 28–31; Nadia Kurd, 'Sacred Manifestations: The Making and Meaning of Mosques in Canada', *Journal of Canadian Art History/Annales d'histoire de l'art Canadien* 33.2 (2012): 148–69. Hasan-Uddin Khan and Kathryn Moore's upcoming publication on the religious architecture of Islam from a global perspective will feature a section on mosques in the Americas. See Moore and Khan, *The Religious Architecture of Islam*. For more on Canadian mosques, see

Nadia Kurd, 'Competing Visions, Common Forms: The Construction of Mosque Architecture in Canada and the United States' (Ph.D. diss., McGill University, 2013).

38 Renata Holod and Hasan-Uddin Khan, *The Mosque and the Modern World: Architects, Patrons and Designers since the 1950s* (London: Thames and Hudson, 1997); Martin Frishman and Hasan-Uddin Khan, ed., *The Mosque: History, Architectural Development and Regional Diversity* (New York: Thames and Hudson, 1994).

39 Holod and Khan, *The Mosque and the Modern World*, 35–37.

40 For sections on Latin America in this volume, see texts by Caroline 'Olivia' Wolf (on modern and contemporary case studies) and Michael Schreffler (on colonial) in Moore and Khan, *The Religious Architecture of Islam*. See also Courtney Lesoon, 'Masjid and Mezquita: Translating the Mosque in Chile (1986–2006)', in Wolf, *Expanding Dialogues of Diaspora*.

41 Kishwar Risvi, *The Transnational Mosque: Architecture and Historical Memory in the Contemporary Middle East* (Chapel Hill: University of North Carolina Press, 2015). For application of the paradigm of the transnational mosque in the context of Latin America, see Caroline 'Olivia' Wolf, 'Monumental Mosques in Latin America', *Khamseen: Islamic Art History Online*, August 28, 2020, https://sites.lsa.umich.edu/khamseen/short-form-videos/2020/monumental-mosques-in-latin-america-key-modern-and-contemporary-case-studies/; Courtney Lesoon, 'Masjid and Mezquita: Translating the Mosque in Chile (1986–2006)', in Wolf, *Expanding Dialogues of Diaspora*.

42 For more on the Brazil Mosque, see Wolf, 'Modern and Contemporary Mosques in Latin America'.

43 Khalidi, 'Fantasy, Faith and Fraternity'.

44 Omar Khalidi, 'Mosques in North America', *American Studies Journal* 52 (2008), http://www.asjournal.org/52-2008/mosques-in-north-america/.

45 Kahera, *Deconstructing the American Mosque*, 68–72.

46 Khalidi, 'Import, Adapt, Innovate', 26–27.

47 'The Islamic Center D.C.', Islamic Center of Washington, accessed March 2, 2021, https://theislamiccenter.us.

48 Kahera closely analyzes the Islamic Center of Washington in Kahera, *Deconstructing the American Mosque*, 68–72.

49 Ibid.

50 For a transregional overview of the history of Islam in the Americas, with emphasis on the United States and Brazil, see Sylviane Diouf, 'First Stirrings of Islam in America', in *The Oxford Handbook of American Islam*, ed. Yvonne Haddad and Jane Smith (Oxford: Oxford University Press, 2015), 15–28. For more on the Muslim legacy and contemporary religious practice in Brazil, see Da Rocha Pinto, 'Muslim Identities in Brazil'.

Part 3

Historiography and Context

Chapter 8

Cultural Encounters, Local Practice, and Historical Process in the Ancient Middle East

Dell Upton

Having taught world architectural history for twenty-five years, I have puzzled over ways to turn an enterprise traditionally framed as a catalogue of cultures and styles into a genuinely global history. Many world architectural historians have relied on historical models created for smaller-scale architectural history. These include biography; culture, defined as a static and bounded entity; social, political, or religious power; or simple semiotics. They have then attempted to finesse the leap from the local to the global by veneering terms such as 'encounter', 'hybridity', and 'cross-cultural exchange' over these inherited models. Yet, neither these models nor the precise ways they apply to architectural change have received much thought. This chapter raises some historiographical questions that architectural historians often overlook. It is a first step in a long-term project to consider how we account for architectural change over long distances and long periods of time.

We might begin by looking at a site in western Asia, which has traditionally been depicted as a crossroads and generator of religions, cultures, goods, and ideas. The Sanctuary of Bel at Palmyra (Tadmor, Syria), a major entrepôt on the trading routes between the Mediterranean and the lands to the east, raises the kinds of questions that are less visible in customary treatments of traditions erroneously presented as self-contained, such as those of Pharaonic Egypt or Renaissance Italy. The Sanctuary of Bel was the largest surviving ancient structure at the site until its main temple was destroyed by Da'esh in 2015. Dedicated in 32 CE but constructed primarily between 17 CE and the early second century, the sanctuary stood for nearly 2000 years. During its long life, it served indigenous, Christian, and Muslim worshippers. The complex occupies an artificial platform used for sacred purposes since the third millennium BCE. The *temenos* (sacred precinct) was enclosed by an outer *peribolos* wall (sacred enclosure) and approached through a monumental gate. The interior of the *peribolos* wall was lined with a colonnade, giving the space the feel of a very large forum or *agora* in a pre-planned Roman or Hellenistic city, or even of a monumental version of the *sahn*s (courtyards) and *riwaq*s (arcades) found in the mosques that were built in the region centuries later [Figure 8.1]. A banqueting hall, ablution fountains, and the main temple were situated in the open space.

To the casual observer, the main structure looked like a Greco-Roman temple [Figure 8.2]. Its rectangular *cella* (inner chamber), oriented roughly north-south, was embellished at the narrow ends with Ionic columns bracketed by shallow *antae* (engaged square pillars). A peristyle of Corinthian columns was crowned by pediments on the short ends, implying the presence of a gable roof. However, the pediments screened a flat roof terrace with towers at the corners and with *merlons* (stepped pyramidal ornaments) along the eaves [Figure 8.3]. The

Figure 8.1: Temple of Bel (*c.*first–second centuries CE), Palmyra (Tadmor), Syria. Reconstructed portion of *peribolos* wall (sacred enclosure) with interior colonnade. Source: Dell Upton.

entrance was marked by a colossal doorway, set off-centre among the columns on the long west side and opening into a double-ended sanctuary. Inside, a *thalamos* (raised, stage-like shrine) at the north end was bracketed by stairways that led to the terrace, and another *thalamos* at the south was approached by a ramp that may have facilitated the removal of a sacred image for use in processions [Figure 8.4].

How might one account for the construction of this sanctuary, in this place, and at that time? Most historians and archaeologists have resorted to associating each of the architectural elements I have mentioned with a particular culture or region. The temple's peripteral colonnade and pediments reflect Roman or Hellenistic building practices; the entrance to the temple owes something to Ptolemaic architecture; the *merlon*s, the transverse entry, and the habit of repeatedly building over earlier sacred sites derive from ancient Mesopotamia; and the roof terrace as well as the enormous *peribolos* that accommodated crowds of worshippers during periodic festivals belong to 'the East' in general. These attributions imply that architecture changes as 'influences' come and go, as the presence of certain people or ideas in certain times or places causes – by some unspecified process – builders to use certain architectural forms.

To explain the Sanctuary of Bel in this manner, we tend to assign relative values to the influences and calculate a kind of weighted average. For some scholars, the sanctuary was

Figure 8.2: Temple of Bel. Note *merlons* (stepped pyramidal ornaments) above colonnade at right. Source: Dell Upton.

'constructed in a fairly orthodox Roman style', and was thus an example of the process archaeologists call 'Romanization', but modified by expressions of 'the particularity of Palmyrene identity'.[1] Thus, the site exemplified 'the genius of Roman authority, which was adept at blending the talents and creative faculties of the most brilliant people in the empire' and it was 'the best example of cultural exchange' in the eastern Roman Empire.[2] To others, it was an appropriation of Greco-Roman architectural forms reinterpreted for Syrian purposes, a 'Hellenized veneer masking an indigenous form'.[3] The visual references to Classical architecture were 'purely superficial', and, '[a]part from superficial decorative details', the Sanctuary of Bel 'belonged wholly within an eastern tradition'.[4] Yet, it may have been 'an eccentric form', that was 'unquestionably an original design, marked by the Syro-Mesopotamian tradition', or even a herald of 'a completely new architectural language'.[5]

Embedded in these descriptions are the most common kind of architectural-historical explanation, marshalled particularly for architecture that does not fit into the modern Western model of individualized architectural creation.[6] The tendency to catalogue and weigh influences stands in as an explanation for the Sanctuary of Bel, the Dome of the Rock, a South Asian bungalow, or any other so-called hybrid building. But this strategy is unsatisfactory as an account of historical change, providing an example of what the philosopher David Hume called argument from contiguity, based on 'a comparison, and a discovery of those [observed]

Figure 8.3: Temple of Bel. Reassembled corner *merlon* (stepped pyramidal ornament). Source: Dell Upton.

relations, either constant or inconstant, which two or more objects bear to each other'.[7] The repeated conjunction of independent events or entities, be they architectural forms or ethnic, cultural, or other religious practices, implies causation. Yet in Hume's view, contiguity is, in itself, 'imperfect and unsatisfactory' as a causal explanation, for it is observation, not explanation.[8] Put simply, contiguity describes chronological and geographical change without specifying the historical processes by which change occurs. Moreover, this account of historical change stumbles in using heterogeneous, extrasomatic, totalizing concepts. Influence, culture, ethnicity, or other more specific kinds of political, religious, and intellectual ideas are used to account for choices of structure, plan, ornament, or any other architectural quality, even though the influences and the specific practices are of different orders of magnitude.

Influence-as-explanation fails to account for the particular combination of elements that characterize each building. The Sanctuary at Baalbek and the Temple of Artemis at Gerasa were both built at roughly the same time as the Sanctuary of Bel, and despite the differences between the three complexes, the descriptions of their main features might read very similarly. By focusing my description on the elements of the Sanctuary of Bel that could be traced to broad influences, I overlooked significant elements of the complex that were grounded in the local. Those elements have to do with the translation of influences, customarily understood as cultural ideas, into stones and mortar, walls and ornament. I did not discuss building materials,

Figure 8.4: Temple of Bel. *Cella* (inner chamber) and south *thalamus* (raised, stage-like shrine). Source: Dell Upton.

craft techniques, or any other aspects of the construction process. By ignoring these material aspects of architectural creation, I left the misleading impression that ideas flow freely, unconstrained by local economics, materials, or labour. I omitted the interplay of the local and the extralocal that Oleg Grabar, for example, evoked in his discussion of the origins of the Dome of the Rock. Grabar acknowledged the physical and the local but separated the Dome's attributes into an elite or translocal realm of ideas and a local, everyday practice of construction, which inflected ideas. As he put it, these distinctions generated 'the equilibrium, or tension, [the Dome] exhibits between local and pan-Islamic traditions and practices', in what he referred to as 'a constant leitmotiv in explanations of the Dome of the Rock'.[9] In this tension, Grabar implied a hierarchical separation of intellect and craft such as that characterizing the ideology of the modern architectural profession. The notion of influences survives in his account, but the local and the cosmopolitan compete with one another rather than one yielding to the other.

A better approach to historical process might begin with architectural practice. Culture is learned from both one's predecessors and one's contemporaries and architectural ideas are actualized in stone and mortar by individual agents whose bodies mediate ideas and materials. At the same time, no building is ever the product of a single person's performance. Each can be uniquely mapped at the intersection of disparate forms of practice or expertise that encompass but are not limited to ritual, craft, intellect, engineering, law, social practice, or taste. None of these factors is shared by all the makers.[10] These forms of knowledge are cultural and therefore learned, existing only through specific transformations of materials. The tensions among makers and realms of expertise during the construction of many buildings stimulate gradual change within a relatively stable architectural environment. At any given time, most buildings are locally similar, but few are precisely alike; over time, local building practice moves away from its initial state.[11] Many historians call this dynamic stability 'structure'. Structure is multiform and only partially integrated, as are modes of practice. Many gradual changes are absorbed and normalized in a way that gradually transforms them.

Occasionally, irregularly, and unexpectedly, structures are shaken by occurrences so disruptive that they alter existing structures in irreversible ways without actually destroying them. Historian William H. Sewell, Jr., calls such occurrences 'events'.[12] In architecture, events might include the incursion of radically different but powerfully imposed ideologies (such as the aggressive proselytization and official enforcement of Christianity and Islam) changing labour relations, new building technologies, or even the use of novel materials such as concrete. Events rarely erase existing structures of architectural praxis, but they do transform them into something that is profoundly the same, yet also different. The interaction of structured practices and disruptive events always operate at the local level.[13]

This model has two implications for the ways we conceive of architectural-historical processes at a local or a regional scale. First, a reworking or even abandonment of the idea of tradition, which too often characterizes long-term structural change as stasis, is demanded.[14] Second, an understanding of individual buildings as fluid rather than fixed is implied: as long as people use the buildings, their meanings will change and their physical fabric will be altered. There is no such thing as the canonical or ultimate form of any building.[15]

These issues become more urgent – and more vexing – as we expand our histories chronologically and geographically. Is it possible to write a global history that integrates structures, places, practices, and events? If architectural history is grounded in the local performance of heterogeneous ideas and practices, how can historians continue to write global histories structured around a parade of exceptional buildings? Instead, we would need to account explicitly for the discontinuous and multi-scaled historical processes that generate particular buildings. This would require us to relinquish many of the analytical concepts that we customarily use, which act much as macros do in computing by compressing discontinuous and multi-scaled historical processes into a bolus of unexamined categories and descriptors such as I have criticized above. The resulting summary labels often conceal more than they reveal. Some readers might argue that categories such as Islamic, modern, Asian, American, or other national entities, culture, influence, hybridity, and many others form the foundations of architectural historical practice; they are the skeletons without which our narratives would be formless. Our work would be 'unthinkable if [we] do not take for granted some primary premises, categories, or presumptions', as the historian Joan Wallach Scott has put it.[16] Scott goes on to suggest that for some historians, 'nihilism, anarchy, and moral confusion are the sure alternatives to these givens, which have the status (if not the philosophical definition) of eternal truths'.[17] Perhaps there could be no such thing as architectural history without these truths, although human actors would surely continue to make architecture as a physical object, regardless. At present, I can only acknowledge the dilemma as we seek a better model.

Notes

This chapter was previously published as Dell Upton, 'Cultural Encounters, Local Practice, and Historical Process in the Ancient Middle East', *International Journal of Islamic Architecture* 11.1 (2022): 5–12.

1. Jaś Elsner, *The Art of the Roman Empire, AD 200–450* (New York: Oxford University Press, 2018), 107, 116.
2. Félix-Marie Abel, *Histoire de la Palestine depuis la conquête d'Alexandre jusqu'à l'invasion arabe*, vol. 2 (Paris: J. Gabalda, 1952), 115, quoted in Maurice Sartre, *The Middle East Under Rome*, trans. Catherine Porter and Elizabeth Rawlings (Cambridge, MA: Harvard University Press, 2005), 171; Andreas Schmidt-Colinet, 'Aspects of "Romanization": Tomb Architecture at Palmyra and Its Decoration', in *The Early Roman Empire in the East*, ed. Susan E. Alcock (Oxford: Oxbow Books, 1997), 157.
3. Kevin Butcher, *Roman Syria and the Near East* (Los Angeles: Getty Publications, 2003), 281.
4. Warwick Ball, *Rome in the East: The Transformation of an Empire* (Abingdon: Routledge, 2000), 329, 330.
5. Butcher, *Roman Syria*, 361; Sartre, *The Middle East Under Rome*, 314; Schmidt-Colinet, 'Aspects of "Romanization"', 157, 361.
6. On description as explanation, see Allen Megill, *Historical Knowledge, Historical Error: A Contemporary Guide to Practice* (Chicago: University of Chicago Press, 2007), 79, 83, 86–92.
7. David Hume, *A Treatise of Human Nature*, ed. Ernest C. Mossner (London: Penguin Classics, 1985), 121.
8. Ibid., 125.
9. Oleg Grabar, *The Dome of the Rock* (Cambridge, MA: Harvard University Press, 2006), 63.
10. On the wide variety of expert knowledge and actors that shape contemporaneous buildings, see Howard Davis, *The Culture of Building* (New York: Oxford University Press, 2006).
11. My thinking on this aspect of architectural change is influenced by Pierre Bourdieu's concept of praxis in *The Logic of Practice*, trans. Richard Nice (Stanford: Stanford University Press, 1990), and Peter Galison's discussion of intercalation in *Image and Logic: A Material Culture of Microphysics* (Chicago: University of Chicago Press, 1997), especially Chapter 9.
12. See William H. Sewell, Jr., *Logics of History: Social Theory and Social Transformation* (Chicago: University of Chicago Press, 2005).
13. See Ibid., 124–151, 218, 219, 227, 244, 245. For a brief consideration of this issue in an architectural context, see Nasser Rabbat, 'Continuity and Rupture in Islamic Architecture', *International Journal of Islamic Architecture* 10.1 (2021): 47–48.

14 For an earlier formulation of this position, see Dell Upton, 'The Tradition of Change', *Traditional Dwellings and Settlements Review* 5.1 (1993): 9–15.
15 Compare, for example, the static and discrete view of Renaissance palaces in Florence offered by standard architectural histories with the much more contingent description offered in Richard Goldthwaite, 'The Florentine Palace as Domestic Architecture', *American Historical Review* 77 (1972): 977–1012, which points out that domestic spaces did not respect the apparent boundaries among buildings. For an analysis of the sanctuary at Baalbek from this viewpoint, see Dell Upton, 'Noah, Solomon, Saladin and the Fluidity of Architecture', *Journal of the Society of Architectural Historians* 68.4 (2009): 457–65.
16 Joan Wallach Scott, 'The Evidence of Experience', *Critical Inquiry* 17.4 (1991): 780.
17 Ibid.

Chapter 9

Neo-Eurocentrism and Science: Implications for the Historiography of Islamic Art and Architecture

Samer Akkach

A recently published and impressive two-volume set, *A Companion to Islamic Art and Architecture*, edited by Finbarr Flood and Gürlu Necipoğlu, reveals an unprecedented collaborative attempt by leading scholars to revamp the field and renegotiate its established frameworks in new terms.[1] The lengthy introduction by Flood and Necipoğlu revisits many of the key issues that have haunted the discipline since its inception, presenting a carefully argued resetting of the field's conceptual and methodological parameters. In their lucid discussions, the editors placed particular emphasis on the inter-connected issues of unity versus diversity, periodization, key thresholds of change, and dealing with the 'modern'. With reference to S. D. Goitein, they used periodization as a 'scientific prerequisite' to establish a seemingly 'neutral' chronological structure that avoids the pitfalls of conventional dynastic, regional, or media-based taxonomies, and through this they aim to dismantle the taxonomic logic underlying the old canons found in art history surveys and art catalogues. In their preferred chronological timeframe, they considered the Mongol sacking of Baghdad in 1258 as representing *the* most significant threshold of change, 'a watershed in the development of Islamic art and architecture',[2] according to which they divided their collection into two volumes: the first is titled *From the Prophet to the Mongols*, and the second, *From the Mongols to Modernism*.

While their preoccupation with periodization appears as a less controversial issue of preference, their discussions of the 'Islamic' and unity versus diversity – the most recurrent issues of debate in the field – appear more divisive. Their discussions reveal a two-sided position: on one hand there is a clear distancing from the earlier works of the field's orientalist founders and their close followers who sought a unifying meaning of the 'Islamic', as well as from the works of the essentialists and/or universalists who seek an ahistorical understanding of the 'Islamic'; on the other hand there is a growing rift between two camps, who are united against uniformity, essentialism, and universalism, but in growing disagreement about the increasing 'unwieldiness' of the field as a result of its increasing diversity.[3] Arguing against Blair and Bloom's concern over unwieldy diversification, Flood and Necipoğlu saw in the field's transition to a 'multifocal and multivocal arena of inquiry […] a mark of its coming of age'.[4] In emphasizing the importance of the field's growing diversity and richness, they compared Islamic art to western art both in the inherent ambiguity of its label and in its richly diversified historical developments, and highlighted the necessity of including the long-neglected 'early modern' and 'modern' in their newly articulated chronological model. Flood and Necipoğlu's timely conceptual and methodological reframing raises many important questions that will no doubt stimulate healthy and vigorous debates.

In this brief essay I want to dwell on the question concerning the threshold of modern change as it relates to the historiographies of Islamic civilization in general, and of Islamic art and architecture in particular. My aim is to go beyond the debate of inclusion and exclusion, and to examine its implications for periodization and the place of the 'Islamic' in the evolving narratives of global or world history. I argue that despite the general consensus among Islamic art historians concerning the necessity of including the modern and the contemporary in the historiographic scope of Islamic art, the various positions on how to deal with the 'modern' have remained rather ambiguous.[5] The question of modernity brings us back to Eurocentrism and orientalism, which once were hotly debated topics occupying the centre stage in the field.[6] As rigorous postcolonial and post-orientalist critiques have effectively dealt with the issues of misrepresentation and marginalization, the debates of these topics among Islamic art and architecture historians have receded in recent years.[7] Inclusion, equal exposure, and celebration of cultural difference are increasingly becoming acceptable mainstream strategies for dealing with the fallouts of the early (mis)conceptualization of the field by Eurocentric orientalists. Yet as my reflections will show, Eurocentrism has not disappeared; it has morphed into a new, more robust form, *neo-Eurocentrism*, demanding a rethinking of the conceptual and methodological parameters of the fields on yet again new grounds.

Thresholds of Change and Neo-Eurocentrism

Preferences for a certain periodization model and the related identification of key thresholds of change call into question the viewpoint from which such preferences are made. Flood and Necipoğlu have made it clear that they 'do not insist that the global turn in the broader discipline of art history should make globalization a new requirement in the Islamic field'.[8]

Giving preference to the internal logic of the Islamic narrative over the external logic of the global narrative certainly has merit; one can even disregard and dismiss global history's narrative, structure, and periodization as being blatantly Eurocentric. But if we consider history writing as essentially a narrative-making exercise presented from a particular perspective rather than a neutral presentation of historical facts, then disengaging with the global narrative – biased and prejudiced as it may be – can only be done at the expense of becoming increasingly irrelevant to an intensely inter-connected and inter-dependant world. In the global narrative, the key threshold of change is crystallizing to be the 'early modern', and this is increasingly becoming universally relevant to all civilizational developments. The implications of the early modern change are too profound and complex to be addressed by mere inclusion. Arguing for similarities in civilizational developments across the western and Islamic contexts raises expectations of intertwining periodization, in which early modernity can be seen as a central node where the historical lines of all civilizational developments may converge before each re-emerging on a new trajectory.

Global history narratives are changing with 'neutral' periodization being used as a new methodological tool.[9] Some global historians are even going beyond periodization to constructing genuine non-Eurocentric cross-cultural narratives.[10] Yet Eurocentrists are also evolving; they are reconceiving European exceptionalism in new ways. The emergence of 'early modern science' remains the most difficult hurdle for non-Eurocentric historians to negotiate, as it represents a seismic shift in the course of human history that cannot be ignored. European exceptionalism has been anchored in this historical episode, as expressed in the widely popular narratives of the *Great Divergence* and the *European Miracle*.[11] The emergence of early modern science has been linked to a complex web of changes at the religious, economic, political, institutional, intellectual, and cultural levels with profound implications for global narratives. From this perspective, the Mongol's sacking of Baghdad, and the conquests of Constantinople and Granada, while significant in their own context, are of relatively minor consequence globally. The Islamic modes of thinking, of knowledge-making, of institutional structure, and of cultural production have not changed markedly at these historical thresholds, let alone the rest of the world, as they did after the threshold of modernity. Thus these historical markers arguably carry little significance for the Islamic grand narrative that is yet to be constructed for global history.

In recent years, some Eurocentric historians have rethought the problematic narrative of the rise of the west in early modernity and related issues of cross-civilizational exchange, with the aims of addressing the orientalist prejudices and of reinventing European superiority and cultural difference. Labelled as 'neo-Eurocentrism', the new shift in thinking has sought to reinstate European/western exceptionalism on new grounds.[12]

Eurocentrism, as commonly known, was a product of the intellectual project of the European Enlightenment, which constructed European exceptionalism on the basis of racial, cultural, and intellectual superiority. It maintained a dismissive attitude towards the so-called uncivilized non-European other. Under the sustained and rigorous critiques of post-orientalists and post-colonialists, however, the conceptual foundations of Eurocentrism have collapsed and related conventional approaches have now largely been abandoned – in academic circles at least. In response, Eurocentrism has mutated into a new form of thinking with sounder, less penetrable, science-based arguments for European exceptionalism. In an insightful article on the challenges facing global dialogical history – developed as a non-Eurocentric response to Samuel Huntington's 'clash of civilizations' thesis – historian John Hobson has outlined the strategic shifts that studies in the history of science have made to sidestep the long-criticized and now defunct propositions of Eurocentrism and orientalism.[13] This has led to the emergence of neo-Eurocentrism as a conceptual orientation that managed to rework the long held Eurocentric premises, assumptions, and arguments in order to reassert European cultural distinction in the grand narrative of global history.

Neo-Eurocentrism has given up two foundational Eurocentric beliefs: that all changes in early modern Europe were endogenous, and that Europeans are distinguished by their rationality and inventive genius. With these ideas having been discarded, so too go representations of the east as static, exotic, non-rational, and non-inventive. The belief that Europeans are the leaders of change and the pure source of original ideas has also been abandoned. Neo-Eurocentrism has thus shifted the theoretical terrain away from the old claim of 'pure European inventive genius' and replaced it with the idea of 'European creative adaptability'.[14] Ownership of original ideas no longer matters from the neo-Eurocentric perspective; what matters now is the ability to assimilate and deploy these ideas – from whatever sources they might come – for greater purposes. The new challenge, Hobson writes,

> is of a picture of Europe that is no longer the master of invention and the creator of everything. Rather, the picture that is emerging is one of a Europe that is superior and exceptional precisely because of its ability to imitate and borrow from others before subsequently adapting these to higher ends.[15]

Imitation and borrowing, once regarded as the hallmarks of allegedly backward civilizations, have now assumed a new and powerful agency in Europe's breakthrough to the modern world. Neo-Eurocentrism has thus significantly shifted the coordinates of the old discourse and changed the terms of the debate. Neo-Eurocentric theorists have given up their long-protected centrality and supremacy in favour of a more adaptive and accommodative position, thereby providing a new space for the non-European *other* to explore new modes of encounters that appear to be conducive to more intellectually productive, cross-cultural trajectories. There is great potential for such thinking to fundamentally change the way scholars consider art and architectural history in the Islamic world and beyond.

Neo-Eurocentrism and the Historiography of Science and Art

There are many examples of neo-Eurocentric works like the above cited *Great Divergence: China, Europe, and the Making of the Modern World Economy*, wherein author Kenneth Pomeranz deconstructed the view of Europeans as the sole makers of their own miraculous rise. In it he revealed the degree to which Europeans relied on external influences to achieve the *great divergence* that set them apart from other regions of the world. Historians of science, as well as art historians adopting their storyline, however, present examples more pertinent to my discussions. I refer here to the works of the German art historian Hans Belting (*Florence and Baghdad: Renaissance Art and Arab Science* [2008], and of the American historian of science Toby Huff (*The Rise of Early Modern Science: Islam, China and the West* [1993] and *Intellectual Curiosity and Scientific Revolution: A Global Perspective* [2011]).[16] Belting and Huff, though from different fields of study, share a fundamental neo-Eurocentric thesis: that a revolutionary discovery that changed the course of human history – though relying on a scientific advancement from the Arab-Islamic world – was only possible in the enabling cultural and intellectual environment of Europe. Belting refers to the discovery of linear perspective and its reliance on Ibn al-Haytham's advanced optics, while Huff refers to the discovery of the heliocentric planetary model and its reliance on Ibn al-Shatir's advanced mathematical astronomy.[17] Both discoveries are shown to have led to quantum leaps in their respective fields; perspective laid the foundations for the emergence of modern art, architecture, photography, and film production, and heliocentrism did the same for modern astrophysics and space technology.[18] Belting boldly dismisses as a 'myth' the old Eurocentric claim that geometrical perspective was 'invented' *ex nihilo* in Renaissance Europe.[19] Huff uses similar arguments with regard to heliocentrism. Both see the culturally enabled, adaptive creativity essential to these developments as being 'surreptitiously encoded' in the DNA of the west. To them it is this distinction that sets it apart from all other cultures.

Ironically, neo-Eurocentrism has appealed to a wide spectrum of Muslim and Arab scholars. That Arab-Islamic science was central to the making of modern Europe has given them something to brag about. Indeed, this has been the focus of countless publications, forming a recognizable genre in popular Arabic literature.[20] Yet, the intractability of neo-Eurocentrism has also generated a paralysing effect, forcing some Islamic intellectual historians to drop Europe altogether from their historical narrative.[21] The bold recognition of the key role Arabic sources played in the revolutionary inventions, which were previously upheld as purely European, is a positive, albeit deceiving, shift. A danger lies in the concomitant proposition that it was exclusively the Europeans who were able to make the adaptive leap into the modern world, precisely because of their exceptional cultural disposition.[22] The Arabs/Muslims, despite having been afforded the honour of working out the theoretical foundations of the above discoveries, were deemed *culturally incapable* of the revolutionary breakthrough due to various religious constraints, intellectual inhibitions, and institutional inadequacies.

As Hobson explains, the old markers of Eurocentric world history constructed their theoretical framework using the European logics of 'immanence' and 'inventive exceptionalism'. With the neo-Eurocentric markers of the west, the likes of Huff and Belting, the old anchors have been replaced by the logics of 'emergence' and 'adaptive/imitative exceptionalism'.[23] Europe is no longer immanently superior; it has emerged superior after embracing and extending external advances. This new shift not only 'recognizes and subsumes the insight of the external, Eastern input into the rise of the West', but can also use the insights of dialogical history effectively to enhance the neo-Eurocentric approach.[24] What matters in the end 'is not the number of Eastern inventions that have been borrowed but the point that Europe was able to work with them and assimilate them to higher ends'.[25]

The upshot of Hobson's analyses is that neo-Eurocentrism, having effectively addressed the shortcomings of Eurocentrism, has blunted the non-Eurocentric approaches' sharpness and stripped their arguments' sense of purpose. These approaches have simply lost their core narrative of anti-Eurocentrism. An acrimonious debate that broke out between two eminent historians of science – Toby Huff and George Saliba – has shown that neo-Eurocentrism can work effectively with dialogical history's findings, narratives, and even critique of Eurocentrism, but not the other way around. Huff can easily and constructively cite Saliba's arguments and findings to strengthen his position, but Saliba cannot do the same, nor can he accept or effectively address Huff's conclusions.[26] This is because, as Hobson points out, the most profound challenge neo-Eurocentrism has posed is its ability 'to offer an *explanation* of the rise of the West that is missing within global dialogism'.[27] He concedes that articulating a non-Eurocentric theoretical explanation of the rise of the west 'is an enormously difficult challenge', for it involves producing 'a non-Eurocentric theoretical explanation of the things that"Europe did right"', without this pointing, explicitly or implicitly, to what other civilizations did wrong that eventually leads back to the old rise-and-decline, boom-and-bust, and Eurocentric-and-non-Eurocentric debates.[28]

Neo-Eurocentrism and Cultural Relativity

Neo-Eurocentrism poses a difficult challenge to non-Eurocentric art and architectural historians generally – and Islamic art and architectural historians in particular – in presenting early modernity as *the* threshold of change around which periodization models must be organized in order to address not just the hard question concerning the rise of the west, but also the profound subsequent changes to modes of thinking and production.[29] If the Islamic world does not have an independent timeline of its own, as Flood and Necipoğlu assert, then negotiating a common chronology of cross-civilizational development becomes mandatory. Ignoring or dismissing this challenge as Eurocentric and irrelevant to the internal logic of Islamic history leads to maintaining a culturally relative position that relies on the field's peculiarities to legitimise preferences. Cultural relativity tends to compound the difficulties of the conventional, non-Eurocentric approaches, which are grounded in cultural history. Within the frameworks of cultural history the question of the 'modern' remains within the bounds of inclusion and exclusion, and the rise of the west continues to appear less significant or critical than the sacking of Baghdad or the fall of Constantinople.

Interest in cultural history rose during the 'cultural turn' of the 1980s, which saw scholars in the humanities and social sciences, including art and architecture, actively seeking to make 'culture' – loose and malleable of a concept as it may – the focus of contemporary debates. In fact, one of the recognized legacies of the influential Islamic art historian Oleg Grabar has been the field's refocusing on culture. The cultural turn also witnessed a rise in interest in Said's influential critiques of orientalism and cultural imperialism, especially among non-western cultural historians. The popularity of the cultural perspective has enabled a range of non-Eurocentric approaches in the field of Islamic art and architecture that hinge on three principles: seeing art and architecture as 'cultural' products; conceiving the problem of Eurocentrism as one of (mis)representation; and articulating the responses within the conceptual and methodological framework of cultural history.[30] Cultural history provides no productive framework to construct a convincing global narrative explaining the rise of the west and transition into modernity without sacrificing the assumed equality of cultural difference. It has always been vague in its theoretical focus and methodological parameters, reflecting the vagueness inherent in the concept of 'culture', which, since its emergence in the eighteenth century, has come to mean several things, including a specific way of life – be it of a group, a period, or humanity in general; a general process of intellectual, aesthetic, and spiritual development; and the works and practices of intellectual and artistic activity.[31] With the democratization of the concept of 'culture' in twentieth-century anthropology and the rise of cultural relativity, whereby all peoples are seen to have different yet equally valuable ways of life and cultural expressions (including art and architecture), providing equal exposure to cultural difference has been conceived as a way to neutralize the historiographical bias inherent in Eurocentric (mis)representations.[32]

Globalizing the scope of cultural history to encompass all cultures (whether globally or within a particular tradition, like the Islamic, for example) and staging them on an all-inclusive, flat, unbiased, and symmetrical chronological platform has been adopted as a strategy to sidestep the traps of geographic, national, regional, dynastic, or stylistic categories in organizing the collected data. Cultural relativity reigns in this global view, yet equality and symmetry can only be maintained up to the threshold of early modernity after which point the narrative tends to lose its constructed balance. The recent *A Global History of Architecture* is a case in point.[33] It shows that equal cultural exposure does not compensate for the civilizational narrative of progress towards modernity. At the moment cultures are no longer equally different, no amount of exposure to under-, non-, or mis-represented cultures will neutralize the historiographical bias inherent in the Eurocentric and neo-Eurocentric global narrative of modernity.[34]

The linear chronology and periodization of history cannot be a neutral organizer of civilizational developments, as historical narratives are normally constructed to describe human progress, the trajectories that lead humanity to the achievements of the present. Currently, only the European line can show uninterrupted continuity at the levels of both thought and practice, especially around the critical node of early modern change. This global narrative takes into account the storylines of intellectual history and the history of science, which have been to some degree distant from that of cultural history. The early modern history and theory of European art and architecture have already been incorporated into European intellectual history and the history of science through the writings of Enlightenment figures such as Rousseau, Laugier, Chambers, Chardin, Diderot, and others, whereas non-western cultures have not crossed the threshold into intellectual history until the late-nineteenth and early-twentieth centuries.[35] Thus, it is not adequate to *include* the 'early modern' as an historical period on an assumed neutral timeline, as this sidesteps the difficult task of addressing the intellectual implications of the rise of modern science and subsequent emergence of European Enlightenment. Arguing for intertwined historical timelines and parallels with western art presupposes an engagement with the implications of Jean-Jacques Rousseau's statement in his *Discourse on the Arts and Science* (1750): 'It was the stupid Mussulman, the eternal scourge of letters, who was the immediate cause of their revival among us.'[36]

The current asymmetry in the construction of the western and non-western global narratives has made it even harder to evolve the non-Eurocentric art and architectural history discourse beyond the limitations of cultural relativity. The current conceptualizations of art and architectural history in cultural and cross-cultural frameworks have distanced the non-Eurocentric efforts from intellectual history, where Eurocentrism was originally

Figure 9.1: The Auburn Gallipoli Mosque in Sydney, Australia. Constructed from 1986 to 1999 for the Australian-Turkish community, the building presents a mediocre replica of classical Ottoman architecture. The absence of narrative-giving agency to Muslims in the making of modernity traps the popular imagination in the past in the search for expressions of cultural identity. Source: Wikimedia Commons/J Bar.

rooted, and hindered the scholars' ability to transcend the limitations of their method [Figures 9.1 and 9.2].

Implications for Islamic Art and Architectural Historiography

In the face of dominating globalism aided by the universalism of modern science, technology, and transnational economy, interest in cultural difference has, as we have seen, not faded away. Quite to the contrary. The west is actively engaged in reasserting its intellectually adaptive exceptionalism, cultural difference, and civilizational superiority. Although this is unfolding specifically in the field of history of science, its implications extend to intellectual, economic, and cultural histories. Islamic art and architecture historians have

Figure 9.2: The Australia Islamic Centre and Mosque, Newport, Victoria, Australia, by Pritzker Prize-winning Australian architect Glenn Murcutt with Hakan Elevli Associates (2016). Exterior (top) and prayer hall (bottom). Despite its novel modern design, the discourse associated with the meanings of its formal composition remains profoundly polarized by tradition and modernity, Islam and the west. Source: Anthony Browell/Architecture Foundation Australia.

yet to engage with the challenges this phenomenon is posing, which demand a substantial rethinking of established conceptual positions, theoretical framings, and methodological tools. Here one may indeed question the need to construct a grand Islamic narrative that makes good sense in a non-Eurocentric global history. Such questioning, however, will inevitably bring Islamic art and architecture historians to negotiate, in one way or another, the early modern not just as a category of art but as a critical threshold of change that demands civilizational repositioning.

In parallel with the rise of neo-Eurocentrism, continual realignment of the conceptions of Asia and the Middle East has been taking place. The old spatial politics of national and regional boundaries as well as the intellectual framing of geographies and cultural difference are becoming increasingly less relevant to the new political, cultural, and intellectual concerns of the twentyfirst century. In this context, the long preoccupation with cultural identity – which has continued to entertain wide popularity in the field of Islamic art and architecture – now demands re-conceptualization in order to advance modes of understanding and thinking relevant to societies profoundly transformed by revolutionary developments in spatial and social connectivity. Also, the increasingly transformative role that technology is playing in our daily life is challenging our once instinctive sense of being human. As we become more and more preoccupied with 'smart' everything, we are driven to question the very core of our humanity (as we have come to know it). The recent emergence of *transhumanism* has foregrounded our relationship to technology in an unprecedented manner, shifting our attention away from cultural difference to the commonalities that make us human.[37]

Furthermore, the significant intellectual shift represented by the recent rise of the critique of postmodernism and deconstructionism further emphasizes the importance of our collective sense of humanity. These still popular theoretical approaches have long provided a legitimate and empowering space for the relative, the marginal, the constructed, and the different to challenge the validity and legitimacy of the universal, the official, the dominant, and the similar. As the passionate postmodern drive for individuality, identity, difference, and cultural relativity has eroded much of the shared understanding of fundamental human values – such as freedom, equality, and justice – there is now a renewed interest in communality and togetherness, in what brings people together rather than what sets them apart despite cultural difference. This is an important move that forms with neo-Eurocentrism and transhumanism a new juncture for cross-cultural thinking to ponder.[38]

In this new juncture, advocates of non-Eurocentric, cross-cultural approaches to art and architecture need to deal with new sets of questions. How can a reconciliation of human commonality and cultural difference enable a constructive rethinking of enduring Eurocentric narratives of global history? Should cultural history be brought closer to both intellectual history and history of science in search of new productive conceptual and methodological intersections? Can an intertwined history of modernity avoid the pitfalls of cultural relativity and grant both western and non-western cultures agency in the making of the modern world? Can neo-Eurocentrism be seen and exploited not just as a divisive expression of an imagined civilizational contest, but as an opportunity to gain new insights into the workings of cross-cultural encounters? These and other related questions should aim to make us less sensitive to, and concerned with, the leaders and followers in any civilizational encounter, but more attuned to how difference makes us collectively better. As the field of Islamic art and architecture expands and diversifies while moving forward into an unstable global future, scholars and practitioners would do well to consider these collective humane concerns.

Notes

This chapter was previously published as Samer Akkach, 'Neo–Eurocentrism and Science: Implications for the Historiography of Islamic Art and Architecture', *International Journal of Islamic Architecture* 10.1 (2021): 203–15.

1. Finbarr Flood and Gürlu Necipoğlu, eds, *A Companion to Islamic Art and Architecture, vol. 1, From the Prophet to the Mongols* (Hoboken, NJ: Wiley Blackwell, 2017), 56.
2. Ibid., 9.
3. See Sheila Blair and Jonathan Bloom, 'The Mirage of Islamic Art: Reflections on the Study of an Unwieldy Field', *Art Bulletin* 85.1 (2003): 125–84.
4. Flood and Necipoğlu, *A Companion to Islamic Art and Architecture*, 1:6.
5. See Jonathan Bloom and Shiela Blair, eds, *Islamic Art: Past, Present, and Future* (New Haven: Yale University Press, 2019).
6. See Nasser Rabbat, 'The Hidden Hand: Said's *Orientalism* and Architectural History', *Journal of the Society of Architectural Historians* 77.4 (2018): 388–96.
7. Orientalism and Said's broad-brush generalizations are still being debated outside the field of Islamic art and architecture. See Wael Hallaq, *Restating Orientalism: A Critique of Modern Knowledge* (New York: Columbia University Press, 2018).
8. Flood and Necipoğlu, *A Companion to Islamic Art and Architecture*, 1:33.
9. See, for example, Robert Tignor et al, *Worlds Together, Worlds Apart: A History of the World from the Beginnings of Humankind to the Present* (New York: W. W. Norton & Company, 2013).
10. See, for example, Peter Gran, *The Rise of the Rich: A New View of Modern World History* (Syracuse, NY: Syracuse University Press, 2009).
11. See Kenneth Pomeranz, *The Great Divergence: China, Europe, and the Making of the Modern World Economy* (Princeton: Princeton University Press, 2000); and Eric Jones, *The European Miracle: Environments, Economies and Geopolitics in the History of Europe and Asia* (Cambridge: Cambridge University Press, 1981).
12. The following discussions of neo-Eurocentrism are based on John Hobson, 'Global Dialogical History and the Challenge of Neo-Eurocentricity', in *Asia, Europe, and the Emergence of Modern Science*, Arun Bala, ed. (Basingstoke: Palgrave Macmillan, 2006), 13–35.
13. Ibid.
14. Ibid., 17.
15. Ibid., 19.

16. Hans Belting, *Florence and Baghdad: Renaissance Art and Arab Science*, trans. Deborah Lucas Schneider (Cambridge, MA: Belknap, 2011); Toby E. Huff, *The Rise of Early Modern Science: Islam, China and the West* (Cambridge: Cambridge University Press, 1993); Toby E. Huff, *Intellectual Curiosity and Scientific Revolution: A Global Perspective* (Cambridge: Cambridge University Press, 2011).
17. Both discoveries occurred within a span of one hundred or so years during the European Renaissance. Fillipo Brunelleschi carried out his famous experiment of perspectival drawing of the Florentine Baptistery in 1415, while Nicolaus Copernicus published his *De revolutionibus orbium coelestium* (*On the Revolutions of the Celestial Spheres*) in 1543.
18. Belting, *Florence and Baghdad*, 1–12. On the history of perspective and its role in architectural representation, see Alberto Pérez-Gómez and Louis Pelletier, *Architectural Representation and the Perspective Hinge* (Cambridge, MA: MIT Press, 1997).
19. Belting, *Florence and Baghdad*, 26.
20. This genre includes translations of books by eminent western authors. See, for example, Montgomery Watt, *Faḍl al-Islām ʿalā al-ḥaḍāra al-gharbiyya*, trans. Ahmad Amin (Beirut: Dār al-Shurūq, 1983). Eminent western-based Arab authors are also included. See, for example, George Saliba, *Al-ʿUlūm al-Islāmiyya wa qiyām al-nahḍa al-ūrubiyya*, trans. Mahmud Haddad (Beirut: al-Dār al-ʿArabiyya li-l-ʿUlūm, 2014). See also writings by influential Arab authors, like ʿAbbas Mahmud al-ʿAqqad. See, ʿAbbas Mahmud al-ʿAqqad, *Athar al-ʿArab fī al-ḥaḍāra al-ūrubiyya*, which appeared in numerous editions.
21. See, for example, Ahmad Dallal, *Islam without Europe: Tradition of Reform in Eighteenth-Century Islamic Thought* (Chapel Hill: University of North Carolina Press, 2018).
22. An example of the effectiveness of this trap can be clearly seen in Ibn Warraq, *Defending the West* (New York: Prometheus Books, 2007).
23. Hobson, 'Global Dialogical History', 20.
24. Ibid., 19.
25. Ibid.
26. See George Saliba, 'Seeking the Origins of Modern Science?', *Bulletin of the Royal Institute for Inter-Faith Studies* 1.2 (1999): 139–52; Toby Huff, 'The Rise of Early Modern Science: A Reply to George Saliba', *Bulletin of the Royal Institute for Inter-Faith Studies* 4.2 (2002): 115–28; George Saliba, 'Flying Goats and other Obsessions: A Response to Toby Huff's Reply', *Bulletin of the Royal Institute for Inter-Faith Studies* 4.2 (2002): 129–41.
27. Hobson, 'Global Dialogical History', 21.
28. As an example of such attempts, see Peter Gran, *The Rise of the West: A New View of Modern World History* (Syracuse, NY: Syracuse University Press, 2009).
29. Some Islamic historians have begun to emphasize early modernity in their historical narratives. See, for example, Virginia Aksan and Daniel Goffman, eds, *The Early Modern Ottomans: Remapping the Empire* (Cambridge: Cambridge University Press, 2007). For a comparative perspective on early modernity, see Shmuel Eisenstadt and Wolfgang Schluchter, 'Paths to Early Modernities: A Comparative View', *Daedalus* 127.3 (1998): 1–18.
30. See Nasser Rabbat, 'The Hidden Hand: Said's *Orientalism* and Architectural History', *Journal of the Society of Architectural Historians* 77.4 (2018): 388–96.

31 See Raymond Williams, *Keywords: A Vocabulary of Culture and Society* (New York: Oxford University Press, 1976), 76–82.
32 As an example of this, see Francis Ching, Mark Jarzombek, and Vikramāditya Prakāsh, *A Global History of Architecture* (New Jersey: John Wiley, 2011).
33 Ibid.
34 See Vikramāditya Prakāsh, 'The "Islamic" from a Global Historiographical Perspective', *International Journal of Islamic Architecture* 6.1 (2017): 17–24.
35 See Paul Hyland et al.,'Art, Architecture and Nature', in *The Enlightenment: A Source Book* (New York: Routledge, 2003), 259–95.
36 Ibid., 262.
37 See Beatriz Colomina and Mark Wigley, *Are We Human?* (Zürich: Lars Müller Publishers, 2016); Max More and Natasha Vita-More, eds, *The Transhumanist Reader* (West Sussex: Wiley-Blackwell, 2013).
38 Adding to this the existential threat of climate change humanity is presently facing, some may argue that the pressing questions today are rapidly converging on one central issue, human survival, against which western exceptionalism, cultural difference, and cross-cultural debates fade into insignificance.

Chapter 10

Carving an Epistemological Space for Southeast Asia: Historiographical and Critical Engagements

Imran bin Tajudeen

In a 2016 issue of the *International Journal of Islamic Architecture*, Abidin Kusno questioned the assumptions behind the construction of 'Islamic architecture' as a discipline of study in its perceived preference for the monumental and historical.[1] Kusno drew attention to the contemporary phenomenon of community-built mosques and *musholla* (prayer room) in the informal slum and squatter neighbourhoods of Jakarta as a means of highlighting an alternative site for investigation, away from the question of aesthetics to the socio-political role that these new landmarks played in stabilizing and legitimizing the claims of their neighbourhoods to permanence. In his critical reading, these settlements and their *musholla* constitute 'invisible geographies' that lie outside the privileging of imperial monuments and large-scale elite edifices that typically characterize the study of Islamic architecture.

Conversely, however, this critique of the scope of 'Islamic architecture' can be extended in a different direction. This chapter explores how maritime Southeast Asia's[2] mosques, mausoleum complexes, palaces, and gardens built by its Muslim communities, rulers, and other patrons from the fifteenth to the nineteenth centuries constitute 'invisible geographies' of a different sort. Namely, maritime Southeast Asia, along with a number of other maritime regions, is invariably omitted from the map of Islamic architecture, with the important exception of two surveys,[3] calling to mind an important critique of art history's 'disciplinary gaze' with particular attention to its narrow geographic scope, among other issues.[4]

I contend that the region's inclusion goes beyond merely expanding the inventory Islamic architectural history, to also serve as the grounds for methodological and conceptual engagements with the discipline of (Islamic) architectural history in three ways. First, the history of maritime Southeast Asia's Islamic architecture in the fifteenth to nineteenth centuries can serve as an ontological critique of the emphasis on the monumental in 'Islamic architecture' in the same manner that the study of non-western architecture and art more generally has served as a critique of the very term 'architecture' and 'art' as categories defined from the European or 'Western' perspective.[5] Second, Southeast Asia provides a site to investigate the assumptions behind the appellation 'Islamic' and its attendant conceptual frameworks in Islamic architectural history. These frameworks derive from received scholarly compartmentalizations according to disciplinary categories based on religion or geographical divisions that are imposed upon (non-western) architecture, which leaves the architecture of maritime Southeast Asia in limbo.[6] Third, Southeast Asia presents a variation on the maritime theme in the study of the Islamic world that currently focuses on the continental oceanfront littoral of the Indian Ocean. It presents instead an 'archipelagic crossroads' situation, in which both transregional/transoceanic and translocal/intra-regional networks and actors intersect in more complex ways. This requires retracing the socio-cultural formations in cosmopolitan port-polities that are rooted in translocal-regional idioms even while they are connected transregionally.[7]

Beyond Exceptionalism

Despite the fact that translation and diversity lie at the core of Islamic architectural culture's ontological constitution, even within its present canon, there is an entrenched tendency to regard the translation of pre-Islamic architecture and material culture for Islamic use in Southeast Asia as exceptional.[8] This parallels the prevailing assumption in the study of Islam and Southeast Asia, and Java in particular, that the region's sociocultural practices are perceived to be at variance with or to deviate from a perceived Islamic normative core or orthodoxy that is located in an anachronistically imagined Arab Islamic heartland. Such a view has been severely criticized by scholars who point out that the negotiation between Islamic sharia and local, pre-Islamic mores, designated by the Arabic-derived term *adat* (*'ada*) in Malay and Javanese, is a condition obtained across all Muslim societies – including in the Arab lands.[9] The implications of such a rethink for architectural study are evident.

The anxiety to justify the Islamic character of Southeast Asia's mosques and mausolea through some connection to Middle Eastern referents, to draw some conjectural source in the Islamic heartlands, or to construct schemas that speak of 'pure and diluted' Islamic character in the arts according to racial lines,[10] are misplaced. Islamic architecture everywhere is constituted from the adaptation, reworking, and transfiguration of formal, spatial, and technical conventions that preceded it. Thus the multi-tiered pyramidal or hip-roof mosques (*tajug* and *limas*, respectively) of maritime Southeast Asia are neither more nor less a part of Islamic architecture's story than is the domed or hypostyle hall of West Asia: each formal-spatial type pre-dated Islam and had been used for other faiths. Studies could instead investigate translation as a site of inquiry across religious boundaries and conversion. Indeed, recent scholarship has begun to expand investigations into Islamic architecture's position in relation to pre-Islamic Arabia's developments.[11]

Translation as Site of Inquiry: Buildings and/as Texts and the Architectural Dialectic

The focus on translation as the site of inquiry into the formation of Southeast Asia's Islamic architecture shifts the discussion from asking what makes some element fundamentally Islamic to how, when, why, and under what circumstances – material, technological, socio-economic, or political – certain forms or meanings were reworked or re-signified. The dialectic between two factors would be pertinent to the study of architectural translation for

Islamic use: first, the way building conventions operate as constraints and contexts for material fabrication; and second, the agency of builders and patrons in the initial conception or deployment and reworking of existing and new sources for discursive purposes. In this regard, the notion of 'the culture of building' and of 'building communities' provides the analytical frameworks for investigating the contexts of production and the dialectical relationship between the embeddedness of a building culture in its community's socio-political and economic configurations and its disciplinary autonomy in the inter-connections between technical-structural systems, socio-spatial conventions, and formal-ornamental symbolic references.[12]

The above architectural dialectic points to how the processes and outcomes of cultural encounter that is manifested in forms for Islamic religious or secular use may be studied: first, through clues in nomenclature and formal-spatial elements, and second, via discursive and descriptive engagements with texts. A caveat has to be inserted about the utility of texts vis-à-vis the building. Aspects of a building's materiality, imagery, or technical innovation might contribute to its meaning or cultural historical significance in ways that exceed what textual sources can tell us.[13] Further, in the absence of textual referents or documentation, a comparative framework for extant buildings helps to elucidate such dimensions. Inherited building conventions – including the spatial anthropological perspective on building features for indigenous religion in maritime Southeast Asia[14] – inform the bases for architecture for Islamic or Muslim secular use in Southeast Asia. Such insights escape the attention of the Islamic frame of architectural analysis. Conversely, builders and patrons adapt and transfigure both old and new elements.[15] Through such innovations, parallel or multiple meanings may be evoked arising from their deliberate re-signification or the coexistence of both older and newer symbolic associations when they are translocalized in a new setting or re-situated in new discursive contexts [Figure 10.1].

Capitals, Satellites, and Rural Sites in Post-imperial Contexts and Networks

The study of Islamic architecture in Southeast Asia also needs to move beyond an isolated focus on mosque halls and their wooden construction as discrete objects. Islam in Southeast Asia took root as the religion of the *negri* – port polities and royal capitals – oriented to international and intra-regional interactions that had developed in the wake of the disintegration of the region's major pre-Islamic empires that were active participants in transoceanic maritime commerce and diplomatic relations.[16] The growth, and in some cases the founding, of these post-imperial harbour polities was frequently predicated upon either the repudiation of the yoke of their former vassalage under pre-Islamic polities, or the emphasis of continuity with and the assumption of their mantle of political legitimacy based on myth construction and material cultural manifestations. Simultaneously, the prosperity of the new regimes was closely connected with the trade wealth and connections involving Muslim merchant networks. With the establishment of

Figure 10.1: The Telok Manok Mosque, at Narathiwat, in the former Malay state of Patani in today's southern Thailand, reputedly from the eighteenth century. Source: Imran bin Tajudeen.

Muslim rule, mosques were also used to spatially stake out jurisdictions and structure the realm politically. Their role and position in urban spectacle and ritual further constitute the ways by which mosques and other structures can be situated within wider contexts that are not yet documented or discussed thoroughly.[17] Analysis should thus encompass associated structures ranging from pools and waterworks or urban-scale canal systems, to ancillary buildings, complexes, and courtyards as well as gateways, cemeteries, and urban *waqf* endowments. Building complexes should also be discussed in relation to urban or settlement contexts [Figure 10.2].

Beyond the scale of individual buildings and their contexts, there is also a need for more rigorous investigation of the variety in urban form beyond the usual focus on the Javanese-type *alun-alun* town. Although a number of articles and monographs have analysed the socio-economic and political histories of different port capitals and studied some historical maps closely,[18] the diverse urban forms known from the historical sources have not been discussed comparatively in a more sustained manner. Such comparisons would help to situate the

Figure 10.2: Remaining structures and ventilation towers connected to underwater tunnels at the ruins of Taman Sari, the eighteenth-century royal water gardens of Yogyakarta, Central Java, Indonesia. Source: Imran bin Tajudeen.

translocal flows and connections chronologically and spatially. Studies of the urban contexts of Southeast Asia's Islamic architectural culture would also need to account for the interactions of various agents. These include: local potentates and the builders they patronized; merchant-princes known or reputed to be of foreign origin who fraternized and intermarried with local rulers and nobility, some of whom appear in the historical sources as *patih*s in the Javanese *pesisir* (north coast region) and *khoja*s in the Malay-speaking towns; and the proselytizers and religious teachers who became rulers or who led the construction of mosques and other structures [Figure 10.3].[19]

An 'Archipelagic Crossroads': Beyond Singular Narratives

The discussion of Islamic architecture in the region has not sufficiently contextualized the port cities in their regional, translocal milieu. Existing studies have been concerned mainly with transregional or global Muslim diaspora from elsewhere – particularly, the interest has been to trace or detect 'influences' from Arabia, India, and China without sufficiently recognizing

Figure 10.3: The third gateway along the *qibla* axis of Kudus Mosque, in Central Java, Indonesia, from the sixteenth century and today found within the enlarged mosque hall. Source: Imran bin Tajudeen.

the translocal regional dynamic and without considering developments arising from neighbouring allies and rivals in the analysis.[20]

The notion of a crossroads is most famously invoked by Denys Lombard in his *longue durée* study of Java. However, its focus was on global historical connections centred primarily upon the island. I propose the term 'archipelagic crossroads' to articulate the dual and dialectical aspect of maritime Southeast Asia's geography as the framework for the sociocultural and political-economic contexts of its Islamic architecture. While this proposed framework is cognizant of the macro-perspective of cross-regional interactions across the Indian Ocean, the South China Sea, and beyond, the invocation of the 'archipelagic' equally gestures towards the region's

Figure 10.4: The 65-metre-high Limo Kaum Mosque in the Minangkabau highlands of West Sumatra, Indonesia, from the nineteenth century. Source: Imran bin Tajudeen.

internal diversity and geographical nuances. Within this perspective, the Java Sea emerges as a centrally positioned arena that functions not as a core, but as a connector in a polycentric world comprising sub-regions linked and defined by waterways that simultaneously served as primary conduits, to varying degrees, of international commerce and the spice trade, from the Straits of Melaka to the Natuna Sea and the Banda and Maluku Seas.

With this framework, it is necessary to move beyond a singular narrative centred on the fifteenth-century Mosque of Demak in Central Java as a mythical origin point. In Java-centric accounts (primarily from Indonesia), fifteenth-century Demak is touted as the earliest Islamic state that provided the model for mosque form across the archipelago, notwithstanding its anachronism.[21] This simplified Demak-as-prototype narrative obscures a more critical discussion of the architectural expressions that present entirely different formal, spatial, and symbolic or material characteristics or the historical networks that did not revolve around Demak and thus detract from the narrative of Demak's prominence or precedence [Figure 10.4].

As a corollary to more rigorous attention to such tangible distinctions and chronological precision, a critical approach to historical accounts and their assertions is also needed. First, the narrative of Demak's primacy should be contextualized in terms of its political utility. The Central Javanese Mataram kingdom's strategic narrative-posturing in the eighteenth-century text *Babad Jaka Tingkir* served to highlight the importance of the mosque that the dynasty adopted as its ritual heirloom.[22] Second, beyond the Demak-centred narrative, attention should be given to accounts of multiple origins and conventions of Southeast Asia's historical mosque forms and complex translocal networks involved in the circulation of specific nuances of architectural details, especially beyond Java.[23]

The significance of the architectural and ornamental evidence in such a fluid setting with multiple translations can only be properly understood against a more nuanced understanding of translocal differentiations and their circulation. With the relative paucity of remnants of urban form from earlier periods, architectural evidence may be studied for aspects pointing to translocal interactions. Such clues may be found in spatial layouts, construction techniques, and structural features, as well as specific motifs and formal profiles.

Beyond Stratigraphic Assumptions

Current mainstream scholarship on Islamic architectural history does not reflect the sociocultural diversity of the Muslim world. This is lamentable given that architectural histories involve more than inquiries into aesthetic or formal concerns; the investigation of architecture also provides insights into the political-economic contexts of the production of buildings and the manifestation of sociocultural conditions.[24] The lacuna on the study of Southeast Asia's historical Islamic architecture, along with the aforementioned 'other' regions of the Muslim world in the writing of the history of Islamic architecture, constitutes a missed opportunity to engage the humanistic understanding of the diversity of the Muslim world through Islamic architecture as it developed and transformed historically. Conversely, the periodization of Southeast Asian history and material culture, with its demarcation into the pre-Islamic and Islamic periods not only in chronological terms but also through its division into separate disciplinary domains of study,[25] is inadequate to deal with the complexity of the formation of Southeast Asia's Islamic architecture. The emergence of new Islamic art and architectural forms in Southeast Asia did not create a new chronological-material layer that replaced, displaced, or was overlaid upon its older non-Islamic forms and their associations. The two cultural complexes and their material production and systems of meaning existed in parallel and interacted across space and time with different combinations and incorporating yet newer elements from other sources into the nineteenth and early twentieth centuries. This continuing dynamic can only be properly analysed through a scope of study that does not adopt religion as an exclusionary frame, but instead engages the conceptual and methodological tools afforded by Islamic art and architecture as a field of scholarly inquiry in the study of Islamic Southeast Asian material without subsuming the region's independent trajectories under ready-made narratives and analytical categories adopted from the latter field, as has been done in some existing works.[26]

In fact, the conversion of Southeast Asia's various sub-regions and localities to Islam was not a straightforward or instantaneous process. There were contestations, reversions, and a process of accommodation between religions. We may observe at least three modalities, and this bears implications on the formation of Islamic architecture in the region. First, a ruler might remain non-Muslim, but permits or even fosters the entry and work of Islamic proselytizers. This occurred in fourteenth–fifteenth-century Majapahit (in East Java) and sixteenth-century Campa (present-day central and south Vietnam). Second, a ruler might convert and cause the populace to do the same, but retain or further apply overtly Sanskrit-derived names and references for buildings, places, and titles, as seen in sixteenth-century Aceh and Banten and seventeenth-century Perak. Third, there have been instances of outright revivals of pre-Islamic religious affiliations in court culture as observed in fifteenth-century Melaka with the second and third Malay rulers re-adopting old Hindu rites and newly fashioned Hindu titles, before the latter's defeat by another prince of part Indian-Muslim descent, who subsequently assumed the throne. Instead of the received periodization of history, which characterizes the thirteenth to fifteenth centuries as the 'transition' period from the Indic to the early Islamic, I suggest that we acknowledge what I have referred to elsewhere as a temporal paradox and that we witness not the supplanting or replacement of one visual, symbolic, and formal cultural complex with another, but their continued negotiation and coexistence. This is in reference to the further elaboration of Javanese and Sumatran Indic elements long after Islamic conversion, and the exuberance of their revival and new inventions based on the older inheritance well into the sixteenth and seventeenth centuries. This was a result of both continuities in the culture of building from the pre-Islamic period and the deliberate choice for these elements for political posturing. Such forms of posturing include the artistic choices by Javanized foreign Muslim elites, as demonstrated in a recent, excellent analysis of feline sculpture of Java's fifteenth- to seventeenth-century mausoleum complexes from the north coast area (*pesisir*).[27] Competing centres thus may choose to utilize certain motifs, including the revival of elements that had fallen out of use in the late Indic classical period of Southeast Asia. This refashioning is still poorly understood – for instance, the significance of the lion as a decorative element in the Wali Songo mausolea of Java's north coast region is still unclear [Figure 10.5].

Rooted Muslim Cosmopolitanisms and Their Limits

The 'new historiography' of Southeast Asia challenges the assumption of a general political, economic, and social decline in its societies and polities from the mid-eighteenth century to the mid-nineteenth century, during a period of intense competition with the imperial ambitions of the Dutch and English East India trading companies preceding the so-called 'high colonial' period. Instead, the new perspective emphasizes the continued growth of the region and its

Figure 10.5: One of numerous stone roundels at Mantingan Mosque, north coast Central Java, Indonesia, likely from the sixteenth century. Source: Imran bin Tajudeen.

agency in dynamic association with several new actors and socioeconomic formations.[28] The discussion of mosque architecture in Southeast Asia has not situated its developments since the eighteenth century against these contexts. Instead, there is usually a simplified and confused narrative of hybridity with foreign elements.

The eighteenth- to early twentieth-century history of Southeast Asia's mosque architecture is significant for the continued vitality of Javanese and Malay architectural and ornamental idioms for mosques that were built by and for foreign merchant communities. The creative incorporation of elements and forms derived from other building cultural conventions – in

Figure 10.6: Mosque of Kampung Hulu, Melaka, Malaysia, from the eighteenth century. Source: Imran bin Tajudeen.

combinations and expressions that are distinct from what is observed in earlier periods – point to a rooted Muslim cosmopolitanism that emerged despite the very different political-economic and urban social configurations that obtained in this later period.[29] Such accommodations and their limits can be investigated by comparing, on the one hand, examples from port cities that had already come under European administration and control with the port towns and royal centres that remained autonomous, and, on the other hand, the major highland regions with their own dynamics of economic activity and mobility that participated in a variety of ways with Islamic, indigenous, and European colonial centres and networks. Thus, in addition to the transoceanic and transregional networks, as well as port capitals and their associated secondary settlements and peripheries, the third significant axis of historical social and political relations with a bearing on the development of mosque architecture is that of the coastal-inland links and what their study might reveal about the selection, incorporation, and fashioning of transcultural references in comparison with more heterogeneous settings in the coastal centres [Figure 10.6].

Museums, Archaeology, Regimes of Knowledge, and Prospects for Rapprochement

Two institutions have played defining roles in delimiting the scope of study and comparative frame for maritime Southeast Asia's Islamic architecture: museums through catalogues of exhibitions and collections and archaeological research centres through their inventories and reports. Four museum exhibition catalogues constitute important references on Southeast Asian Islamic architecture and ornament, despite the fact that very few architectural fragments or components are found in museum inventories.[30] The venues for travelling exhibitions and the sources for their exhibit loans, in one instance involving more than a dozen institutions, illustrate the established and emerging sites and circuits of discourse and artefact holdings.[31]

However, much of the evidence must still be documented from the field. Yet, whereas archaeology enjoys greater dominance in the study of mainstream Islamic architecture because of the importance of masonry ruins, this discipline plays a more limited role in Southeast Asia because of the predominance of wooden construction and ornament. Much of the archaeological contribution is on gravestone art and Javanese tomb complexes with masonry elements, which typically receive greater attention in reports and inventories of 'antiquities', although the restoration of wooden structures on Java was also conducted by the Dutch colonial archaeological departments in the early twentieth century.[32] Given that there are few art historians and archaeologists from dedicated programs of study working on Southeast Asian Islamic material,[33] independent researchers who venture far beyond the confines of museum storage play an immense role in documenting widely dispersed examples. Some works are driven by ideological-polemical assertions within national historiographical debates.[34] Other works straddle religious frames to engage regional anthropological perspectives on a situated Islam and are not constrained by the frame of Islamic aesthetics centred on Middle Eastern or Mediterranean paradigms. Such works are written by collectors, woodcarvers and builders, journalists, area studies historians and anthropologists, or lecturers in architecture or art schools.[35]

The question of disciplinary approaches is also pertinent to the study of textual sources for Islamic Southeast Asia. Because these texts require specialized knowledge of regional cultural history typically expected of 'area studies' scholars,[36] one scholar has rhetorically questioned whether the situated study of Islam in Southeast Asia is better served by the rubric of 'Asian Studies' rather than that of 'Islamic Studies'.[37] This rumination points to a core assumption in the study of Islamic societies and their cultural production: the normalization of a limited group of peoples and their cultural formations and their practices as the normative core of the Islamic to the exclusion of much of the rest of the Muslim world. Critiques of these assumptions have been reviewed earlier.[38] Conversely, we could similarly ask whether Islamic architectural history's investigations into Arab, Persian, and Turkish translations from pre-Islamic sources might be better lodged as Middle Eastern, Persian, Anatolian, or Mediterranean area studies instead.

The point of this critique is to ask what dialectic exists between regional or area studies and pan-Islamic conceptual frames or methodological approaches that transcend the internal dynamics of Arab, Persian, Ottoman, or Mediterranean studies – and consequently how the study of Southeast Asia's Islamic architecture could have similar or different dynamics. How would 'Islamic architecture' as frame compare with a regional historical frame built upon knowledge of local building cultures encompassing vernacular and Indic architectural practices and conventions to contextualize Southeast Asia's mosques, mausoleum complexes, palaces, and royal gardens? Such regional-historical investigations look across and transcend religious lines – for example with Hindu and Muslim in South Asia, where the question of translation from one religious system of meanings and forms to another is examined through the circulation, selective reuse, recombination, and transfiguration of motifs, techniques, and elements,[39] and for pre-Islamic and Islamic elements in South Arabia.[40]

Unfortunately, existing publications on mosques in Southeast Asia do not engage these questions critically. They are divided by modern nation-state boundaries and simply present information for each building discretely as separate entries.[41] An intermediate scale of study is needed that engages individual examples while keeping sight of larger questions and conceptual issues, as well as methodological dexterity across vernacular/anthropological frameworks of inquiry, and the widened ambit of the 'building culture' perspective. Thus, such a study, in the face of the paucity of written sources specific to each building, would consider instead the craft/material and economic contexts of production and what is known about the socio-political perspectives of the discursive contexts of architectural posturing and patrons' projects. Through such analytical approaches and investigations, the study of Southeast Asia's Islamic architecture may engage wider discussions without forsaking questions and issues of more local or 'area studies' interest, both in its material-formal constitution and discursively.

Acknowledgements

The author acknowledges and appreciates support from a MOE AcRF Tier 1 R295-000-150-114 Research Grant and the Al-Mutawa Visiting Research Fellowship, Oxford Centre for Islamic Studies.

Notes

This chapter was previously published as Imran bin Tajudeen, 'Carving an Epistemological Space for Southeast Asia: Historiographical and Critical Engagements', *International Journal of Islamic Architecture* 10.1 (2021): 217–32. The text has been updated for this publication.

1. Abidin Kusno, 'Invisible Geographies in the Study of Islamic Architecture', *International Journal of Islamic Architecture* 5.1 (2016): 29–35. This essay is reproduced in the present volume.
2. A note has to be made about the term used to designate the region, 'maritime Southeast Asia'. Older names for this region are Nusantara – translated in Francophone studies as

'Nusantarienne', and Jawī, the adjective for Muslims from Bilād al-Jawā. Other terms include Malayo-Indonesian.

3   Martin Frishman and Hasan-Uddin Khan, eds, *The Mosque: History, Architectural Development & Regional Diversity* (London: Thames & Hudson, 1994); and Finbarr Barry Flood and Gülru Necipoğlu, eds, *A Companion to Islamic Art and Architecture*, 2 vols. (Hoboken, NJ: Wiley Blackwell, 2017).

4   Robert Nelson, 'The Map of Art History', *The Art Bulletin* 79.1 (1997): 28; Heghnar Z. Watenpaugh, 'Resonance and Circulation: The Category "Islamic Art and Architecture"', in *A Companion to Islamic Art and Architecture*, ed. Finbarr Barry Flood and Gülru Necipoğlu (Hoboken, NJ: Wiley-Blackwell, 2017), 2: 1224–25; John Tagg, *The Burden of Representation: Essays on Photographies and Histories* (Basingstoke: Palgrave Macmillan, 2007).

5   Gulsum Baydar, 'The Cultural Burden of Architecture', *Journal of Architectural Education* 57.4 (2004): 19–27; William Siew Wai Lim and Jiat-Hwee Chang, *Non West Modernist Past: On Architecture and Modernities* (Singapore: World Scientific, 2012).

6   Imran bin Tajudeen, 'Java's Architectural Enigma: The Austronesian World and the Limits of "Asia"', in *Architecturalized Asia: Mapping a Continent through History*, ed. Vimalin Rujivacharakul, H. Hazel Hahn, Ken Tadashi Oshima, and Peter Christensen (Hong Kong: Hong Kong University Press, 2013), 121–38.

7   See for instance Engseng Ho, *The Graves of Tarim: Genealogy and Mobility Across the Indian Ocean* (Berkeley: University of California Press, 2010).

8   Ahmed Wahby, *The Architecture of the Early Mosques and Shrines of Java: Influences of the Arab Merchants in the 15th and 16th Centuries?* (Bamberg: Opus, 2008); Zakaria Ali, *Islamic Art in Southeast Asia 830 A.D.–1570 A.D.* (Kuala Lumpur: Dewan Bahasa dan Pustaka, 1994).

9   William Roff, 'Islam Obscured?: Some Reflections on Studies of Islam and Society in Southeast Asia', *Archipel* 29 (1985): 7–34; Chiara Formichi, 'Islamic Studies or Asian Studies? Islam in Southeast Asia', *The Muslim World* 106.4 (2016): 696–718; Daniel Martin Varisco, *Islam Obscured: The Rhetoric of Anthropological Representation* (New York: Palgrave Macmillan, 2005).

10 Harlina Md Sharif, 'Mosques in Island Southeast Asia, 15th–20th Century' (Ph.D. diss., SOAS, University of London, 2013); Zakaria Ali, *Islamic Art*.

11 'Ali Ibrahim al-Ghabban, *Roads of Arabia: Archaeology and History of the Kingdom of Saudi Arabia* (Paris: Musée du Louvre, 2010).

12 Howard Davis, *The Culture of Building* (Oxford: Oxford University Press, 2006); Alka Patel, *Building Communities in Gujarāt: Architecture and Society During the Twelfth through Fourteenth Centuries* (Leiden: Brill, 2004).

13 Finbarr Barry Flood and Gülru Necipoğlu, 'Frameworks of Islamic Art and Architectural History: Concepts, Approaches, and Historiographies', in *A Companion to Islamic Art and Architecture. Volume I: From the Prophet to the Mongols*, ed. Finbarr Barry Flood and Gülru Necipoğlu (Hoboken, NJ: Wiley Blackwell, 2017), 23.

14 Gaudenz Domenig, *Religion and Architecture in Premodern Indonesia: Studies in Spatial Anthropology* (Boston: Brill, 2014).

15 Hélène Njoto, 'Mythical Feline Figures in Java's Early Islamisation Period (Fifteenth to the Early Seventeenth Centuries): Sinitic and Vietnamese Imprints in Pasisir Art', *Arts Asiatiques*

73 (2018): 41–60; Trevor Marchand, *The Masons of Djenné* (Bloomington: Indiana University Press, 2009).

16 Namely, south-east Sumatra's Srivijaya and Malayu, and East Java's Majapahit kingdoms. See George Coedès and Louis-Charles Damais, *Sriwijaya: History, Religion & Language of an Early Malay Polity: Collected Studies* (Kuala Lumpur: MBRAS, 1992); and Sri Soejatmi Satari, 'Some Data on a Former City of Majapahit', in *The Legacy of Majapahit*, ed. John N. Miksic and Endang Sri Hardiati Soekatno (Singapore: National Heritage Board, 1995), 31–41.

17 Important exceptions are the studies by Robert Wessing, 'The Gunongan in Banda Aceh, Indonesia: Agni's Fire in Allah's paradise?', *Archipel* 35 (1988): 157–94; and 'An Enclosure in the Garden of Love', *Journal of Southeast Asian Studies* 22.1 (1991): 1–15.

18 Claude Guillot, *Banten: Sejarah dan Peradaban Abad X-XVII*, trans. Hendra Setiawan, ed. Daniel Perret (Jakarta: Kepustakaan Populer Gramedia [KPG], 2011); Pierre-Yves Manguin, 'Demografi dan tata perkotaan di Aceh pada abad 16: Data baru menurut sebuah buku pedoman Portugis tahun 1584', in *Panggung Sejarah: Persembahan kepada Prof. Dr. Denys Lombard* (Jakarta: Yayasan Obor Indonesia, 1999), 225–44; Anthony Reid and Takeshi Ito, 'A Precious Dutch Map of Aceh, c. 1645', *Archipel* 57 (1999): 191–208; and Pierre-Yves Manguin, 'Of Fortresses and Galleys: The 1568 Acehnese Siege of Melaka, After a Contemporary Bird's-eye View', *Modern Asian Studies* 22.3 (1988): 607–28.

19 Religious teachers who became progenitors of dynasties include Sunan Giri in Gresik, East Java, and Sunan Gunung Jati in Cirebon and Banten, West Java. On the mosque and burial complexes associated with them, see Aminuddin Kasdi, *Kepurbakalaan Sunan Giri: Sosok akulturasi kebudayaan Indonesia asli, Hindu-Budha, dan Islam abad 15–16* (Surabaya: Unesa University Press, 2008); and Hasan Basyari, *Sekitar komplek makam Sunan Gunung Jati dan sekilas riwayatnya* (Cirebon: Zul Fana, 1989).

20 Wahby, *Early Mosques*; Handinoto and Samuel Hartono, 'Pengaruh Pertukangan Cina Pada Bangunan Mesjid Kuno Di Jawa Abad 15–16', *Dimensi Teknik Arsitektur* 35.1 (2007): 23–40; Kees Van Dijk, 'The Changing Contour of Mosques', in *The Past in the Present: Architecture in Indonesia*, ed. Peter J. M. Nas (Rotterdam: NAi Press, 2007), 45–66.

21 The narrative of Demak as prototype is accepted in Abdul Halim Nasir, *Mosque Architecture in the Malay World*, trans. Omar Salahuddin Abdullah (Bangi: Penerbit Universiti Kebangsaan Malaysia, 2004); and Sharif, 'Mosques in Island Southeast Asia', 8.

22 Nancy K. Florida, *Writing the Past, Inscribing the Future: History as Prophecy in Colonial Java* (Durham, NC: Duke University Press, 1995).

23 Imran bin Tajudeen, 'Trade, Politics, and Sufi Synthesis in the Formation of Southeast Asian Islamic Architecture', in *A Companion to Islamic Art and Architecture, Volume II: From the Mongols to Modernism*, ed. Finbarr Barry Flood and Gülru Necipoğlu (Hoboken, NJ: John Wiley & Sons, 2017), 996–1022.

24 This is in line with Kusno's own recent exhortation in the context of the study of vernacular architecture. See Abidin Kusno, 'Reframing the Vernacular and Other Tales', in *Reframing the Vernacular: Politics, Semiotics, and Representation*, ed. Gusti Ayu Made Suartika and Julie Nichols (Cham: Springer, 2020), 1–12.

25 Tajudeen, 'Java's Architectural Enigma'.

26 For instance, Malay *ukir* motifs is discussed as a form of arabesque in Heba Nayel Barakat, *The Arabesque: An Introduction* (Kuala Lumpur: Islamic Arts Museum Malaysia, 2018).
27 Njoto, 'Mythical Feline Figures'.
28 Anthony Reid, ed., *The Last Stand of Asian Autonomies: Responses to Modernity in the Diverse States of Southeast Asia and Korea, 1750–1900* (New York: St. Martin's Press, 1997).
29 Imran bin Tajudeen, 'Mosques and Minarets: Transregional Connections in Eighteenth-Century Southeast Asia', *Journal 18* 4 (2017), http://www.journal18.org/2056.
30 Abdul Halim Nasir, *Masjid-masjid di Semenanjung Malaysia* (Kuala Lumpur: Berita Publishing, 1984); Helen Ibbitson Jessup, *Court Arts of Indonesia* (New York: Asia Society Galleries, 1990); Farish A Noor and Eddin Khoo, *Spirit of Wood: The Art of Malay Woodcarving: Works by Master Carvers from Kelantan, Terengganu and Pattani* (Hong Kong: Periplus, 2003); and Barakat, *The Arabesque*.
31 See the exhibition circuits of *Court Arts of Indonesia*, *Spirit of Wood* and *The Arabesque*, with catalogs bearing the same titles referenced above.
32 Othman Mohd. Yatim, *Batu Aceh: Early Islamic Gravestones in Peninsular Malaysia* (Kuala Lumpur: Museum Association of Malaysia, 1988); Daniel Perret and Kamarudin bin Ab. Razak, *Batu Aceh, warisan sejarah Johor* (Johor Bahru: École française d'Extrême-Orient; Yayasan Warisan Johor, 1999); and Daniel Perret and Kamarudin Ab. Razak, *Batu Aceh Johor dalam perbandingan* (Johor: École française d'extrême-Orient; Yayasan Warisan Johor, 2004).
33 Exceptions are Zakaria Ali, *Islamic Art* and Njoto, 'Mythical Feline Figures'.
34 Agus Sunyoto, *Atlas Wali Songo: Buku pertama yang mengungkap Wali Songo sebagai fakta sejarah* (Jakarta: Pustaka Iiman, 2012).
35 Ashadi, *Warisan Walisongo: telaah kritis atas 'Cinanisasi' dalam proses islamisasi di Jawa melalui penelusuran sejarah dan transformasi arsitektural* (Bogor: Lorong Semesta, 2006); Noor and Khoo, *Spirit of Wood* writes on the work, philosophy, and collection of the woodcarver Nik Rashiddin.
36 C. Formichi, 'Islamic Studies or Asian Studies? Islam in Southeast Asia', *The Muslim World* 106.4 (2016): 696–718. Meanwhile, Barry Flood and Gülru Necipoğlu have pointed to the need for greater engagement between Islamic Studies' textual scholars and Islamic art and architecture historians who focus on visual culture. Flood and Necipoğlu, 'Frameworks', 21.
37 Drewes, *Adminitions of Seh Bari*; Denys Lombard, *Aceh*; Michrob, *Banten*; Guillot, *Banten*.
38 Watenpaugh, 'Resonance and Circulation'; Gülru Necipoğlu, 'The Concept of Islamic Art: Inherited Discourses and New Approaches', *Journal of Art Historiography* 6 (2012): 1–26, https://arthistoriography.files.wordpress.com/2012/05/necipogludoc.pdf.
39 Finbarr Barry Flood, *Objects of Translation: Material Culture and Medieval 'Hindu-Muslim' Encounter* (Princeton: Princeton University Press, 2009).
40 Ghabban, *Roads of Arabia*.
41 Such catalogue surveys include Taufiq Hidayat and Harry Widodo, *Masjid-masjid Bersejarah dan Ternama Indonesia* (Jakarta: Permata Communications, 2005), and Junus Satrio Atmodjo, *Masjid Kuno Indonesia* (Jakarta: Direktorat Perlindungan dan Pembinaan Peninggalan Sejarah dan Purbakala, 1999).

Part 4

Fieldwork and Documentation

Chapter 11

A Field without Fieldwork: Sustaining the Study of Islamic Architecture in the Twenty-First Century

Nancy Um

'Can I wear it over my glasses?', I asked. Nick responded affirmatively and helped me put on the heavy headset. He then gave me two controllers, one for each hand. Soon, I was flying above the surface of the earth, looking down upon the globe. He told me that I could go anywhere that I wanted to and showed me how to navigate through the sky using the various triggers and buttons. I immediately soared east, toward the Arabian Peninsula.

Mocha, the Red Sea port city that is often associated with the coffee trade, has been the focus of my research for 25 years [Figure 11.1]. Yet, the last time I visited Yemen was in 2002, having paused between research trips to complete writing projects for tenure and promotion while also caring for two young children. Those life and career circumstances resulted in an unintended and extended absence, which has greatly stoked my desire to walk again through Mocha's streets and revisit its monuments in person. So, when given the opportunity to wear a hi-tech headset and use the Google Earth VR application, I headed straight for Mocha.[1] As I flew above the city, its familiar details came into view: the crescent-shaped harbour which has silted up considerably over the centuries, the straight road that cuts across the southern edge of the city, its modern jetty, and the small white specks which are the roofs of historic buildings [Figure 11.2].

In its virtual reality (VR) version, the Google Earth application provides users an expansive bird's-eye view, but also the ability to tread on the ground. Other colleagues who tested the same application reported that they were able to glide over to Asia and then walk through the neighbourhoods of Hong Kong, but also to peruse our own campus landmarks here in Binghamton virtually.

'How do I land?', I asked, as I hovered above the port. Nick instructed me how to move from flying to a standing posture using the controllers. Yet, as I tried to enter the city of Mocha, the application stalled. Rather than offering me a seamless passage from air to land, I received the message: 'Street view unavailable', which shattered the immersive illusion that had surrounded me. Apparently, this application, which offers 'to put the whole world within your reach', provides entry into certain sites, while others are only partially available.[2] I could only hover just above the surface of the city but could not enter it. I then tried to visit the UNESCO World Heritage city of Sanaa and other key sites in Yemen, but found that they were also inaccessible from the ground. Distant views from the sky would have to suffice there too.

It goes without saying that the virtual experience of place cannot stand in for the actual encounter that one would have on the ground at that site. But, VR can offer a meaningful

Figure 11.1: View of Mocha, with Bayt Sidi Nunu in the foreground and the Mosque of al-Shadhili in the background, in 1996. Source: Nancy Um.

spatial experience, whether it is convincingly realistic or utterly artificial. In this case, my virtual engagement with Yemen mirrored my limited physical access to my research sites. The fiction of unencumbered travel that Google Earth VR offers, with its ambitious tagline 'Go anywhere', was immediately dispelled. Yemen remained inaccessible, even through this virtual portal.

Using my own personal obstacles to travel (both actual and virtual) as launching points, this essay queries where the field of Islamic architectural history is today and where it might possibly go amidst certain practical and institutional challenges; some field specific and others shared across the humanities. This essay is not concerned with the fundamental and contentious intellectual concerns that govern the field today. Rather, it is meant to question some of the core expectations about the way that we work and the institutional structures within which we operate, with the interest of asking how the field of Islamic architectural history might adapt to grapple with the challenges that stand before it.

Figure 11.2: View of Mocha, screenshot from Google Earth VR, 2019. Source: Google.

The Question of Access

As a graduate student of Islamic art and architecture in the 1990s, I understood clearly that one needed to earn the credentials to become an accepted scholar by passing through certain stages that were codified in my program's regulations. They entailed completing a sequence of coursework, fulfilling foreign language requirements, successfully filing written and oral exams, submitting a proposal, and completing a doctoral dissertation, all in addition to other minor benchmarks along the way. Yet, as we all know, there is an unwritten curriculum that operates in parallel to these stated academic protocols. This 'hidden curriculum', as it is sometimes called, is learned independently and often through social channels, sometimes conveyed by mentors outside of the seminar room or acquired by observing peers and attempting to model their most successful behaviours. This unwritten curriculum governs a whole range of dispositions that go far beyond the professional sphere, including the way we dress and present ourselves, as well as the kinds of social and professional networks that we form and sustain.

As in many other fields in the humanities, part of the 'hidden curriculum' of studying Islamic architectural history is the expectation of extensive original fieldwork in the region, one of the cornerstones of advanced research in a subfield that has rarely welcomed the type of dissertation that can be undertaken without leaving one's campus, oriented primarily on topics such as historiography or theory. The contribution of architectural and urban fieldwork is evaluated, at least in part, on the researcher's capacity to document and study buildings that have yet to be published or those that have been misinterpreted in the past. In this way, Islamic architectural historians are faced with a different set of expectations than those for art historians who work primarily with known objects that are housed in global (or local) museums, libraries, and archives, but may never set foot in the Middle East. In most cases, this requirement to conduct extensive and original fieldwork hinges on the ability to travel, which assumes that one can cross national borders and safely gain direct physical access to sites. In this way, passport stamps earned may be added to one's informal roster of credentials.

It should also be noted that the actual practice of field research is rarely taught to us. Whereas archaeology offers a significant amount of training in the field, most architectural historians arrive at their field sites equipped only with the detached intellectual disquisitions that they were exposed to in the classroom. This background rarely provides guidance on how to solve practical problems on the ground, such as figuring out how to document a structure on the verge of collapse or how to work with custodians to gain access to historic monuments (some of which may be inhabited or in use).

To be sure, in Islamic architectural history, one's choice of research topic has never been driven by intellectual curiosity in any pure sense, but hinges largely on access. Students are avidly (and rightly) discouraged from studying certain places, not because they lack architectural or cultural value, but rather because of the dangers posed by local conflicts or because research permits are unobtainable. These issues of access have greatly determined patterns of research in the field, and thus governed its internal hierarchies and the unevenness of the sub-specialties represented within it. I chose to work in Yemen, namely because of my interest in maritime trade and Yemen's key place on the Arabian Peninsula at the edge of the Indian Ocean world. At the time that I began my field research in 1996, after the end of the 1994 civil war, Yemen was relatively stable. My early research inspired me to envision a continuing career there and to look forward to a whole host of possible future projects. There were, of course, certain difficulties: the local institutions that supported academic research were sparse, foreigners were sometimes kidnapped, and movement within the country was frequently restricted. Even so, I had not considered that a violent war would begin in 2015, yet again tearing the country apart and, as a consequence, upending the research trajectory to which I had aspired.

If I were to start again today, rather than in the 1990s, those decisions would be even more fraught, as fieldwork in the Middle East and North Africa, and across West and South Asia, has become increasingly complicated – with multiple on-going conflicts throughout the region, which have resulted in staggering human loss and mass displacement, and in certain cases widespread hunger and disease. Moreover, the job of the art and architectural historian is under great pressure because cultural heritage is not a mere casualty of these conflicts, but has even been targeted directly by warring parties that seek to instigate cultural anguish and loss of identity.[3] We are also witnessing increased constraints on scholarly expression and widespread violations of academic freedom that further threaten research possibilities across the Middle East.[4]

To be clear, the problem that I identify is not just about access to Islamic architectural sites for foreign researchers, an issue which has a much longer history and only affects some scholars who work in the field (including some of the most privileged ones). But, regional conflicts have also made it extremely difficult for colleagues in certain Middle Eastern institutions to continue their research. Some have fled the area for fear of their own safety or concerns about their ability to speak and write freely. As an indication of the increasing severity of this issue, the Scholars at Risk Network was established in 1999 and has continuously expanded its programs to protect the precarious lives and rights of scholars who are threatened, including those in the Middle East.[5] Moreover, I am identifying the chilling effects of a rising sensibility that seeks to build barriers and to police passage through them aggressively, precisely at a time when there are more and more reasons to travel or migrate, in order to pursue opportunity, but also out of utter despair. These barriers have effectively stymied movement in various directions, not just from the west to the east. As an example, one of my advanced doctoral students, who holds an Iranian passport, was scheduled to begin dissertation fieldwork in Tehran in 2017. Right before the time of her departure, newly inaugurated US President Donald Trump committed one of his first major acts in office: Executive Order 13769, the policy referred to more commonly as the 'Muslim travel ban', which barred the citizens of certain countries from entry into the United States. While this restriction would have no effect on this student's voyage to Iran, it could certainly have affected her ability to re-enter the United States after the trip was completed and thus hindered the successful completion of her dissertation and graduate studies. Amidst the chaotic months that followed, when multiple attempts were made to block the implementation of this order, the student eventually made the bold decision to embark on this research trip, but shortened it due to these uncertainties. As one of her advisors, it was agonizingly difficult to provide her with reasonable counsel during this challenging situation. It also pushed me to wonder, as borders close down and various types of mobility are impaired, how can a community of scholarly refugees, so to speak, sustain research in this field? How can Islamic architectural history continue as a field of study as we lose access to sites of interest and the very monuments that we study are under siege?

As I write this, the COVID-19 pandemic is destabilizing the world, further affecting travel, connection, and mobility across borders, thereby suggesting that these questions stand to become more, rather than less, fraught even if some of the political conflicts mentioned above may be resolved.

Working as an Islamicist

We also must acknowledge that the humanities have been subject to major structural changes, particularly during the past decade. It is no longer surprising to hear about the closure of humanities programs and departments at American universities.[6] Fewer students elect to major in the humanities or to take humanities courses because they are compelled to seek experience in areas that they believe will yield more secure and lucrative career possibilities. By extension, the number of tenure-track academic jobs for new Ph.D.s is diminishing, particularly in fields such as art and architectural history. The positions that are advertised are increasingly contingent, short-term, or precarious.[7]

At the same time, the field of Islamic art and architectural history has grown considerably over the past generation, a trend that is discernible in the list of dissertations that the College Art Association (CAA) maintains and publishes yearly.[8] This list, which has a history of almost 60 years, is by no means exhaustive and is limited to North America, but it provides certain indications about the direction of the field.[9] As such, its contents are worth delving into. The list was initially published in the CAA's *Art Journal* in 1963 and then migrated to *The Art Bulletin*.[10] Yet, 'Islamic art' appears as a distinct and consistent category (which included Islamic architecture as a major component) only in its 1992 roster, with three US dissertations being written in the subfield.[11] In 2018, the last time that the list was consulted for this essay, 36 dissertations were either being written or had been completed [Figure 11.3].[12] It is clear that the field has been on the rise over the past three decades, with growing numbers of doctoral students specializing in Islamic art, even though not all of the dissertations that were begun were completed and this rise has not been a steady one. At the same time, the number of institutions granting degrees in this field has expanded considerably, from only five in the 1990s to 33 in the twenty-first century [Figure 11.4].

Of course, this growth is not limited to Islamic art history, but is indicative of a much-broadened field of art and architectural history in general. *The Art Bulletin* listing of dissertations, in total across sub-fields, both in progress and completed, was six pages long in 1992, but then grew to 33 pages in 2008, the last time the roster was published in that journal. Even so, it is worth considering what this expansion might mean for our subfield. Indeed, such growth can be seen, on one hand, as a welcomed development, as it demonstrates the increased profile of Islamic art within the classically Eurocentric discipline of art history. But, we must also ask how that expansion can be sustained in the current climate when the possibilities for full-time academic positions have substantially decreased. How can we continue to accept students into doctoral programs and to issue degrees to freshly minted Ph.D.s who increasingly emerge into an academic market that is already saturated and extremely precarious?

Moreover, the landscape of scholarly publishing is shifting radically. Even reputable and seemingly well-funded establishments, like Stanford University Press, have been pushed to justify their existence, which portends diminished possibilities for disseminating scholarly research through traditional channels.[13] The market for books on Islamic architectural history has never been vast, but is currently subject to further contraction in an academic publishing environment that is mindful of its bottom line. Even if scholars wish to speak only to a small group of like-minded peers, publishers are growing much more resistant to such a limited scope of dissemination. With this in mind, we must ask who our audiences are and question if the forms and venues for scholarly expression that we generally employ are appropriate for the contemporary moment, along with our expectations for tenure and promotion in the academy.

I do not find oft-repeated proclamations about the impending death of the humanities to be particularly useful. But I do believe that we should recognize the various precarities that threaten the academic structure to which many of us have grown accustomed, rather than simply waiting for things to change. Indeed, we ought to acknowledge the unlikelihood that the previous state of academic hiring or humanities support will be restored in

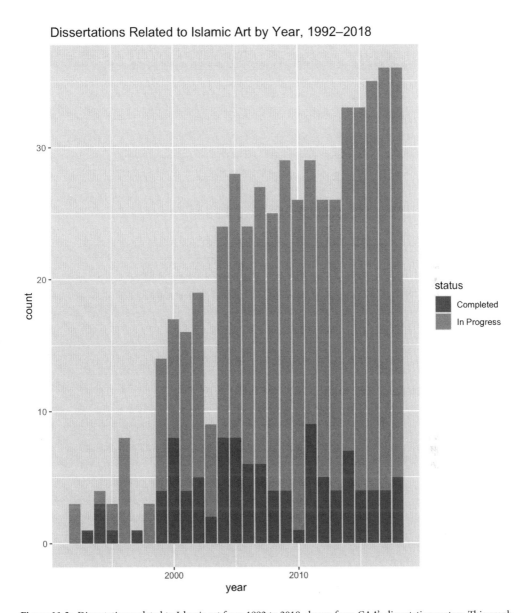

Figure 11.3: Dissertations related to Islamic art from 1992 to 2018, drawn from CAA's dissertation rosters. This graph includes each title that appeared on the CAA roster under the categories Islamic Art, Art of the Middle East/North Africa, Middle Eastern/West Asia, and West Asia, so certain titles were reported several times while in progress and at completion. Source: Graph created by Nancy Um. Data from *The Art Bulletin* annual roster and *caa.reviews*.

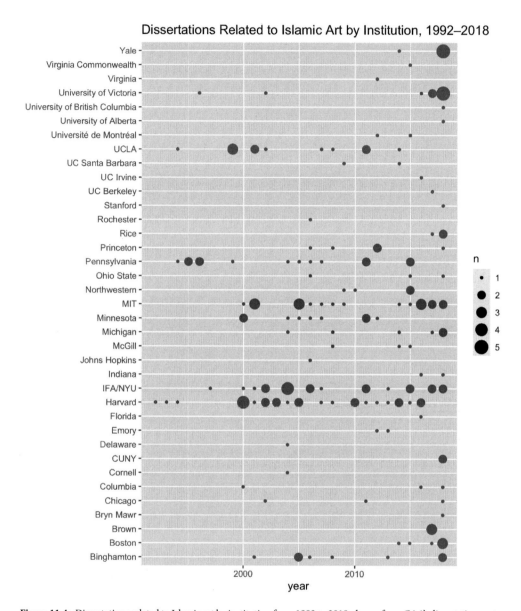

Figure 11.4: Dissertations related to Islamic art by institution from 1992 to 2018, drawn from CAA's dissertation rosters. This graph includes each dissertation author only once and also includes dissertations that were not completed. Source: Graph created by Nancy Um. Data from *The Art Bulletin* annual roster and *caa.reviews*.

the near future. We have ethical responsibilities to both the profession and to our students to recognize what has shifted and to engage in frank discussions about how to move forward. As one specific example, the graduate students in the Department of English and Comparative Literature at Columbia University pushed the faculty to reckon with this crisis in a pointed manner. In May 2019, 84 alumni and students, who were undoubtedly vulnerable in their positions, wrote a letter to protest the admission of a large cohort of new graduate students into the program at a time when so few advanced students had been placed in stable professional positions during that hiring season.[14] The department was forced to acknowledge the students' concerns and responded by holding a town hall meeting. One outcome of this gathering was that the department agreed to provide job search support for advanced students, which would include possibilities for non-academic careers. It has yet to be seen if these responses will be adequate in preparing students for the job market of the future, but it indicates that we need to think about training graduate students in more holistic and practical ways than we have in the past and recognize that emerging scholars are situated in a very different position than their mentors were at the early stages of their own careers.

Sustaining Islamic Architectural History

This essay has cited two concerns about the sustainability of Islamic architectural history as a subfield. The first concern – access to field sites and the capacity to conduct on-site research – is oriented around personal mobility and current restrictions on it in an age of war and closed borders. The second concern overlaps with the first, by identifying the structural changes that are affecting higher education, and particularly the humanities. While admittedly posing more questions than answers, I wish to present both conditions as real and significant and to prompt a discussion about the future of the field. How should we conduct and evaluate research in the contemporary moment? How will Islamic architectural history ensure its own robust continuation into the twenty-first century?

It seems clear that some answers will be oriented around technological innovation, even if our VR headsets do not provide adequate surrogates for on-the-ground experiences that architectural historians require. Yet, we need to explore technologies for remote engagement more seriously, as anthropologists have done with the development of digital anthropology. For them, technology has opened up possibilities for virtually connected fieldwork that does not rest upon the expectation of unencumbered travel, and so must it for us.[15] Moreover, open and dynamic formats for digital publishing may provide promising pathways for the production and dissemination of scholarship in an increasingly networked world. But, regardless, we need to acknowledge that the future of the field will not look like its past, while also envisioning what the next generation of Islamic art and architectural historians will need in order to succeed and flourish.

Notes

This chapter was previously published as Nancy Um, 'A Field Without Fieldwork: Sustaining the Study of Islamic Architecture in the Twenty-First Century', *International Journal of Islamic Architecture* 10.1 (2021): 99–109. The text has been updated for this publication.

1. On May 30 and July 12, 2019, I used the HTC Vive VR System and the Google Earth VR application, made available by the Binghamton University Libraries. I am deeply grateful to Nick Eggleston, Binghamton University Libraries Systems Specialist, for facilitating these experiences.
2. 'Introducing Google Earth VR', Google, accessed July 8, 2019, https://vr.google.com/earth/.
3. See, for example, Lamya Khalidi, 'Destruction of Yemen and its Cultural Heritage', *International Journal of Middle East Studies* 49 (2017): 735–38; Heghnar Zeitlian Watenpaugh, 'Cultural Heritage and the Arab Spring: War over Culture, Culture of War and Culture War', *International Journal of Islamic Architecture* 5.2 (2016): 245–63.
4. As one record of these violations, see 'Committee on Academic Freedom', Middle East Studies Association, accessed July 10, 2019, https://mesana.org/advocacy/committee-on-academic-freedom.
5. 'About', Scholars at Risk Network, accessed March 1, 2020, https://www.scholarsatrisk.org/about/.
6. These changes have been taking shape globally, but I treat the US case because it is the one with which I am the most familiar. Eric Kelderman, 'Can Closing a Humanities College Save a University?', *Chronicle of Higher Education*, April 13, 2018, https://www.chronicle.com/article/Can-Closing-a-Humanities/243113.
7. Bryan Alexander, *Academia Next: The Futures of Higher Education* (Baltimore: Johns Hopkins University, 2020), 36–40; Kevin Carey, 'The Bleak Job Landscape of Adjunctopia for Ph.D.s', *New York Times*, March 5, 2020, https://www.nytimes.com/2020/03/05/upshot/academic-job-crisis-phd.html.
8. This chapter deals with the rosters that have been issued by CAA, published in the organization's journals. Since the original publication of this essay in 2021, the Society of Architectural Historians has issued a comprehensive study of trends in architectural history in the United States, which adds more perspective to the findings based on the CAA dissertation roster. See *Architectural History in the United States: Findings and Trends in Higher Education* (Chicago: Society of Architectural Historians, 2021), https://www.sah.org/docs/default-source/default-document-library/sah-data-report-book-final_digital.pdf.
9. For more information about the dissertation roster and its history, see Nancy Um, 'What Do We Know about the Future of Art History: Let's Start by Looking at its Past, Sixty Years of Dissertations', *caa.reviews*, August 18, 2020, http://www.caareviews.org/reviews/3797; Nancy Um and Emily Hagen, "What Do We Know about the Future of Art History? Part 2: Dissertations since 1980," *caa.reviews*, June 28, 2021, http://www.caareviews.org/reviews/3924.

10. 'Dissertations in Progress', *Art Journal* 22.3 (1963): 168–69. The list was issued by *Art Journal* until 1980. *The Art Bulletin* published it yearly in its June issue from 1981 to 2008, when it was migrated fully to the online forum *caa.reviews*.

11. 'American and Canadian Dissertations, 1992', *Art Bulletin* 75.2 (1993): 354. Before 1993, Islamic topics were included under 'Art of Asia'. For instance, see Nancy Micklewright's dissertation, 'Turkish Costume History', in 'Dissertation Topics, 1982', *Art Bulletin* 65.2 (1983): 360.

12. It must be noted, however, that CAA changed the categories several times over this period. So, the areas that have been included in this query aggregate the results of Islamic Art, Art of the Middle East/North Africa, Middle Eastern/West Asia, and West Asia, which, in some cases, include certain topics that sit outside of, or on, the chronological or geographical fringes of Islamic art.

13. In April 2019, Stanford's provost, Persis Drell, announced that Stanford University Press's request for continuing funding would not be approved. She constituted a committee to develop a plan for the press's continuation. On October 15, 2019, that committee issued a report proposing that the press should be funded for another five years, although it raised concerns about the press's mission and financial viability. It should be noted that Stanford's Faculty Senate constituted a second committee with the same charge, which also issued a report on this matter. See 'Report from the Provostial Committee on the Future of the Stanford University Press', unpublished report, October 15, 2019, accessed March 8, 2020, https://provost.stanford.edu/wp-content/uploads/sites/4/2019/10/SUPress-Report.pdf.

14. Serena White, '"An Ethical Quandary": In Face of National Humanities Decline, English Department Reckons with Future of Graduate Students', *Columbia Spectator*, November 1, 2019, https://www.columbiaspectator.com/news/2019/10/31/an-ethical-quandary-in-face-of-national-humanities-decline-english-department-reckons-with-future-of-graduate-students/.

15. Marieke Brandt, *Tribes and Politics in Yemen: A History of the Houthi Conflict* (Oxford: Oxford University Press, 2017), 6–7.

Chapter 12

Architectural History in Turkey: Between Fieldwork and Archival Research

Patricia Blessing

Fieldwork is, quite obviously, a major component of architectural history, since much of its research needs to take place where the structures being studied are located. Considerable challenges can arise due to political circumstances, from local restrictions on research to violent conflict. Such events often require major adjustments to research agendas and sometimes render fieldwork impossible, as Nancy Um notes in the present volume. In the last decade, this has been the case in Yemen and Syria, both of which are completely off limits to foreign scholars and enduring conditions that make it impossible for local scholars to work there. The consequences for the conservation of monuments are vast and archaeological sites are at great peril.[1] Further, ethical questions loom large as to what extent work with material previously gathered can and should be done in light of human suffering on-site.[2]

Previously, I wrote on my fieldwork experiences for the Society of Architectural Historians' blog while I was a 2015–16 H. Allen Brooks Travelling Fellow making my way to diverse places such as Armenia, Bosnia, Kosovo, North Macedonia, Morocco, Spain, and Turkey.[3] At that point, the most dramatic recent event in the political history of Turkey, and in the urban development of Istanbul, had been the Gezi Park protests of 2013.[4] Quickly suppressed, these protests had been triggered by a project to reconstruct Topçu Kışlası (1806), a military barracks located until 1909 on the site of one of the few parks in central Istanbul that had been established in the 1930s.[5] Just north of Taksim Square, Gezi Park survives, but its vicinity has been redeveloped, with the reconstruction of the Atatürk Kültür Merkezi and the construction of a mosque that opened in spring 2021.[6]

In preparation for writing this essay, as I revisited these blog posts, written as real-time reflections while traveling to various sites, I realized how profoundly things on the ground have changed in the last five years. Events since 2013 have further transformed the political landscape in Turkey. In January 2016, numerous scholars signed a petition to ask the Turkish government to stop attacks on Kurdish areas, especially the historical Sur area of Diyarbakır, as the peace process with the Kurdistan Workers' Party (abbreviated as PKK in Kurdish) collapsed.[7] Many of these signatories, known as 'Academics for Peace', lost their positions at Turkish universities, some had to leave Turkey, and others have faced time in prison. Charges against those not yet convicted were eventually dismissed in 2019.[8] In the aftermath of the military coup attempt on July 15, 2016, more scholars lost their positions, as did public servants in various areas of administration. The following year, a referendum led to the establishment of a presidential system with Recep Tayyip Erdoğan, who had been prime minister, at its head. The resulting restructuring of public institutions also affected museums and archives, such as the Ottoman archives in Istanbul, which was moved into the purview of the Office of the President.

Financial difficulties as the Turkish economy struggles to recover from the COVID-19 pandemic will certainly affect universities and museums, as well as the ability to conduct restoration projects on historical monuments in cities across Turkey. These are some of the political realities that underpin research in Turkey today. Obviously, they are much more difficult to face for scholars who live and work in Turkey, than for those, like me, who conduct research there during summers and sabbaticals.

Fieldwork in the City

The urban realities are equally striking. In Istanbul, a city with (officially) about 15.5 million inhabitants and an expanding highway and public transportation system, monument preservation is a constant, pressing issue.[9] The third bridge across the Bosporus (opened in 2016) and the new airport near the Black Sea (opened in 2019) have had far-reaching urban impacts, as traffic patterns have shifted and forests were cut down for new construction. The ecological impact has been extensive: wild boars were seen swimming across the Bosporus fleeing construction, and the airport endangers migratory birds [Figure 12.1]. Currently, the Kanal İstanbul project, which aims at connecting the Black Sea to the Sea of Marmara on the western edge of Istanbul, poses further threats to the environment. If completed (which is doubtful given the current state of Turkey's economy and state coffers), the effects will be immense. While the built fabric of Istanbul will be largely spared because the site is far from the parts of the city that contain historical monuments, the ecological impact makes the project highly problematic.[10]

Increasing population, traffic, and construction within the city pose constant challenges to the preservation of Istanbul's historical monuments, including Topkapı Palace, Hagia Sophia, and its many Ottoman and Byzantine sites. One of the most recent interventions of government policy in heritage management was the removal of Hagia Sophia's museum status in the summer of 2020 and its renewed use as a mosque. It is far from clear how this change in status will affect ongoing and future restoration projects and scholars' ability to conduct research as has been noted in a number of scholarly reactions since the controversial change was announced.[11]

Every step taken within the city brings encounters with a historical and present-day urban fabric. Seen from the terrace behind the Süleymaniye Mosque (1550–57), a view of the Bosporus emerges over the domes of one of the four madrasas that belong to the complex.[12] Shifting the view slightly to the left, the foreground remains very similar, yet the background changes: the skyscrapers of the business centres and malls in Maslak and Levent emerge in the back, and the metro bridge (opened in 2014) cutting across the Golden Horn. The changes in the sightlines caused by such projects – as necessary as they may be in order to improve public transportation – are considerable. Thus, the contemporary, living city is ever present

Figure 12.1: Migrating storks in Sarıyer, in the northern section of Istanbul's European side, photographed in March 2015. Source: Ali Yaycıoğlu.

around the historical monuments, and at times within them; the fifteenth-century Mahmud Pasha Hammam, for instance, houses clothing stores [Figure 12.2]. Such contemporary uses keep monuments alive, but can also damage them, depending on the nature of activities and interventions involved. In the mid-eighteenth-century Serpuş Han in Karaköy, for instance, metal-working workshops occupy historical rooms and a fig tree growing on the roof threatens the structure. Nevertheless, amidst the increasing gentrification of this part of Istanbul, expelling the workshops to restore the building and then letting it stand empty would likely bring more problems than solutions.[13]

On the brighter side, the election of Ekrem İmamoğlu as mayor of Istanbul in June 2019 brought new hope for the city. Elected in a landslide victory after a first election in March 2019 was cancelled by the government, İmamoğlu has become a symbol of democracy and progressive politics for many in Turkey. Celebratory stencilled graffiti soon appeared around the city [Figure 12.3]; in this example, the text reads 'Hope is everywhere. #EkremAbi34'. The hashtag contains the mayor's first name, and a colloquial spelling for the affectionate but also respectful 'older brother' form of address in Turkish (*ağabey*). The number 34 identifies Istanbul on car license plates. Thus, the simple stencil reflects its maker's hope for change in the city, but also for Turkey at large. For art historians, and for any resident of Istanbul, this graffiti immediately evokes the stencils that appeared in Istanbul during the Gezi Park protests in 2013.[14] Perhaps this change in leadership will bring about new opportunities for scholars to engage in monument preservation at the municipal level, and new resources for municipal institutions such as the İBB (İstanbul Büyükşehir Belediyesi) Atatürk Kitaplığı, which holds historical documents, manuscripts, and photographs.

Elsewhere in Turkey, other challenges can emerge as restoration projects can be controlled by various authorities, from municipalities to national institutions. During my research in central Anatolia, I encountered a range of such projects, and realized the utmost importance of working with historical photographs, even though these are somewhat challenging to find for cities in that region.[15] I should also note that 'historical photographs' here denotes not just nineteenth-century photographs taken by travellers and by well-known Ottoman photographic studios such as Sébah and Joaillier.[16] Later photographs taken by scholars including Kurt Erdmann in the 1950s, Walter B. Denny from the 1960s onward, and Bernard O'Kane from the 1980s and later have become invaluable resources, as the urban context in many cities in Anatolia has profoundly changed over the course of the twentieth century.[17] In these cases, the pre-modern urban fabric has been obscured by the construction of apartment buildings and of large boulevards that were added in the 1950s and 1960s in order to open cities to cars.[18] These interventions of course affect our ability to analyse the historical context, as monuments appear as isolated traces of the past, but archival images can help.

One example of such changes that affect the ways in which historical buildings can be studied is the central Anatolian city of Sivas. There, the urban fabric is characterized by apartment buildings and thoroughfares, and historical monuments stand isolated, without any traces of pre-modern residential architecture or city walls.[19] Medieval buildings such as the Çifte Minareli Medrese (1271) and the Buruciye Medrese (1271) have been restored multiple

Figure 12.2: The interior of the Mahmud Pasha Hammam (1462), Istanbul, photographed in 2016. Source: Patricia Blessing.

Figure 12.3: Stencilled graffiti celebrating the election of Istanbul mayor Ekrem İmamoğlu in June 2019, photographed in Istanbul in July 2019. Source: Patricia Blessing.

Figure 12.4: The Gök Medrese (1271) in Sivas, photographed in 2008. Source: Patricia Blessing.

times, most recently between 2008 and 2013. The Gök Medrese is one monument that underwent multiple restorations: the first one, recorded in an inscription, in 1823–24 [Figure 12.4].[20] The French Jesuit Guillaume de Jerphanion photographed structures in Sivas in 1905 and 1910, including a detail of the Gök Medrese.[21] The photograph, one of the earliest of it that I have been able to find, clearly shows how far the soil level has risen, covering part of the portal. This is even more evident in Albert Gabriel's photograph from the 1920s, and residential structures are shown to encroach on the monument.[22] In the 1960s, when Kurt Erdmann photographed it, some restoration work must have been already done, as the madrasa appears free of abutting structures and an area around it has been excavated to the level of the original foundations.[23]

A documentation, excavation, and repair project was carried out on the Gök Medrese in 1979–80; its effects are seen in Walter Denny's photographs from the 1980s, which are available on Artstor.[24] That project, directed by architect and archaeologist Orhan Cezmi Tuncer was published in detail, although not until 2008. Nevertheless, Tuncer's book is highly valuable – nothing similar is available for other monuments in Sivas. The project was abandoned, according to Tuncer, when he moved to a new university position in 1980–81.[25] A final, highly controversial project was carried out between 2007 and 2021, with numerous delays; while the project dealt with necessary repairs to structural issues, it also garnered criticism for excessive intervention, especially in cleaning the portal and the use of concrete.[26] More recent photographs, for instance those published on the website associated with the project 'Crossing Frontiers: Christians and Muslims and their Art in Eastern Anatolia and the Caucasus', show the extent of cleaning and repairs.[27] Thus, older photographs make it possible to trace a history of the monument that is only in part published and not visible on site today. The same is true for a great number of buildings across Turkey (and surely elsewhere) as research on architectural history is influenced by local and national politics, and sometimes aggressive interventions in urban space over time.

Archives in Turkey and Beyond

Archival research is thus crucial within architectural history, not as a replacement for what can be studied on-site, but as a complementary form of investigation. For the Ottoman context, relevant archives and libraries are of course found within Turkey, but also in regions that were formerly under Ottoman rule in the Balkans, Hungary, North Africa, and several other Arab countries.[28] Documents can be in multiple languages: Ottoman Turkish, Arabic, Persian, Greek, and more, depending on the nature and age of documents.[29] To advance research on architectural history that traces changes over time, photographic archives are especially crucial; such archives exist across the world, with various degrees of online accessibility. For most archives in Turkey, good knowledge of modern Turkish is essential in addition to knowledge of the research languages that one needs. For the most part, navigating the archives without knowing Turkish would be difficult, especially as the catalogues and search interfaces are often only available in Turkish. Similarly, knowledge of the currently dominant local language is often crucial for archives located in other countries. The linguistic situation can be a further barrier to research, restricting accessibility to scholars from different backgrounds and with different training. Knowledge of one (or more) languages over others can also direct research agendas in a way that might generate blind spots, further adding to the complexities of research projects in this part of the world. Relatedly, scholars' citizenship or visa status might prevent them from traveling to certain locations, even more so as travel restrictions increased during the COVID-19 pandemic.

Within Turkey, historical records are available in the Ottoman archives in Istanbul, the archive of the Vakıflar Genel Müdürlüğü (Directorate of Pious Foundations) in Ankara, or the Topkapı Palace Archive. Further, manuscript libraries such as the Topkapı Palace Library, the Nadir Eserler (rare books) department of Istanbul University Library, and the Süleymaniye Library can be essential depending on the topic of research. On-site access to these large archives tends to be relatively straightforward, even though occasional delays in getting responses to requests for research permits can arise. The Ottoman archives (formerly Başbakanlık Osmanlı Arşivi, now officially named Türkiye Cumhuriyeti Cumhurbaşkanlığı Devlet Arşivleri Başkanlığı Osmanlı Arşivi Külliyesi) has by far the most streamlined process for receiving a permit and accessing digitized copies of documents on site in Kağıthane.[30] Were one conducting transhistorical or comparative research on former Ottoman territories, such as Tunisia or Algeria, one may further find related materials archived in Tunis and Algiers. If investigations extend into the realm of post-Ottoman imperialism, one might even need to access archives in Paris, Nantes, or Aix-en-Provence, in the case of France and its former colonies.[31]

Other archives can be more difficult to access, as Pınar Aykaç outlines, and even those that are generally accessible may deny requests for specific projects for a number of reasons.[32] Further, documents that might be useful cannot always be traced, and archaeological excavations in particular often remain unpublished for many years (and sometime permanently). In my dissertation research, for instance, I tried and failed to find excavation records for work completed at the Çifte Minareli Medrese in Sivas in the 1960s.[33]

Thus, research is often guided by what can be accessed. This is true as well when it comes to photographic archives. Some are available online, including the vast collection of SALT, a research centre and library in Istanbul, which offers a sleek interface in both Turkish and English.[34] Another major online source is Akkasah, an open-access photographic archive connected to NYU Abu Dhabi. The archive of architectural historical Aptullah Kuran (1927–2001) is located at Boğaziçi University, and it is currently in the process of being digitized. Once available, it will be a major resource for researchers. Some of the papers of İbrahim Hakkı Konyalı (1896–1984), who wrote several books on the history and monuments of cities in Anatolia, including Konya and Erzurum, including letters, photographs, and newspaper clippings, are preserved in the İbrahim Hakkı Konyalı Kütüphanesi in Üsküdar, Istanbul.[35] Much of the documentation used in the writing of his books is also printed in the volumes themselves; these include a great number of photographs of monuments and documents.

Conclusion

To a great extent, historiography, archives, and fieldwork are deeply interconnected. Without understanding the background and trajectory of the many scholars who have worked on any given place and period so far, and without access to their publications, it is extremely difficult to situate the material gathered during fieldwork and archival research. Architectural history must acknowledge buildings as the product of the time in which they were first built, of the time that has passed since then, and of human interventions and effects of natural disasters and climate change. To this end, archival work is crucial for tracing how monuments have developed over time, and especially how they have been affected by rapid urbanization during the twentieth- and twenty-first centuries. Acknowledging the complexities of access to sites and materials, the linguistic challenges inherent in a multi-lingual field covering a diverse and historically rich geography, and in a time of considerable change and instability, is an important part of doing work in, and on, today's Islamic word.

Acknowledgements

I thank Daniel E. Coslett and Mohammad Gharipour for their comments on earlier drafts of this essay, and for including me in this volume. I also thank the Society of Architectural Historians for the research support that enabled my initial reflections on fieldwork and archives in 2015–16.

Notes

1. Stephennie Mulder, 'War and Recovery', in *The Oxford Handbook of Islamic Archaeology*, ed. Bethany J. Walker, Corisande Fenwick, and Timothy Insoll (Oxford: Oxford University Press, 2020), doi: 10.1093/oxfordhb/9780199987870.013.28.
2. I admit that my own research has not been affected in this dramatic way. A large part of my scholarly fieldwork since I began working on my dissertation in 2008 has taken place in Turkey, where I have studied Islamic architecture dating from the twelfth to the sixteenth centuries.
3. Patricia Blessing, 'Byzantium in Istanbul, or: Istanbul is Constantinople (Among Other Things)', Society of Architectural Historians blog, March 28, 2016; Patricia Blessing, 'Creating an Ottoman Capital: Istanbul in the Late Fifteenth Century', Society of Architectural Historians blog, February 26, 2016; Patricia Blessing, 'Istanbul: Sultans' Mosques and Urban Expansion', Society of Architectural Historians blog, January 25, 2016, all accessible at https://www.sah.org/publications-and-research/fellowship-reports/brooks-fellowship-reports#Blessing.
4. Ömür Harmanşah, 'Urban Utopias and How They Fell Apart: The Political Ecology of *Gezi Parkı*', in *The Making of Turkey's Protest Movement: #occupygezi*, ed. Umut Özkırımlı (New York: Palgrave MacMillan 2014), 121–33; Elif Çiğdem Artan, '#OccupyGezi Architecture' and Archival Tactics of Resistance', *International Journal of Islamic Architecture* 9.2 (2020): 409–30.
5. Berrak Kırbaş, 'Gezi Parkı'nın Musallat Hayaleti: Taksim Topçu Kışlası', *mimar.ist* 16.56 (2016): 23–30; Malte Fuhrmann, 'Taksim Square and the Struggle to Rule Istanbul's Past', *Critique & Humanism* 46 (2016): 163–90.
6. Can Bilsel, 'The Crisis in Conservation: Istanbul's Gezi Park between Restoration and Resistance', *Journal of the Society of Architectural Historians* 76.2 (2017): 141–45; Eray Çaylı, 'Inheriting Dispossession, Mobilizing Vulnerability: Heritage amid Protest in Contemporary Turkey', *International Journal of Islamic Architecture* 5.2 (2016): 359–78.
7. For general information on the petition, see 'Peace Petition Scholars, Turkey', Scholars at Risk Network, accessed July 6, 2021, https://www.scholarsatrisk.org/actions/academics-for-peace-turkey/. On Sur, see Serra Hakyemez, 'Sur', *Middle East Report* 287 (Summer 2018), https://merip.org/2018/10/sur/.
8. Tansu Pişkin and Hikmet Adal, 'Constitutional Court in Turkey: Freedom of Expression of "Academics for Peace" Violated', *Jadaliyya*, July 29, 2019, https://www.jadaliyya.com/Details/39843/Constitutional-Court-Freedom-of-Expression-of-Academics-for-Peace-Violated.

9 'Istanbul Population 2021', World Population Review, accessed July 15, 2021, https://worldpopulationreview.com/world-cities/istanbul-population.
10 Tessa Fox, 'Erdoğan's "Crazy Project": New Istanbul Canal to Link Black and Marmara Seas', *Guardian*, February 17, 2020, https://www.theguardian.com/environment/2020/feb/17/canal-istanbul-erdogans-crazy-plan-to-plot-route-between-black-and-marmara-seas.
11 See the collection of relevant essays in 'Hagia Sophia: From Museum to Mosque', *Berkley Forum*, July 17, 2020, https://berkleycenter.georgetown.edu/posts/hagia-sophia-from-museum-to-mosque; İpek Kocaömer Yosmaoğlu, 'Aghia Sophia and a Reckoning with History', *Platform*, July 27, 2020, https://www.platformspace.net/home/aghia-sophia-and-a-reckoning-with-history.
12 Gülru Necipoğlu, 'The Süleymaniye Complex in Istanbul: An Interpretation', *Muqarnas* 3 (1986): 92–117.
13 Khalid Abbood, 'Neoliberal Gentrification and Socio-Spatial Transformation in Karaköy', Prezi, October 30, 2019, https://prezi.com/p/noprntrhks73/neoliberal-gentrification-and-socio-spatial-transformation-in-karakoy/; Veli Baçaru, 'Galata Serpuş Han ve Tavan Resimleri', *Sanat Tarihi Dergisi* 29.1 (2020): 51–79.
14 As the protests were brutally suppressed, the graffiti were erased and survive only in photographs gathered by activists, journalists, and scholars. Christiane Gruber, 'The Visual Emergence of the Gezi Movement', *JADMAG Pedagogy Publications* 1.4 (2013): 29–36.
15 Istanbul and Bursa are very well represented in collections of nineteenth-century photography of the Ottoman Empire.
16 Such photographs are, for instance, collected in the Pierre de Gigord albums, which have been digitized by the Getty Research Institute. See 'Pierre de Gigord Collection of Photographs […]', Getty Research Institute, accessed July 15, 2021, https://primo.getty.edu/permalink/f/mlc5om/GETTY_ALMA21118428440001551.
17 On a personal note, I am very grateful to Walter Denny who shared with me some of his photographs. In a conversation on July 16, 2021, Richard McClary and I noted how the materials from our dissertation projects, gathered between roughly 2008 and 2014, have become historical documentation due to new restoration campaigns.
18 Patricia Blessing, 'Recording the Transformation of Urban Landscapes in Turkey: The Diaries of Kurt Erdmann and Ernst Diez', *Studies in Travel Writing* 16.4 (2012): 415–25.
19 Full discussion in Patricia Blessing, *Rebuilding Anatolia after the Mongol Conquest: Islamic Architecture in the Lands of Rūm, 1240–1330* (Burlington, VT: Ashgate, 2014), 69–122.
20 Ibid., 105.
21 Unpublished photograph, held in the archives of the Pontificio Istituto Orientale, Rome. I thank Vincenzo Ruggieri for allowing me to study Jerphanion's photographs in 2009. Some of Jerphanion's photographs are published in Guillaume de Jerphanion, *Mélanges d'archéologie anatolienne: Monuments prehelléniques, gréco-romains, byzantins et musulmans de Pont, de Cappadoce et de Galatie* (Beirut: Imprimerie catholique, 1928).
22 Albert Gabriel, *Monuments turcs d'Anatolie* (Paris: E. de Boccard, 1931), 2: plate LIII.
23 Unpublished photographs, Kurt Erdmann Archive, Otto-Friedrich University, Bamberg. I thank Lorenz Korn for allowing me to study Erdmann's photographs.
24 Artstor also contains photographs by Sheila Blair and Jonathan Bloom.

25 Orhan Cezmi Tuncer, *Sivas Gök Medrese* (Sahip Ata Fahrettin Ali Medresesi) (Ankara: Vakıflar Genel Müdürlüğü Yayınları, 2008).
26 '750 Yıllık Çiniler Asitle Kazındı', *Hürriyet*, May 24, 2017, https://www.hurriyet.com.tr/gundem/750-yillik-ciniler-asitle-kazindi-40467756
27 Maxime Durocher, 'Gök Medrese', Crossing Frontiers, accessed July 15, 2021, https://sites.courtauld.ac.uk/crossingfrontiers/crossing-frontiers/turkey/sivas/gok-medrese/. The project was funded by a Getty Connecting Art Histories grant and directed by Antony Eastmond (Courtauld Institute). I was a project member from 2016 to 2018.
28 For information on archives and libraries relevant for Islamic studies, including ones in Turkey, see Hazine, accessed July 15, 2021, https://hazine.info/. Information may be outdated, but it is a good start.
29 Even in the Ottoman context, for instance, *waqfiyas* (foundation documents) continue to be written in Arabic into the early sixteenth century.
30 Not everything has been catalogued, let alone digitized, although work continues on both fronts. Original documents are not normally made available to researchers. Online access is available, but does not always work in my experience, especially from outside Turkey. The catalogue also provides digital copies of documents in the Topkapı Palace Archive. For more (slightly outdated) information, see 'Ottoman State Archives', Hazine, October 10, 2013, https://hazine.info/basbakanlik-arsivi/.
31 Zeynep Çelik, *Empire, Architecture, and the City: French-Ottoman Encounters, 1830–1914* (Seattle: University of Washington Press, 2008) is a good example of a work that does this and engages material from many archives scattered across Ottoman and European imperial geographies. For a study of nineteenth-century Ottoman Anatolia that makes extensive use of Turkish and European archives, see Peter H. Christensen, *Germany and the Ottoman Railways: Art, Empire, and Infrastructure* (New Haven: Yale University Press, 2017).
32 Pınar Aykaç, 'Archives as Fields of Heritage-Making in Istanbul's Historic Peninsula', *International Journal of Islamic Architecture* 9.2 (2020): 361–87.
33 Mentioned in Michael Meinecke, *Fayencedekorationen seldschukischer Sakralbauten in Kleinasien* (Tübingen: Verlag Ernst Wasmuth, 1976), 2: 450–56. Meinecke's archive is preserved in the Museum für islamische Kunst in Berlin.
34 For a broader overview of resources that are helpful in teaching Islamic architecture, see: Patricia Blessing, 'Teaching Islamic Architecture', *Journal of Medieval Worlds* 2.3–4 (2020): 124–33.
35 For biographical information, see Erdem Yücel, 'Konyalı, İbrahim Hakkı', *Türkiye Diyanet Vakfı İslâm Ansiklopedisi*, accessed July 15, 2021, https://islamansiklopedisi.org.tr/konyali-ibrahim-hakki; İsmail Hakkı Avcı, *İbrahim Hakkı Konyalı (1895–1984)* (Istanbul: Akıl Fikir Yayınları, 2015). His books include İbrahim Hakkı Konyalı, *Abideleri ve kitabeleri ile Erzurum tarihi* (Istanbul: Erzurum Tarihini Araştırma ve Tanıtma Derneği, 1960); İbrahim Hakkı Konyalı, *Abideleri ve kitabeleri ile Konya tarihi* (Konya: İbrahim Hakkı Konyalı, 1964); İbrahim Hakkı Konyalı, *Abideleri ve kitabeleri ile Niğde Aksaray tarihi* (Istanbul: Fatih Yayınevi Matbaası, 1974–75).

Chapter 13

Documenting Islamic Architecture: Objectives and Outcomes in a Time of War

Sharon C. Smith

Documenting Islamic architecture and the impact of its loss on material and visual culture has been, and will continue to be, an on-going study of tremendous importance. Written while the loss of life, destruction of architecture, and theft of cultural objects throughout large portions of the Middle East are increasing, this essay illustrates the demand for increased attention on an international level. Its aim is to explore issues such as intent and challenges at the broadest level. In other words, the goal of this brief reflection is to inspire more scholars, architects, and other interested groups to continue this work with heightened urgency. Penning this essay, I acknowledge that I will raise more questions than I answer. In laying out the polemical state of the field, my hope is to encourage discussion.

Approaches

Cultural heritage and the built environment throughout the Middle East are at tremendous risk. The ravages of war have become part of our vernacular through the advancements of technology. As the public is inundated by the daily profusion of media from, and on, the Middle East – presented in a rapid-fire fashion from a plethora of producers and meant to be consumed wholly and without cognizance of the creators' intent – context and meaning are lost along with local voice and original narrative. It is these issues that will be examined here along with the opportunities, constraints, intentions, and consequences – planned and not – of the production, presentation, and dissemination of these materials, with a focus on the digitization of the same materials from or about the Middle East writ large.[1]

To talk about institutional frameworks in the realm of documenting Islamic architecture is to talk about a complex world in flux. One encounters difficulties in this exploration almost immediately, upon just reading the title. Ontologies, taxonomies, translations, and transliterations are issues that must be addressed immediately when dealing with the wider Middle East. Regions, boundaries, colonization, histories (rewritten and not), and dynasties are all issues that one needs to consider in this examination.[2]

I come to this topic as an architectural historian and as someone who has been actively involved in both the digital world and documentation of the Middle East for some time. Some readers might know that I was the founding director (2011–18) of the Aga Khan Documentation Center (AKDC) at the Massachusetts Institute of Technology and served as Primary Investigator (PI) and co-director of Archnet, a post shared with my colleague at the Aga

Khan Trust for Culture. As the head of AKDC, my mission was to present Muslim visual and material culture, with a decided focus on architecture, including historical, geographic, and temporal specificity, i.e., in its context. As a framework for such work, Archnet and the Aga Khan Trust for Culture were far ahead of their time. Conceived in 1999 as an open-source online research tool for researchers, students, and scholars alike, the tool originally launched *c.*2003. The site was redeveloped and re-launched in 2013 [Figures 13.1 and 13.2]. Until relatively recently, Archnet stood uniquely in the realm of digital access to materials on and about the Middle East. There are now newer efforts, each, for the most part, finding its own niche in this ever-growing field.

Websites such as the Digital Library of the Middle East, while still in nascent states, are working to not only document destruction of cultural heritage, but also to focus on the illegal looting and illicit trafficking resulting from the chaos of the moment.[3] The Middle East Materials Project (MEMP), an important collection hosted by the Center for Research Libraries, seeks to

> preserve collections in digital and microform format of unique, rare, hard to obtain, and often expensive research material for Middle East studies. It also preserves deteriorating printed and manuscript scholarly materials. The geographic scope of MEMP coverage includes Arab countries, Israel, Turkey, Iran, and related areas not covered by other cooperative materials projects.[4]

Some websites are regional, such as Qatar National Library,[5] for example; and yet others are monumental in scope, such as Access to Middle East and Islamic Resources (AMIR), which is a blog-style compilation of numerous collections and websites.[6] Some are highly curated by experts, some not; however, they are all of value, even if many lack the focus and authoritative nature of Archnet, and fail to remain fully open and anonymous for users, as Archnet does.[7]

Digital Proliferation and the Role of Digital Humanities

Digital resources have grown steadily over the past decade and will continue to proliferate in the future. Enveloped within the larger rubric of digital humanities, digital projects are most often seen as philanthropic. While these projects are rightfully praised for increasing researchers' ability to access resources that once were reached only via travel – often prohibitive either in cost and/or accessibility – or preserving materials no longer extant, one should also be aware of who or what is driving them.[8] Consideration of the source leads to questions of authenticity of the collected, how and why the images are displayed, and why they are presented online. Furthermore, the material should be evaluated for what is not there. What is missing? Joshua Craze, for example, looked at government redaction in documentation in his article 'Excerpts from a Grammar of Redaction'. His point regarding 'the annoying suppressions that get in the way of significance' can and should be acknowledged in what is presented.[9] Redaction leads to decontextualizing, which, in turn, removes meaning.

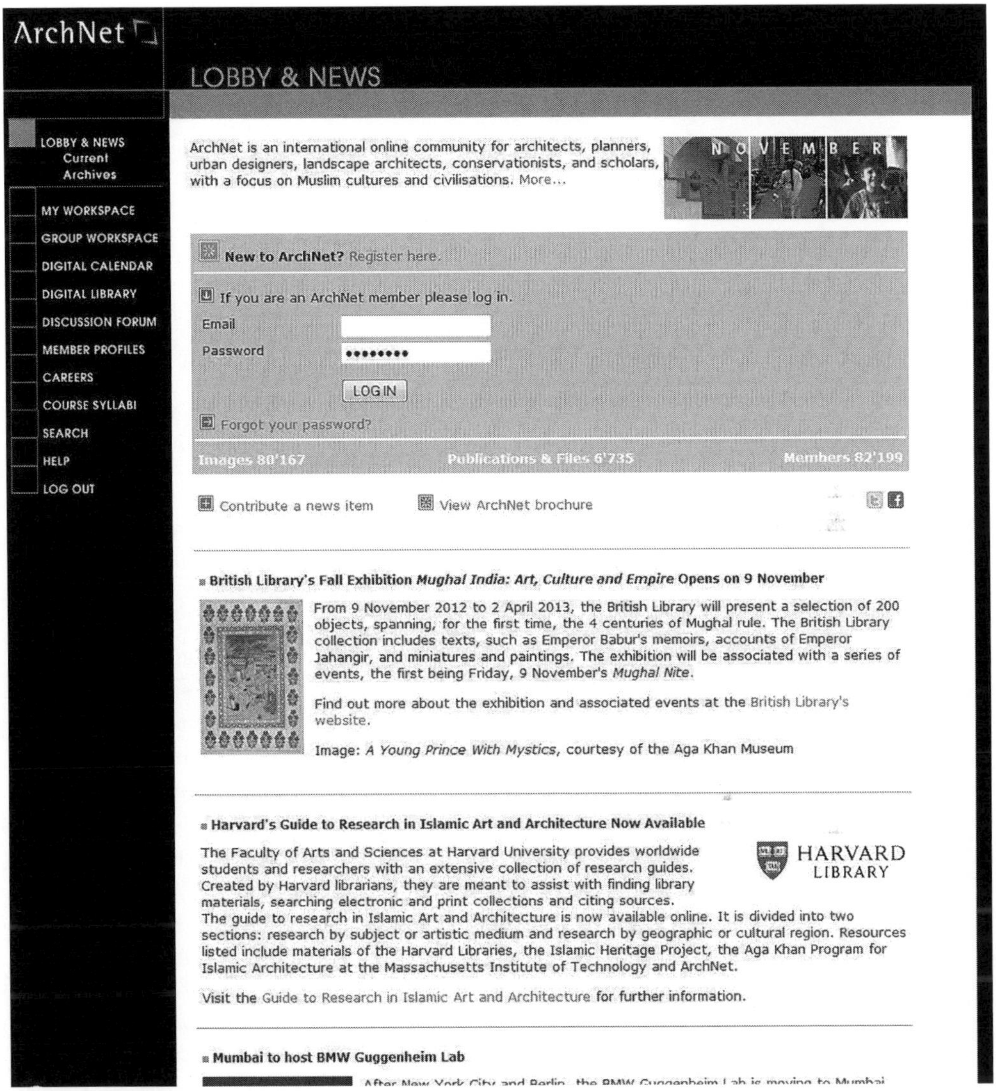

Figure 13.1: The original login page for Archnet, c.2003. Source: Aga Khan Trust for Culture.

For too long, digitization/digital projects have escaped the rigors of traditional academic evaluation, resulting in a simplified reading of the digital process and the resulting output. One must critically evaluate the impact of digitization, particularly in terms of the production of knowledge and its attendant effects in historiographic practices. The effects of digital humanities on constructed knowledge have not yet been thoroughly evaluated. However, we might not have the time, as digital humanities could be causing irreparable damage to local contexts by

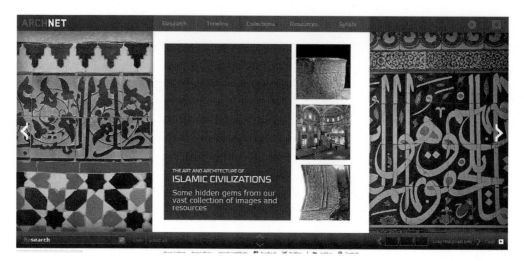

Figure 13.2: The Archnet home page *c.*2014. Source: Aga Khan Documentation Center at MIT.

changing narratives through selective examinations. For example, the use of the ancient Roman-era triumphal arch from Palmyra has become shorthand for the war in Syria and the supposed dominance of the western forces against ISIS and other militant groups [Figure 13.3].[10] This representation, displayed internationally through the use of 3D modelling and other digital humanities tools, is aimed at a western public audience with generally limited understandings of the situation. The monument's reconstructed presence of course foregrounds issues of vulnerability and the need for safeguarding cultural heritage, but as a decontextualized ornament appearing in odd places, it arguably becomes meaningless as signifier of the reality – the horror – of the present conflict necessitating its ersatz deployment. Furthermore, the arch, while important to Syrian culture and as an acknowledgement of Khaled al-Asaad (1935–2015), the scholar who was brutally murdered for guarding the antiquities of ancient Palmyra, the use of it is problematic for other reasons. The triumphal arch is not exactly a signifier of modern Syria and the horrific battles fought there today, nor is it an Islamic monument. Witnessing the actuating ascendancy of Islamophobia in the larger western world, this image-cum-stand-in for war and the Syrian people has validated the ignorance and inertia of the western audiences to the events in Syria and the violence, deaths, and destruction of cultural heritage, because by focusing attention on ancient buildings in jeopardy, viewers from afar need not acknowledge the brutal realities of the on-going war and humanitarian crisis [Figure 13.4].

Ethics and the Digital Divide

Sarah Bond echoes these sentiments regarding the Palmyra arch's appearance in New York's City Hall Park in 'The Ethics of 3-D Printing Syria's Cultural Heritage', where she notes that

Figure 13.3: The triumphal arch in Palmyra, Syria, c.1980s–1990s. Source: Yasser Tabbaa Archive, Aga Khan Documentation Center at MIT.

'Many question whether the 3D replica truly celebrates the antiquities of Syria and defies the destructive actions of ISIS, or is a form of "digital colonialism".[11] Digital colonialism can be perceived as the use of all those images collected to document a now destroyed ruin in the current craze to recreate, through the digital, cultural signifiers – particularly those that emphasize the existence of the heroic colonial power in the centre of newly created and reinterpreted narratives. The placement of a 3D printed gate from Palmyra in a random setting, such as a park or a square in the west, is to present the monument without its context and thus exposes it to unintended and potentially unhelpful meaning and interpretation. Such action takes one down a slippery slope toward digital colonization, and fast. Context is always a disruptive element in the newly created narrative – both in New York and beyond – and a reminder of the existence of the pre-crisis local and differing voices.

Of course, the much talked-about digital divide is another contributing factor in this colonization process, with its very real social and economic inequities and their consequences.[12] While the space of digital humanities is envisioned as utopian, romantic, and inclusive, the truth is that if you do not read English, French, German, or other western languages, you might not have a chance to access this knowledge. If you read only Arabic, the result might be that you are at least ten years behind in scholarly production, because of the lack of accessibility.

Islamic Architecture Today and Tomorrow

Figure 13.4: Palmyra's triumphal arch recreated in Trafalgar Square, London, UK, in 2016. Source: Sharon C. Smith.

Indeed, the idealistic vision of digital humanities as a unifying global phenomenon might not be realistic.[13] Another phenomenon, identified recently with the extraordinarily loaded phrase of 'ruin porn', may further illustrate the colonialist nature of contemporary digital humanities.[14] Colonialism (digital and otherwise) has always resulted in destruction and loss – loss of identity, loss of cultural heritage, and a residue of ruin.[15] The two notions – digital colonialism and ruin porn – are not exclusive. As offensive and reductive as that sounds, one cannot but wonder if this is true.

What are the effects of the day-to-day barrage of images and information regarding destruction and wars that are no longer measured by days or months, but by decades? We 'use' it – representations of death, destruction, and devastation willingly and wilfully in teaching, in art, and casually on social media. I do not have an answer. In her article, Bond talks about the ethics of this work. Would our work as architectural historians working in the Middle East today be better framed as a question of ethics? And what does that even mean? digital humanities producers operate through a web of politics, people, institutions, power, and production (technology) – a network of uneven relations – that must be accounted for. Ethics are certainly relevant and should frame, and question, our and others' intentions.

Certainly this is not dismissing the genuine need for documenting what can be considered war crimes against people, cultural heritage, and the built environment, occurring today in places such as Iraq, Syria, Palestine, Yemen, etc. Sadly the list is too long. However, one cannot deny the asymmetry of points of production vis-à-vis the points of destruction. Critique needs to be fixed and penetrating. Indeed, a normative process in digital documenting production is necessary.

Today, when many digital humanities projects are developed to reveal the horror of war in the Middle East, we must be careful how we (western cultures writ large) view ourselves in these projects. Too often, the notion that we are feverishly working to document the destruction of sites in Syria, for example, with heavy focus on the destruction of (pre-Islamic) antiquity, has led to a 'ruination of ruins' phenomenon. As Yasser Tabbaa posted on his Facebook feed at the time of Palmyra's destruction, 'The destruction of art is becoming the hot new thing in art history'.[16] Sadly, there is truth to his statement. Far too often, the hot new thing is to frantically recreate cultural heritage sites by any means possible, but, again too often, these efforts play out as narratives assigned and reassigned by others without the local voice, depriving the locals of the right to define their own history, loss, and identity.

The Allure and Its Challenges

The allure of digital humanities is romantic. It is a global knowledge network. It is a utopian vision of shared knowledge, culture, and semantic content.[17] It is feel-good, warm, and fuzzy. In a blog post, a University of Connecticut history professor asserted that 'people in the digital humanities are nice'.[18] What does 'nice' mean vis-à-vis a serious scholarly endeavour?

In fleshing out the notion of nice, the author continues by stating that those engaged with digital humanities are nice because they are more concerned with method (tools, data visualization) than with theory.[19] It is this lack of theorization and focus on the final product (method and data collection) that may reflect a populist dimension to the outcome. Seeking immediate emotional impact on the audience rather than committing to firm academic standards allows even the horrors of war to become a form of popular media production. Furthermore, as digital humanities is still in the formulation process, most of the production is done by earlyand mid-career academics. Their focus on creating a demonstrable impact has been valued higher than theorizing the field.[20]

Frankly, from my perspective and others, digital humanities is simply Humanities of this time. A comment I have heard more than once – and one that is particularly irksome – is that in this time, our time, a scholar of liberal arts, humanities, or art history must learn code in order to remain a vital part of the academic community. I completely disagree; in today's world, we must collaborate to achieve great things. Not only an opportunity for collaboration, but a collaboration that must be highly interdisciplinary – for those in the humanities, this could be described as 'hinter-disciplinary', as we rarely found reason to engage with technologists, engineers, and programmers to any degree in the past. The potential for missed opportunities cannot be overstated.

So, what are the desired outcomes of utilizing digital humanities in documenting the Middle East in this moment? Immediately apparent to most is the role that these projects can play in the realm of social justice. How do these projects defend social justice? Clearly, the use of such media in a crisis aided Aga Khan Program for Islamic Architecture Bibliographer at Harvard University, András Riedlmayer, when he testified numerous times at The Hague regarding the

Figure 13.5: A street in Aleppo, Syria, 2016. Source: Ibrahim Kalin, 'Aleppo Burning', *Middle East Monitor*, May 11, 2016, https://www.middleeastmonitor.com/20160511-aleppo-burning.

systematic eradication of cultural monuments and destruction of cultural heritage in Bosnia-Herzegovina during the Bosnian war of the early 1990s.[21] His pioneering work set the standard for such cases.[22] The work done by Riedlmayer has been collected not only by himself and others, but has formed a permanent collection within Archnet that is now digitally accessible [Figure 13.6].[23] The notion that his contribution to the field has a permanent presence on the web brings us to the essential issue of the sustainability of online projects.

In the digital realm, important projects often simply disappear. The issues of sustainability and preservation are typically not paramount when creating digital projects, and they are inherently speculative, since we have no way of knowing exactly what technology, storage, distribution, and presentation modes will be like in the distant future. This flaw in the system may be related to a project's agenda or practitioner; too many focus on gaining instant yet temporary audience attraction and have more to do with self-achievement than demonstrating a sustainable and long-term impact on the local targeted subject, i.e., the heritage site itself, the surrounding communities, or the hosting nation.

Preservation, sustainability, and storage are challenging tasks, both expensive and complicated. This reasoning supports the undesired yet widely accepted notion of the oft-thought transitory nature of digital humanities projects; however, at AKDC, these issues were deeply

Figure 13.6: The work of András Riedlmayer presented as a permanent collection on Archnet. Source: Aga Khan Documentation Center at MIT.

explored and commitment made to sustainability on a grand scale. We are beginning to witness a shared shift in these notions. Without overtly stating (but with some bias, perhaps) that AKDC and the Center's work on Archnet were a driving force behind the shift, Archnet and AKDC's policies were on the frontline in addressing these challenges. There are many examples within the site, including Riedlmayer's aforementioned work at The Hague, which will not fade away, but have already become a collection on Archnet and will continue to develop there.[24]

Outcomes

We know roughly what we want digital humanities to do with regard to the destruction and disruption of the Middle East, but is there a clear roadmap for getting there? While sounding new and different, a catchphrase of the day if you will, digital humanities and those who practice it are still attached to the humanities – art historians, historians, linguists, and so on – and tried and true praxes should remain in place. As historians, we recall E. H. Carr's reminder that we ought to navigate history-making events with as little judgment as we can, knowing full well we can never be totally removed. Indeed, we all come with prepossessed notions and biases as much as we try to avoid them. In moments of great social injustice, it is virtually impossible.[25]

Having said all this, what is the point? My aim is to urge us on, to continue documenting the visual and material culture of Muslim societies of yesterday, today, and tomorrow. While documenting the current destruction and information even though the online form is rather *pro forma* and rigid until now, the data collected can, and should, be used in the narrative that contextualizes the story – we must not forget to capture visual and material culture that is quietly slipping away, that which is not lost to the ravages of war, but altered by natural events or simply the passing of time.

In conclusion, yes, we need digital humanities, but we have always needed documentation, digital or otherwise. It is the capital H in the digital humanities that brings context and meaning to an often-misconstrued barrage of images that reinforces the notion that the Middle East is a place defined by violence and destruction. This contemporary drift to non-content, non-project work – digital humanities for the sake of the Digital – must be avoided. There has been a myopic focus on tools and technology even found in the halls of some of our most esteemed institutions that must be broadened to recognize the necessity of context and curation for these projects to hold pedagogical worth. Let us privilege the theory over the method (tools) with critique, content, context, and meaning, and work to develop a systematic, holistic approach to documenting Islamic architecture as well as providing access to all.

Long-held models must be broken: knowledge is not to be hoarded; intellectual property must be shared openly; and the scholar/architect/etc. as hero is no more. No longer can one person, or one institution, claim sole ownership of knowledge and data. As radical as it sounds to some, we must partner, share, and collaborate because the quantity of data is too great and the quality is too easily manipulated for personal, political, or state gain, even if it means we must no longer be quite so nice.

Notes

This chapter was previously published as Sharon C. Smith, 'Documenting Islamic Architecture: Objectives in a Time of War', *International Journal of Islamic Architecture* 10.1 (2021): 159–70.

1. Walter Benjamin, *The Work of Art in the Age of Mechanical Reproduction* (n.p.: Prism Key Press, 2010), 18. Penning this book in 1935, the philosopher and cultural critic Benjamin grappled with these issues as he analysed changing experiences impacting art and modern society, with concern for the inundation of images and their impact on unwitting viewers.
2. For a clear and concise introduction to all of these issues, see Christian Hedrick's pedagogical tools developed for Archnet. These PowerPoint presentations are freely downloadable and editable, meaning the instructor does not necessarily need to follow Hedrick's structure, although I strongly recommend they do. See Christian A. Hedrick, 'Teaching Islamic Architecture: An Introduction to Introducing the Subject', *Archnet*, 2015, http://archnet.org/collections/825/publications/10038.

3   Digital Library of the Middle East, accessed February 18, 2020, https://dlme.clir.org/. See also 'About', Digital Library of the Middle East, accessed February 18, 2020, https://spotlight.dlme network.org/library/about/about.
4   Middle East Materials Project, accessed February 18, 2020, https://www.crl.edu/programs/memp.
5   Qatar Digital Library, accessed February 18, 2020, https://www.qdl.qa/en.
6   Access to Mideast and Islamic Resources (AMIR), accessed February 18, 2020, http://amirmide ast.blogspot.com. AMIR, a monumental undertaking as described on their site: 'This project began as a consequence of a series of conversations in 2010 between Charles Jones and Peter Magierski at NYU about the need for a tool to assemble and distribute information on open access material relating to the Middle East'. Further, they encourage active participation.
7   'Archnet is an open access, intellectual resource focused on architecture, urbanism, environmental and landscape design, visual culture, and conservation issues related to the Muslim world. Archnet's mission is to provide ready access to unique visual and textual material to facilitate teaching, scholarship, and professional work of high quality. Archnet is an authority, a growing repository, and a tool for teaching and learning about the architecture of Muslim societies, past, and present'. 'About', Archnet, accessed February 18, 2020, http://archnet.org/pages/about.
8   Arn Keeling and John Sandlos, 'Shooting the Archives: Document Digitization for Historical-Geographical Collaboration', *History Compass* 9.5 (2011): 423–24.
9   Joshua Craze, 'Excerpts from a Grammar of Redaction', in *Dissonant Archives: Contemporary Visual Culture and Contested Narratives in the Middle East*, ed. Anthony Downey (London: I. B. Tauris, 2015), 385–400.
10 Mohamad Meqdad, Aga Khan University Institute for the Study of Muslim Civilisations (AKU-ISMC), personal correspondence, 2016
11 Sara Bond, 'The Ethics of 3D-Printing Syria's Cultural Heritage', *Forbes*, September 22, 2016, https://www.forbes.com/sites/drsarahbond/2016/09/22/does-nycs-new-3d-printed-palmyra-arch-celebrate-syria-or-just-engage-in-digital-colonialism/.
12 See, for example, Steve Lohr, 'Digital Divide Is Wider than We Think, Study Says', *New York Times*, December 4, 2018, https://www.nytimes.com/2018/12/04/technology/digital-divide-us-fcc-microsoft.html; Sanjeev Dewan and Frederick J. Riggins, 'Digital Divide: Current and Future Research Directions', *Journal of the Association for Information Systems* 6.12 (2005): 298–337.
13 Mohamad Meqdad, personal correspondence, November, 2016.
14 See Joann Greco, 'The Psychology of Ruin Porn', *City Lab*, January 6, 2012, https://www.city lab.com/design/2012/01/psychology-ruin- porn/886/; Siobhan Lyons, 'What "Ruin Porn" Tells us About Ruins—and Porn', *CNN*, November 1, 2017, https://www.cnn.com/style/article/what-ruin-porn-tells-us-about-ruins-and-porn/index.html; Richard B. Woodward, 'Disaster Photography: When is Documentary Exploitation?', *ARTnews*, February 6, 2013, https://www.artnews.com/art-news/news/the-debate-over-ruin-porn-2170/.
15 Daniel Macmillen Voskoboynik, 'Colonialism Can't Be Forgotten – It's Still Destroying Peoples and Our Planet', *openDemocracy UK*, October 18, 2018, https://www.opendemocracy.net/en/opendemocracyuk/colonialism-can-t-be-forgotten-it-s-still-destroying-peoples-and-our-pl/.

16 On Yasser Tabbaa, see 'Yasser Tabbaa', Archnet, accessed February 24, 2020, http://archnet.org/authorities/2874.
17 Alexander Maedche and Vanentin Zacharias, 'Clustering Ontology-based Metadata in the Semantic Web' (paper presented at the *Principles of Data Mining and Knowledge Discovery, 6th European Conference, PKDD 2002*, Helsinki, Finland, August 19–23, 2002), available at https://www.researchgate.net/publication/220699521.
18 Jamie 'Skye' Bianco, 'This Digital Humanities Which Is Not One', Debates in the Digital Humanities, accessed October 10, 2016, http://dhdebates.gc.cuny.edu/debates/text/9.
19 Ibid.
20 Mohamad Meqdad, personal correspondence, November, 2016.
21 On András Riedlmayer's impact on the issues and his time at The Hague, see András Riedlmayer, 'Information on Cultural Destruction in Bosnia-Herzegovina', February 9, 1995, http://www.hartford-hwp.com/archives/62/068.html; András Riedlmayer, 'Human Rights Project', April 19, 2004, https://hrp.bard.edu/andras-riedlmayer/; Mirko Klarin, 'Targeting History and Memory', *Sense*, 2016, http://www.heritage.sense-agency.com/; 'Destroying All Traces of Mosques and Churches', *Sense Tribunal*, June 2, 2010, https://archive.sensecentar.org/vijesti.php?aid=11720.
22 Riedlmayer's project has been documented on Archnet. See András Riedlmayer, 'Kosovo Cultural Heritage', *Archnet*, accessed February 24, 2020, http://archnet.org/collections/22. The collection will continue to grow as documents from The Hague are released and added.
23 Craze, 'Excerpts'.
24 Riedlmayer, 'Kosovo Cultural Heritage'.
25 Edward Hallett Carr, *What Is History?* (New York: Random House, 1961).

Part 5

Education and Pedagogy

Chapter 14

Reorienting Perspectives: Why I Do Not Teach a Course Titled 'Islamic Architecture'

Jelena Bogdanović

'Islamic architecture' is usually defined and studied through divisive concepts of 'otherness' – as architecture made by those whose religion is Islam, for patrons who live in predominantly Muslim lands, or for Muslims who live outside these territories. The concept of 'otherness' inevitably includes the notion of 'distance'; for architecture, especially relevant is that 'otherness' reinforces spatial distance. This distance is not only geographically framed in terms of the physical remoteness of predominantly Islamic lands from Europe and the United States, it is also framed both culturally and in terms of identity.[1] Instigated by early studies of Islamic architecture, spatial distance is outlined by the peripatetic and antiquarian nature of research that initially focused predominantly on the architecture of the Arabs, Ottoman Turks, and Muslims in Spain, Sicily, or Persia. Ever since the earliest writings on Islamic architecture were published in the nineteenth century – mostly by Europeans – recurrent images of Islamic architecture in books and textbooks and, since 1991, on the internet have shown almost exclusively object-focused, objectified, and essentially distanced exterior views of structures most often devoid of people and by extension devoid of human scale and sense of presence.[2]

For religious architecture in particular, the inner experience of being and one's physical presence within a place are recurrently articulated by the interior space that architecture frames. Still, only few experts in the field would recognize the award-winning interior of the Šerefudin White Mosque in Visoko, near Sarajevo, in Bosnia and Herzegovina, which was built in 1979 [Figure 14.1]. The subtle, almost abstract modelling of the interior volume of the space of worship is articulated flawlessly in the Šerefudin Mosque and is architecturally conveyed by delicate treatment of the atmospheric light there. While many people typically think that architects design buildings, architects themselves would expand this notion to highlight that they design 'spaces that the physical structure of a building forms'.[3] Hence, the Šerefudin White Mosque is not only an Islamic building, but it is also an architecturally significant one. In 1983, only a few years after its completion, the Šerefudin White Mosque was presented with the Aga Khan Award for Architecture, a major prize for Islamic architecture likely familiar to many readers.[4] Yet it was another 35 years before a western architectural authority, the Museum of Modern Art, also recognized it as one of the exceptional examples of modern architecture generally.[5] This architectural masterpiece was commissioned by the Muslim community in Visoko in 1969, in what was then Yugoslavia, and was designed by architect Zlatko Ugljen. His portfolio, like those of many professional architects, includes significant residential, commercial, and cultural projects in addition to Islamic and Christian religious buildings.

Figure 14.1: Zlatko Ugljen's Šerefudin White Mosque in Visoko, Bosnia and Herzegovina, 1969–1979. This project won the Aga Khan Award for Architecture in 1983. Interior view. Source: Vladimir Kulić.

'Theory' and Its Relevance to the Study of 'Islamic Architecture'

The example of the Šerefudin White Mosque reminds us of the plurality and fluidity of architectural designs and practices, where spatiality takes precedence over temporality. Additionally, the Šerefudin White Mosque points to the complexity of identity issues associated with architecture, which always go beyond the 'I vs. the Other' binomen of epistemic identity.[6] Similarly, although sociopolitical studies of 'otherness' elucidate power mechanisms and identity constructions, as elaborated in Edward Said's critical book *Orientalism*, they also maintain the exclusionary dichotomies between 'I' and the 'Other' that have led to a monolithic and somewhat oversimplified definition of Islamic as 'non-Western'.[7] 'Islamic architecture' in 'Western' academia is most closely tied to Said's critique of the western construction of the 'Orient'. 'Orientalism' and 'otherness' emerged almost concurrently with 'post-colonial' studies in the 1970s and 1980s and became significant currencies within the academy. At the same time, the space of 'Oriental' or 'Islamic architecture' lost geographic and cultural specificity. Defined in opposition to 'Western' space, 'Oriental' and 'Islamic' space has floated over time from the Middle East to Bosnia and Herzegovina and from Japan and to Chicago.[8]

Nineteenth-century antiquarian and colonial interest in everything exotic was the impetus for at least two later major phenomena.[9] One was the cultural phenomenon of sincere interest in everything new and different from the *self*, whereby otherness also reveals alterity, the *other-self*. The other was increasing scholarly interest and the formation of appropriate school departments in 'Oriental studies'. Following the expansion of 'Oriental studies' as a field, increasing specialization, and critique of the western construction of the 'Orient' in the 1970s and 1980s, these departments changed their names to seemingly more geographic-specific, more neutral, and politically more acceptable names such as Near Eastern, Middle Eastern, or East Asian studies.[10] The major focus of these regional or area studies remained on languages, international security, and religion and politics as expressions of privileged knowledge and power. Within area studies, architecture is subsidiary, elective, and frequently studied by non-architects. At best, architecture is entrapped in methodologies of its own alongside the seemingly complementary but distinct disciplines of art history and archaeology.[11] Occasionally, Islamic architecture is studied together with Byzantine architecture as its eastern Christian or medieval counterpart within the wider Mediterranean region.[12]

These studies of architecture are not necessarily negative as they often assert genuine interest in various architectural accomplishments across the globe. The discipline of history of architecture exploded after the 1950s and again especially after the 1980s, when it was supported by the post-1980s disciplinary formations.[13] Yet despite the advance of scholarly methods to collect, document, and classify significant buildings during this period, studies of 'non-Western' architecture(s) were left under-theorized. They were instead made to catch up with what was often presented as the more sophisticated studies of 'Western' architecture, in what was itself an echo of 'Orientalist' colonialism.[14]

Rey Chow wonderfully reasons that the prestige and authority of 'theory' is in a way an 'allegory of colonialism' and further clarifies:

The turn toward otherness that seems to *follow* from the theoretical dislocation of the sign is, strictly speaking, the very historicity that *precedes* the poststructuralist subversion: the supplementary look at Europe's other reveals anew the violence that was there, long before the appearance of 'theory', in the European imperialism of the past few hundred years.[15]

Therefore, the major issue for the twenty-first century is not the lack of knowledge or faulty knowledge of 'non-Western' architecture(s) but rather of their relation to self-proclaimed 'Western' architecture.[16] If theory and so-called Islamic architecture(s) are related not through genealogy and fulfilment but through contingency and parallel existence, they often instigate uncomfortable proximity and co-existence.[17] Such scholarly uneasiness resolves itself by simplifying Islamic architecture into a somewhat homogeneous monolithic entity.

Myths from the Classroom and Beyond

My experience of teaching architectural history in a professional school of architecture produces again and again what Mark Jarzombek calls 'the shock of the immaturity of the discipline' and demonstrates 'the need to restructure it from the bottom up'.[18] Institutionally, little place is given for studies of the Islamic 'I' in architecture *with*, not *against*, the 'Other' architecture(s). This approach results in three myths: that there is no 'Islamic architecture' after the 1600s or, sometimes alternatively, after the 1750s; that 'Islamic architecture' is only religious in nature; and that 'Islamic' is always the same as the 'Orient'.

The intellectual and institutional arrogance of situating architectural history and the methods of its study within Eurocentric concepts of modernism – concepts closely intertwined with notions of nation-states, authority, and regimes of control – produced terms such as 'non-Western' and 'pre-Modern' architecture.[19] The historicist logic of everything 'non-Western' is then reduced to 'pre-Western' or 'pre-Modern'. Despite genuine attempts to recognize the non-monolithic quality of Islamic architecture by including 'non-Western' examples of architecture in major textbooks, the organization of these texts continues to highlight the centrality of the Middle Ages and the Middle East when presenting Islamic accomplishments.[20] Somewhat better and more feasible propositions include additional course sections that engage with the cultural and geographical frameworks of Africa, Asia, and even Europe and America.[21] Yet 'non-Western' modern architecture, whether its threshold is placed in the 1600s or 1750s, and 'non-Western' contemporary architecture, again regardless of chronological threshold, are still presented as rather over-simplified reactions to 'Euro-American' architecture and its causes.[22] Often my students respond that there is no such thing as modern or contemporary Islamic architecture, even when I show them the image of the Burj Khalifa in Dubai, United Arab Emirates, finished in early 2010 [Figure 14.2].[23]

The world's tallest building at the time of its construction, this skyscraper is an example of architecture made for patrons whose religion is Islam and who live in predominantly Muslim lands. Yet, for most of my students it is an example of modern but not Islamic architecture simply because it is not a 'religious building'; it is a skyscraper; and it does not 'look Islamic'.[24] Their

Figure 14.2: Adrian Smith and Bill Baker's Burj Khalifa (known as the Burj Dubai until 2010) in Dubai, United Arab Emirates, 2010. Exterior view. Source: Wikimedia Commons/Donaldytong.

textbooks additionally highlight the identity of the architects and architecture as imports from the west.[25]

The fact that Islamic architecture, defined as such, is essentially religious in nature raises several supplementary issues. These issues are revealed in the latest 2020 National Architectural Accrediting Board (NAAB) requirements for professional schools of architecture, wherein religious contexts are not mentioned as relevant for architectural frameworks, even within study of the histories and theories of architecture.[26] Simply put, NAAB criteria, which can be theorized by the Lefebvrian concept of the production of space,[27] provide little to no place for studies of religious architecture. By extension, they also dismiss ontological, teleological, and similar sorts of arguments in architecture. Should we then only study modern 'vernacular Islamic architecture'? If so, is there such a thing as 'vernacular Islamic architecture', and how can it be defined as a special typological category in architectural studies? This is a vexing question, which goes beyond the scope of this essay.[28]

Widespread academic compliance with teaching architectural history and theory in this limited way is somewhat discouraging. With a professional engineering degree in architecture, several graduate degrees, and a body of scholarship on the subject, I am qualified to teach the history and theory of architecture. Among my courses are electives and general education on architectural history to the 1750s. The latter is a globally inclusive course that is bracketed off as 'History of Pre-Modern Architecture'. Colleagues at my own institution are surprised to learn that I am an architect, having assumed that such courses are taught exclusively by art historians and archaeologists. Then, too, students themselves assume that 'Islamic' is the 'Orient'. Especially in introductory courses, they are often confused about the meanings of 'Orient', 'Orientalism', and 'oriental', the latter best known to them as a politically incorrect racial slur.

Not feeling empowered enough to touch upon such delicate topics, architectural students, who mostly study to later work as design professionals in the architectural industry, rarely have an opportunity to venture towards lesser known facets of Islamic architecture. Some are also hesitant to engage in discussing what they view as potentially uncomfortable subjects. Bright exceptions to the norm are those scholars who examine Islamic architecture not as a mere historical citation but rather as an active paradigm in architecture. For instance, focusing on the aspects of sustainability and technology, a team led by architect Leslie Forehand won the 2018 Joan B. Calambokidis Innovation in Masonry Design Award for the project *Mashrabiya 2.0*.[29] Inspired by lattice screens, *Mashrabiya 2.0* is a 3D-printed ceramic element of a 'smart' façade, which can be integrated into buildings' mechanical systems for evaporative cooling and control of light, airflow, and privacy [Figure 14.3].

Remaining Critical Questions and Approaches

Methodologically, questions of the 'Other' in architecture are numerable, including those revolving around the major one: what is the 'Other' of the 'Other'? In terms of double negation, there is simply no 'Other' to the 'Other' or, if there is, this 'Other' leads from exclusionary

Figure 14.3: *Mashrabiya 2.0–3D-Printed Ceramic Evaporative Façade*, by Leslie Forehand with Shelby Doyle, Erin Hunt, and Nick Senske, won the Joan B. Calambokidis Innovation in Masonry Design Ward (Young Architect/Engineer Category) in 2018. *Mashrabiya 2.0* (inset, top right) and its potential application to a standard storefront window. Source: Leslie Forehand.

alterity back to mere deference. The alterity of God has been little theorized in the Islamic context of the religious 'Other'. Despite these open theoretical questions, it is important to remember that the major interest of architects and architectural students is, of course, architecture, and Islamic architecture *is* architecture. Instead of circling between socio-political 'Orientalism' and culturalism, it is possible for scholars and students of architecture to broaden their architectural perspectives. Such an aim is already visible within the 2020 NAAB criteria for the professional degree in architecture, which encourage acknowledgement of parallel 'architectures', 'histories', and 'theories' of architecture.[30] There is already a useful perspective built into architectural education. Because a majority of architectural students are preparing to work in the architectural industry, their education must by necessity focus on architectural spaces that are specific, in addition to the imaginary and abstract spaces of theory. Site-specific and context-specific understandings of architecture eventually lead towards the recognition that any 'context is ultimately boundless'.[31]

Instead of a Conclusion, Some Opinions on Teaching Architecture and a Student's Response

My rationale for not teaching a course titled 'Islamic architecture' is a gentle nod towards the discourse that speaks about the Islamic 'I', not *against* but rather *with* the 'Other'. Such an approach allows architectural historians to localize and examine architecture and its practices within distinct sociopolitical and geographic regions in more subtle ways. It allows for engagement with the current typologies of non-religious and non-monumental 'Islamic architecture'. Without privileging specific locales, it enables the examination of larger thematic questions about the technological, economic, gender, or philosophical aspects of architecture. In the process, it allows for the study of 'Islamic architecture' side by side with other architectures, both 'Western' and 'non-Western'. Emphasis is on the idiosyncratic qualities of architecture and on the different criteria and vibrant processes we may use to study it beyond such binary definitions.

In teaching, this approach is not a simple effort at political correctness, but rather a three-step process that can be accomplished within the tight curriculum for architectural students. In introductory general education courses such as *Architectural History* – rather than presenting only the most basic information about Islamic architecture in a single lecture focused on Umayyad pre- 750s architecture in the Middle East – several lectures touching upon various aspects of Islamic architecture geographically and historically can be dispersed throughout the semester.[32] Junior-level courses allow for more detailed discussions beyond descriptions of the objects and annotations of major contexts. These courses can place emphasis on cross-cultural and religious themes in architecture and artistic hybridity in a given region as well as on questions of cultural legacies as embodied, represented, or perceived through archi- tecture.[33] Senior- and graduate-level classes, such as the course *Meaning and Form in Architecture*, which I initially developed for architectural students at

Figure 14.4: I. M. Pei's Museum of Islamic Art in Doha, Qatar, 2008, and the Mosque of Ibn Tulun in Cairo, Egypt, 879 and later. Comparative analysis of urban settings with a focus on (at left) the Museum of Islamic Art and the minaret of the Fanar Mosque, built in 2008 in Doha, and (at right) the thirteenth-century sabil (ablution fountain) and the ninth-century (and later) minaret of the Ibn Tulun Mosque complex in Cairo. Source: Rami Mannan.

Iowa State University, can allow for critical analysis of meaning and form in architecture and of the built environment in various cultural contexts examined from historical and theoretical perspectives. Emphasis can be placed on thematic approaches and work initiated by architectural students themselves, who by then feel empowered to voice their own opinions. Not long ago, Rami Mannan, a former undergraduate student of mine, published a mature critical analysis, developed in our class, of the Museum of Islamic Art in Doha, Qatar, built in 2008.[34] He also scrutinized I. M. Pei's use of architectural precedents from the Ibn Tulun Mosque complex in Cairo, Egypt, dated to 879 and later times, for a museum in Qatar [Figure 14.4].

I will end this reflection piece with Rami's thoughts on the subject:

> We need to [...] move past approaching architectural elements rich in history in a shallow manner by traditionalizing the modern or modernizing the traditional through the use of some symbolic architectural elements in a building – domes, arches, minarets and other elements indicative of a certain [i.e., Islamic] civilization.[35]

This revised approach, he writes, would call into question

> our choices of precedents when it comes to exemplifying the essence of Islamic architecture. A mosque is considered a sacred building typology that traditionally embodies the Islamic architectural elements that are perhaps deemed as iconic. On the other hand, building typologies that would be considered secular typology can still embody Islamic virtues and the frameworks that guided the masters to create the initial forms that are recognized as iconic Islamic architectural elements. This [...] perhaps urges us to attempt to adopt the frameworks that resulted in the forms we know today rather than simply adapting architectural elements while excluding them from their context for the sake of the continuity of Islamic

architecture. Then again, Islam has always accepted and built upon the successes and failures of previous experiences in a continuous process – a rather iterative process, with continuous improvements. Rejection of previous experiences and other outlooks is considered a waste in Islam, as Islam values continuous transformation and metamorphosis of modes of understanding, while not appreciating and perhaps condemning cycles of destruction. In that regards, MIA's formal interpretation of Islamic architecture and its continuity would be deemed as a good start in the attempt of furthering Islamic architectures continuity.[36]

Deeply aware that basing a Qatari architectural identity on precedents drawn from Egypt in the twenty-first century is highly problematic, Rami's work moves beyond identitarian topics to those intricately related to architecture itself. His work, as well as that of my other students, reorients attention towards the thoughtful command of the material at hand, seeks to understand (Islamic) architecture on its own terms, and eschews established and problematic methodological frameworks and architectural precedents. This is meaningful progress worth acknowledging and supporting.

Acknowledgements

This essay originated from a presentation at the 108th College Art Association Annual Conference in Chicago in February 2020. It was given as part of the panel 'Deconstructing the Myths of Islamic Art' organized by Onur Öztürk and Xenia Gazi. I am grateful to Onur and Xenia for inviting me to share my experience at the large public venue, to Daniel E. Coslett and Mohammad Gharipour for their interest in documenting it here, as well as to my students for their participation in classes I teach and for their feedback and encouragement. I also thank April Eisman, Rami Mannan, Leslie Forehand, and Vladimir Kulić for use of their research materials and scholarly communications. The cited references are illustrative and by no means exhaustive. Erika Zinsmeister edited this text. My family members, as always, granted their support to this project.

Notes

This chapter was previously published as Jelena Bogdanović, 'Reorienting Perspectives: Why I Do Not Teach a Course Titled "Islamic Architecture"', *International Journal of Islamic Architecture* 10.1 (2021): 113–26. The text has been updated for this publication.

1 Several historiographical studies detail the development of scholarly research on Islamic architecture and highlight its geographic contexts. These important texts include Robert Hillenbrand, 'Studying Islamic Architecture: Challenges and Perspectives', *Architectural History* 46 (2003): 1–18; and Sheila S. Blair and Jonathan M. Bloom, 'The Mirage of Islamic Art: Reflections on the Study of an Unwieldy Field', *Art Bulletin* 85.1 (2003): 152–84. See also,

Sheila S. Blair and Jonathan M. Bloom, 'The Study of Islamic Architecture: Reflections on an Expanding Field' in this volume.

2   A random review of some 200 images used on the covers of books about Islamic architecture at Amazon.com, accessed on March 30, 2020, revealed only a handful of covers depicting architectural interiors or people in architectural space. Among these, the exceptional decoration of domes and *mihrab*s (prayer niches) was repeatedly highlighted in somewhat flattened images of mosques and the depictions of people were focused on prayer rites or the otherwise communal settings of religious architecture. On the new sensitivity to visual representations of Islamic architecture beyond these stereotypes, see, for example, Jonathan M. Bloom and Sheila S. Blair, eds, *Islamic Art: Past, Present, Future* (New Haven: Yale University Press, 2019); Stefan Maneval, *New Islamic Urbanism: The Architecture of Public and Private Space in Jeddah, Saudi Arabia* (London: UCL Press, 2019); and Mohammad Gharipour, *The Bazar in the Islamic City: Design, Culture, and History* (New York: American University in Cairo Press, 2012).

3   Branko Mitrović, 'Visuality, Intentionality, and Architecture', *Journal of Art Historiography* 14 (2016): 15.

4   'Sherefudin's White Mosque', Aga Khan Development Network, accessed April 1, 2020, https://www.akdn.org/architecture/project/sherefudins-white-mosque; Sherban Cantacuzino, ed., *Architecture in Continuity* (New York: Aperture, 1985), 102–09.

5   Mejrema Zatrić, 'Šerefudin White Mosque', in *Toward A Concrete Utopia: Architecture in Yugoslavia 1948–80*, ed. Martino Stierli and Vladimir Kulić (New York: The Museum of Modern Art, 2018), 164–67.

6   Mark Jarzombek, 'The Identitarian Episteme: 1980s and the Status of Architectural History', in *After Effects: Theories and Methodologies in Architectural Research,* ed. Helene Frichot, Gunnar Sandin, and Bettina Schwalm (London: Actar Publishers, 2018), 99–109.

7   Edward W. Said, *Orientalism* (New York: Vintage Books, 1994).

8   *A Complete 'Guide' to the Egyptological Exhibit: In The Cairo Street Concession at the World's Columbian Exposition, Chicago: With a Résumé of Egyptian History from the Earliest Date of the Present Day* (Chicago: [publisher not identified], 1893) records early interest in 'exotic East'.

9   Summary on Egyptology and Egyptomania in Jelena Bogdanović, 'Art and Architecture', in *Egypt: Middle East in Focus* (formerly *Egypt: A Global Studies Handbook*), ed. Mona Russell (Santa Barbara, CA: ABC–Clio, 2013), 239–73, esp. 259–61. One is also reminded of the nineteenth-century mania for everything Japanese. Christopher Bush, 'The Other of the Other?: Cultural Studies, Theory, and the Location of the Modernist Signifier', *Comparative Literature Studies* 42.2 (2005): 162–80. *Japonisme* is comparable to Egyptomania as fervent taste for everything Egyptian, including its Islamic component.

10 See 'Near Eastern Studies', Princeton University, accessed May 9, 2020, https://gradschool.princeton.edu/academics/fields-study/near-easternstudies; 'History of Department', Department of East Asian Studies, Princeton University, accessed May 9, 2020, https://eas.princeton.edu/about-us/history-department.

11 Jarzombek, 'The Identitarian Episteme'.

12 Hillenbrand, 'Studying Islamic Architecture', 1–18, esp. 7.

13 According to WorldCat (https://www.worldcat.org/, accessed March 30, 2020), there are 749,393 books published on the topic of architecture; of these, 10,071 (1.3%) are on Islamic

architecture and 3,958 (0.5%) are on Byzantine architecture. The catalog of Princeton University library (https://catalog.princeton.edu/, accessed March 30, 2020) avoids repetition of titles across various editions and highlights those used in academic discourse and yet still shows statistics similar to WorldCat: 237,869 books have been published on the topic of architecture; of these, 4,357 (1.84%) are on Islamic architecture (the first was published in 1815) and 1,537 (0.64%) are on Byzantine architecture (the first was published in 1607). Trends have remained seemingly static over the last twenty years. Of 122,841 books on architecture published after the year 2000 and catalogued by Princeton, 2,290 (1.86%) were on Islamic architecture and 770 (0.62%) were on Byzantine architecture. Yet substantial jumps in book production related to modern and contemporary architecture are also observable, which leave Islamic and Byzantine architecture significantly behind. Since the 1950s, 23,490 or some 10% of architectural books contained 'modern' in the title (the first use of 'modern' architecture in a title is recorded in 1471). During the last twenty years, there was also a dramatic 90% increase in titles using the wording 'contemporary architecture'.

14 Jarzombek, 'The Identitarian Episteme'.
15 Rey Chow, *Ethics After Idealism: Theory, Culture, Ethnicity, Reading* (Bloomington: Indiana University Press, 1998), 5 (emphasis original). As a reminder, by World War I, approximately 85% of the globe was controlled by Europeans.
16 I discuss western self-proclaimed centrality also in Jelena Bogdanović, 'On the Very Edge: Modernisms and Modernity of Interwar Serbia' in *On the Very Edge: Essays on Modernism and Modernity in the Arts and Architecture of Interwar Serbia (1918–1941)*, ed. Jelena Bogdanović, Lilien F. Robinson, and Igor Marjanović (Leuven: Leuven University Press, 2014), 1–29.
17 I agree with Bush, 'The Other of the Other?'.
18 Jarzombek, 'The Identitarian Episteme', 107.
19 Mark Jarzombek, 'The Rise of the so–called Premodern', in *2000+ The Urgencies of Architectural Theory: A Symposium Convened by Mark Wigley*, ed. James Graham (New York: Columbia University, 2015), 132–43.
20 See also Hillenbrand, 'Studying Islamic Architecture'.
21 Richard Ingersoll, *World Architecture: A Cross–Cultural History* (Oxford: Oxford University Press, 2018), 231–43, 285–98, 365–73, 443–56, 485–504, 932–58.
22 Ibid., 932–58.
23 Ibid., 950–52.
24 Rest assured that students will also deny the existence of modern and contemporary Christian architecture.
25 Ingersoll, *World Architecture*, 950–52. I am using Ingersoll's text in my course as I find it to be the best option available on the current market because of the breadth of the material it covers, the multiple narrative threads it presents in understandable language, and the degree to which it goes beyond the description of individual architectural examples. The format and scope of the book are ultimately manageable for a twosemester survey of architectural history.
26 National Architectural Accreditation Board, Inc., *Conditions for Accreditation: 2020 Edition*, accessed April 3, 2020, https://www.naab.org/wp-content/uploads/2020-NAAB-Conditions-for-Accreditation.pdf. In Section 3.1, the program criteria

include 'PC.4 History and Theory—How the program ensures that students understand the histories and theories of architecture and urbanism, framed by diverse social, cultural, economic, and political forces, nationally and globally'. Ibid., 2.

27 Henri Lefebvre, *The Production of Space* (Malden: Blackwell, 2016).
28 As a kind of short annotation, in religious societies, houses often have designated space of worship. In my work, Jelena Bogdanović, 'On the Architecture of the *Konaks* in Serbia (1804–1830s)' *Serbian Studies* 21.2 (2007): 161–80, I demonstrate how *konaks*, residential palaces in the Balkans, had a prayer niche known as *ikonluk*, a special niche for religious icons, thus indicating that the occupants were Christians, while in Muslim houses *abdesluk* or *avdesana* was a space for performing the rituals of prayers, handling and reading the Qur'an, as well as ablution.
29 'Mashrabiya 2.0–3D Printed Ceramic Evaporative Façade', Chronicle of Leslie Forehand, accessed May 9, 2020, https://leslieforehand.com/portfolio/mashrabiya-2-0-3d-printed-ceramic-evaporative-facade/; Faye Oney, '3-D Printed Ceramics Could Provide Buildings with Airflow, Evaporative Cooling', American Ceramic Society, March 27, 2018, https://ceramics.org/ceramic-tech-today/3-d-printed-ceramics-could-provide-buildings-withairflow-evaporative-cooling; International Masonry Institute, '3D-printed Ceramic Façade Offers Evaporative Cooling to Buildings', YouTube, April 5, 2019, https://www.youtube.com/watch?v=PHjGDwStCYY.
30 See note 26.
31 Jonathan Culier, *On Deconstruction: Theory and Criticism After Structuralism* (Ithaca, NY: Cornell University Press, 1982), 123.
32 Titles of some lectures in an introductory-level course are: 'The Sacred Rocks and Soaring Minarets: Islamic Architecture'; 'Multicultural Spain; The Living Architecture of the Sub-Saharan Africa'; 'The Ottoman Architecture in Europe, Asia and Africa'; and 'Islamic Architecture of Asia'. When given an opportunity to teach architectural history after the 1750s, lectures can include antithetical lectures to those that essentially reinforce 'Orientalism'. Instead, the focus can be on the parallel developments of modernism and modernity rather than on architecture in Islamic territories as a reaction to architecture in Europe and America.
33 Some topics at this level for courses in medieval architecture are Architectural History of the Middle East Before 1600; Byzantine Architecture; and Medieval Architecture in Western Europe, with each including discussions of Islamic architecture.
34 Rami Mannan, 'Museum of Islamic Art in Qatar by Pei: Tradition and Modern Development in Islamic Architecture', *NCUR 2019 Proceedings* (Kennesaw, GA: Kennesaw State University, 2020): 271–79, https://www.ncurproceedings.org/ojs/index.php/NCUR2019/article/view/2790.
35 Ibid., 278.
36 Ibid.

Chapter 15

Decolonizing Architectural Knowledge: Situating Middle Eastern Pedagogies in a Globalizing World

Ashraf M. Salama

Since the seventeenth century, architecture has been approached from four profoundly different standpoints – those of the academic architect, the craftsman-builder, the civil engineer, and in recent years, the social scientist. From the academic viewpoint, architecture has been traditionally viewed as a fine art in which principles of formal composition, stemming from the classical (i.e., Greek and Roman) traditions, are considered to be of greatest importance. Furthermore, both the craftsman and the engineer have tended to place more emphasis on utilitarian and structural ends than on formal design; the craftsman-builders often came from a background of handicraft and folk traditions while the engineer would usually come from one of technology and applied mathematics. Since the advent of sociology, founded in the early nineteenth century by Henry de Saint-Simon and named by his disciple, August Comte, in the 1830s, the social implications of architecture have increasingly influenced the concepts of mass housing and urban design.

Congruent with the preceding historical approaches to architecture, four different types of architectural education were developed: academic, craft, technological, and sociological. Academic education underscores the study of compositional theory and the traditional principles of formal design as the most important aspects of an architect's education. These principles, considered to be most satisfactory, are acquired in schools or academies, where practicing and experienced professors are well acquainted with major design principles. In contrast, craft training in architecture has stressed the achievement of proficiency in the building trades, a proficiency that can either be learned on the job under a master craftsman, or more commonly nowadays, in architectural or craft schools. The primary aim of this type of architectural education is to train craftsman-builders who can erect buildings rather than make designs to be carried out and built by others.[1] However, while the design taught in the academies was primarily based on formal considerations with 'beauty' as the ultimate goal, in technical schools, emphasis was placed on the application of scientific principles to specific problems, with utility and economy as end goals. Under the influence of the new disciplines of sociology and social science, architectural schools were expected to emphasize pragmatic principles; thus, they not only stressed the social function of buildings and the proper relation of these to socio-physical contexts, but also, gradually, paid careful attention to planning and designing for different types of users.[2]

Formal architectural education as we know it today has changed the ways in which architecture has been approached and practiced historically. In essence, modern training has developed as a result of government initiatives as was the case of the Ecole des Beaux-Arts and the Art Academies in France, or craft and guild movements as was the case of the Bauhaus in

Germany and its counterpart Vkhutemas in Russia [Figure 15.1]. In terms of approach, content, and focus, these schools represent the principal models of architectural education and have been developed into variations that were adopted and adapted in other parts of Europe, North America, and later to other parts of the world including the Middle East.

Contemporary Problematization

Far from homogeneous, architectural education in the Middle East has ensued along different schools of thought depending upon the region and the national setting. This makes it almost impossible to capture one unique image of the qualities and characteristics of architectural education in Middle Eastern countries. Various studies suggest that in many cases it began during colonial periods, adopting educational models of the ruling colonial power.[3] In other cases, systems of education were wholly imported, following approaches that seemed suitable at the time. In a few cases, some nations within their broader region have influenced others. Currently, each nation, or group of nations, pursues its own educational practices that are based on a combination of inherited traditional models and contemporary regional or international affiliations.[4]

The majority of the academic content, educational structures, curricula, modes of delivery, and learning styles within the educational process of architecture in the Middle East are developed based on western models. From a critical perspective, the main body of knowledge on architectural education and design pedagogy is predominantly fashioned and developed in the English-speaking world and is interrogated, debated, and reproduced mainly in the larger context of Western Europe and North America. The architectural academic community in other parts of the world, including the Middle East, is intensely predisposed by such a discourse as well as by various pedagogical trends typically introduced in western academia to reflect the needs of future professionals and the profession at large. Mainly, these represent tendencies that are instigated and practiced within the contextual particularities of western academia including the ambitions and constraints of academic institutions, the professional milieu, and the way in which architecture is practiced and produced. Classically, such an influence manifests itself in the fact that in any discussion about architectural pedagogy in Middle Eastern academia the discourse which characterizes the Global North dominates; it thus overshadows opportunities for developing another parallel, or in fact different but equally important and critical discourse which can be generated and developed to address other unique particularities relevant to the Middle East.[5]

Questions Arise

The notion of 'Islamic architecture' and the 'Islamic city', which occupies the collective psyche of architectural educators in the Middle East, was first produced within western orientalist

Decolonizing Architectural Knowledge

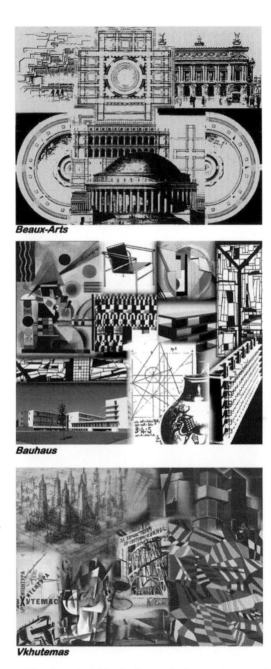

Figure 15.1: A representation of the inherited models of architectural education. Source: Ashraf M. Salama, *Spatial Design Education: New Directions for Pedagogy in Architecture and Beyond* (London: Routledge, 2015), 63, 65, and 68.

discourse and was later questioned in national postcolonial debates. Such ideas were then revisited amidst the rise of nationalist particularism, international architecture, cosmopolitanism, and globalization, all constructs that, despite their consequences, liberated the discipline of architecture from the older, fixed prototypes and embraced the influences of different world orders on the production of architectural knowledge.

An integral part of the discussion within the preceding contextualization and problematization is a number of questions and possible topics, which can trigger thinking about architectural education in the Middle East and its contents, structures, processes, routine practices, and religious and cultural particularities. These may include:

- How do various contemporary interests – such as tradition, identity, modernity, vernacularism, post-colonialism, poverty, sustainability, and globalization – originate within architectural curricula?
- How do the preceding interests act as drivers or catalysts for studio projects and processes?
- How do international accreditation approaches and processes address the particularities of the Middle East? And how do schools develop contextualized approaches to international standards?
- How do international partnerships and summer schools inform studio practices and enrich cross-cultural dialogues between students from the Middle East and students from other parts of the world?[6]

Responding to these questions goes beyond the scope of this discussion. Yet, there have been a few studies that instigated efforts toward providing responsive answers relevant to the content and context of the Middle East. However, these studies represent individual attempts rather than general trends.[7]

Sustained Negative Idiosyncrasies

Following models inherited from the west and adopting techniques practiced by their western counterparts, architectural educators in the Middle East strive to impart the knowledge requisite for successful practice; however, the approach to this is often divergent and may depend on the priorities and ideals of the educator. Nevertheless, despite the amount of knowledge that may be imparted, it is the way in which such knowledge is transmitted that actually has significant professional and social implications.[8] Concomitantly, there is an urgent need to confront issues that pertain to the nature of reality – 'what' and the way in which knowledge about that reality is conveyed to future professionals – and 'how'. Traditional teaching practices suggest that gaps frequently exist between 'what' and 'how'.

In the traditional design pedagogy typically followed in the Middle East, architecture students are habitually encouraged to utilize site visits and walkthroughs of the built environment to observe different phenomena. Unfortunately, however, research indicates that such casual visits and exercises are often not structured to support any form of investigation or inquiry. Likewise, for large classes, a site visit is often confronted with logistical difficulties that may result in little opportunity for individual student mentoring. In this context, two major idiosyncrasies can be envisaged; these continue to characterize teaching practices in many schools around the world, but in particular within the Middle East and can be outlined as follows.[9]

Learning theories about the phenomena versus getting an in-depth understanding of the phenomena's behaviour: When teaching any body of knowledge, there is a frequent tendency to present it as a body of facts and to present architectural theories as a process of criticism. Knowledge is usually presented to students in a retrospective way, through the extensive exhibition of the performance of an architect's work over time. Often abstract and symbolic generalizations used to describe research results do not convey the feel of the behaviour of the phenomena they describe. Additionally, knowledge acquired in this rote manner is often internalized, as it has no outlet for application.

The real versus the hypothetical: Educators tend to give hypothetical design projects which result in the neglect of apprehending many important contextual variables. Typically, educators focus on offering students ready-made interpretations about the built environment rather than providing them with genuine opportunities to explore issues that are associated with the relationship between culture and the built environment. Even if they do give them such a task, they place emphasis on one single culture, which is usually their own. To ameliorate this glaring pedagogical shortcoming, learning from the actual environment should be introduced wherein students experience active learning in parallel to problem solving.

Many architectural educators in the Middle East are aware of this lack and advocate for introducing real-life issues to architectural education. While published experiences have debated innovative practices in the design studio,[10] there has been less emphasis placed upon the way in which structured experiences could be introduced in theory and lecture-based classes.

Appreciative Inquiry (AI): A Milieu for the Critical Thinker

While many pedagogical concepts have been developed by western scholars within the western context, the notions I am introducing here are very relevant to the Middle East as they are centred on the particularities of the context both in terms of the content of knowledge and the content of experience.

Emerging from the fields of organizational behaviour and management, Appreciative Inquiry (AI) has been described as 'the art and practice of asking questions that strengthen a system's capacity to apprehend, anticipate, and heighten positive potential'. It is also viewed as a form of action research that is visionary in nature and aims to create new ideas and images that aid in developmental change.[11]

Inquiry-based learning (IBL) can be considered under the rubric of AI, as an instructional method developed during the 1960s in response to a perceived failure of more traditional forms of instruction and rote learning wherein students were required to simply memorize and reproduce instructional materials.[12] Active and experiential learning are sub-forms of inquiry-based learning: in this methodology progress is assessed by how well students develop experiential and critical thinking and analytical skills rather than how much knowledge they have acquired. A number of recent studies challenge university educators to develop integrative teaching approaches that more fully represent transformative pedagogies: educators need to move away from thinking of students as passive listeners and encourage them to become active learners.[13] However, despite this being easier said than done, the incorporation of active learning strategies into the daily routine of classroom instruction has now become a necessity.

The most significant characteristic of active learning is student involvement: students are actively engaged in individual or group activities during the class session. These may include reading, discussing, commenting, and exploring tasks, ideas, and theories. Rather than a declamatory orator, the instructor takes on the more active role of facilitator and/or monitor and can thus provide students with immediate feedback.[14] Notably, in active learning sessions students are involved in accessing higher order thinking; this simultaneously involves the analysis, synthesis, and evaluation of a wide spectrum of issues and phenomena. In the context of an active-learning university classroom, students are engaged not only in doing things, but also in reflecting and thinking about what they are doing.

Experiential learning has developed into an important paradigm based on the works of John Dewey, Jean Piaget, and David Kolb.[15] They argued that a practical, hands-on experience should be an integral component of any teaching/learning process; this rationale must apply to classroom settings. Therefore, experiential learning goes against learning in which the learner only reads about, hears about, talks about, or writes about these realities but never comes in contact with them as part of the learning process. Experiential learning is first-hand learning in which the learner is directly in touch with the realities being studied.[16]

Moving Forward with Responsive Approaches

In the context of architectural education in the Middle East there are educators who mistakenly equate experiential learning only with 'off campus' or 'non-classroom' learning, not conceiving how it could be very effectively applied to the classroom setting. For example, instead of providing students with lectures about theories of architecture and the work of famous architects, a class in the history of architecture or urban design or a class in design theories might incorporate periods of student practice in theory exercises and critical thinking problems. Likewise, a class in 'principles of architectural design' or in 'human-environment interactions' might involve critical analysis exercises on how people perceive and comprehend the built environment. Both classes could require field visits to buildings and spaces during which students are in close contact with the environment, thus enabling them to better explore aspects of culture, diversity, and people's behaviour, while actively being part of that environment. Hence these mechanisms involve an experiential learning component, which, in turn, enables students to experience and explore first-hand the problems they examine or discuss in the classroom.

Learning through experience involves not merely observing the phenomenon being studied but also doing something with it or to it, for example testing its dynamics or applying a theory to learn more about it and/or achieve desired results. Assessment of environments as a valuable research vehicle needs to be introduced in lecture courses; this can help establish a solid knowledge base about the built environment, which will enable students to have more control over their learning, knowledge acquisition, assimilation, and utilization in future experiences.

The previous discussion suggests that active and experiential learning as concepts and instructional strategies are actually two sides of the same coin: both underpin inquiry-based learning. While they may differ in certain terminology, both nevertheless represent interactive learning mechanisms that share similar aims and qualities, and both can be part of an AI process. Both increase student motivation by placing strong emphasis on the exploration of attitudes and values, knowledge production, and critical thinking skills rather than simply focusing on knowledge transmission or regurgitation.

While including assessment research and active and experiential learning as interactive learning mechanisms, it is also important to involve architecture and design students in assessment processes that are conducted objectively and systematically; casual interviews or observations may only reveal what is already known, not what has been learned and internalized. Through experiential learning, students are actively engaged; they learn about the problems and potentials of existing environments and how or whether they meet user needs, enhance and celebrate their activities, and foster desired behaviours and attitudes.

Underlying AI, relevant aspects of organizational change are important in the context of classroom instruction within a course or a program in architecture. Students are given the opportunity to organize themselves in teams, make selections of environments they see relevant to assess, collaborate effectively in group discussions, and collectively develop arguments and make qualitative and quantitative judgments about those environments. Addressing these aspects in assessment exercises or projects enable the development of skills that include listening and respecting the views of others and negotiating and reaching consensus in making judgments about the qualities of an environment. All of these skills are essential for successful architects and urban designers.

Towards a Decolonized Architectural Education

Architectural education in the Middle East continues to operate within a global world. There are significant opportunities to experience, experiment with, and learn from traditional and vernacular contexts. However, content should not be treated as the ultimate end-goal, but the approach to grasp and comprehend that content should be viewed as an important driver for contextualizing issues relevant to the particularities of the Middle East.

A considerable portion of students' education in architecture is based on 'experience', 'making', and 'active engagement'. Students are encouraged to study the existing built environment and attempt to explain it through theories or typologies, by always looking at and even referring to outstanding examples. However, underlying these approaches are hidden assumptions about the built environment. It is in this grey area, in this vague and often inchoate relationship, wherein lies the 'lesson' to be learned. Hence, the integration of structured learning experiments could effectively produce a more profound learning and foster the establishment of links between the existing dynamic environments, the concepts and theories that purportedly explain them, and the resulting learning outcomes. Accordingly, the contribution of AI lies in the fact that the inherent, subjective, and hard-to-verify conceptual understanding of the built environment can be refined and harmonized by the structured, documented interpretation performed in a systematic manner that promotes critical thinking and reflection. The dynamics of cities in the Middle East allow for the integration of AI and afford the introduction of structured experiments, which may range from experiencing the engagement with communities in unplanned urban settlements to learning from urban conservation projects in historic districts.

Experience through appreciative inquiry has the capacity to decolonize the content of the curriculum and the way in which knowledge is produced and reproduced. As approaches to learning, they enable the development of contextual knowledge that challenges the established canons of architectural education with a fundamental intention to instigate parallel architectural narratives that are not aimed at competing with, but are equally important to, western architectural authority. In this context, while critiquing context-specific values, norms, and practices, the thrust would be to develop typologies of knowledge that directly respond to unique opportunities – such as urban growth potentials and emerging satellite settlements or sustainable tourism development – and challenges – such as spatial justice and access to social infrastructure, ethnic and regional conflicts, mass displacements of refugees, and political and economic instability – among other undecorated realities facing Middle Eastern societies. The starting point would be the utilisation of the key, recently developed knowledge that interrogates the realities of architecture and urbanism in the Middle East and the wider Global South.[17]

Notes

This chapter was previously published as Ashraf M. Salama, 'Reflections on Architectural Education of the Muslim World within a Global World', *International Journal of Islamic Architecture* 8.1 (2019): 33–41. Updates, where appropriate, have been made to the present version.

1 The term 'civil engineer' was first used in 1763 by the English Engineer Joan Smeaton to distinguish civil from military engineer. See Donald Drew Egbert, *Beaux-arts Traditions in French Architecture* (Princeton: Princeton University Press, 1981), 117.

2   See expanded discussion on the history, evolution, and contemporary practices in architectural education in Ashraf M. Salama, *Spatial Design Education: New Directions for Pedagogy in Architecture and Beyond* (London: Routledge, 2015).
3   See for example Ali Djerbi and Abdelwahab Safi, 'Teaching the History of Architecture in Algeria, Tunisia, and Morocco: Colonialism, Independence, and Globalization', *Journal of the Society of Architectural Historians* 62.1 (2003): 110–20; and an earlier collection of essays published in Ahmed Evin, ed., *Architectural Education in the Islamic World* (Singapore: Aga Khan Trust for Culture, 1986).
4   See *Summary Report: Survey of Architectural Education and Professional Practice in Selected Areas of the Muslim World* (Geneva: Aga Khan Trust for Culture, 2007).
5   An earlier similar argument was introduced in an editorial of a special issue of *Charrette: Journal of the Association of Architectural Educators*. See Ashraf M. Salama, 'From the Global South: Pedagogical Encounters in Architecture', *Charrette* 5.1 (2018): 1–7. Currently, a comprehensive discourse is developed to capture the salient features of architectural pedagogies of the Global South with a view to contract a parallel, non-competing, but equally important content on the opportunities that teaching practices in the Global South can offer. See Harriet Harriss, Ashraf M. Salama, and Ane Gonzalez Lara, eds, *The Routledge Companion to Architectural Pedagogies of the Global South* (London: Routledge, forthcoming).
6   Salama, 'From the Global South'.
7   *Architecture Education in the Islamic World* seems to be the first of its kind, an important edition that was based on Seminar Ten in the series of Architectural Transformations in the Islamic World, held in Granada, Spain, in 1986. The book offers important arguments that contextualize architectural education within unique cultural and religious locales, with contributions from world-renowned scholars, theorists, and art and architecture historians including Christian Norberg-Schulz, Gulzar Haider, Hasan-Uddin Khan, Ismail Serageldin, Jamel Akbar, Mohammed Arkoun, Renata Holod, and Spiro Kostof. Issues related to architectural education and the content of knowledge needed in an Islamic milieu are debated, including discussions on the history and evolution of architectural education in Bangladesh, Egypt, India, Iran, Iraq, Morocco, Pakistan, Saudi Arabia, Syria, Tunisia, and Turkey. This is coupled with a discussion of the content and structure of the Aga Khan Program for Islamic Architecture at Harvard University and the Massachusetts Institute of Technology, and how architectural education in the countries represented in the book was influenced by various schools of thought and curriculum models within the Global North including France, Germany, Switzerland, United Kingdom, and the United States. See Evin, *Architectural Education in the Islamic World*. Additional surveys were undertaken by the Aga Khan Trust for Culture in 1992 and 2007.
8   Sanjoy Mazumdar, 'Cultural Values in Architectural Education', *Journal of Architectural Education* 46.4 (1993): 230–37.
9   Ashraf M. Salama, 'Seeking New Forms of Pedagogy in Architectural Education', *Field* (University of Sheffield) 5.1 (2013): 9–30.
10 Ibid.
11 The work of David Cooperrider is a manifestation of the growing interest in Appreciative Inquiry. See David Cooperrider, *An Appreciative Inquiry: Rethinking Human Organization* (Champaign, IL: Stipes Publishing, 2000), 42.

12 See Russell A. Ackoff, *Redesigning the Future: A Systems Approach to Societal Problems* (New York: John Wiley & Sons, 1974); Jerocie S. Bruner, 'The Act of Discovery', *Harvard Educational Review* 31.4 (1961): 21–32.
13 Salama, 'Seeking New Forms of Pedagogy'.
14 See Charles Bonwell, 'Building a Supportive Climate for Active Listening', *The National Teaching and Learning Forum* 6.1 (1996): 4–7; Euda Dean, 'Teaching the Proof Process: A Model for Discovery Learning', *College Teaching* 44.2 (1996): 139–44.
15 Classic writings on learning from experiences include John Dewey, *Experience and Education* (New York: Kappa Delta Pi, 1934); Jean Piaget, *The Psychology of Intelligence* (London: Routledge and Kegan Paul, 1950); David A. Kolb, *Experiential Learning: Experience as the Source of Learning and Development* (Upper Saddle River, NJ: Prentice Hall, 1983).
16 Ashraf M. Salama and Laura A. MacLean, 'Integrating Appreciative Inquiry (AI) into Architectural Pedagogy: An Assessment Experiment of Three Retrofitted Buildings in the City of Glasgow', *Frontiers of Architectural Research* 6.2 (2017): 169–82.
17 See Mohammad Gharipour, ed., *Contemporary Urban Landscapes of the Middle East* (London: Routledge, 2018); Ashraf M. Salama and Marwa M. El-Ashmouni, *Architectural Excellence in Islamic Societies: Distinction through the Aga Khan Award for Architecture* (London: Routledge, 2020).

Chapter 16

Educating the Public about Islamic Art and Architecture through Museums

Sheila R. Canby

The question of whether the public can learn about Islamic art and architecture from museums starts with what museums consider their educational goals to be, as expressed in their mission statements. One hundred and fifty years ago the Metropolitan Museum of Art (Met) was founded 'for the purpose of establishing and maintaining in [New York City] a Museum and library of art, of encouraging and developing the study of the fine arts, and the application of arts to manufacture and practical life, of advancing the general knowledge of kindred subjects, and, to that end, of furnishing popular instruction'.[1] As this statement demonstrates, the museum's mission to educate the public has been central to its identity since its inception. Nonetheless, a 2015 revision of the Met's mission statement hardly refers to 'education', favouring exhortations such as 'connect the broadest audience to our scholarship' and 'position our collection, scholarship, and expertise to create greater access, dialogue, and understanding around these resources'.[2] While the underlying aim to present works of art to the public, accompanied by explanatory information, is implied in these statements, the vision of how visitors might use or benefit from the collections is no longer crucial to the bullet points that comprise the 'core values' and 'guiding principles' of the twenty-first-century document. The Met's new mission statement seems to recognize the diversity of the museum's audience and the need to offer a variety of avenues to comprehending the art it presents. Similar aims are articulated better in the mission statement of the Museum of Fine Arts, Boston (MFA): 'The Museum creates educational opportunities for visitors and accommodates a wide range of experiences and learning styles',[3] while the Smithsonian Institution, the largest organization of museums and research centres in the United States, prefaces its fiscal year 2017 annual performance plan as follows: 'MISSION STATEMENT *The increase and diffusion of knowledge* VISION STATEMENT *Shaping the future by preserving our heritage, discovering new knowledge, and sharing our resources with the world*'.[4] The goal of sharing its collections with the world implies an expectation of engaging with an exceptionally broad range of people, underpinned by the creation and spread of knowledge. Whereas the Met and MFA announce their commitments to diverse audiences, the Smithsonian's statement affirms its commitment to knowledge and assumes its reach is global.

To comply with the tenets of their museums' mission, curators of Islamic art in the Americas and Europe face a singular challenge. Not only do they have to familiarize their local and national audiences with the history and culture of periods and regions not their own, but they must also find ways to attract visitors to their galleries in the first place. Major renovations, such as the Met's galleries for the art of the 'Arab Lands, Turkey, Iran, Central Asia and

Later South Asia' that opened in 2011 receive abundant attention in the press and on social media and result in large visitor numbers.[5] Likewise, special exhibitions bring in crowds as long as they are advertised and scheduled appropriately within the calendar year.[6] For some segments of museum management, visitor numbers are the most important metric. Yet, the curator hopes to provide an environment in which a visitor's curiosity will be piqued and answers will be provided to their questions about the works on view, in essence a learning experience. Any worthy museum installation starts with the works of art, but case design, lighting, wall colour, and materials all have an impact on how visitors perceive objects. Long before an object is brought to a gallery, its position in a vitrine, on a pedestal, or on a wall is mocked up so the curator and designer can see what placement and combination with other works show each to best effect. This is a process not only of producing a visual hierarchy or rhythm in a case or on a wall, but also of drawing attention to the most significant work in a group of related pieces.

Assessing the Audience

How can a museum provide enough information to explain the historical and cultural context in which a work of art was produced while promoting the enjoyment of the work itself? Modern museums have myriad tools at their disposal, including written labels, audio guides, and apps that connect viewers to a museum's website on their mobile devices, docents who give gallery tours, and curators who lead more focused tours on an occasional basis. Seasoned museumgoers are accustomed to reading labels or listening to audio guides, while the app route most likely appeals to the young and tech-savvy. In contrast to labels and their limited word length, docents and curators can speak at length about specific objects or their historical milieu and, more importantly, answer people's questions. Thus, various forms of information are on offer to address the different ways people seek knowledge in galleries of Islamic art. Some visitors make plans while others literally get lost only to find themselves in one of the Islamic galleries. The former group may join a tour or read up on the galleries on the website before coming to the museum; the latter arrive by serendipity.

A survey conducted at the Metropolitan Museum of Art in 2010 in anticipation of the new galleries dedicated to the Arab Lands, Turkey, Iran, Central Asia and Later South Asia posed one question about the type of information visitors were seeking when looking at works of Islamic art and architectural fragments. The answers indicated that about half the people interviewed wanted historical background, while the other half wanted help in understanding the details and 'story' of the piece before them. Most people also preferred a chronological installation to a grouping of objects by theme or media without a geographical or chronological order. Instead, they favoured arrangements of objects from the same time and place in order to understand the life of that era. The survey reinforced the decision to organize the galleries according to geography and chronology. For this reason, the Met chose to name the galleries not after the religion of Islam, but in accordance with the geographical sources of the works on view. The galleries do not contain art from sub-Saharan Africa, Southeast Asia, or from an Islamic context in the Americas, nor are other galleries in the Met that contain Christian and Buddhist art named after those religions. Thus, the name, although long, indicates what will and will not be seen in this suite of rooms.[7]

By 2010 one of the main reasons that visitors came to the Met to see Islamic art was to learn more about the history of the regions mentioned so often in the news media. This interest spiked after 2001 and included Saudi Arabia, Afghanistan, Iraq, and Iran. By 2011 the Arab Spring had turned the world's attention to Tunisia, Egypt, and Syria. Its aftermath and the rise of Da'esh/ISIS implicated Turkey. The large population of South Asians in North America is also reflected in the visitorship to the galleries of the Islamic and Asian Art Departments at the Met. No matter whether people have travelled in or only read about the regions represented in the Met's collection, they all arrive with some preconceived notions or questions about these areas and their art. Current affairs have led to a general familiarity with the countries of the Middle East but little knowledge of the specific histories of the regions from Spain to Southeast Asia where Islam is or has been the religion of large segments of the population. One heartening phenomenon is that visitors are generally seeking to broaden their understanding of the Middle East and North Africa and to familiarize themselves with the cultural heritage of these places. Although the word 'Islamic' is used to define the field, most of what is on view was not produced for religious purposes. Likewise, not every work with an Arabic inscription is a piece of religious art. These points are made throughout the galleries, starting with the first piece that most people see: a tenth-century ceramic bowl from Nishapur, Iran, inscribed in Arabic with an adage, 'Planning before work protects you from regret; prosperity and peace' [Figure 16.1].

Perhaps the most common misconception about Islamic art is that the depiction of the human form is prohibited and thus has never occurred. Seventh- and eighth-century Islamic textiles from Egypt and metal bowls from Iran, for example, include human figures, while Iraqi lusterware dishes of the ninth and tenth centuries feature drinkers, musicians, and men with banners. Most of the objects decorated with human figures had secular, quotidian uses. The increasing use of paper after the tenth century led not only to an upsurge in the production of Qur'ans, but also to the growth of illustrated manuscripts. The subjects of these books ranged from scientific and medical texts to volumes of fables, historical texts, and poetry. Illustrations to these manuscripts, especially in historical or pseudo-historical texts, include depictions of the Prophet Muhammad, a hot-button issue after the 2005 publication in the Danish newspaper *Jyllands-Posten* of cartoons featuring disrespectful images of Muhammad.[8] The contemporary cartoons imply that Muhammad espoused terrorism, or would do so if he were alive today, and thus equate the religion of Islam with violent acts. In fact, the images in historical Iranian, Turkish, and South Asian texts depict him at key moments of his life or in Shi'i-inflected scenes with his son-in-law 'Ali and his grandsons Hassan and Hussein and emphasize the Prophet's role as a transformational leader of men and messenger of God. Since the Met's permanent galleries opened in 2011, the museum has consistently shown at least one of these images.[9] Exhibited in the context of other paintings of the same period and style,

Figure 16.1: Bowl with Arabic Inscription. Iran, Nishapur, from the tenth century. Earthenware; white slip with black-slip decoration under transparent glaze, h. 7 in. (17.8 cm); diam. 18 in. (45.7 cm). Source: Metropolitan Museum of Art, Rogers Fund, 1965, 65.106.2.

these works have never elicited a negative response. As tools for educating the public, they allow the museum to counter assumptions that the Prophet Muhammad was never depicted or was shown only with his face veiled.

In the present day, the exhibition of a comprehensive collection of Islamic art in a large museum such as the Met carries with it the responsibility to confront negative attitudes toward Muslims, their religion, and their cultural heritage. To achieve this without writing object labels in the form of political manifestos, one must prefer to say little or nothing, believing that the

Figure 16.2: View of two *mashrabiya* screens in gallery 453 at the Metropolitan Museum of Art, New York. The screen above the doorway is Egyptian, from the eighteenth–nineteenth century; while at the left is one of a suite of screens produced in Egypt in 2010–2011 specifically for the windows in the Islamic galleries that give light onto a central atrium. Source: Metropolitan Museum of Art.

art can and will speak for itself. In addition, striving to create a mood with a hint of the places of origin of the works on view is desirable and conducive to concentration. One visitor surveyed before the galleries opened put it this way:

RESPONDENT.   [I am] hoping there would be an atmosphere, an atmosphere of peace and harmony and the atmosphere I find in Islamic countries. I'd like information to be clear and short and artistic and straight to the point. Illuminating. I like facts and I hope to learn.
INTERVIEWER.   What would you hope to learn?
RESPONDENT.   I don't know that much so it is a good question. I'd like more of a timeline and the origins of Islamic art. Broad world view, put it in perspective.[10]

With architectural touches, such as *mashrabiya* (lattice) screens and arched doorways, the designers of the galleries provided subtle details that evoke Islamic architecture and create an atmosphere but do not distract from the art on view [Figure 16.2]. Likewise, wall colours and flooring were chosen with the art in mind, all the while with the notion that the setting needs to support the experience of looking at the art.

Beyond Labels: Public Programs and Outreach

In addition to gallery talks, public programs for families and adults that take place in the galleries attract audiences. For example, museum educators organize programs for children and families that may involve close observation of works on view followed by making art or crafts inspired by what the group has seen. Curatorial departments, on the other hand, plan and execute programs that emphasize history and art history or the broader cultural milieu of the collection. At the Met the Islamic Art Department initiated a monthly series of free one-hour concerts in the small Moroccan Court by musicians playing instruments and music from the various regions represented in the galleries. Between one and three musicians would perform for an audience that grew from about 25 people to over 150. The growing number of people in the gallery space began to endanger works of art that were not under glass, and the insistence of colleagues responsible for production of events in the 750-seat museum auditorium that large sound boards be installed for each concert led to their discontinuation, much to the dismay of the loyal audience.

At other times a museum's educational mission is best advanced by responding to current events in a way that uses the collections to open a window on a particular part of the world. Following former President Donald Trump's travel ban in January 2017, which restricted the travel of people from a series of Muslim-majority countries to the United States, the Met's Departments of Ancient Near Eastern and Islamic Art joined forces and planned a series of pop-up talks on art from the countries subject to the ban. These ten-minute talks focused on individual objects and enabled curators to discuss the art in the context of the history and culture of the affected countries. The talks took place once a week for several months, and like the popular Moroccan Court concerts, their audiences grew over the course of that period. In many cases, the speakers discussed how a particular technology or style originated in one of the banned regions and was later adopted in Europe and the rest of the Europeanized world. Even a nugget of information could grab a visitor's attention and change his or her understanding of how modern artistic styles, technologies, and institutions developed.

Training

A final aspect of educating people about Islamic art and architecture in museums involves training. For many years graduate and senior fellowships in museums have given students and scholars the opportunity to spend an academic year conducting research on an aspect of the museum's collection. Pivoting to a broader educational mission, in 2015 the Met and Columbia University jointly organized a closed-door workshop in Istanbul to which museum professionals from Syria and Iraq were invited to discuss their greatest needs in the wake of the invasion of Daʿesh/ISIS and destruction of monuments and museum collections. The one area in which participants in the workshop all agreed that they needed help was the documentation of their collections. In the following year, money was raised to produce ten documentation packs, consisting of a backpack containing a laptop computer, camera, iPhone, photographic lights, and the necessary batteries for photographing and cataloguing the works in their care. Then ten museum professionals were invited to Istanbul (and later Amman), where they were trained to use the equipment and take 'museum-quality' photographs of their collections. The idea was not only to save the information in the cloud so it could not be destroyed in case of hostilities, but also to publish small pamphlets of their collections that could be sold. At least three of the Iraqi museums expected to have published brochures by autumn 2019[11] and several others planned to follow. While these collections contain far more than Islamic art alone, the information and images that will become available through the published catalogues will help expand knowledge both in Iraq and elsewhere.

Conclusion

Museum curators fervently believe in the importance of seeing works of art first-hand. As anyone who has visited Giza knows, photographs cannot begin to capture the scale and impact of standing in front of the pyramids. Likewise, Islamic art in a museum invites the visitor to look and enjoy the virtuosity of a piece's making, the richness of its colour, and the elegance of its design. Furthermore, through labels and other means the visitor can learn about how the object fits into a larger narrative that in some cases has nothing to do with politics but reflects the lives of people unknown to us today. Other arts such as music and poetry enhance the visual and often express the same emotions as the works of art. Despite the fascination with computer screens and other media as adjuncts to works of art, they change the viewer's experience without necessarily broadening his or her knowledge. Finally, beyond the walls of one museum, say the Met, or borders of one country, lie others in the regions covered by the museum in question. In areas where cultural heritage is threatened, helping museum professionals with the documentation and safeguarding of their collections is a form of education that may ultimately improve the ability of the Met or its sister institutions to educate its audience about Islamic art and architecture.

Coda: Islamic Art in Museums in the Era of COVID-19

As with every other sector of the global economy, COVID-19 transformed art museums. Forced to close for six months of the spring and summer of 2020, most museums had to cancel exhibitions, lay off staff, and offer retirement packages to people over 55 or 60 years old, while losing significant amounts of money.[12] The Met, for example, reopened at the end of August 2020 with timed entry for its visitors. At that time the docent tours were all shelved in the interest of social distancing, and uncertainty about future programs was substantial. Fortunately, a number of exhibitions that had been scheduled for the previous spring were rescheduled.

For those wary of travelling, many museum websites have expanded their offerings, providing online exhibition tours and lectures on works in the collection. These do not replace the first-hand encounter with works of art, but they are a way to engage the audience. Perhaps one good outcome of the pandemic has been the realization on the part of museums that publicly available collection databases are key to maintaining public awareness and interest in their holdings. Students and professors mine these databases for their research and lectures. Members of the general public scan them for answers to their questions or material for social media. In the face of radically altered circumstances, museums can and do still educate the public about Islamic art, reaching out online with an array of platforms that highlight their collections. No matter what happens next, museums will likely continue to enhance their websites to ensure the broad accessibility of their collections and the fulfilment of their educational mission, all the while hoping for a return to pre-pandemic norms.

Notes

This chapter was previously published as Sheila R. Canby, 'Can Museums Educate the Public about Islamic Art?', *International Journal of Islamic Architecture* 9.1 (2020): 21–28. Updates, where appropriate, have been made to the present version.

1. Charter of The Metropolitan Museum of Art, State of New York, Laws of 1870, Chapter 197, passed April 13, 1870, and amended L.1898, chapter 34; L. 1908, chapter 219, as stated in Metropolitan Museum of Art, *Annual Report for the Year 2017–2018* (2018), 11, https://www.metmuseum.org/-/media/files/about-the-met/annual-reports/2017-2018/annual-report-2017-18.pdf.
2. Metropolitan Museum of Art, *Annual Report for the Year 2015–2016* (2016), 11, https://www.metmuseum.org/-/media/files/about-the-met/annual-reports/2015-2016/annual-report-2015-16.pdf.
3. Museum of Fine Arts (Boston), 'Mission Statement' (1991), accessed October 28, 2019, https://www.mfa.org/about/mission-statement.
4. Smithsonian Institution, *Annual Performance Plan: Fiscal Year 2017*, 2, https://www.si.edu/Content/Pdf/About/FY2017_performance-plan.pdf. Capitalized text and punctuation as in the original.
5. By February 2013 one million people had visited the galleries for the art of the Arab Lands, Turkey, Iran, Central Asia and Later South Asia. The numbers decreased gradually but thousands of people still visit the galleries annually.
6. As I have observed in over four decades working in museums, the best time slots for exhibitions of medieval or early Islamic art are in the fall or winter, during the academic year, when

professors can incorporate a visit to the exhibition into their curriculum and not compete with exams and school vacations.

7   The name of the galleries reflects what is on view and conforms to one style of designating galleries in the Metropolitan Museum of Art, to wit, Asian, European Paintings, American Wing, etc. Discussions of the title involved Trustees, donors, museum administrators, and curators. For administrative reasons the name of the department that curates this collection has remained the Department of Islamic Art.

8   Christiane Gruber, *The Praiseworthy One: The Prophet Muhammad in Islamic Texts and Images* (Bloomington: Indiana University Press, 2018), 24, 312. Christiane Gruber, ed., *The Image Debate: Figural Representation in Islam and Across the World* (London: Gingko Library, 2019); Christiane Gruber and Avinoam Shalem, eds, *The Image of the Prophet between Ideal and Ideology: A Scholarly Investigation* (Berlin: De Gruyter, 2014).

9   Because none of the Met's seven representations of Muhammad was on view at the time of the Danish cartoons' publication and subsequent demonstrations and violence, the museum was accused by a tabloid newspaper in New York of being afraid to exhibit its pictures of Muhammad. See Isabel Vincent, '"Jihad" Jitters at the Met', *New York Post*, January 10, 2010, https://nypost.com/2010/01/10/jihad-jitters-at-met/.

10 Anonymous visitor, Metropolitan Museum of Art, June 2010.

11 The first brochures to appear were to be those of the National Museum of Iraq, Baghdad; Slemani Museum, Suleymaniyah; Basra Museum, Basra; and Mosul Museum, Mosul.

12 Alex Greenberger, 'Metropolitan Museum of Art Lays Off 81 Employees Amid Financial Uncertainty', *ARTNews*, April 22, 2020, https://www.artnews.com/art-news/news/met-museum-layoffs-coronavirus-1202684559/.

Part 6

Curation and Publication

Chapter 17

Displaying Islamic Arts in Global Cities

Jorge Correia

The *International Journal of Islamic Architecture* (*IJIA*) recently celebrated its tenth anniversary. Scholarship and practice that concern the wider field of Islamic architectural studies rejoiced in the journal's efforts over the last decade. Indeed, its articles, position papers, and reviews have managed to mediate disciplines elegantly, to negotiate concepts within a broader geography, and to push towards a new approach to the 'Islamic' built environment in a transdisciplinary way.

When I was invited to write this short essay (initially for *IJIA*), I could not help but return to its first issue and rediscover what Hasan-Uddin Khan had said in the journal's inaugural editorial.[1] In his opening address as academic editor of *IJIA*, Khan outlined some of the persistent interpretations of the subject – such as the conflict or synergy between religion and civilization – and he acknowledged the significant shifts and perceptions of the arts of Islam in the previous decades. Still, he underlined the need for their rereading. In fact, as he put it later in the text, cultural histories of Islam and its arts have to be further deepened within Muslim societies in order to better address the issues of the secular and sacred within the total human experience, so that we might craft a new narrative that searches for new paradigms and proposes novel positions of Islam in global art history.

The reference to a compartmentalization of knowledge that refuses to see the arts, and particularly architecture or urban studies, as a hinge for discussing contemporary societal challenges and expressions has been recurrent. This aspect is vividly mirrored in the dichotomy between the image of the city and the curatorial options of museums, both in the Middle East and in western countries. While cities have gone global, whether within the Arab geography or on the European continent, museums have encapsulated an enduring vision that is, in a certain way, an orientalist gaze towards the lands of the Islam. So, what is the epistemological canvas of knowledge now: city or display? What is the becoming?

On Context: Globalization, Orientalism, and Mobility

The frame of globalization has introduced parallel phenomena of cosmopolitanism in geographies traditionally divided by cultural barriers inherited from colonialism. Migrations and increasing mixture of nationalities (including the emergence of second and third generations of immigrants) in the northern Atlantic sphere, together with the ascent of the Gulf states' financial capacity – energized by petro-dollar economies – have gradually diminished the 'otherness' and the 'apartness' with which the Islamic world had traditionally been labelled. As Khan puts it in his second editorial, globalization 'raises the issue of whether national or social identity or indeed notions of Islamic identity still mater, for they play an apparently small role in the economically driven city'.[2] In fact, this statement remains valid today despite timid signs of change.

Mobility has enabled critical masses to debate new perspectives for new realities; the Erasmus generation within/to/from Europe generated links that have steadily produced cultural changes in practice and thought.[3] Moreover, expat fluxes to Gulf Coast countries have introduced new scenarios and dynamics of artistic reception and perception [Figure 17.1]. Gradually, cities have become territories of overlapping cultures and crossroads for new nomads. Historically cosmopolitan, today they continue to act as fertile vehicles of information and knowledge. Stagnant views of Middle Eastern cities encapsulating frames of immovable social and physical scenography have become gradually obsolete as a novel imagery is conveyed not only by media, but also by the shortening of distance by human mobility, displacement, communication tools, or the internet.

Curiously, one and a half centuries ago, travelling was perceived in the opposite way and helped perpetuate erstwhile static impressions. In the late 1800s, French writer Gustave Flaubert defined the orientalist in the figure of the well-travelled western man.[4] During the nineteenth century, the east represented the realm of exoticism, fantasy, and mystery. Literature and painting provided perfect vehicles for fertile explorations of the unknown. In Europe, the writings of Flaubert, Victor Hugo, and Gérard de Nerval, and the paintings by Eugène Delacroix, among others, fashioned visions of the 'oriental' world. A voyage to the orient was considered a step back in time, towards the remains and ghosts of western history. Orientalist tropes that generated the notion of the 'Islamic city' well into the twentieth century were based on a static, unchanging type of city [Figure 17.2]. This derived neither from some originating city form or representation, nor from some established set of rules or ordinances to be found in the culture.[5] Instead, the city in the Muslim world was a negative construct, born of the projection of otherness: that which was not the western, the modern, the capitalist. Thus, traditional cities in the Islamic sphere have generally gathered orientalized receptions and perspectives, picking up from misconceptions and stereotypes that evolved during the second half of the nineteenth century and were perpetuated by colonialism.

One century after Flaubert, Palestinian-American academic Edward Said proposed a much wider concept of orientalism, defining the term as a product of the west characterized by a patronizing attitude towards Middle Eastern, Asian, and North African cultures, often manifested in literary and pictorial imagery of the Islamic world.[6] Scholarship on urban studies soon joined this thread. Works revising the orientalist approach emerged through conferences and scholarly meetings that brought together academics from different backgrounds, including people from Arab and Turkic countries, among others.[7] More recent scholarship has shed light on the urban organization and composition of such tissues, most of them confined to old quarters or historical centres of thriving contemporary cities within Dar al Islam.

Figure 17.1: A street in Dubai, UAE, photographed in 2015. Source: Jorge Correia.

Figure 17.2: John Beasley Greene, View of Houses in Cairo, Egypt, 1854–1855. Source: Canadian Centre for Architecture, PH1991:0255.

In fact, today these are cities that struggle to fit into traditional taxonomies, such as 'Middle Eastern', that too broadly emphasize geographical perspective, or, even less, 'Arab cities'.[8] This latter label underlines specific cultural aspects that can no longer be isolated from the main forces shaping contemporary cities. Indeed, the emphasis on socio-religious interests – such as in 'Islamic' or 'Muslim' cities, or even 'Islamicized' or 'Islamicate'[9] – has been contested.[10]

New Museums, Old Collections: The Resurgence of the Arts of Islam

Fuelled in large part by the global petro-economy, established urban centres in some Arab countries are now able to recreate regional narratives and thus abandon decades of submission to what the west has dictated. Overall, one observes a legitimate claim to lead its own cultural agenda from one of the most important demographic universes in the world – the Muslim – delicately balanced between the conservative tradition and the contemporary proposal. That is

Figure 17.3: The Museum of Islamic Art in Doha, Qatar, photographed in 2017. Source: Jorge Correia.

the case of Qatar, which positions itself as a cultural hub for the region with its museums, most notably the Museum of Islamic Art in Doha [Figure 17.3]. Nevertheless, unlike cities, museums are struggling to move towards global ends. The economically emergent territorial axis from the southern Mediterranean to the Gulf shores has been sponsoring local, regional, and/or national views, which exacerbate cultural values with a limited geographical range and lack critical distance to reposition them in a contemporary global context. Despite efforts, the problem is not exclusive of the formerly colonized countries, but can be verified in the west too, in formerly colonizing nations. Furthermore, it appears that in spite of growing human mobility, increased exchange of knowledge, and shared museological practices, both geographical poles of this issue continue to behave traditionally. In fact, European or North American institutions, impermeable to their countries' internal demographic changes, keep displaying according to chronological and regional conventions.

Recently, institutions have devoted an unprecedented level of care to the reconfiguration of the display of the arts of Islam.[11] Political questions translated into a growing presence of the Arab-Persian-Turkic spheres in global media have fostered the search for meanings and answers to current social challenges. In recent years, much attention has been devoted to the rediscovery and realignment of so-called 'Islamic art' through curatorial redesigns and temporary exhibitions associated to the theme.[12] Such was the case of the Metropolitan Museum of Art (the Met) in New York and the Louvre in Paris, both of which have renovated their galleries in the aftermath of 9/11 and related events. The former presented new galleries dedicated to the 'Art of the Arab Lands, Turkey, Iran, Central Asia, and Later South Asia' in 2011, using a neutral terminology soon to be redenominated as 'Islamic art' in the collection description.[13] Less than one year later, the Louvre opened 3,000 square metres of new exhibition space, declaring it the museum's greatest architectural work since the Grand Louvre, and calling it 'Arts de l'Islam'.[14] In 2018, London's British Museum refurbished two galleries at its very heart to house 'The Albukhary Foundation Gallery of the Islamic World', aiming to bring together stories of interconnected worlds across time and geography, that of the traditional Islamic world, i.e., exclusively a series of regions stretching from north-west Africa to Southeast Asia.

Overall, difficulties in integrating global history into broader curatorial discourses or narratives persist, and resilient linear histories are presented. Even when terminologies try to avoid traditional denominations, physical seclusion remains and the question of how to narrate the arts of the Islamic world has yet to be addressed. I argue that the time has come for museums to rethink their curation praxis. Beyond orientalizing stereotypes and displays in galleries dedicated to the arts of Islam, are museums questioning the position of Dar al Islam in a global perspective? Are they, in fact, reviewing their entire exhibition concept?

Almost a century has passed since the 'Tree of Architecture, showing the main growth or evolution of the various styles' was published in the first edition of Sir Banister Fletcher's *A History of Architecture on the Comparative Method* in 1896, which marginalized other cultures in favour of the western branch.[15] Critical distance offers now a morphological turn. It allows us to reflect on the construction of identities beyond Europe and to question veils of isolation, as well as canals of communication and travel, undoubtedly fostering scholarship to acknowledge diversity in time, place, and pattern. The question is how to mediate between an epistemological revision of concepts, ideas, and even terminologies, and the emergent scholarship on Africa, the Middle East, and Asia. On the question of who maps the world, museums have a fundamental role in establishing or deleting borders, notions, and ideas.

Although a body of scholarly thought on the need and potential for change in museological approaches has been produced, the *modus operandi* seems not to follow it operatively. On the one hand, a slow and sometimes lethargic ontological revolution of the west still struggles to accept its own artistic and cultural production as contribution rather than matrix. On the other hand, many institutions in countries inhabited mostly by Muslims still identify themselves with the cultural label of 'Islamic' even if, at the same time, they nourish the seeds to its very same revision. Besides museums, parallel cutting-edge research and teaching programs present the very same seclusion of the arts and architectures of Islam in the university curricula of the Middle East and North Africa, considering it a separate section of world art history.

Museology vs. Built Environment: Global Divergences

There is an urgent need for a new conceptual cartography in museums that is able to remap and to reflect the cities hosting them, whether in Europe, North America, or the Middle East, and to interrogate the traditional arrangement of contents. If the architecture of museums has for so long now attended to a conceptual turn that has placed them as global cornerstones of contemporary design, why are permanent collections' displays not following the movement? Actually, this quest should be a claim from the cities themselves. It ought to emerge from the civil societies that no longer recognize themselves in the canonical chronological and/or thematic organization and sequence of galleries or rooms that somehow materialize segregation rather than the social-demographic changes that the built environment is expressing. Throughout the world, urban-becoming has shared models, sketches, and agents, making for a diversified architectural lexicon by which museums and galleries are designed, available to all. The hiring of reputable architects in North Africa and the Middle East is just one of the symptoms of the overcoming of former physical distances and gaps between western and eastern poles. In fact, the Gulf region has become one of the architectural crossroads for so-called 'starchitects' responding to a growing demand for signature buildings, notably new museums and galleries. Yet, this change has yet to be joined by their internal exhibition display message.

While the effects of colonialism still reverberate, keeping alive a past when global art historiography confirmed such paradigms by reducing peripheral subjects almost to chapters of curiosities, more recent postcolonial efforts to reverse this status quo have ended up being postmodern,[16] and fostered expressions of traditional language as a source for architectural design and artistic expression. The resurgence of confidence in Islam from the 1970s fuelled this phenomenon from Morocco to Oman. Paradoxically, it also led to forms of neo-colonialism by exacerbating moralist expressions and aesthetic forms, thus legitimizing the narrative of the difference by the former centres of power in the north Atlantic sphere.[17] In the case of museums, as in many other vectors of cultural agendas, neo-colonialism has not been translated into practices of cultural imperialism over developing countries, but rather through the expression of cultural colonialism mirrored in their own displays in European or North American museums. Wealthy nations control values and perceptions of others through these cultural means. By claiming leadership on the matter, and thus dictating hegemonic standards, they continue to reaffirm the canon and its artistic compartments to the world, corroborating a deficient vision for the present.

In a challenging twenty-first century, museums should act as agents of change while searching for their own essence as contemporary institutions with a pedagogical and social responsibility. The performance of the exhibition display is not yet following the digital turn and nomadic lifestyle that cities manifest on a daily basis. Digital does not merely mean turning museums more virtual, interactive, and wired, but urgently creating mechanisms to follow and join the globalist tendency of the built environment in which they are housed or that surrounds them. Anywhere in the world, and particularly in the context of the Middle East, contemporary cities can no longer be isolated from the global forces shaping them. Thus, the revision of concepts like 'Islamic city', or 'Islamic architecture' for that matter, as seen earlier, was driven by a globalization of design ideas, agents, and patronage. It was the evolution of urban morphology and building typologies observed on the ground that, ultimately, have revaluated culturally embedded terminology.

As reflectors of society, museums must question the identity of places where they are located and the public to which they cater, which is now a varied mixture of nationalities, backgrounds, and interests. As mentioned before, it seems that while museums have somehow come closer to a worldly standard when it comes to their architectural design, liberating themselves from Islamic languages in their forms or decorative aspects, the narrative they are conveying inside seems less progressive. The place of the artefact is yet to be addressed in a global history that is now displayed in global museums. Whereas established institutions, such as the Louvre or the Met, have insisted on secluded arrangements of objects and structures, new spaces in the Middle East and North Africa (MENA) still produce anthological representations of regional, national, and local histories, or simply copy the western standard whenever they present a global perspective, often with a vernacular touch oriented towards the specificities of the country in which they are located. Museology in the MENA region has a unique opportunity today: to lead a revolution in art display. Collections can now be reflectors of the Islamic Arts found in the places where they were originally produced, thus providing a broader scope of circulation, transfer, and mutation that puts into perspective classical arrangements, fosters a transversal reading of history, and breaks the traditional vertical structure of knowledge that has represented them as peripheral curiosities.

Cutting-edge exhibition discourses will be those that negotiate the object and the subject, the artefact and the public, the inside and the outside of the museum walls. The heritage piece of art, with its immutable historical value, will be required to engage more and more with the societal metamorphosis of the areas where they are exhibited, refusing to serve representations of nationalist pride. Ultimately, museums should act as beacons of the time and the cultures they narrate, pushing towards a revision of concepts that would irreversibly foster a common path between the reality of the globalization of cities' built environment and their cultural museology institutions. Aligning contemporary exteriors of new museums with coherent, progressive presentations in galleries would definitely better suit the cosmopolitan momentum of our time.

Notes

This chapter was previously published as Jorge Correia, 'Displaying Islamic Arts in Global Cities', *International Journal of Islamic Architecture* 10.1 (2021): 137–46. The text has been updated for this publication.

1. Hasan-Uddin Khan, 'Editorial: Towards a New Paradigm for the Architecture and Arts of Islam', *International Journal of Islamic Architecture* 1.1 (2012): 5–22.
2. Hasan-Uddin Khan, 'Editorial: Identity, Globalization and the Contemporary Islamic City', *International Journal of Islamic Architecture* 1.2 (2012): 211.
3. Having recently celebrated its 30th anniversary, the Erasmus Program (EuRopean Community Action Scheme for the Mobility of University Students) is a European Union student exchange

program established in 1987. Mobility between Europe and North Africa or the Middle East has been particularly framed within specific programs such as Erasmus Mundus or Erasmus Plus. The latter is the new program combining all the EU's current schemes for education, training, youth, and sport, and was started in January 2014.

4   Gustave Flaubert, *Dictionnaire des idées reçues* (Paris: Conard, 1913, repr., Éditions du Boucher, 2002), 70.
5   Mark Crinson, 'The Mosque and the Metropolis', in *Orientalism's Interlocutors: Painting, Architecture, Photography*, ed. Jill Beaulieu and Mary Roberts (Durham, NC: Duke University Press, 2002), 80–81.
6   Edward Said, *Orientalism* (New York: Pantheon Books, 1978).
7   See Albert Hourani and Samuel Miklos Stern, eds, *The Islamic City: A Colloquium [held at All Souls College, June 28–July 2, 1965]* (Oxford: Cassirer, 1970); R.B. Serjeant, ed., *The Islamic City, Selected Papers from the Colloquium Held at the Middle East Center, Faculty of Oriental Studies, Cambridge, United Kingdom, 19–23 July 1976* (Paris: UNESCO, 1980); Ismail Serageldin, Samir El-Sadek, and Richard Herbert, eds, *The Arab City: Its Character and Islamic Cultural Heritage, Proceedings of a Symposium Held in Medina, Kingdom of Saudi Arabia, 24–29 Rabi II, 1401 AH, 28 Feb.–5 Mar., 1981 AD* (Arlington: I. Serageldin, 1982). Besim S. Hakim, *Arabic-Islamic Cities: Building and Planning Principles* (London: KPI, 1986) established the groundbreaking systematization of the knowledge so far, seeking the derivation of the urban structure of cities, still generically defined as 'Islamic', in Islamic law. Though potentially contested today, including in André Raymond's *The Great Arab Cities in the 16th to 18th Centuries* (New York: New York University Press, 1984), Hakim created the cornerstone of urban studies on the subject. For further survey of later works, see Murat Cetin, 'Contrasting Perspectives on the Arab City', *Urban Morphology* 15.1 (2011): 79–84.
8   Such was the case of the symposium 'Architecture and Representation: The Arab City' organized at Columbia University in 2014, and the subsequent edited volume. See Amale Andraos and Nora Akawi, eds, *The Arab City: Architecture and Representation* (New York: Columbia Books on Architecture and the City, 2016).
9   This term was coined in Marshall Hodgson, *Venture of Islam*, vol. 1 (Chicago: University Chicago Press, 1974), 59, in reference to 'the social and cultural complex historically associated with Islam and the Muslims, both among Muslims themselves and even when found among non-Muslims'.
10 On this, see Noha Nasser, 'Cairo Ville Crée en Islam? A Reinterpretation of an Islamicate Urban Paradigm', in *The Planned City? ISUF International Conference*, vol. II (Bari: Union Corcelli Editrice, 2003), 566–72.
11 See 'Installing Islamic Art: Interior Space and Temporary Imagination', special issue, *International Journal of Islamic Architecture* 7.2 (2018).
12 As an example, at the Calouste Gulbenkian Foundation in Lisbon, there were two temporary exhibitions dedicated to or regarding this theme very recently: 'Art and Architecture between Lisbon and Baghdad: The Calouste Gulbenkian Foundation in Iraq, 1957–1973' (October 20, 2017 through January 29, 2018) and 'The Rise of Islamic Art 1869–1939' (July 12 through October 7, 2019).

13. 'The Met Collection', Metropolitan Museum of Art, accessed April 28, 2020, https://www.metmuseum.org/art/collection.
14. On this topic, see Nancy Demerdash, 'Serving Harmony: The Arts de l'Islam at the Musée du Louvre', *International Journal of Islamic Architecture* 2.1 (2013): 228–32.
15. There are several versions of the tree that were published. For one example, see Banister Fletcher, *A History of Architecture on the Comparative Method* (London: B.T. Batsford, 1905).
16. Nasser Rabat explores these notions in '"Islamic Architecture" and the Profession', *International Journal of Islamic Architecture* 3.1 (2014): 37–40. This essay is reproduced in the present volume.
17. 'Neo-colonialism' was first coined by Jean-Paul Sartre in 1956. It is further developed in Jean-Paul Sartre, *Situations V. Colonialisme et Néo-colonialisme* (Paris: Gallimard, 1964).

Chapter 18

Curating the 'Islamic': The Personal and the Political

Leslee Katrina Michelsen

Few scholars of the Islamicate world probably imagine themselves relocating to Honolulu for work. Since 2017, when I took up my current post and repositioned myself within a pan-Pacific framework both physically and mentally, the ebbs and flows of curating the arts of the Islamic world have continued to increase, as they have substantially, and globally, over the past ten years [Figure 18.1]. Yet this changed geographic viewpoint has provided a welcomed repositioning that has informed my current insights into museums, exhibitions, collections, and the shifting roles that they play in education – not only of my peers, but also of the general public. Within the context of the present volume, it seems reductive to note that a sea-change has occurred in the field of curating the arts of the Islamic world since 2001.[1] A truly staggering number of new museums, art fairs, and digital platforms has mushroomed.[2] Substantial rehangs of historic collections and spaces seem to open annually; curatorial training programmes and residencies have grown exponentially; and the enormous sums of money underwriting all of the above are also coursing through auction houses and commercial art galleries whose expanded footprints eagerly embrace the 'Islamic' [Figure 18.2].

How, then, to edit from the 'global' and the 'inter/trans' into a more manageable dialogue, to share something of substance within the confines of the present brief essay? Within the scope of this work, I have chosen to fixate on the hyper-local and the very personal: my own experiences in curating the arts of the Islamic world over the past fifteen years. This retrospective includes spaces – physical and digital – ranging from a historic caravanserai to international museums, from a former private home to Instagram, and how this curatorial practice, writ very small, might factor in to, comment on, and reflect the larger shifts in both contemporary curatorial practice and perspective. To me, whether of exhibitions or of installations, curating is inherently about narratives. These, in turn, are shaped most clearly by geographies. For this commentary, I have arranged my wide-ranging thoughts on museums and curation into an exploration of *spaces*, i.e., the past, present, and future spaces of exhibitions of 'Islamic' art and the related reverberations in ambition, reach, ways of knowing, and praxis. It is of the utmost importance to me that curating is also seen and discussed as an action that bends toward tangible and communal outputs – not as a thought exercise, or the preciousness of exclusive and excluding prestige, but as a community action whose spaces are shared and public in both ethos and physicality. Taking over a space, holding space, sharing space, inviting others into a space, giving space, making space: all are ways of connecting curatorially with communities and, I would argue, impose an ethical responsibility on the part of those of us privileged to care for collections and artworks.

Figure 18.1: The Shangri La Museum of Islamic Art, Culture & Design in Honolulu, Hawaiʻi – a programme of the Doris Duke Foundation for Islamic Art. Source: David Franzen, Doris Duke Foundation for Islamic Art.

Figure 18.2: Anne Samat, *Varada*, *The Goddess of Love*, and *Abhaya* (left to right), 2017, yarns, PVC, paper, and plastic. These works were exhibited here at India Art Fair in 2018. This fair, held annually since 2008, is the largest showcase of modern and contemporary art from greater South Asia. Source: Richard Koh Fine Art.

The Hyper-local and the Personal

Trained and educated in the United States and France, but having worked for most of my life in Muslim-majority nations including Afghanistan, Turkmenistan, Turkey, and Qatar, my perspective on curation has been deeply shaped by circumstance and opportunity as much as by theory and methodology. My first brief forays into curation happened within institutional frameworks including a co-curated exhibition with my fellow graduate students in a formal exhibition space within the Rare Book Library at the University of Pennsylvania and in public gallery spaces at the Philadelphia Museum of Art. These 'traditional' spaces of curation followed a process and format that have varied little since the days of the *Wunderkammer* (cabinet of curiosities): a lengthy period of object-based research, specialist writing and editing, and preservation-based displays, which largely reached audiences both self-selected and extant. From this pleasant but rather placid training ground, my next curatorial opportunities took place in an art school in Kabul: suddenly the works were contemporary, the artists vocal and engaged, the exhibition spaces challenging and non-hushed, and the audiences spirited and opinionated. Curatorial choices were debated, inclusion and exclusion of submitted artworks were critiqued, and the hanging was accomplished with the materials at hand. I found myself for the first time enmeshed and encircled by communities and audiences of makers deeply knowledgeable of the subject material, assertive of their own opinion, and completely undistracted by shifts in light levels or unconventional wall colours: it was the content, and not the exhibition atmosphere or parameters, that was key. I had been an art historian, but there I was understanding what it meant to be a curator.

After Kabul, I spent a few years teaching at an art school in Paris. I enthusiastically participated in critiques, guerrilla exhibitions with communities of artists from refugee and immigrant backgrounds in garages and abandoned spaces, and the heady whirl of *nuits blanches* when the entire city seemed to be pulsing to the beat of hundreds of exhibitions of arts of all media. I aim not to indulge my own reminiscing, but to present this as part of my training, which continues to inform my curatorial practice. It was only when I began to spend significant time with artists and makers who rejected the notion of the museum-as-institution that I could begin to see its flaws, as well as its possibilities. I needed to leave, to be external, before I could return. Certainly many of my peers were surely more critical and already aware of these issues during my graduate training, but I was not – and more importantly, I did not know that I was not. Art for me had been subsumed within a more general academic classification, parsed without the aid of social engagement or advocacy. I am personally convinced that curation remains one of the trades in which apprenticeship is absolutely key. Furthermore, that apprenticeship without a thorough grounding in theory, languages, or other research tools that formal training provides, is ultimately inadequate.

Context and Contextualization

Regardless of the path(s) a curator of Islamic art follows, it should come as no surprise that the very sobering sociopolitical realities of the twenty-first century offer up significant challenges for, with, and in regard to the greater Middle East/North Africa/South and South East Asia (MENAS/EA) region. These countries, cities, monuments, artworks, and artists may be familiar to our audiences on one level, entering our living rooms and pockets through myriad media and devices, and yet they are the subjects of erroneous public assumptions due to perceived differences in cultures, histories, and indeed shared experiences and understandings. There are also thorny issues intimately connected with complicated questions about heritage and identity, especially as filtered through the lens of the political and social upheaval of the twentieth and twenty-first centuries. How best do we address these complex issues in a museum setting? What are our goals and motivations as curators and as educators?

Shedding light on these issues is one of the positive achievements of the field of Islamic art curation in the past ten years. Rejecting and explaining the limits of the imperfect label 'Islamic' art either directly or indirectly – and embracing the rich heterogeneity of cultures, languages, religions, and peoples whose myriad art forms emerge from communities of direct/diasporic/ descendant artists from the MENAS/EA regions – is a crucial part of sharing multiple narratives with our audiences and of refocusing the cultural discussion away from one based solely on faith.[3] Communicating these complex issues to the visitors to our museums can be challenging, especially within the traditional confines of a 150-word label. Nor does cultural or religious context provide much cover; in Qatar I was frequently asked by a wide variety of multi-national residents and visitors why we did not host more religiously themed exhibitions at the Museum of Islamic Art or require female visitors to cover their heads. In Honolulu I commonly encounter variants on the exclamation by many visitors that it is 'bizarre' to have a collection of Islamic art in Polynesia. Quite frankly, curators do not always help advance more complex and thought-provoking conversations about the cultures whose artworks are represented in our spaces. Ruminating on reductive and quasi-universalist themes such as 'light' or the meditative effects of tessellations without a larger, robust conversation contextualizing these themes can do much harm. Acknowledging that twenty-first-century Detroit and Sydney are just as much a part of the Islamic world as seventeenth-century Istanbul and tenth-century Baghdad – and that the former two might have much more in common with twenty-first-century Cairo or Jakarta than the middle examples – is not always a comfortable conversation for some curators who prefer not to engage with contemporary sociopolitics.

Yet however much I might wish to concentrate solely on my research areas, to disappear into the wondrous worlds of medieval Samarkand or the contemporary streets of Beirut, the simple fact is that, as a museum curator, my job is to balance my academic work with engaging and expanding public audiences. I not only provide specialized knowledge on objects, but I also work to interpret them for and with a general audience, composed of a wide variety of learners. I want to excite and engage visitors to look closely, think deeply, and engage personally with the artworks. The days of a curator being a narrowly focused specialist toiling alone in a dusty storage room are – mostly – over. A large portion of my work consists of communicating and collaborating with the public, and that really means everyone. An argument can be made that disappearing into the world of Ottoman botanical manuscripts *without also engaging with* the contemporary ramifications of such knowledge production and cultural capital, is essentially not serving the ethical requirements of a curator at a public institution.

Institutions and Exhibitions

It seems ironic to write a commentary on curation while discussing institutions when so much of current practice is very firmly – and deliberately – ex-institutional. Few museums have the staff, budget, or support to mount large-scale exhibitions of the visual and material cultures of the Islamic world on a regular basis, even when they can and do achieve the targeted visitor numbers that vaunt such an event into 'blockbuster' status.[4] Most departments of Islamic art, or, as it seems increasingly common, South Asian and Islamic art, are staffed by one curator and, perhaps, an assistant. Dedicating the resources of such limited staff to the multi-year investment of time and money that traditional exhibitions require is a serious investment on the part of a museum. In making such commitments, the museum must also take into careful consideration resources that divert from other areas of curatorial work, such as collections research, acquisitions, and donor cultivation. The exceptions – both in larger encyclopaedic collections, such as the British Museum or the Metropolitan Museum of Art, as well as in museums dedicated to the field, such as Mathaf, the Barjeel Foundation, the Aga Khan Museum, or the Museums of Islamic Art in Berlin/Cairo/Doha/Malaysia – frequently provide, therefore, the bulk of the larger exhibitions. These can be permanent galleries or temporary exhibitions, and they can focus on historic materials or on contemporary works, or some combination of the two.

In many ways, this is simply the zeitgeist in regard to exhibitions from historic and modern periods in competition – and I use this term deliberately – with those focused on the contemporary. Few members of the public are probably aware of the extent of investment of time, people, and money that exhibitions require, or of the chorus of voices who have input and decision-making power along each step of the multi-year process. While a resulting exhibition is an opportunity to connect deeply with multiple publics, to give space for a variety of narratives, and to share the object biographies of artworks – from materials science, to provenance, to makers – it must also contribute to the bottom line of the institution, either through ticket sales (rarely) or, more likely, through the petitioning for and receiving of grants, some of which may come from problematic sponsors.[5] My own curatorial practice has been free from donor cultivation, with my current and former workplaces funded by foundations of one form or another. I know that my position is privileged, and I am pragmatic enough to understand that a museum must have funds to keep the lights on and the doors open. For many curators, however, there are concessions or choices, sometimes painful, to make.

In Sheila R. Canby's excellent article on this subject, she discusses the multi-layered outreach and learning programmes initiated by the Metropolitan Museum of Art – from pop-up lectures on sociopolitics to music-making in the galleries – some of which were so successful that they needed to be discontinued.[6] The dynamic among curators, collections, and programmes, as well as the training programmes for such interactions, depends heavily, if not entirely, on museum administrative support. The topicality, if such a term can embrace fully the realities of the late twentieth and early twenty-first century, of the arts of the Islamic world has made the roles of education and access in collections and/or museums even more impactful.

Additional Platforms

Yet another positive development in the past decade is the proliferation of digital platforms and 'alternative' exhibition spaces – from the street to the art fair – where exhibitions of art from the Islamic worlds, past and present, can be shared with a different scale of cost as well as, frequently, different or at least expanded audiences from the traditional museum space. This is also a space in which the artist can sidestep the traditional curator or the institution, and connect directly with the public. Perhaps most evident in the long tradition of street artists, it can also be born of necessity, such as artists creating work in response to social upheaval. Artists reach wide audiences through social media platforms and create graphics that draw attention to the creative dissent coursing through the region. Often the art is executed at sites that have been the focus of cultural destruction, in an effort to highlight, to acknowledge, and to reclaim. Spaces of exhibition can be forms of resistance; codes of conduct in galleries and museums can be avoided by non-traditional spaces, and hierarchies of architecture can be subverted to reach new audiences. Within the art fair/biennial spaces, curators must make art accessible and communal to the shared experience of the event, which is participatory by design.

Increased opportunities often arrive along with increased scrutiny. I am not sure how many curators were completely comfortable with perhaps the largest-scale pop culture reference of contemporary curation being the famous museum scene from the film *Black Panther*.[7] Unflattering it may have been, but I do not think it can be accused of dishonesty – aside, perhaps, from the coffee drinking in the gallery. The scene speaks to a moment in contemporary culture in which museums – long perceived as either neutral or positive – are increasingly scrutinized. Alternative tours, museum hacks, vocal critiques of curatorial hires, and a public increasingly concerned with museum funding have created a situation that is fraught, but also rich with possibility. What I sense most clearly is a demand for *urgency*, which I both admire and support. Museums matter. Our audiences care about how we exhibit and interpret art. I see this as a rich time for increased collaboration and communication with the multiple publics with whom a museum must and should engage. When museums get this right, it resonates. The rehang of MoMA, and its increased attention on global pluralism and a rethought canon, has been well received.[8] The Block Museum's recent exhibition *Caravans of Gold, Fragments in Time: Art, Culture, and Exchange across Medieval Saharan Africa*, centred on a dramatic historic recalibration of the past through the reinterpretation of artefacts and artworks from the African continent, was a stunning achievement. As Seph Rodney noted in *Hyperallergic*, it 'pulled us all back from the precipice of amnesia'.[9] When curators are able to communicate clearly and participate with their communities in the preservation, elevation, and amplification of the works they care for, museums thrive.

Conclusion

Curation is often about letting others speak, be they objects or people. If museums of the twenty-first century are spaces of public engagement, then they must also be advocates of social justice and platforms for fairer representation as well as exhibitions of the contemporary conversations swirling around arts and cultures. It is important that curators see these issues as crucial and not dismiss them as trendy. Islamic art in particular is deeply tied to questions of identify and heritage, of inclusion and representation, and of social transformation. It is a microcosm of the global. It demands not only connection and heterogeneity but also transparency, including transparency about what this label means and how it is shared and with whom.

Like many curators of Islamic art, I work in an institution established on colonized land and founded by a patron who collected according to the legal and ethical mores of her time [Figure 18.3].[10] The work that my colleagues and I are undertaking in Honolulu – to reassert the global connections of Islamic art, to support our diverse learning communities, and to amplify artists from a wide spectrum of backgrounds – is a small step toward acknowledging the changing global landscape and our roles within it. I can think of no discipline that is more intimately tied to these challenges, nor one that has more opportunities because of it, than those of us who curate Islamic art. The past decade has been transformative, and so must the next decade be.

Figure 18.3: Bahia Shehab, *My People*, 2018, acrylic and latex on wood. This two-part mural at the Shangri La Museum of Islamic Art, Culture & Design, represents a verse from a work by Palestinian poet, Mahmoud Darwish (1941–2008). A poem originally written in Arabic, Shehab has interpreted the title and content of the text as a challenge to power – 'The 'Red Indian's' Penultimate Speech to the White Man' (1992) – and selected this evocative phrase for her piece: 'My people will return as air and light and water'. The mural uses an artist-created script that has both pixelated and added figurative roots to tenth-century floriated Kufic calligraphy to make a site-specific commentary about colonization, displacement, and loss of land, people, and identity. Source: David Franzen, Doris Duke Foundation for Islamic Art.

Notes

This chapter was previously published as Leslee Katrina Michelsen, 'Curating the "Islamic": The Personal and the Political', *International Journal of Islamic Architecture* 10.1 (2021): 127–36. The text has been updated for this publication.

1. A recent issue of *IJIA* devoted to curating the arts of the Islamic world provides a number of topical explorations on this point. See *International Journal of Islamic Architecture* 7.2 (2018).
2. In the museum sector, galleries of Islamic art – once frequently relegated to a single cramped gallery in the back – are being revamped at a truly astonishing rate. In the past ten years alone, the Metropolitan Museum of Art, the Musée du Louvre, the British Museum, and the David Collection have unveiled their new, larger, and grander Islamic art galleries, and the V&A, Museum fur Islamisches Kunst, and the Freer/Sackler Gallery, are at varying stages of redoing their own such galleries. In addition, the Aga Khan Museum opened in Toronto in 2014, while the countries in the Persian Gulf seem to be in an expensive 'arts race', with the Museum of Islamic Art in Doha opening in Qatar in 2007, and the Louvre Abu Dhabi in 2017. Museums that have had collections of Islamic art, but no Islamic art curators, have also been adding them, with at least six new positions in the past decade. Biennials and art fairs include over 30 from the MENAS/EA region. See 'Directory of Biennials', Biennial Foundation, accessed February 1, 2020, https://www.biennialfoundation.org/home/biennial-map/.
3. While we in the field understand the lengthy and deep discussions about the term 'Islamic' art, this is frequently very new for museum audiences who conflate the term – if they are aware of it at all – with the practice of the faith of Islam. This is of course an important part of the discipline and its corresponding artworks, no doubt, but one which does not consider the much greater heterogeneity implicit in the label and representative in the breadth of artworks from the myriad cultures and faiths we explore.
4. One such example was the splendid *The Art of the Qur'an: Treasures from the Museum of Turkish and Islamic Arts* exhibition at the Freer/Sackler Gallery in 2016.
5. See, for example, Martin Bailey, 'How Ethical Can Museums Afford to Be?', *The Art Newspaper*, September 3, 2019, https://www.theartnewspaper.com/news/how-ethical-can-uk-museums-afford-to-be.
6. Sheila R. Canby, 'Can Museums Educate the Public about Islamic Art?', *International Journal of Islamic Architecture* 9.1 (2020): 21–28. This essay is reproduced in the present volume.
7. For a brief overview, see Mary Carole McCauley, '"Black Panther" Raises Difficult Questions in Museum Community', *The Baltimore Sun*, March 2, 2018, http://www.baltimoresun.com/entertainment/movies/bs-fe-black-panther-museums-20180227-story.html.
8. See, for example, Holland Cotter, 'MoMA Reboots With "Modernism Plus"', *New York Times*, October 10, 2019, http://www.nytimes.com/2019/10/10/arts/design/moma-rehang-review-art.html.
9. Seph Rodney, 'In Centering West Africa, an Exhibition Tells Another Story of the Medieval Period', *Hyperallergic*, March 15, 2019, https://hyperallergic.com/488133/caravans-of-gold-fragments-in-time-art-culture-and-exchange-across-medieval-saharan-africa/.
10. Bahia Shehab, *My People*, 2019. This artwork, in the entrance courtyard at the Shangri La Museum of Islamic Art, Culture & Design in Honolulu, is a site-specific commentary on

colonized land. Taking a quotation from Mahmoud Darwish's poem 'The "Red Indian's" Penultimate Speech to the White Man', Shehab has created a pixelated and rooted foliated Kufic script that reads 'My people will return, as air, and light, and water'. *My People* speaks to how Shangri La is the intersection of cultural aesthetics and a place to explore political concerns across indigenous contexts. Shehab's inventive and energetic interpretation of Arabic epigraphy richly illustrates the ways that art can be a space for marginalized voices.

Chapter 19

Islamic Architecture on the Move: Publishing Architectural History in the Digital Age

Nancy Micklewright

Architecture is an art form that is meant to be experienced in three dimensions, to surround the body, to confound or satisfy expectations as the space unfolds, sometimes to dazzle the eye with colour and pattern, to manipulate a view, or to introduce sound. Over the centuries, sophisticated two-dimensional conventions have been developed to represent three dimensional structures, but no matter how detailed and accomplished floor plans, elevations, and renderings may be, they do only a fair job at best of conveying the spatial and sensory identity of a building.

With the advent of photography, an additional imaging mode came into play for representing architecture. Still two dimensional, photography was nonetheless immediately hailed as ground-breaking in the documentation of ruins and great monuments, and indeed the early history of photography includes a diverse array of architectural images, from those depicting major monuments to images of more quotidian structures [Figure 19.1]. Photography is a complex medium: apart from the obvious issues around indexicality, the relationship between photography and architecture, the purpose, circulation, and consumption of images of buildings, the way in which depictions of the same site change over time depending on context, photographer, and a host of other factors have been the subject of a rich scholarly genre over the past decades.[1] Notwithstanding their interpretive challenges, photographs and related formats such as panoramas, first in black and white and then in colour, became a standard way of documenting and studying architecture.

Early Forays into Digital Publishing: *JSAH* and *AO*

The emergence of digital imaging in the 1990s, beginning with digital photography and quickly moving to a multitude of new imaging tools (three-dimensional or 3D images, 360° views, animations, video, sophisticated GPS mapping, photogrammetry, etc.), would seem to have ushered in more effective ways of experiencing the spatial characteristics of architecture from a distance. Yet scholars in the field of architectural history, including those working in the history of architecture in the Islamic world, have been slow to adopt these digital imaging modes in publishing their research. Here I explore how digital platforms and digital research methods[2] have been used in the production and creation of research in the area of Islamic architecture,[3] beginning with scholarly journals.[4]

In 2005–06 Mariët Westermann and the late Hilary Ballon completed a white paper entitled 'Art History and Its Publications in the Electronic Age', considering the current state

Figure 19.1: Felix Bonfils, *Damascus Fountain*, c.1850. Albumen print. 28.5 x 22.9 cm. Source: Freer Gallery of Art and Arthur M. Sackler Gallery Archives FSA A2017.07.

of electronic (digital) publications in the field of art history and the potential for moving the field forward.[5] This was shortly followed by a three-day convening at the University of Virginia that looked in depth at what would be involved in adding digital options to the existing roster of art history publications. Bringing together scholars, publishers, librarians, technology experts, and others for detailed conversations, the Scholarly Communication Institute published a report of its findings later in 2006. One key result of this convening was the decision on the part of the Society of Architectural Historians (SAH) to develop a digital component of its *Journal of the Society of Architectural Historians* (*JSAH*). The *JSAH Online* became the first 'print plus multimedia' journal with its publication in 2010.[6] Funded by grants from the Andrew W. Mellon Foundation (which also funded the Westermann and Ballon white paper and the Scholarly Communication Institute) and the National Endowment for the Humanities, the development of *JSAH Online* was a complex endeavour that involved user group interviews to identify desirable features, the selection of a publishing partner, the creation of a new publishing platform, completely new software to create the journal, and a new business model for the SAH. It was a nearly full-time endeavour over the course of an entire year for a team of scholars, SAH staff, software developers, publishers, and others.[7]

The online version of the journal, which shared the same design as the print version, was intended to include zoomable colour images, 3D models, video, sound, panoramas, and links to Google Earth maps. Additionally, a new feature of the journal, Multimedia Reviews, was added. The first issue launched in March 2010, and included a study of the 1559 panorama of Istanbul by Melchior Lorichs, entitled 'Constructing Melchior Lorichs's Panorama of Constantinople'.[8] The article included three panoramas: Lorichs's 1559 image, a photographic panorama by the Istanbul photographic firm of Sebah and Joaillier, circa 1880, and a 2009 photographic panorama by one of the authors [Figure 19.2]. All three were zoomable. The presentation of the Lorichs panorama, comprised of 21 sheets of paper, involved a time-consuming stitching together of the individual photographs and was an impressive accomplishment for the time.

It proved more difficult than expected to acquire the enhanced illustrations that had been envisioned for the new online journal. Even the transition to colour photographs was not immediate.[9] In order to encourage authors to consider new ways of presenting their work, SAH produced three short instructional videos on how to prepare videos, 3D models, and panoramas for publication in the journal. It also offered subsidies to offset the cost of producing such material.[10] In the time since the launch of *JSAH Online*, apart from the online format itself, which provides access to readers globally, the most enduring features of the online format are zoomable colour photographs and the Multimedia Reviews column. Incorporating more complex digital content has remained challenging.[11]

In 2012, two years after *JSAH Online* appeared, *Ars Orientalis* (*AO*) began experimenting with online content by offering four articles online as a supplement to the printed volume. Volume 42, which appeared in October 2012, presented a selection of papers from the 2010 convening of the Historians of Islamic Art Association (HIAA) online. The digital component comprised three papers from a session entitled 'Cinematic Realism in the Middle East', which included

Islamic Architecture Today and Tomorrow

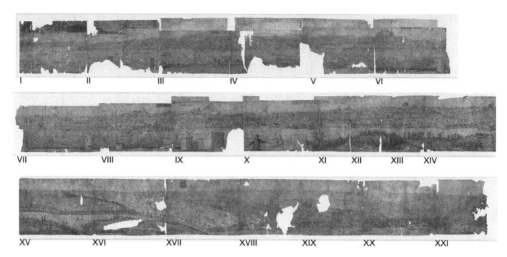

Figure 1 Melchior Lorichs (Lorck), *Panorama of Istanbul, Byzantivm sive Costantineopolis*, 1559; sheets I–XXI. See *JSAH* online for a zoomable image (University of Leiden, the Netherlands)

Figure 2 Sebah and Joaillier, *Panorama de Constantinople, pris de La Tour de Galata*, ca. 1880, detail (Library of Congress, Prints & Photographs Division, Abdul Hamid II Collection, LOT 8931 no. 1 [H size]). See *JSAH* online for a zoomable image of the entire panorama

Figure 3 Istanbul peninsula from top of Galata Tower, 2009 (author). See *JSAH* online for a zoomable color image

Figure 19.2: The Istanbul panoramas as presented in *JSAH*. Source: Nigel Westbrook, Kenneth Rainsbury Dark, and Rene van Meeuwen, 'Constructing Melchior Lorichs's Panorama of Constantinople', *Journal of the Society of Architectural Historians* 69.1 (2010): 63.

video clips, and a study on the Freer Siege Scene plate illustrated with some of the conservation tests that were part of the project. Four years later in 2016 the first fully digital volume of *AO* appeared, together with a re-designed print version. The two were related in terms of design, but not identical, and the digital version included content not available in the print copy: the new Digital Initiatives column and expanded images that took advantage of the digital platform.

In the six years (2010–16) between the first issue of *JSAH Online* and the publication of the digital *AO*, much had changed. While it took a considerable amount of work to make the switch from the traditional print-only *AO* format to print-plus-digital, that work involved identifying new designers, copy editors, printers, a new distribution model, and a new business plan, as well as working with the platform host on design details. The editorial team could choose among multiple online hosts, and there was no need to build new software for the journal. The transition was a relatively seamless one, and one year later in 2017, *AO* moved to an open access/print-on-demand model, with the digital version becoming primary.

The decision to make the switch to a digital-first publication model for *AO* was driven by several different objectives, first among them being a desire to make the content more easily accessible to a global readership. Almost equally important was an interest in expanding the options for authors in terms of presenting their research by providing the capability for enhanced visual materials. There was also a desire to nudge the fields served by the journal in the direction of the digital by reviewing new digital projects or resources and showcasing research that took advantage of digital research tools.

The journal's success in meeting these objectives was mixed, even keeping in mind that at the time of this writing there had only been four digital volumes. There is certainly a more global readership, a trend that is very satisfying. Including enhanced illustrative materials in the journal proved challenging. *AO*'s practice of including high numbers of images continued, and was expanded, with colour, zoomable illustrations now the norm. Videos appeared in a handful of articles that had a more anthropological focus, but it was difficult to move beyond these formats. Volume 46 (2016) featured an animation of a Buddhist pagoda to allow the reader to see how a person would move through the structure, but this is so far the only representation of architecture that goes beyond a flat image, plan, or elevation [Figure 19.3]. The 2020 volume of *AO* included a suite of seven articles all focused on digital technologies in Chinese Buddhist art and architecture – the first time the journal published scholarship that depends on digital tools for the investigation and publication of research questions.

Ten Years Later

Considering the examples of *JSAH Online* and *Ars Orientalis* is instructive when thinking about where we stand with embracing the digital in publishing architectural history. Despite the many advances that have taken place in digital humanities, and digital art history in particular between 2010 and the present, it is still challenging to find authors interested in adding enhanced visual material to their work. Based on informal conversations with publishers and

Animation shows the five sets of icons aligned vertically along the central axis of the structure that can be observed in a continuous sequence as one ascends the pagoda clockwise in circumambulation. SketchUp model built by Zhenru Zhou.

Figure 19.3: Zhenrou Zhou's Pagoda SketchUp model animation that illustrates the alignment of the structure's interiors and its icons, in addition to the path one takes in ascending the tower. Source: Wei-cheng Lin, 'Performing Center in a Vertical Rise: Multilevel Pagodas in China's Middle Period', *Ars Orientalis* 46 (2016), http://dx.doi.org/10.3998/ars.13441 566.0046.005.

colleagues, apart from some journal editors seeking content, there does not seem to be a significant demand for this kind of enhancement on the part of readers. Authors have to decide how best to spend their all-too-limited research time and funds, and must consider whether the investment in time and money to create an animation of a piece of architecture or a video tour of a site will be time better spent than on other more traditional ways of advancing their research and publication records. The research trip usually wins out over the animation. It seems difficult to see how this will change, as long as enhanced visual material is understood as an afterthought to the main work of the research project.

On the other hand, projects that depend on sophisticated digital research tools require a steep investment in digital technology on the part of the scholar and may require publication capabilities that are beyond what many online platforms can offer, apart from venues designed for the purpose. Most often such projects involve teams of scholars working together over several years, requiring coordination of research time and funding streams.

Deciding how best to publish research results is an on-going question, as technology and the publication landscape are constantly changing. In many ways, digitally based research projects are not very different from any other large-scale collaborative research projects in that they require greater financial support, usually have longer timelines, and can be more challenging to publish.

Looking Further Afield for Digital Engagement

Academic journals may not be publishing new digitally based scholarship in Islamic architecture in large numbers, but it would be a mistake to imagine that the field is not engaging with the digital. How, then, are digital tools being deployed in this field? For what audiences are digital outputs being developed and who is using them? Researchers in the field of Islamic architecture have long been able to depend on significant digital resources for their work, most particularly MIT's Archnet and the SAH's SAHARA archive of digital architectural images. Smaller scale projects provide access to particular sets of images, for example the Manar al-Athar project, based at the University of Oxford. Digitized collections of historic and modern photographs at major research institutions around the world are key resources for the study of architecture and urbanism, as are digitized collections of maps and legal documents. The ready availability of digitized research material has changed how scholars carry out their research, but has also given rise to reinvigorated conversations around the definition of the archive and the politically inflected practices of archiving.

The use of digital tools to document architecture in the face of political conflict or environmental disaster and to plan conservation work of historic monuments is much more common than in other areas of architectural history. Photogrammetry and other non-invasive imaging techniques permit highly accurate mapping of building surfaces as a means of documenting current conditions and assessing the need for intervention.[12] Mapping projects such as 'Monuments of Mosul in Danger' allow the documentation of lost buildings for sites that have been caught in the crossfire of political conflict.[13] A particularly impressive project is the Maldives Heritage Survey (led by R. Michael Feener of the Oxford Centre for Islamic Studies), which involves international researchers and a Maldives-based team using digital tools such as laser scanning and GIS (Geographic Information System) to inventory and document the endangered cultural heritage of the Maldives. The open access website includes an extensive database of the sites that have been surveyed, 3D models of some structures, and a host of other information [Figure 19.4].[14]

The Digital in the Classroom

College and university classrooms provide rich sites for engagement with the digital, whether through the use of some of the many resources for the field that have become available

Figure 19.4: Screenshot image of fieldwork underway in an Islamic cemetery by members of the Maldives Heritage Survey team. Source: R. Michael Feener, 'Kōagaṇṇu Cemetery, Hulhumeedhoo', Maldives Heritage Survey, accessed February 26, 2020, https://maldivesheritage.oxcis.ac.uk/index.php/cemetery/.

recently, or by empowering students themselves to create new content.[15] Smart History has a significant amount of content concerning Islamic architecture that uses some video and links to other formats, particularly the Turkish site 3D Mekanlar with 3D views of hundreds of buildings and sites.[16] The Global Architectural History Teaching Collaborative (GAHTC), which now includes more than 200 lectures emphasizing transnational and trans-geographical perspectives in the teaching of architectural history, is an outstanding example of using a digital platform to connect people across time and space and to address a specific teaching need.[17] A particularly innovative example of course design that takes full advantage of digital possibilities is the 2018 collaboration between Stephennie Mulder (University of Texas at Austin), Alex Dika Seggerman (Rutgers University-Newark), and Leslee Michelson (Shangri La Museum of Islamic Art), in which students were assigned to write or update Wikipedia articles on topics in Islamic art and architecture. A semester's worth of collaborative research culminated in a two day Wiki 'edit-a-thon' and the publication of fifteen new or revised articles, about half of which concerned architecture. The project continued in 2019 with 52 students from the University of Texas, Rutgers University-Newark, and Temple University (under the supervision of Emily Neumeier) updating and expanding 40 entries in Wikipedia, approximately half of which focused on architecture.[18]

The 2020–? COVID-19 pandemic continues to wreak havoc on academic life, having forced university education – and indeed most scholarly endeavours – online beginning in

March 2020 and continuing well into 2021. The pandemic has been a global public health disaster with lasting personal, social, and economic impacts, but the unprecedented circumstances have led to significant advances in the use of digital platforms for teaching and scholarly research. Two particularly notable examples in the field of Islamic art and architecture are *Khamseen: Islamic Art History Online* and the 'Virtual Islamic Art History Seminar'. *Khamseen* is spearheaded by Christiane Gruber and a small editorial team, hosted by the University of Michigan with funding support from The Andrew W. Mellon Foundation. The project, which had been in its fledgling stages early in 2020, gained new urgency with the onset of the pandemic and a first collection of teaching resources was launched in the summer of 2020. New content has been added continually. The site hosts short-form multimedia presentations created by scholars across the field 'with the aim of bringing new voices, subjects, and audiences to the field of Islamic art history'.[19] The 'Virtual Islamic Art History Seminar', which launched in May 2020, was established by Mira Xenia Schwerda and Melis Taner, who were later joined by Alexander Brey. Hosted online by Harvard University,

> the virtual seminar series was founded to allow scholars to connect during a time when most of us are physically disconnected. Since then, it has demonstrated a capacity to bring together researchers from around the world, filling a new niche in academic discourse.[20]

It has been an extremely effective way of connecting scholars globally at a time when most were physically isolated, but it has also demonstrated the effectiveness of a new model for sharing research, exploring new parameters in the field, and increasing diversity and access to the field as a whole.

Opening Access

It goes without saying that publishing in the twenty-first century is a fast-paced, constantly changing endeavour. The peer-reviewed scholarly journals that have been the mainstay of academic publishing since the late nineteenth century are no longer the only place where serious scholarship appears. While the efforts of journals like *JSAH* and *AO* to provide both print and digital access for their material are important, today there are many other publishing platforms for architectural history. These include standalone, project-specific websites such as those mentioned above, but also new-born digital peerreviewed publications such as *Nineteenth-Century Art Worldwide* and *British Art Studies*, both of which include the built environment in their remit. The open access peer-reviewed journal of the European Architectural History Network, *Architectural Histories*, began publication in 2013.[21] While the journal is organized into annual volumes (one issue per year), content is published online as soon as the peer review and editing processes are completed, which is a departure from traditional publication practice. Moving further away from the academic journal model, *Places Journal* is a non-profit journal that positions itself at the intersection of scholarship and journalism, presenting content in a range of formats with a focus on contemporary issues in the built environment. Founded in 1983, it went online and open access in 2009, and in 2017 eliminated its peer review process in order to strengthen its commitment to public scholarship.[22]

With the exception of *JSAH*, all of the publications mentioned here are open access. In the past, scholarly journals in art history have been supported through a combination of subscription fees, membership dues, and institutional support, either from a host institution or foundations, or both. This remains the case for the majority of art history journals today. Moving to an open access format requires a different business model that involves a much greater dependence on support from host institutions, in the case of *AO*, *British Art Studies*, *Architectural Histories*, and others, as well as from foundations and individual donors. In some cases, foundations underwrite specific aspects of a journal, as for example the support provided first by the Andrew W. Mellon Foundation and then the Terra Foundation for the digital humanities articles published in *Nineteenth-Century Art Worldwide*.

To a certain extent, scholarly journals in art history are in a different position vis-à-vis the conflicts currently roiling the publishing business in the sciences and some areas in the humanities.[23] The decision to produce an open access journal in art history, at least at the moment, has more to do with the desire to reach a broader and more diverse audience than it does the need to circumvent an economically unsustainable level of subscription cost and author fees. However, some of the same challenges face open access publications in art history as they do in other disciplines. First among these is the perception that open access (and digital) publishing is less rigorously peer reviewed and thus less prestigious than traditional print publishing. This perception, and the accompanying concern that open access and digital publications do not carry the same weight in tenure and promotion review, certainly affects submission rates. While the field has begun addressing this through publication prizes, conference sessions, and other means, the perception remains. Secondly, there is a very real concern about the longevity of online scholarly journals, particularly those published without accompanying print versions. Given the ever-changing nature of web-based interfaces, how can publishers ensure that their content remains accessible? This concern extends across web-based publishing; addressing it requires on-going financial commitment and attention to infrastructure maintenance and storage that is very different from the logistical work involved in print publishing. In the 2012 article 'Towards Digital Islamic Art History', Hussein Keshani provided an insightful and comprehensive assessment of the field's engagement with the digital at that moment. He laid out the significant barriers as well as the advantages of the digital turn, ending with this: 'It is clear that digital humanities is here to stay, along with its ways of knowing about the world, but what is less clear is how the field of Islamic art will adapt to the digital turn'.[24] Nearly a decade later, a certain amount of progress has been made in embracing digital research methods and publication, but certainly the institutional frameworks needed to support the research of digitally minded scholars remain inadequate and many publication platforms are limited in the digital formats that they can display. The on-going expansion of the digital turn in the study of Islamic architecture will rest with our 'digitally born' and trained graduate students and the intrepid established scholars who are engaging with new research methods and tools.

Notes

This chapter was previously published as Nancy Micklewright, 'Islamic Architecture on the Move: Publishing Architectural History in the Digital Age', *International Journal of Islamic Architecture* 10.1 (2021): 147–58. The text has been updated for this publication.

1. For an excellent introduction to the complexity of interpretation of architectural photography, see Claire Zimmerman, 'Reading the (Photographic) Evidence', *Journal of the Society of Architectural Historians* 76 (2017): 446–48.
2. In considering the digital turn in the humanities it is important to make the distinction between digital publishing and digitally based research. While there can certainly be a relationship between the two, they are not the same. Digital publishing allows the incorporation of a variety of imaging formats and interactive features in the presentation of a particular subject, while digitally-based research involves the incorporation of digital research tools such as network analysis or complex mapping into the research design, often allowing new questions to be asked of the project data. For an excellent discussion of the relationship between the two, and the challenges of reconciling them in publication, see Emily Pugh, Elizabeth Buhe, and Petra Chu, '*Nineteenth-Century Art Worldwide*'s "Digital Humanities and Art History": Reflections on Our First Articles', *Nineteenth-Century Art Worldwide* 15.1 (2016), https://www.19thc-artworldwide.org/spring16/pugh-on-digital-humanities-art-history-our-first-articles.
3. There is an extensive literature in defining Islamic art and architecture. For two relatively recent discussions of what constitutes 'Islamic architecture' or how it should be/is defined, see Nasser Rabbat, 'What is Islamic Architecture Anyway?', *Journal of Art Historiography* 6 (2012): 1–15, and Hasan-Uddin Khan, 'Towards a New Paradigm for the Architecture and Arts of Islam', *International Journal of Islamic Architecture* 1 (2012): 5–22.
4. My interest in this topic has been sparked by my experience as editor-in-chief of *Ars Orientalis* from 2010–19, during which time the journal moved to a digital platform and we began seeking innovative digital presentations of our authors' work. I am grateful to the colleagues who responded to my queries about work in progress, field-wide updates, and other insights. Thank you to Renata Holod, Sana Mirza, Emily Neumeier, D. Fairchild Ruggles, Nancy Um, and Ethel Sara Wolper. Despite best efforts, I am sure that I have overlooked exciting projects that deserve mention here, and I apologize for that unintentional oversight.
5. Hilary Ballon and Mariët Westermann, *Art History and Its Publications in the Electronic Age*, 2006, http://cnx.org/content/col10376/1.1/.
6. The development process is described by Pauline Saliga and Ann Whiteside, 'Collaboration at its Best: How Dozens of Digital Humanists Helped a Learned Society Create Three Online Academic Resources in Four Years', *Visual Resources* 2.1–2 (2013): 120–28.
7. I am grateful to David Brownlee, the Frances Shapiro-Weitzenhoffer Professor Emeritus of Nineteenth-Century European Art at the University of Pennsylvania and the *JSAH* editor who oversaw the creation of the online version of the journal, for sharing his recollections of the project with me.

8   Nigel Westbrook, Kenneth Rainsbury Dark, and Rene van Meeuwen, 'Constructing Melchior Lorichs's Panorama of Constantinople', *Journal of the Society of Architectural Historians* 69:1 (2010): 62–87.

9   Correspondence with David Brownlee, November 13, 2019.

10   These videos may still be seen online. See David Brownlee and Chris Cook, 'How to Prepare Videos for JSAH Online', Society of Architectural Historians, http://www.youtube.com/watch?v=2gCNEPcltYc; 'How to Prepare 3D Models for JSAH', Society of Architectural Historians, http://www.youtube.com/watch?v=ge0MdGPE4PA; and 'How to Prepare Panoramic Photographs for JSAH', Society of Architectural Historians, http://vimeo.com/24138383#.

11   Correspondence with Pauline Saliga, Executive Director of the Society of Architectural Historians, February 1, 2020.

12   See for example, Hakan Karabörk, Lütfiye Karasaka, and Esra Yaldız, 'A Case Study: Documentation Method with Close Range Photogrammetry of Muqarnas Which is to be Ornamentation Type Specific to the Islamic Architecture', *Procedia Earth and Planetary Science* 15 (2015): 133–40.

13   'About the Project', Monuments of Mosul in Danger, accessed December 10, 2019, http://www.monumentsofmosul.com/about-the-project-i.

14   'Maldives Heritage Survey', Maldives Heritage Survey, accessed December 15, 2019, https://maldivesheritage.oxcis.ac.uk.

15   Space limitations preclude the discussion of digital applications for the presentation of architecture in museum or onsite settings, but this is a rich area for the incorporation of the digital, with some exciting work already having taken place.

16   'Sites in 3D', 3D Mekanlar, accessed February 25, 2020, http://www.3dmekanlar.com/sites.html.

17   'About GAHTC', Global Art History Teaching Collaborative, accessed December 10, 2019, http://gahtc.org/pages/about-gahtc/.

18   The project is described here in 'Meetup StudentsofIslamicArt', Wikipedia, accessed January 27, 2019, https://en.wikipedia.org/wiki/Wikipedia:Meetup_StudentsofIslamicArt#Articles_with_new_photos.

19   'About', Khamseen, accessed June 14, 2021, https://sites.lsa.umich.edu/khamseen/about/.

20   Email correspondence from Mira Xenia Schwerda to the seminar email list, June 2, 2021.

21   *Architectural Histories*, accessed February 24, 2020, https://journal.eahn.org/.

22   'Our Commitment to Public Scholarship', *Places Journal*, 2017, https://placesjournal.org/our-commitment-to-public-scholarship/.

23   For a concise account of these issues, see Brian Resnick and Julie Belluz, 'The War to Free Science', *Vox*, July 10, 2019, https://www.vox.com/the-highlight/2019/6/3/18271538/open-access-elsevier-california-sci-hub-academic-paywalls.

24   Hussein Keshani, 'Towards Digital Islamic Art History', *Journal of Art Historiography: Islamic Art History* 6 (2012): 1–24.

Chapter 20

Illustrating Islamic Architecture: On Visual Presentation and Scholarship

Lorenz Korn

Any thorough occupation with architectural history, and any publication in the field, comes with illustrations of buildings through photographs, plans, bird's-eye views, and visual reconstructions. The field of Islamic architecture is by no means different. Still, the situation of the Islamic world has shaped architectural publishing in a particular way. This has to do more with the general conditions under which architectural historians have worked and with their personal attitudes than with the nature of the studied buildings. In the present essay, I attempt to assess some of these conditions and to give a short overview of the way in which the visual presentation of Islamic architecture in publications has developed. The essay focuses on Iran and neighbouring regions, in accordance with my own principal field of research, but other regions of the Islamic world will be considered in terms of overarching developments. Obviously, the selection of examples is bound to omit many important cases.

To my knowledge, a history of the way in which Islamic architecture has been depicted – be it in scholarly or other contexts – has not yet been written, and one might speculate about the reasons for this absence. A detailed history of this kind would have to deal with many issues, ranging from orientalist and self-orientalizing viewpoints of illustrators, to the depiction of buildings in a way that highlights features of their aesthetics in an art-historical framework, to a technical documentation for purposes of heritage conservation.[1] Looking at publications on Islamic architecture, it becomes clear that these aspects actually overlap and interfere with each other. In the following, I argue that scrutinizing the different ways in which architecture has been illustrated is worthwhile, and I will indicate some of the dimensions through which this scrutiny could proceed – de-constructing orientalist stereotypes being merely one of the lines of inquiry that is much dwelt upon. I also aim to show that the illustration of Islamic architecture is not in itself a success story with a clear development – from the imperfect to the highest standards – but that varying interests (and capacities) have produced representations (in the broader sense) of varying qualities.

Early Illustrations and Plans

While the history of photography has extensively dealt with orientalist manners of depicting the Islamic world, architectural drawings have hardly been considered in the history of Islamic art history. On-going debates and research on the history of the scholarly field are mostly silent on the ways in which architecture has been documented, presented, and interpreted through its depiction in drawings.[2] As an exception, Eva Troelenberg has analysed publications of the façade of Mshatta in the early twentieth century, postulating that these images reflect on the way in which a history of ornament was created. She relates this use of drawings to that in natural history, as an instrument for categorizing the world, as Bruno Latour has interpreted them.[3] Meanwhile, textbooks on the history of Islamic art use architectural drawings – mostly ground plans – tacitly without addressing their character. This is not surprising, as the illustration of architecture has been part and parcel of scholarly literature on architecture from its beginnings, and the customary depiction of structures includes a ground plan, an exterior main view, and details that are relevant for the discussion. This applies for Islamic architecture as much as for any other field of architectural history, so there seems to be no *a priori* need for discussion. The fact that architectural drawings have been part of the construction and design industry for centuries is also not discussed with regard to the representation of extant buildings in scholarly contexts. While very few premodern architectural drawings have been preserved in the Islamic world, it is clear that they were used (and were sometimes executed in a quite sophisticated way) for the designing of buildings and their decoration, at least from the tenth and eleventh centuries onwards.[4] Yet, these drawings did not play a role in the foundational historiography of Islamic architecture. As a scholarly discipline that developed in Europe, it built upon the visual tradition current among European artists and architects – no matter whether scholars recorded 'Occidental' or 'Oriental' monuments.

The documenting of Islamic architecture began long before art historical scholarship with depictions in travelogues to the lands of the Bible. The quality of the drawings by Konrad Grünemberg (*d*.1494) shows their high potential as sources for the history of Islamic architecture, had they not been so geographically and culturally limited.[5] In a similar way, although not primarily tinted with religious interest, the drawings by Engelbert Kaempfer (1651–1716), Carsten Niebuhr (1733–1815), and the *Description de l'Égypte* (*Description of Egypt*, researched 1798–1801)[6] – just to name three outstanding cases – were apt to give an exact impression of buildings as an integral part of the cultural geography of Islamic lands. 'Exact drawings' in this context should be taken as images that reproduce the visual appearance. It was possible for them to render the situation of buildings in their topographic context, as with Kaempfer's *Planographia*, which served to reconstruct the layout of Safavid Isfahan [Figure 20.1]. They could focus on details such as inscriptions, as can be seen in Niebuhr's drawings. His reproductions of the Persepolis inscriptions, for example, sufficed to enable Georg Friedrich Grotefend's deciphering of Old Persian cuneiform in 1802. The *Description de l'Égypte* combined elevations and ground plans to document buildings of military interest such as fortifications, aqueducts, and bridges, whereas cities and villages were depicted in general views that integrated architecture with picturesque scenes of 'daily life'. Some monuments such as the Nilometer and several major mosques were documented in ground plans or even in sections, as well as in elevations and drawings of architectural details [Figure 20.2].

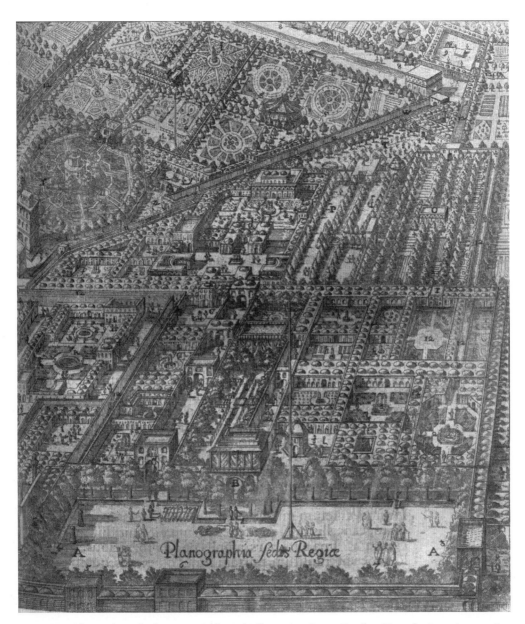

Figure 20.1: The Maydan and palace area in Isfahan in bird's-eye view. Source: Engelbert Kaempfer, *Amoenitates exoticae* (Lemgo: Meyer, 1712), 179. Bibliotheksverbund Bayern.

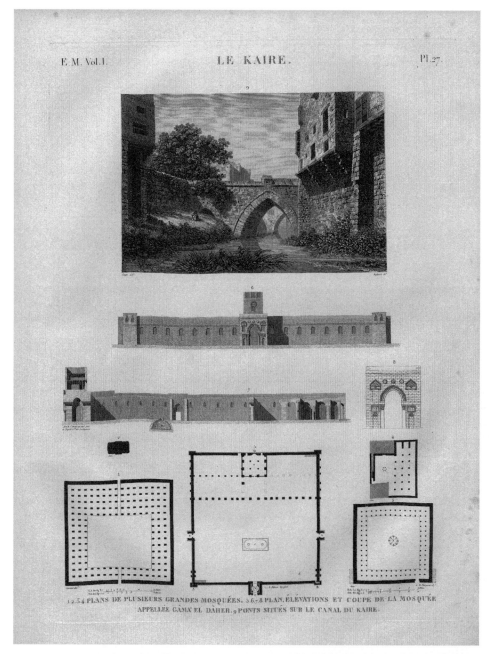

Figure 20.2: View of the canal with bridges in Cairo, and plans of various mosques. Source: Edme François Jomard, ed., *Description de l'Égypte* vol. 4.2.1: *Planches: Etat moderne* 1 (Paris: Imprimerie Impériale, 1809), Plate 27. Heidelberger historische Bestände.

In the plates of the *Description*, a division between romantic views and documentary images can be observed. This distinction increasingly came to characterize representations of the 'Orient' during the following decades. David Roberts's romanticizing images from Egypt and the Holy Land depict many Islamic monuments in a manner that appears convincing, or even 'correct', from an architectural point of view – however without interest in their historical value, their technique of construction, or their decoration. They appear as part of a larger visual experience of the 'Orient'.[7] As a contrast, architectural drawings and photographs published from the 1880s onwards in the *Exercices* of the Comité de conservation des monuments de l'art arabe (Committee for the Conservation of Arab Art Monuments) were intended to document buildings as objects of historical inquiry and of conservatory efforts. The documentary approach, driven by art historical interest, found its preliminary climax in the publications of K. A. C. Creswell (1879–1974) on Islamic architecture, with their particular focus on Egypt.[8] Creswell's writing draws attention to the properties of each building and thus values it as a work of architecture in its historical and aesthetic dimensions. Creswell illustrated his meticulous descriptions of monuments not only with photographs and plans, but also with some information such as the measures of diagonals between corners of a courtyard – which appear in the plans – enabling the viewer to partly retrace the process of documenting.

For Iran, an approach comparable to that of the *Description de l'Égypte* can be recognized, one generation later, in the works of Eugène Flandin and Pascal Coste.[9] While Flandin's drawings were obviously intended to give a picturesque impression of landscapes, urban scenery, and buildings, Coste was more interested in architectural documentation. His drawings are considered sufficiently true to serve as archaeological evidence. For example, the plate depicting a tomb tower at Rayy has been taken as a basis for reconstructing the text of its Arabic inscription, for which no other documents exist.[10] Coste himself did not shy away from reconstruction drawings, for example in the case of the 'Blue Mosque' of Tabriz, which he depicted in a general view in its dilapidated state and in plans. In the ground plan, extant parts and conjectured walls can be discerned, and the elevation of the ruined north façade is supplemented with a reconstruction. Coste's drawings vary in their degree of truthfulness. The ground plan of the Great (Friday) Mosque of Isfahan that was published in his *Monuments modernes de la Perse mesurés, dessinés et décrits* (*Modern Monuments of Persia Measured, Drawn and Described*, 1867) was certainly not very exactly measured, as all parts appear in a rectangular layout. It does, however, differentiate faithfully between varying shapes of pillars and widths of aisles. In his documentation of some other Islamic monuments, he went further. The Masjid-i Shah and Madrasa-i Shah Sultan Husayn in Isfahan are represented not only with ground plans but also in sections [Figure 20.3]. In a similar manner, Jane Dieulafoy published the Mausoleum of Öljeitü in Sultaniya and analysed the proportions of the building, however some dimensions were not directly measured, thus rendering the plans somewhat deficient.[11] These plans and sections by Coste and Dieulafoy were also reproduced in the surveys of Islamic architecture published by Henri Saladin (1907) and Ernst Diez (1915).[12]

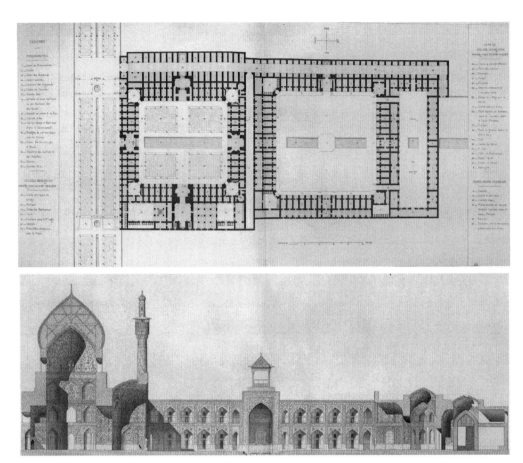

Figure 20.3: The Madrasa of Shah Sultan Husayn at Isfahan. Ground plan (top). North-south section looking west (bottom). Source: Pascal Coste, *Monuments modernes de la Perse* (Paris: Morel, 1867), Plates 19, 20, 30, and 31. Wikimedia Commons.

Towards an Ever More Reliable Documentation?

In principle, the documentation of Islamic architecture went along similar lines as that of other historical monuments, as it developed in the contact zone between archaeologists and architects. The beginning of the heritage conservation movement played an important part for the study of historical forms and constructions, with drawings as an indispensable corollary. Karl Friedrich Schinkel's journey to the Marienburg in 1817 and the publication of John Ruskin's *Stones of Venice* in 1851 can be cited as two milestones among many. Combined descriptions in word and image, essential for the research on individual buildings, appear also in the first coherent histories of architecture, such as Franz Kugler's *Geschichte der Baukunst* (*History of Architecture*, 1856–73).[13] The same academic methods that were used for objectifying the historical monuments of Europe were applied to Islamic architecture in the Middle East and North Africa. In these terms, it seems misguided to discredit plans and images as instruments of 'Orientalist' and 'colonial' appropriation. In the age of historicism, the same instruments were common for an appropriation of the European past. It should be noted, however, that travellers who published material on architecture in the Middle East and North Africa divided their energies unevenly, usually spending more efforts on monuments of pre-Islamic periods. Thus, the Byzantine masterpiece of the Hagia Sophia had been subject to a measured documentation by Wilhelm Salzenberg during the restoration works by the Fossati brothers at the mid-nineteenth century, while the classical Ottoman mosques of the fifteenth through eighteenth centuries had to wait until 1912, when they were published in a large volume by Cornelius Gurlitt.[14] Also, the documentation of Islamic architecture was frequently intermingled with texts containing ethnological description of manners and customs until the early twentieth century – a fact that certainly taints the context of perception, even if it detracts little from the character of the drawings themselves.[15]

In theory, it should be possible to write the history of documentation of Islamic architecture as a progressive development toward ever-more complete documentation and increasingly exact measuring and drawing. Reality, however, yields a very uneven picture. High standards of measuring and drawing that had been attained were difficult to keep under the circumstances of restricted research permits and short-term travels by non-resident scholars. Chaotic organization of public and private archives, with changing responsibilities and interests, contributed to the difficulty of building on previous works of research, as these were (and still are) frequently not accessible.

Thus, it is not surprising that some works of comparatively early date stand out in their exact manner of documentation. Friedrich Sarre, in his volume on the architecture of Iran that mirrors the situation at the turn of the nineteenth century, included some drawings by Eduard Jacobsthal that illustrate the mausolea of Mu'mina Khatun and of Yusuf ibn Kuthayr in Nakhchivan.[16] These images not only give elevations of the façades rendering the minute details of brick ornament, but some of them also illustrate the technique of façade decoration in an analytic reconstruction of the work process [Figures 20.4 and 20.5]. The state of *Bauforschung* (building archaeology) taught at the Technical University of Berlin is visible here.

While there was no single figure like K. A. C. Creswell recording architecture in the regions east of Baghdad, the immense effort of Arthur Upham Pope's *Survey of Persian Art* meant that a host of buildings was recorded in Iran at breathtaking speed during the 1930s.[17] At the same time, André Godard published a couple of Islamic monuments that he recorded in his function as head of the Iranian department of historical monuments.[18] Pope's own photographs, the plans and descriptions by his contributors (mostly Eric Schroeder and Donald Wilber), and the publications by Godard and his colleague Maxime Siroux constitute a body of material on which two generations drew to build their research on the architectural history of Islamic Iran. With regard to the sheer coverage of material, it seems that scholars during the 1930s

Figure 20.4: The upper section of the façade of the Mausoleum of Mu'mina Khatun in Nakhchivan (Azerbaijan). Drawing by G. Krecker after E. Jacobsthal's sketch. Source: Friedrich Sarre, *Denkmäler Persischer Baukunst* (Berlin: Wasmuth, 1910), Plate 4.

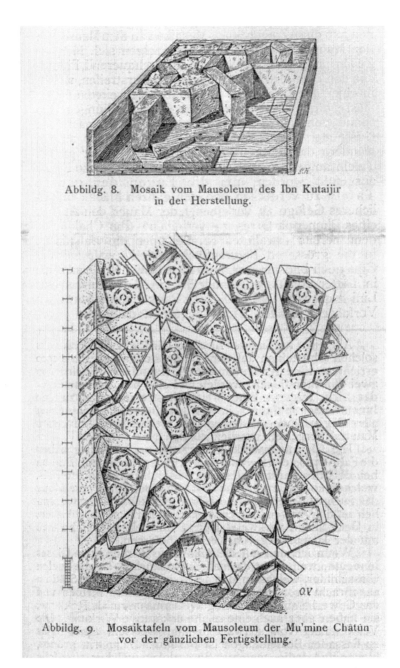

Figure 20.5: The Mausoleum of Yusuf ibn Kuthayr and the Mausoleum of Mu'mina Khatun Khatun in Nakhchivan (Azerbaijan). Details illustrating techniques of façade decoration. Source: Eduard Jacobsthal, *Deutsche Bauzeitung* 33 (1899): 569, Figures 8 and 9.

were making up for the lag that distanced research in Iran from that on architecture in Egypt, Bilad al-Sham, and Turkey.[19]

However, if any pre-war architectural historian of Islamic Iran could claim to be a *Bauforscher* (building archaeologist), it would be Myron B. Smith. His few monographic articles on Seljuq monuments remain unsurpassed in the standard of architectural documentation. Smith noted his observations and depicted them in general plans as well as drawings of architectural details [Figure 20.6].[20] A fanatic of meticulous recording, he even wrote his own manual with instructions for the team in his project to measure the Great (Friday) Mosque of Isfahan, explaining how to use their instruments and how to double-check results.[21] The resulting plan was highly reliable, but also far too large for publication. Smith's drawings (made without the help of photogrammetry) match the quality of those produced later by Michael Burgoyne for Jerusalem and Christian Ewert for architecture in the Islamic west.[22] The fact that Smith's standards did not become the rule for architectural historians and archaeologists of the Islamic period in Iran can be explained partly from the need (or the desire) to record a large number of sites during surveys. Thus, on his journeys during the late 1960s and early 1970s, Wolfram Kleiss documented finds from all epochs – including buildings from the Islamic period – in sketch drawings that obviously did not claim to represent exact measurement, while displaying a high degree of visual judgement.[23]

Photography

One factor that eased the burden of the draftsmen was obviously the rapid development of photography. Monuments in Egypt and in the Holy Land had been subjects of photography as early as the 1850s. In Iran, the monarch himself was the most active photographer and collector of photographs. In 1912–13, the French archaeologist Henry Viollet worked on a photographic mission on Islamic architecture in Iran. Historical monuments in Iran were thus systematically photographed, but the results remained largely unpublished.[24] Among the books that used photographs to illustrate Islamic architecture in Iran were those authored by Friedrich Sarre (1910) and Ernst Diez (1918).[25] From that point onwards, photographs replaced the former drawings of general views, interior views, and architectural details. As 35 mm cameras became common and images became cheaper to produce, the number of photographic illustrations multiplied, though they generally became smaller in format. In Pope's *Survey of Persian Art* from 1938, for example, many photographs are printed full-page, and only few in less than quarter folio size [Figure 20.7]. Thirty years later, the overview of Islamic architecture by Derek Hill and Oleg Grabar was also richly illustrated, but mostly with photographs in small-format.[26]

More recently another change has taken place with the transition to digital photography, which fundamentally altered the character and value of photographic images. While digital images are relatively cheap, and photographs of many monuments can easily be obtained through the internet, copyright laws constitute an obstacle that is sometimes difficult to handle,

Illustrating Islamic Architecture

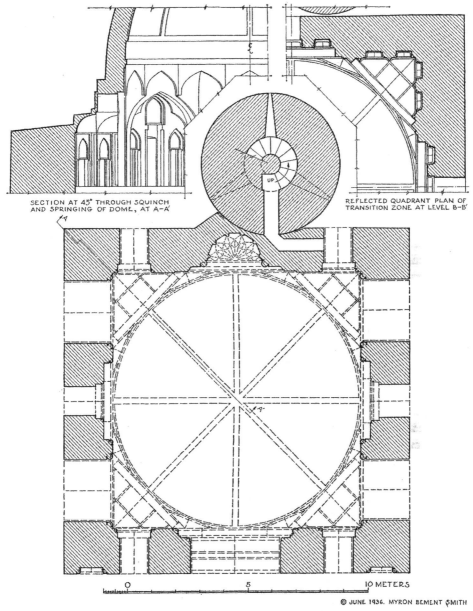

Figure 20.6: The dome hall and minaret of the Great Mosque at Barsiyan. Ground plan, with details of zone of transition in plan and elevation. Source: Myron B. Smith, *Ars Islamica* 4 (1937): 11, Plate 1.

Islamic Architecture Today and Tomorrow

Figure 20.7: The layout of a double page in the *Survey of Persian Art*, depicting the Gunbad-i Qabus. Source: Arthur Upham Pope and Phyllis Ackerman, *A Survey of Persian Art* (London: Oxford University Press, 1938–1939), Plates 337 and 338.

and reliable information connected with the image is not always at hand.[27] Problems have shifted since the reproduction of photographic illustrations is hardly more expensive than the printing of text. At the same time, publishers reduced their capacities in image editing, so that the average expertise in this field has drastically sunken. This can be felt particularly with regard to architectural photography. In many recent publications, it is visible that photographs of buildings have not been rectified, that the clipping of margins is neglected, and that contrast and brightness did not receive the attention that would be needed to give a reasonable idea of the building depicted.

Conceptual Approaches Versus Documentation

The documentation and publication of Islamic architecture in Iran that took place from the late 1920s onwards were fraught with two handicaps, one technological and one ideological. From the technical point of view, the mass of buildings that were 'discovered' and offered themselves for documentation required a certain speed in measuring and drawing. It has already been mentioned that works by André Godard and by Pope's team, determined to cover a great number of buildings, were bound to mirror this relative haste. The point where this can be seen most clearly is in the lack of sections and elevations. As the recording of vertical elements is more time consuming and requires more technical effort than the measuring of ground plans, it is little wonder that sections are as good as absent from publications by Godard and form a rare species in the *Survey*. The other handicap was theory. Both Pope and Godard maintained that the Islamic architecture of Iran was permeated with an inalienable Iranian spirit. Godard in particular put forward the idea that the domed mosque should be interpreted as an expression of a national revival, as it seemed to recur in the shape of the pre-Islamic *chahar taq*. He surmised that the monumental dome halls of the Seljuq period were erected on an empty surface, freestanding with arcades opening on three sides.[28] This theory of the *mosquée kiosque* was not only expressed in words but had its repercussions on architectural drawings. Thus, Eric Schroeder's plan of the north dome of the Great Mosque of Isfahan, published in the *Survey*, shows the walls as if open with triple arcades on all sides.[29] In his reconstruction of the Great Mosque of Burujird, the Seljuq-period dome hall was drawn by Maxime Siroux like an isolated pavilion on the *qibla* side of a large empty enclosure [Figure 20.8].[30] This way, Godard's hypothesis became more tangible and exerted an even stronger influence on the perception of Iranian Islamic architecture.

Later interpretive publications were divided between those approaches that depend less on detailed documentation and those that had a vital interest in receiving more reliable information on form and construction. Among the former, interpretations of architecture along ideas inspired from Sufism are prominent. These publications could do with sketches elucidating principles of design rather than representing individual buildings [Figure 20.9].[31] A different focus was on patronage, underlining the role of architecture as an expression of power. For this approach, the form of the building, its topographic setting, and the details of its architecture are meaningful, but details of construction seem less important.[32] This can be seen in a monograph on a major religious complex in Iran that offers only a schematic sketch of the ground plan.[33] On the other hand, architectural historians who are interested in the structural history of individual monuments and in methods of construction and design continue to use, and to publish, exact plans that are true to measure and that serve to differentiate between individual features. When photographs do not suffice, drawings are also used to give an impression of the three-dimensional appearance, e.g., through axonometric representation.[34] Drawings are also essential for clarifying results of archaeological research on buildings. A prominent case in question is Eugenio Galdieris's extensive study of the Great (Friday) Mosque of Isfahan [Figure 20.10].[35] Here, photogrammetry was also instrumental for the documentation of exterior and interior elevations [Figure 20.11]. On this basis, it also became possible to test hypotheses on the design process and on proportions in architecture, developed in connection with the history of mathematics.[36] The analytic drawings by Kambiz Navai and Kambiz Hajji Qasimi in their book on construction and design in Iranian architecture are also based on meticulously measured sections and elevations.[37]

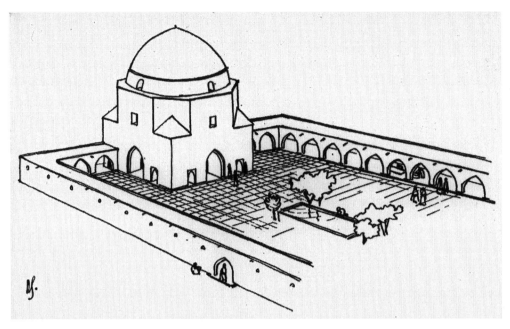

Figure 20.8: Reconstruction of the dome hall of the Great Mosque of Burujird, in its supposed original appearance as a 'mosquée kiosque', according to the ideas of André Godard. Source: Maxime Siroux, *Bulletin de l'Institut français d'archéologie orientale du Caire* 46 (1947): 249, Figure 8.

Conclusion: The Digital Turn

In recent years, digital technologies have greatly facilitated architectural documentation. Three-dimensional laser scanning and digital photogrammetry have been applied on Islamic monuments and promise to give new insights about their construction and design. It is now possible to produce elevations and sections that are considerably more reliable than older material. An example can be seen in the comparison between four sections through the dome hall of the Great Mosque of Burujird [Figure 20.12]. The first one, showing the dome before the construction of the outer shell, was published on a rather small scale.[38] The second and the third are not compatible with each other with regard to profiles of the dome and of the arches, thereby demonstrating that at least one of them cannot go back to correct measuring.[39] The recent drawing resulting from a 3D laser scan renders even smaller deformations of the shell of the dome.[40] Only the latter can serve as a basis for advanced considerations of the construction of the historical parts of the dome and for conclusions concerning its conservation. In general, it can be said that for a holistic understanding of Islamic architecture there is no way around thorough documentation in plans, covering as many dimensions of a building as possible.

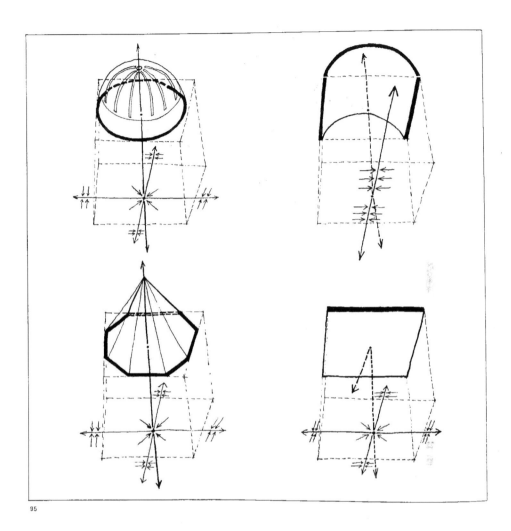

Figure 20.9: Schematic drawings illustrating 'the concept of dome'. Source: Nader Ardalan and Laleh Bakhtiar, *The Sense of Unity: The Sufi Tradition in Persian Architecture* (Chicago: University of Chicago Press, 1979), 74, Figure 95.

The crucial role that drawings and photographs have played in scholarly research on the history of Islamic architecture has been characterized as developing in parallel to (or following the model of) European architectural history – an observation that has many implications beyond the limited scope of the present essay. One of the aspects that could not be addressed here is that of drawings as a medium for envisaging future plans. For the history of European architecture, it is hardly possible to separate the two aspects of documentation and planning

Islamic Architecture Today and Tomorrow

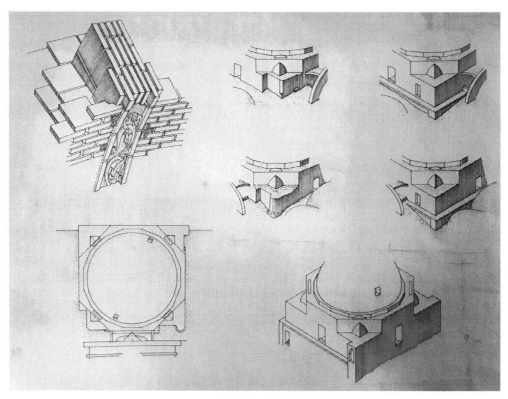

Figure 20.10: Details of masonry and schematic views of exterior north-east, north-west, and south-west corners of the south dome of the Great (Friday) Mosque of Isfahan. Drawing by Eugenio Galdieri in preparation for his publication on the building. Source: Central Archives of the State (Italy): Fondo Eugenio Galdieri, EG PRO 3/3.6–1.2.

from each other, as architects used drawings not just as instructions for building, but also for the presentation of their prestigious works to a larger public – starting with the thirteenth-century elevations of Gothic cathedral façades. The two aspects of the technical drawing and the visualization for a larger public, intertwined from early on, seem to have become ever more closely connected during the last few decades, when plans for architectural projects were published in the press before construction of the building began. With 3D computer graphics for visualization, and the Internet as a medium for publication, the potential has grown for architectural drawings to be popularized. However, the character of these drawings is also changing. It remains to be seen whether ground plans or elevations will continue to be important sources of information on buildings – in the realm of Islamic architecture just as in other fields of construction and design – or whether they will be replaced by animated videos of three-dimensional vistas. As clicking rates are among the decisive factors for prominence, the latter seems more likely.

Figure 20.11: North dome of the Great (Friday) Mosque of Isfahan. Elevation of interior looking east, on the basis of photogrammetric recording. Source: National Organisation for the Preservation of Historical Monuments of Iran – IsMEO – Rasad Survey (1973).

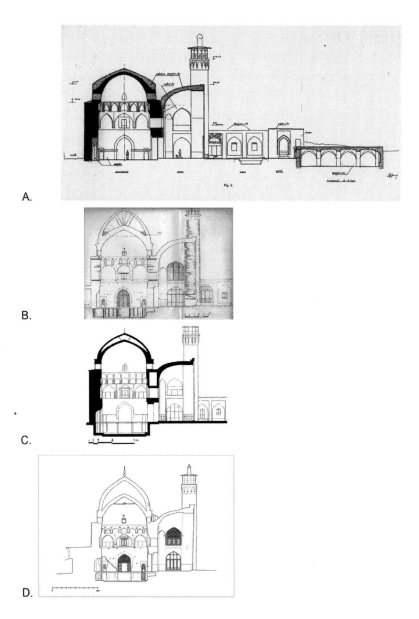

Figure 20.12: The *qibla iwan* and dome hall of the Great Mosque of Burujird. North-south section looking west, in a variety of recordings. Sources: A: Maxime Siroux, *Bulletin de l'Institut français d'archéologie orientale du Caire* 46 (1947): 249, Figure 3; B: Muhammad Muqaddas, Iranian Cultural Heritage Organisation unpublished report (1993), 231; C: Kambīz Ḥājjī Qāsimī, ed., *Masājid-i jāmiʿ. Ganjnāma: Farhang-i āthār-i miʿmārī-i islāmī-i Īrān*, vol. 7 (Tehran: Dānishgāh-i Shahīd Bihishtī, 1383/2004), 108; D: University of Bamberg and Iranian Cultural Heritage, Handicraft and Tourism Organization, drawing after 3D scan by J. Badr and J. Müller (2013).

Notes

This chapter was previously published as Lorenz Korn, 'Illustrating Islamic Architecture: On Visual Presentation and Scholarship', *International Journal of Islamic Architecture* 10.1 (2021): 171–90. The text has been updated for this publication.

1. For the wider problems of the field of the history of Islamic art, see Sheila S. Blair and Jonathan M. Bloom, 'The Mirage of Islamic Art: Reflections on the Study of an Unwieldy Field', *The Art Bulletin* 85 (2003): 152–84; Finbarr B. Flood and Gülru Necipoğlu, 'Frameworks of Islamic Art and Architectural History: Concepts, Approaches and Historiographies', in *A Companion to Islamic Art and Architecture*, vol. I, *From the Prophet to the Mongols*, ed. Finbarr B. Flood and Gülru Necipoğlu (Hoboken, NJ: Wiley Blackwell, 2017), 2–56. For an overview of the study of Iranian-Islamic art, see Yuka Kadoi and Iván Szántó, eds, *The Shaping of Persian Art: Collections and Interpretations of the Art of Islamic Iran and Central Asia* (Newcastle upon Tyne: Cambridge Scholars Publishing, 2013); Iván Szántó and Yuka Kadoi, eds, *The Reshaping of Persian Art: Art Histories of Islamic Iran and Central Asia* (Piliscsaba: Avicenna Institute of Middle Eastern Studies, 2019).
2. See Blair and Bloom, 'Mirage'; Flood and Necipoğlu, 'Frameworks'; Nasser Rabbat, 'Islamic Architecture as a Field of Historical Enquiry', *Architectural Design* 74.6 (2004): 18–23; Moya Carey and Margaret S. Graves, eds, 'Islamic Art Historiography', special issue, *Journal of Art Historiography* 6 (2012).
3. Eva-Maria Troelenberg, *Mschatta in Berlin: Connecting Art Histories in the Museum* (Dortmund: Kettler, 2014); Bruno Latour, 'Visualisation and Cognition: Drawing Things Together', in *Knowledge and Society Studies in the Sociology of Culture Past and Present* 6 (1986): 1–33. I am indebted to Jasmin Holtkötter for drawing my attention to the work of Bruno Latour.
4. Gülru Necipoğlu, *The Topkapı Scroll: Geometry and Ornament in Islamic Architecture* (Santa Monica, CA: Getty Center, 1995).
5. Conrad Grünemberg, *Beschreibung der Reise von Konstanz nach Jerusalem*, MS Karlsruhe, Badische Landesbibliothek St. Peter pap.32, accessed December 15, 2019, https://digital.blb-karlsruhe.de/blbhs/content/ titleinfo/7061.
6. Engelbert Kaempfer, *Amoenitatum Exoticarum Politico-Physico-Medicarum Fasciculi V.* (Lemgo: H. W. Meyer, 1712), 179, with the bird's-eye view of the 'Planographia sedis Regiae'. Note that Kaempfer's large plan of the city of Isfahan has never been printed and is probably lost. See Heinz Luschey, 'Der königliche Marstall in Iṣfahān und Engelbert Kaempfers Planographia des Palastbezirkes 1712', *Iran* 17 (1979): 77; Carsten Niebuhr, *Reisebeschreibung nach Arabien und den umliegenden Ländern*, 2 vols. (Copenhagen: Möller, 1774–78); Edme François Jomard, ed., *Description de l'Égypte: Ou recueil des observations et des recherches qui ont été faites en Égypte pendant l'expédition de l'armée française, publié par les ordres de sa majesté l'Empereur Napoléon le Grand*, vols. 4.2.1–4.2.2: *Planches: Etat moderne* 1, 2 (Paris: Imprimerie Impériale, 1809, 1817).
7. David Roberts and George Croly, *The Holy Land: Syria, Idumea, Arabia, Egypt, and Nubia*, 6 vols. (London: Moon, 1842–49).
8. On Creswell's scholarship, see the articles in *Muqarnas* 8 (1991).

9   Eugène Flandin, *Voyage en Perse de MM. Eugène Flandin, peintre, et Pascal Coste, architecte*, 1 vol. and atlas of plates and maps in 4 vols. (Paris: Baudry, 1843–54); Pascal Coste, *Monuments modernes de la Perse mesurés, dessinés et décrits par Pascal Coste…* (Paris: Morel, 1867).

10 Sheila S. Blair: *The Monumental Inscriptions From Early Islamic Iran and Transoxiana* (Leiden: Brill, 1992), 144–46, 55n, figs. 95 and 96.

11 Jane Dieulafoy, 'Mausolée de Chah Khoda-Bendé', *Revue générale de l'architecture et des travaux publics* 4e série 10 (1883): 97–104, 145–51, 193– 97, 241–43, plates 23–26.

12 Henri Saladin: *Manuel d'art musulman, vol. I: L'architecture* (Paris: Alphonse Picard, 1907), 329, 344; Ernst Diez: *Die Kunst der islamischen Völker* (Berlin-Neubabelsberg: Athenaion, 1915), 83–87, 106, 108, 112, figs. 110, 112–14, 139, 142, and 147.

13 Franz Kugler, *Geschichte der Baukunst*, 5 vols. (Stuttgart: Ebner & Seubert, 1856–73).

14 Wilhelm Salzenberg, *Alt-christliche Baudenkmale von Constantinopel vom V. bis XII. Jahrhundert* (Berlin: Ernst & Korn, 1854); Cornelius Gurlitt, *Die Baukunst Konstantinopels* (Berlin: Wasmuth, 1912).

15 Lorraine Decléty, 'Les architectes français et l'architecture islamique: Les premiers pas vers l'histoire d'un style', *Livraisons d'histoire de l'architecture*, 9 (2005): 73–84.

16 Friedrich Sarre, *Denkmäler persischer Baukunst. Geschichtliche Untersuchung und Aufnahme muhammedanischer Backsteinbauten in Vorderasien und Persien* (Berlin: Wasmuth, 1910), 9–14, figs. 1–8, plates 1–11. Jacobsthal had published the monuments shortly before in a monographic article. See Eduard Jacobsthal, 'Mittelalterliche Backsteinbauten zu Nachtschewân im Araxesthale', *Deutsche Bauzeitung* 33 (1899): 513–16, 521, 525–29, and 549–51 (with a contribution by Martin Hartmann, 'Die Inschriften', ibid: 559–74).

17 See the reports in the *Bulletin of the American Institute for Persian Art and Archaeology* (from 1935 onwards titled *Bulletin of the American Institute for Iranian Art and Archaeology*), and the final result in Arthur Upham Pope and Phyllis Ackerman, eds, *A Survey of Persian Art from Prehistoric Times to the Present*. 6 vols. (London: Oxford University Press, 1938–39). See also Bernard O'Kane, 'Arthur Upham Pope and the Study of Persian Islamic Architecture', in *Arthur Upham Pope and A New Survey of Persian Art*, ed. Yuka Kadoi (Leiden: Brill, 2016), 111–24.

18 See the articles by André Godard in *Āthār-é Īrān* 1 (1936), 2 (1937), 3 (1937), 4 (1949)

19 See Robert Hillenbrand, 'The Scramble for Persian Art: Pope and His Rivals', in Kadoi, *Arthur Upham Pope*, 15–45.

20 Myron B. Smith, 'Material for a Corpus of Early Iranian Islamic Architecture: I. Masdjid-i Djumʿa, Demawend', *Ars Islamica* 2 (1935): 153–71; Myron B. Smith, 'Material for a Corpus of Early Iranian Islamic Architecture: II. Manār and Masdjid, Barsīān (Iṣfahān)', *Ars Islamica* 4 (1937): 7–40; Myron B. Smith, 'Material for a Corpus of Early Iranian Islamic Architecture: III: Two Dated Seljuk Monuments at Sīn (Iṣfahān)', *Ars Islamica* 6 (1939): 1–10.

21 Myron B. Smith, 'Method of Procedure, Plan of M.-i Djumʾa' (unpublished manuscript, 1936), Washington DC, Freer/Sackler archives, M. B. Smith papers, Box 111-1.

22 Michael Hamilton Burgoyne, *Mamluk Jerusalem. An Architectural Study* (Buckhurst Hill: World of Islam Festival Trust, 1987); Christian Ewert and Jens-Peter Wisshak, *Forschungen zur almohadischen Moschee*, 4 vols. (Mainz: Zabern, 1981–95).

23 See his several articles titled 'Erkundungsfahrten […]' in *Archäologische Mitteilungen aus Iran* 2 (1969), 4 (1971), 5 (1972), 6 (1973).

24 On Nasir al-Din Shah as photographer, see Iraj Afshar 'Some Remarks on the Early History of Photography in Iran', in *Qajar Iran: Politcal, Social and Cultural Change, 1800–1925*, ed. C. E. Bosworth and C. Hillenbrand (Edinburgh: University Press, 1983), 261–90. The work by Marine Fromanger, 'L'architecture musulmane en Perse d'après les missions d'Henry Viollet (1911–1912)', 2 vols. (unpublished manuscript, Aix-en- Provence, 1997), was not accessible to me.

25 Sarre, *Denkmäler persischer Baukunst*; Ernst Diez, *Churasanische Baudenkmäler* (Berlin: Reimer, 1918).

26 Derek Hill and Oleg Grabar, *Islamic Architecture and its Decoration, A.D. 800–1500* (London: Faber & Faber, 1967).

27 See Archnet, https://archnet.org/, for the richest example of a database on Islamic architecture.

28 André Godard, 'Les anciennes mosquées de l'Iran', *Āthār-é Īrān* 1 (1936): 187–210; André Godard, 'Les anciennes mosquées de l'Iran', *Arts Asiatiques* 3 (1956): 48–63, 83–88; André Godard, *L'art de l'Iran* (Paris: Arthaud, 1962).

29 Pope and Ackerman, *Survey*, fig. 346.

30 Maxime Siroux, 'La Mosquée Djum'a de Bouroudjird', *Bulletin de l'Institut français d'archéologie orientale du Caire* 46 (1947): 239–58 and fig. 8.

31 Most prominently, Nader Ardalan and Laleh Bakhtiar, *The Sense of Unity: The Sufi Tradition in Persian Architecture* (Chicago: University of Chicago Press, 1979); for a more recent example see Samer Akkach, *Cosmology and Architecture in Premodern Islam: An Architectural Reading of Mystical Ideas* (Albany: State University of New York Press, 2005).

32 An example is Yasser Tabbaa, *Constructions of Power and Piety in Medieval Aleppo* (University Park: University of Pennsylvania Press, 1997). The majority of plans are reproductions of drawings by Ernst Herzfeld.

33 Kishwar Rizvi, *The Safavid Dynastic Shrine: Architecture, Religion and Power in Early Modern Iran* (London: I. B. Tauris, 2011).

34 Robert Hillenbrand, *Islamic Architecture: Form, Function and Meaning* (Edinburgh: University Press, 1994), with many examples, however of varying quality.

35 Eugenio Galdieri, *Eṣfahān: Masǧid-i Ǧum'a* 3 vols. (Rome: IsMEO, 1972–1984).

36 Alpay Özdural, 'A Mathematical Sonata for Architecture: Omar Khayyam and the Friday Mosque of Isfahan', *Technology and Culture* 39 (1998): 699–715. For studies on proportion, see also Mitkhat S. Bulatov, *Geometricheskaya garmonizatsiya v arkhitekture Srednei Azii Ix-xv vv* (Moscow: Izdatel'svto Nauka, 1978).

37 Kāmbīz Navā'ī and Kāmbīz Hājjī Qāsimī, *Khisht va-khayāl. Sharḥ-i mi'mārī-i islāmī-i Īrān* (Tehran: Surūsh, 2011).

38 Siroux, 'La mosquée'.

39 Muḥammad Muqaddas, 'Bar-rasī, taḥqīq va-ta'mīrāt-i anjām shuda dar Masjid-i Jāmi'-i Burūjird. Tā ākhar-i shish māha-i avval-i sāl 1370' (unpublished report, Iranian Cultural Heritage Organisation, 1993); Kambīz Ḥājjī Qāsimī, ed., *Masājid-i jāmi'. Ganjnāma: Farhang-i āthār-i mi'mārī-i islāmī-i Īrān* (*Congregational Mosques. Ganjnameh: Cyclopaedia of Iranian Islamic Architecture*), vol. 7 (Tehran: Dānishgāh-i Shahīd Bihishtī, 1383/2004), 106–11 (in English), 90–95 (in Farsi).

40 See Lorenz Korn, 'Masjid-i jāmi'-i Burūjird. Nukātī dar bāb-i ṭarrāḥī va-sākht-i bināhā-i daura-i saljūqī', *Asar* 40.1 (1398/2019): 89–106.

Part 7

Globalization and Change

Chapter 21

Uneven Geographies and Neoliberal Urban Transformation in Arab Cities

Rami F. Daher

Architects, urban planners, and politicians have been observing the transformation of the Arab city over the past three decades vis-à-vis the emergence of a neoliberal urban restructuring and new order regarding real estate ventures and the creation of public space. The development of new urban islands that cater to the elite and their propensity for excessive consumption, coupled with the internationalization of commercial real estate companies and construction-consulting firms capable of providing high-end services, is the main indicator of the neoliberal urban restructuring that is occurring in places such as downtown Beirut, Abdali in Amman, Dreamland in Cairo, the financial district in Manama, the Bou Regreg River Development in Rabat, Pearl Island in Doha, and even in the heart of the holy city of Mecca through the Jabal Omar Project. Indeed, most cities of the Arab world have been subject to such neoliberal transformations in one way or the other, from Rabat in Morocco to Amman in Jordan. Pierre-Arnaud Barthel has dubbed these real estate ventures 'Arab mega-projects' in reference to their scale, and he considers them to be the main vectors in contemporary Arab town planning.[1] While investors and municipal decision-makers are obliged to create a competitive business climate and first-class tourist attractions in order to lure people to live, invest, and travel to their cities, such development efforts are raising questions about longer-term impacts on spatial landscapes and social fabrics. Driven mostly by corporatization, these urban transformations are not only creating geographies of inequality in cities, but they are also adversely affecting the nature and quality of public space.[2]

This chapter seeks to explain how spatial dynamics reveal forces and transformations that have led to widening socio-economic inequality in various Arab and Islamic communities. My analysis attempts to position localized spatial ordering and restructuring in the Arab city within the recent history of broader global socio-economic and geopolitical transformations. Manifestations of this increasing spatial ordering and inequality have included a substantial reduction in public space, withdrawal of the state from a wide range of social and physical infrastructures (e.g., social housing, water, electricity, and solid waste management) in favour of private for-profit service providers, land speculation, market-based development models, and a general corporatization of the public sector. While in other publications I have addressed these alarming shifts within the context of Amman, my focus here is on similar patterns of urban change in other Arab cities including Beirut, Cairo, Dubai, Damascus, Aqaba, Tunis, and Rabat.

David Harvey, a critic renowned for developing theories of socio-spatial analysis that build on the work of Henri Lefebvre, pointed out that neoliberal economic thought and its political implementation emerged out of a critique of, and backlash against, the welfare state.[3] Accordingly, politicians of the late 1970s, such as Margaret Thatcher, formed a new doctrine, now generally known as 'neoliberalism', that was soon to become the central guiding principle of economic thought and management.[4] Neoliberalism has led directly to excessive privatization, the withdrawal of the state from welfare programmes, the dominance of multinational corporations, and, as far as the so-called 'Third World' is concerned, a change from project-oriented international aid to aid in the form of structural adjustments and policy. In response, a number of forces have emerged that would propel this neoliberal transformation, as exemplified by the dominance of the World Trade Organization (WTO), the World Economic Forum (WEF), the North American Free Trade Agreement (NAFTA) and since 2020 its successor the United States-Mexico-Canada Agreement (USMCA), and similar global organizations, treaties, and instruments. As a direct consequence of neoliberal socio-economics, policy makers and planners across a widening swath of Arab countries – including Jordan, Egypt, and Tunisia – find themselves gradually withdrawing from providing social services (most notably education, healthcare, social security, and social housing) and instead becoming more involved in real estate development as a facilitator, regulator, and provider of indirect subsidies for multinational corporations.

This essay resituates the current urban neoliberal condition in the Arab world in the context of circulating patterns of urban transformation. It introduces a discursive framework whereby various neoliberal projects can be examined and evaluated against one or more of the following indicators: urban lifestyle, emancipatory neoliberal discourse, claims to social sustainability, socio-spatial politics and dynamics, governance and place management, the changing role of the state, and circulation of neoliberal practices.

Manifestations of Neoliberal Urban Restructuring

Gulf investments (before and after the financial crisis of 2008) in mega-projects in cities like Dubai, Amman, Beirut, Cairo, Rabat, and Tunis are manifested through the circulation of Gulf capital, that is, revenue generated from exports of Gulf oil, and huge reserves of money in search of high-yield and secure investments. Between 2003 and 2004, the six states of the Gulf Cooperation Council enjoyed a surplus of about $50 billion, which then rose to $400 billion between 2007 and 2008. In 2009, it plummeted to an estimated $47.4 billion, rising again to $142.2 billion in 2010. It was estimated that between the years 2005 and 2020, the Gulf States invested some $3000 billion in the Middle East and North Africa.[5]

In Amman, for example, one can clearly see evidence of neoliberal urban restructuring and emergent forms of spatial ordering and engineering in the form of high-end – and geographically isolated – business and residential towers that have been expressly designed to stress the concept of exclusivity and endorse specific consumption patterns associated with luxury. Examples of new neoliberal urban transformations include exclusive office and residential spaces that also offer retail, commercial, and tourism activities (e.g., the Abdali real

Figure 21.1: The Abdali development under construction in Amman, Jordan (2015). Source: Wikimedia Commons/Makeandtoss.

estate development);[6] high-end residential 'gated' communities all over Amman (e.g., Green Land and Andalucia); and even lower-income residential housing projects that work to push the poorer segments of society to the outskirts of the city in newly zoned 'heterotopias' (e.g., social-housing developments in Jizza, Marka, and Sahab) [Figures 21.1 and 21.2].[7] These different forms of urban transformation all reflect dominant political and ideological practices of power as regulated by neoliberal tropes and manifested through spatially engineered realities. More importantly, some of these emerging neoliberal city-projects will certainly lead to urban geographies of inequality and exclusion, as well as to spatial and social displacement [Figure 21.3].

A similar case of neoliberal urban restructuring can be seen in Beirut. In the early 1990s, following the end of the Lebanese Civil War (1975–90), major reconstruction works were done at the same time as substantial real estate ventures changed the ravaged historic downtown of Beirut. The downtown Beirut reconstruction undertaken by the Société Libanaise de Développement et de Reconstruction (Solidere), which was presented to the public as a comprehensive post-war reconstruction effort that would serve the entire city, has been criticized as a mere for-profit real estate development project in which centuries of history and heritage are recreated through pastiche representations. While it is true that the project also included the preservation of older buildings and urban spaces from before WWI (typified by 'traditional Lebanese' architecture and the central hallway dwelling or triple-arch typology popular during the nineteenth and early-twentieth centuries) and French Mandate period

Islamic Architecture Today and Tomorrow

Figure 21.2: *Living Well*, by Emad Hajjaj (known as Abu Mahjoub). The full title, *Living Well, an Apartment above the Roof*, satirizes the new series of English magazines popular in Jordan today about social events and the lifestyles of the rich. The image refers to the new neoliberal real estate developments, visible here in the poor man's home, the roof of which he has built using an advertisement billboard. Source: Emad Hajjaj.

(1923–46), it is important to stress that the final outcome is an exclusive urban setting where the notions of urban memory and property ownership have disintegrated. Today, residents or shopkeepers no longer own their own property; instead, they are allocated shares within a company run by a few powerful majority shareholders. Moreover, reminiscent of gentrification that has occurred elsewhere around the globe, the pastiche recreation of the city's long history and heritage caters to a 'boutiqueization' of once-vibrant areas of socio-economic exchange. This reconstruction has essentially created a collaged urban morphology designed for consumption by tourists and the Lebanese people alike. The effect of global Gulf capital is evident in Palestinian cities as well. Rawabi, which has been advertised as the first planned city constructed by and for Palestinians, is a development project near Ramallah in the West Bank with a current investment level exceeding $1 billion. It is considered the largest private-sector project ever to take place in Palestine, though unfortunately at the expense of rich and

Uneven Geographies and Neoliberal Urban Transformation in Arab Cities

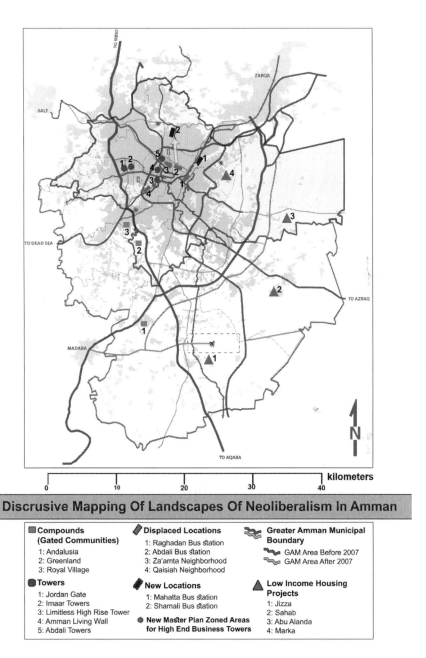

Figure 21.3: Neoliberal developments in Amman, Jordan (2013). Source: Rami Daher.

valuable agricultural land; the project has been heavily critiqued by urban activists and NGOs in Palestine and beyond.[8]

It would be interesting to analyse several of these projects in light of the emerging urban lifestyles of their clientele. In both Amman's Abdali project and the work of Beirut's Solidere – and specifically the residential/retail towers constructed in these areas – the occupants and residents of corporate office space and luxury apartments create their own type of utopia. Their 'privileged position' is, in most cases, quite detached from the rest of the city and its inhabitants. Indeed, the marketing materials for these projects promise, without any ambiguity, a distinctively luxurious lifestyle in a protected and safe environment.

Again, these projects will very likely lead to inequality and exclusion and intensify spatial and social displacement. For example, Amman's Abdali project will almost certainly heighten the city's socio-economic and spatial polarization – not only between East and West Amman, but also between this new 'elitist urban island' and the rest of the city. In fact, it has already led to the displacement of the Abdali transportation terminal, which has effectively distanced its drivers, informal vendors, and occupants to the outskirts of Amman. This shift has created considerable disruption and financial burdens for commuters by complicating and dispersing public-transportation options in the city.

Furthermore, it is important to analyse these projects in terms of a number of knock-on effects. These include changes in urban governance; the emergence of new governing bodies in the city; the production of new subjects and experts devoted to urban management; the privatization of essential urban services; the creation of new types of partnerships between the public and private sectors; and the informalization of decision-making and building-permit processes when it comes to approving large-scale and corporate neoliberal investments in the city. Krijnen and Fawaz observe similar trends in urban governance in Beirut, arguing that additional flexibility is provided for capital investments through the informalization of public decision-making with regard to planning.[9] In essence, more decisions are made by mutual agreement, on an ad-hoc basis, and at multiple levels of the public hierarchy. In cases of high-end residential and corporate projects, informalization is also precipitated by an increasing trend to favour visual communication in the form of 3D images, models, and videos, all of which work to 'glitzify' proposed projects and make them more attractive to investors. The problem with this approach is that it tends to lack any consideration for social and physical sustainability concerns in decision-making processes.[10]

Most of the examples discussed here testify to a clear trend in urban management in the Arab world today: planning processes are being delegated to the for-profit private sector. This private sector then operates in the midst of newly emerging governing bodies of the city (e.g., Mawared in Amman, Solidere in Beirut, ASEZA [Aqaba Special Economic Zone Authority] in Aqaba, and in Tunis the Société de Promotion du Lac de Tunis [a collaboration between the Tunisian government and the Saudi company Al Baraka in the development of the northern lagoon shores of the Tunisian capital]). These emerging governing bodies are replacing older governmental entities, most notably municipalities whose role in urban governance has been extremely marginalized.

From Real Estate Investments to City Infrastructure

More recently, one can observe an even more excessive post-neoliberal corporatization of state public institutions (e.g., electricity, solid waste management, water, and social housing), coupled with a period of deregulation. Jordan, for example, has witnessed a rapid decrease in state subsidies for water, electricity, and essential commodities such as bread. Egypt, on the other hand, has experienced the continuation of structural adjustment programmes after the current regional recession, which has led to increased taxes on both essential and nonessential goods.

While Arab states are increasingly retreating from public works and welfare programmes, large state subsidies are being allocated to neoliberal projects that favour exclusive real estate development projects. In the case of Amman's Abdali project, for instance, Mawared's rhetoric to decrease state involvement also includes a public subsidy for private real estate development that benefits selective urban business elites from Lebanon, Jordan, and the Gulf. Moreover, the financial contribution from Jordan is considerable, with the greater portion of the subsidy devoted to making prime urban space available at very low prices to the 'right' buyer. Other forms of subsidies include tax exemptions, infrastructure provisions, the elimination of many barriers and red tape designed to uphold thoughtful zoning decisions, and the passage of favourable building regulations and zoning ordinances that make it easier for investors to cater to the wealthy. For example, the Tunisian government officially sold 950 hectares of land along the newly sanitized southern lake in Tunis to the Sama Dubai real estate company in the early 1990s for a token sum of 1DT.[11] Similarly, neoliberal urban transformation in Beirut is serving high-end developers by increasing the number of permitted built-up areas, providing tax breaks, and offering considerable public subsidies that favour the development sector. Most recently, newly emerging national and multinational corporate investors are becoming dominant stakeholders in this privatization process. This trend signifies a considerable shift from an interest primarily in investing in real estate development to becoming increasingly involved in urban infrastructure provision, which was previously undertaken by state institutions.

A clear example of this shift can be found in Jordan. There, during a post-neoliberal era,[12] Jordan has witnessed an excessive corporatization of the state's public sector institutions, including utilities for electricity and water, accompanied by what is declared to the general public as 'policy reform' leading to a period of deregulation of public sector institutions. This phenomenon is not restricted to Jordan; in fact, many 'Third World' countries are facing key shifts in the neoliberal era of water governance: first, public water institutions were institutionally reformed through privatization or public-private partnerships; and second, institutions were commercialized or corporatized to utilize market governance logics in water management. In Amman, the corporatization of the water sector has resulted in the selling, buying, and reselling again of state institutions. This shift means a re-working of state organizations from privatization to corporatization and commercialization through public/private partnerships. The shift from the privatized 'LEMA' water companies (a consortium of Lyonnaise des Eaux, Montgomery Watson, and Arabtech Jardaneh), which was strictly a management company responsible for billing, distribution, and customer services (contracts and assets of the water sector remained with the state), to today's Miyahuna, owned by the Water Authority of Jordan (WAJ), is a perfect example.[13] WAJ is now responsible for regulating Miyahuna. Here, this de-regulation is not only significant because the owner is now serving as regulator simultaneously, but also because it marks a critical shift in management's priorities. The real emphasis is now on water provision *and* on cost recovery, especially when the government is not investing in water harvesting projects, but rather in expensive quick fixes that offer no future rewards, such as the Disi Project, which pumps water from the Disi aquifer in the south to Amman and thus depletes one of Jordan's primary water sources.

The post-neoliberal excessive corporatization and de-regulation of public sector institutions can be seen in the electricity sector as well, as is clearly apparent in the Jordanian government's selling of National Electric Power Company (NEPCO) shares to multi-national corporations such as Dubai Capital. Eric Verdeil's critical work on the privatization of the electricity sector demonstrates the need for more empirical research addressing specific examples of neoliberalization.[14] Verdeil has written that the state's involvement in the supply of electricity to urban homes improved by a dramatic proportion, from 39 per cent in 1961, to 78 per cent in 1979, and to 99.7 per cent during the early 1990s. The current privatization of the electricity sector, where the state is no longer subsidizing the sector, stands in stark contrast to previous state involvement in infrastructure provision.[15] Verdeil has also stated that privatization was strongly correlated with the end of subsidies for electricity, leading to increased prices in 2004 and in 2008, and thus to the period's increased levels of urban poverty and inflation. While some things have changed in the years since Verdeil's work was published, these issues remain relevant and many of the challenges stemming from the policy and ownership changes that occurred at that time remain significant.

Conclusion

Increasing numbers of Arab cities are being subjected to newly emerging neoliberal bodies of urban governance, which, despite their rhetoric of emancipation, conceal exclusionary and exploitative social relations and spatial ordering that create new pockets of poverty in the inner city, cause major social and physical displacement of marginalized social groups, and decimate the power and influence of local state authorities. There is, therefore, a significant disparity between the rhetoric of urban policies on the one hand, and the resulting reality on the other. The common thread between these various case studies from Amman, Beirut, Tunis, Ramallah, and elsewhere is that both types of neoliberal projects – whether those targeting high-end clientele or those targeting poorer segments of society – lead to geographies of inequality through the formation of urban islands of excessive consumption and exclusive residential neighbourhoods. The eventual outcome is that poorer segments of society are pushed to the outskirts of the city and into new pockets of poverty away from essential social services and transportation networks. I would argue that several of these projects even demonstrate a search for a particular contradictory utopia (and in most cases, a consumerist utopia), promoted by the rhetoric of neoliberal developers through various mechanisms both within and beyond the city.

In the Arab world, questions concerning the politics of place, urban development, and the environment (to name a few) have, for the most part, remained outside the domains of political and public consciousness and critical debate. My purpose in this chapter is not so much to critique this emerging reality, but to contribute to our understanding of this developing phenomenon of 'neoliberal urban restructuring' in Arab cities.[16] A related goal is to raise the profile of the discourse and public debate about key transformations concerning the built environment. There remain ample opportunities for other researchers to critically investigate such neoliberal urban transformations and engage in comparative analyses of different case studies that will illuminate the nature and implications of the changing urban environment in the Arab world.

Notes

This chapter was previously published as Rami F. Daher, 'Uneven Geographies and Neoliberal Urban Transformation in Arab Cities Today', *International Journal of Islamic Architecture* 7.1 (2018): 29–35. Updates, where appropriate, have been made to the present version.

1   Pierre-Arnaud Barthel, 'Arab Mega-Projects: Between the Dubai Effect, Global Crisis, Social Mobilization, and a Sustainable Shift', *Built Environment* 36.2 (2013): 5–17.

2   Even though publications on the Arab city are numerous, not many have addressed the neoliberal transformations and urban restructurings that have taken place over the past decade. Among the few that have are Yasser Elsheshtawy, ed. *The Evolving Arab City: Tradition, Modernity and Urban Development* (New York: Routledge, 2008). For comparative work on Amman and Beirut, see Doris Summer, 'Neo-Liberalizing the City: Transitional Investment Networks and the Circulation of Urban Images in Beirut and Amman' (MA thesis, American University of Beirut, 2005). On Amman, see Rami Daher, 'Amman: Disguised Genealogy and Recent Urban Restructuring and Neoliberal Threats', in Elsheshtawy, *The Evolving Arab City*, 37–68; Rami Daher, 'Discourses of Neoliberalism and Disparities in the City Landscape: Cranes, Craters and an Exclusive Urbanity', in *Cities, Urban Practices, and Nation Building in Jordan*, ed. Myriam Ababsa and Rami Daher (Beirut: Institut Français du Proche-Orient), 273–96. On Damascus, see Valérie Clerk and Armand Hurault, 'Property Investments and Prestige Projects in Damascus: Urban and Town Planning Metamorphosis', *Built Environment* 36.2 (2013): 34–47. On Tangier, see Pierre-Arnaud Barthel and Sabine Planel, 'Tanger-Med and Casa-Marina, Prestige Projects in Morocco: New Capitalist Frameworks and Local Context', *Built Environment* 36.2 (2013): 48–63. On Cairo, see Khaled Adham, 'Cairo's Urban Déjà Vu: Globalization and Urban Fantasies', in *Planning Middle Eastern Cities: An Urban Kaleidoscope in a Globalizing World*, ed. Yasser Elsheshtawy (New York: Routledge, 2004), 134–68. On energy transition and infrastructure in Jordanian and Lebanese cities, see Éric Verdeil, 'Energy Transition in Jordanian and Lebanese Cities: The Case of Electricity' (paper presented at 'In

Cities and Energy Transitions: Past, Present, Future' conference, Autun, France, June 2009), http://halshs.archives-ouvertes.fr/halshs-00424539/fr/. On Rawabi, near Ramallah in Palestine, see Adam Haneih, *Lineages of Revolt: Issues of Contemporary Capitalism in the Middle East* (Chicago: Haymarket Books, 2013). On Beirut, see Marieke Krijnen and Mona Fawaz, 'Exception as the Rule: High-End Developments in Neoliberal Beirut', *Urban Environment* 36.2 (2010): 117–31.

3   David Harvey, *A Brief History of Neoliberalism* (Oxford: Oxford University Press, 2005).
4   Ibid.
5   Daher, 'Amman'.
6   Abdali is the largest neoliberal real estate development project currently underway in Amman. The project is promoted as 'the new downtown' for Amman and is expected to include high-end offices and residential spaces, in addition to retail, commercial, and other tourist-related attractions. The remodelled area, previously the site of the General Jordan Armed Forces Headquarters, spans over 350,000 square metres in the heart of Amman and will contain a built-up area of approximately 1,000,000 square metres. Rami Daher, 'Neoliberal Urban Transformations in the Arab City: Meta Narratives and Urban Disparities – The Emergence of Consumerist Utopias and Geographies of Inequalities in Amman', *Environnement Urbain/ Urban Environment* 7 (2013): 102.
7   Ibid., a99–a115.
8   See Haneih, *Lineages of Revolt*.
9   Krijnen and Fawaz, 'Exception as the Rule'.
10 Ibid.
11 On the development of Tunis's lakefront in the years leading up to this, see Bechir Kenzari, 'Lake Tunis, or the Concept of the Third Centre', in Elsheshtawy, *Planning Middle Eastern Cities*, 114–33.
12 On just one of the products of this neo-liberal era, see Eliana Abu-Hamdi, 'The Jordan Gate Towers of Amman: Surrendering Public Space to Build a Neoliberal Ruin', *International Journal of Islamic Architecture* 5:1 (2016): 73–101.
13 Rana Tomaira, 'Legacy of a Rentier State: Reforming Jordan's Water, Energy, and Telecommunications Sectors' (Ph.D. diss., University of California, Berkeley, 2008).
14 Verdeil, 'Energy Transition'.
15 According to Verdeil, the Jordanian government rationalizes this privatization due to pressure because of the 'brutal end of the remittances from the Gulf after the second Gulf war' and also because of temporary decrease in international aid. 'After one unsuccessful tender in 2005, Energy Arabia announced in 2007 the purchase of 51 per cent of Central Electricity Generating Company (CEGCO). Energy Arabia (Enara) is a company established by Jordan Dubai Energy, the Energy investment arm of Jordan Dubai Capital (which is owned by Dubai Holding, a giant Emirati financial firm).' Ibid., 6–7.
16 The levels and nature of contestation to these neoliberal urban restructuring projects and transformations in infrastructure provision have been different from one context to another in the Arab world. They have provoked various forms of resistance, particularly by urban activists, research centres, and NGOs. Several of these research centres and their associated activists have worked on the enhancement of public spaces in the cities and their respective

communities, attempting to counteract neo-liberal urban restructuring while granting voice to marginalized populations. Abir Saksouk-Sasso's brochures on the politics of public space and neoliberal transformations on Beirut's waterfront *Dalieh* are an example. See Abir Saksouk-Sasso, 'Making Spaces for Communal Sovereignty: The Story of Beirut's Dalieh', *Arab Studies Journal* 22.1 (2015): 296–319. See also Hadi Makarem, 'The Bottom-Up Mobilization of Lebanese Society Against Neoliberal Institutions: The Case of Opposition Against Solidere's Reconstruction of Downtown Beirut', in *Contentions Politics in the Middle East*, ed. Fawaz A. Gerges (New York: Palgrave Macmillan, 2015), 501–21.

Chapter 22

Affection for *Nouvel* Architecture: On Contemporary (Islamic) Architecture and Affect

Şebnem Yücel

To state that architecture is a global practice today is of course to be stating the obvious. When we are talking about architecture in the Islamic world – no matter how we may define the boundaries of this world – the practice is not strictly localized. To a great extent it is not culturally, let alone religiously, specific to that context. Any attempt to identify a category of contemporary 'Islamic' architecture, in distinction from the rest, is problematic – perhaps bound to fail – and though the term is still used, we are no longer adopting the simplistic and reductionist labels and categories that were once validated within architectural circles.

This does not mean that all we can identify is a 'replication of uniformity', or a single 'world culture'.[1] Rather, it is quite clear that no matter how 'cumbersome' the issues of representation and identity have become, and despite the recognition of architecture's inability to 'fully represent the peoples, nations, and cultures within which it exists',[2] these issues are still at play as various projects illustrate from the global vitrine. The challenge, then, is 'to avoid simplistic explanations of any sort', as architect and university dean Amale Andraos declares in relation to emerging urban centres in the Gulf.[3] According to her:

> ethnicity, tradition, and religious identity are set as the foundation for new transnational formations, variously moderate or extreme as they may be. Using form and content, architecture is expected to reconcile competing forces. Buildings must go up and their forms must, by necessity, involve some kind of settlement.[4]

While it is impossible to know if architecture will ever succeed in reconciling such competing forces, we can at least say that in today's more critical context, kitsch and orientalist clichés – as canonized by architectural historians and practised by colonial administrations at the turn of the century and later re-produced by those that rely on identity politics – lose their appeal and fail to impress. And yet, we cannot declare their total fall from grace. In other words, simplistic and reductionist explanations that produce an eclectic pastiche of domes, minarets, arches, and applied ornaments freely borrowed from different building typologies and regions are losing their relevance in Islamic geographies, and the economy's role in regulating such reconciliation is gaining strength, mostly in the production of unique and attractive cultural destinations.

Affect

Scanning the geographies of Islam through popular architectural media, we come across signature projects by star architects (or 'starchitects') that can easily be read as 'brandscapes'.[5] They are objects in the 'experience economy', advertising what investors – in most cases governments – imagine themselves to be while promising new sensations to their visitors/customers. While the economy has always been an important input in architectural practice, it is now the main locomotive more than ever, driving what, how, and by whom such entities are built. For example, the creation of Saadiyat Island, Abu Dhabi's major tourism and cultural destination, was clearly an important investment, and projects by famous architectural offices from all over the world were an important part of its marketing. The list of prestige projects by global firms includes the Louvre Abu Dhabi by Jean Nouvel; the UAE Pavilion, originally designed for Shanghai Expo 2010, by Foster and Partners; the Zayed National Museum by Foster and Partners; the Guggenheim Abu Dhabi by Gehry Partners; the Abrahamic Family House, composed of a mosque, church, and synagogue, by Adjaye Associates; and the Abu Dhabi Performing Arts Center by Zaha Hadid Associates.[6]

The designers of these projects do wish to see their creations belong 'to a country, to its history, to its geography without becoming a flat translation, the pleonasm that results in boredom and convention'.[7] As they succeed in becoming much more than flat translations, however, the degree to which they manage to belong to a specific culture or context remains secondary to their success. This is not to say that the question of true belonging constitutes a lack or a problem. In fact, given the specifics of their sites, they are perhaps largely successful attempts. But more importantly, their belonging should be understood within a global framework. Because these signature projects do belong to what architectural historian and theorist Douglas Spencer calls the 'scenography of contemporary architecture':

> The friction-free space supposed to liberate the subject from the strictures of both modernism and modernity, to reunite it with nature, to liberate its nomadic, social and creative dispositions, to re-enchant its sensory experience of the world, to conjoin it with a technology itself now operating in accord with the very laws of the material universe, with emergence, self-organization and complexity.[8]

For Spencer, under the guise of a libertarian rhetoric, what surfaces is 'the spatial complement of contemporary processes of neoliberalization'.[9] In this emergence, affect – or rather the creation of affect – plays an important part, forming the link between contemporary architecture and neoliberalism.[10] Through a discussion of contemporary architectural examples and several seminal texts by well-known architects (e.g., Alejandro Zaera-Polo and Farshid Moussavi), architectural critics (e.g., Sylvia Lavin), artists (e.g., Lars Spuybroek), and the prominent figures of affect theory (e.g., Brian Massumi), Spencer charts architectural expression's move away from 'traditionally established modes of articulation' and its new operation through 'supposedly uncoded formal, geometric and tectonic means'.[11] He shows us that architectural form is no longer mediated by 'established cultural or historical code' and now its main task is 'communicating with the "molecular" nature of contemporary reality'.[12] With reference to Moussavi's *The Function of Form*,[13] Spencer points to a trajectory common in most of these works, identifying

> changes within capitalism as key to the development of architectural forms now capable of addressing the 'plurality and mutability' of this reality of product differentiation and mass customization, a reality where capitalism is no longer 'an homogenizing force', but 'contributes to the production of difference and novelty'.[14]

In this new conception, there is a move away from meaning, from interpretation. A search for meaning, especially in artistic works, is replaced by the immersion in sensual experience. And most of all:

> An architecture of affect performs as a power of aestheticization. Its work is to absorb the sensorium in an environmental patterning with which the subject can identify, recognizing itself as a thing among other things, a neoliberal subject as operationally agile and efficient as are the forms with which its milieu is increasingly saturated. […] It is the affirmation of affect, and not the practice of critique, that subtracts from perception in reducing it to a condition of pure aisthesis.[15]

Perhaps one of the best architectural proposals to demonstrate this affective turn has recently emerged in Saudi Arabia. In the circulating computer-generated images of the Sharaan Resort, in the words of its architect, Jean Nouvel, and in the glamourous atmosphere of this high-end luxury destination, one truly finds affect in practice within the context of the contemporary Islamic world.

Nouvel at Sharaan

On October 27, 2020, the news of a new Jean Nouvel resort in Saudi Arabia hit the architectural news media.[16] While this was hardly unusual, especially considering the fact that the architect has designed and completed two prestigious projects in the Gulf Region (e.g., the Louvre Abu Dhabi and the National Museum of Qatar), the accompanying video, including computer-generated renderings of the project and an interview with Nouvel, impressed the architectural audience with its novelty.

The nearly six-and-a-half-minute video opens with a close up of what appears to be the surface of natural stone.[17] As the camera zooms out, first a text appears in capital letters: 'SHARAAN BY JEAN NOUVEL'. As the camera continues its retreat, one gets a better view of a big rocky formation, a butte, probably set within a mountainous zone. As daylight wanes, purple, orange, and yellow lights flicker through fissures on the rock's now-shadowy surface. The light oozes from the cracks, sometimes in a continuous slit, in others in a lace-like pattern. And when the night sky finally settles in, the white text – 'SHARAAN BY JEAN NOUVEL' – becomes even brighter in contrast to its dark background. The cinematographic strip seems to bring to us a vision of a settlement in a galaxy far, far away. The scene fades into total darkness and a new scene opens with a sunrise over a deserted valley of rocky formations. Then we hear the architect of this otherworldly place, who appears dressed in black, in a room with black-and-white walls, speak in French. As Nouvel narrates, we look at an impressive desert landscape, at inscribed writings on walls, at a stone crevice flooded with daylight, at dust moving with the air, and then we see a map of Saudi Arabia superimposed over the scene with a mark identifying the location of AlUla. English subtitles of Nouvel's speech run underneath: 'We are clearly in one of the cradles of civilization', he says, continuing:

> We are in a desert and a desert always means mystery, always means eternity. AlUla is really an open-air museum. What most struck me – beyond the archaeological features – is the work of the wind, of the wind on the rock formations. I'd never seen anything with the same precision before. And for me, these particular rock formations and landscapes are actually works of art. Building here is a real responsibility. The thing that's peculiar to Sharaan is that it's a virgin landscape.

AlUla is a region within Wadi al-Qura, which was home to Nabatean Civilization (second century BCE to first century CE), containing Saudi Arabia's first World Heritage site, Al-Hijr (Madâin Sâlih). In July 2017, Saudis formed the Royal Commission for AlUla 'to revitalize this unique region and to showcase its impressive heritage as part of the Saudi Vision 2030 plan'.[18] 'Saudi Vision 2030', which had been announced in 2016, was an ambitious and comprehensive economic plan to reduce Saudi Arabia's dependence on shrinking oil reserves.[19] On the official website for 'Saudi Vision 2030', Prince Mohammed Bin Salman Bin Abdulaziz Al-Saud described the government's vision, which rested on three pillars: their status in the Arab and Islamic worlds, especially as the host of the holy Islamic sites; their determination to become 'a global investment powerhouse'; and the transformation of their 'unique strategic location into a global hub connecting three continents'.[20] The Saudi government's new interest and investment in the heritage of a pre-Islamic civilization, making it a flagship project intended to present a new face for the country, clearly had its economic benefits.[21] But maybe even more significant than the economic benefits was the celebration of the country's pre-Islamic past, which was a common modernizing step in many other Muslim-majority countries (e.g., Turkey and Iran) at the turn of the twentieth century. As part of the plans, a French-Saudi partnership was formed in order to guide the development of AlUla into an archaeological, cultural, and touristic complex. The French Agency for AlUla was founded in July 2018, and in the same year a design competition for a resort project was organized as part of the bigger development plans for transforming the region into an international tourism destination. Nouvel's design for Sharaan Resort, named after an eponymous nature reserve, was selected by the Royal Commission for AlUla nearly two years before the winning project was publicly revealed.

'When you're a contextualist, which I am, that's the starting point', says Nouvel in the aforementioned publicity video. In his previous projects, too, we can observe him successfully 'work[ing] with what's there'. For example, in reference to his Louvre Abu Dhabi, Andraos calls Nouvel's architecture 'almost immaterial, blending in with the scenarios and atmospheres of its context, both real and imagined'.[22] She calls Nouvel 'a self-declared contextual architect', 'a no-kitsch designer', and talks about how 'his sophisticated knowledge insulates him from any charge of simplistic orientalist'.[23] Furthering this idea in the case of Sharaan, Nouvel explains:

> Building here means enhancing the site, it means giving it an added feature, it means providing a visual focus, and it also means using all that's there, using all the features that are there. And I feel there's something, here, that needs revisiting – through a form of modernity – and this something is 'inhabiting the rock'.

'Inhabiting the rock' is revealed from the outside only at night when interior lighting escapes through the crack-like voids in the stone's surface [Figure 22.1]. Otherwise, the occupation is camouflaged and 'the immediacy of perception' is strong.[24] This is a whole new stage in the creation of the 'friction-free space' that Spencer describes. There is no envelope, other than the one created by nature. The smoothness of the surface, the patterns, the lace-like openings on the surface of the rock – which Nouvel compares to *mashrabiya*s – have all been formed by the wind. The reunification of the subject with nature that Spencer references has reached its ultimate limit. There is no building here. The building is nature. At AlUla, enriching the site means empowering the imagination; this is a sensual enhancement. Nouvel explains again:

> So here, in this resort, we'll be in unique conditions. Emotion is the basis of architecture and it's the basis of art. So, it's clear that on these rock formations, inside these particular rocks, there is something emotional going on.

In the architect's discussion of Sharaan, emotion reads like a precognitive sensory experience that does not see a clear divide between emotion and affect.[25] Here what matters is the architecture's capacity to affect people with emotion. In the interior we notice patterns, both made by people – geometric and calculated – and by nature – organic, serendipitous – throughout (see Figure 22.1). The patterns cover the ground, the ceiling, and the walls, drawing light in, casting shadows, creating visual connections between inside and outside, and linking the interior with sky, land, and water.

The spectacular interior visualizations manifest an atmosphere that is both primeval and new, magical and rational. They are alluring. Borrowing words from human geographer Nigel Thrift's discussion of allure, we can say that the 'calculated sincerity of allure' is attractive in that the renderings 'manifest a particular style that generates enchantment without supernaturalism'.[26] In this sense they are representative of many objects and environments produced by capitalism. Thrift argues that the 'quality of allure' is applied to produce a more magical world that is also more calculated: 'In the process, new "intangible" value is being generated

Islamic Architecture Today and Tomorrow

Figure 22.1: Concept renderings of Jean Nouvel's resort at Sharaan, Saudi Arabia. Included are the view from within the resort (top), the pool area (middle), and an unspecified interior (bottom). Source: Ateliers Jean Nouvel.

for industries that are already some of the world's key means of making money.'[27] The magical qualities of Sharaan come from the site, as much as from the architecture that enhances the site. Nouvel concludes the interview:

> I personally think there is an underlying reason for every piece of architecture. But here, we're within a dimension that's very metaphysical, very poetic, and on a broad geographical scale, as well as within an awareness of a landscape, a world, that we want to enhance, that we want to make even more palpable. […] Here the brief is to disturb, but in a different way, to disturb through emotion, based on a poetic, philosophical, palpable material that's already there, but that should hopefully be more accessible after interventions like this one. As soon as you go into the rock like this, as soon as you go into the geography, as soon as you go into what amounts to a kind of entombment, you are obviously there – in principle – for eternity.

Nouvel smiles as the screen fades to black and the film ends. 'DISCOVER SHARAAN', 'SHAPED BY HISTORY', 'CURATED BY NATURE', and 'SCULPTED BY JEAN NOUVEL' flicker across shadowy footage of sand and sparkling dust.

Orientalizing the Scenography of Contemporary Architecture

All we have so far is the computer-generated images of Sharaan, since the resort is not due for completion until 2024. There is much more that one could say about the project in relation to affect theory, specifically based on these images alone. For example, following architectural scholar Akari Nakai Kidd, one could explore how affective the image-making is, or, in other words, how 'sticky' these images are.[28] Or, following Nigel Thrift again, one might explore the 'glamorous' persona of the starchitect.[29] Indeed, a 2019 *Financial Times* interview with Nouvel gives strong clues about his glamorous persona, from the restaurant he chose for the interview – where the alcove for his table is adorned with a model of the Louvre Abu Dhabi – to calling himself Don Quixote.[30] Whether Nouvel referred to himself this way because of idealistic, romantic, or egotistical perspectives is not clear; but his response to a query on 'building in places where he might not agree with social and political norms' suggested that he saw something chivalrous in his actions:

> It's about culture – it's very important to show that there are different cultural standards, that aren't narrowed by religion or fundamentalism. Being there and creating buildings can help the mentality to evolve. Just because a culture is in the Middle Ages, it doesn't mean you shouldn't go there. Just because they don't treat women in the way we agree with, it doesn't mean you shouldn't go there. I'm an optimist. If one can make things better, one must. I want things to change.[31]

The 'civilizing mission' of colonial-era projects comes back to haunt us in his words. It is true that the words Nouvel chooses to describe Sharaan and its site are full of qualities that were used to describe the 'Orient': from 'the cradles of civilization', to its 'virgin landscape', from being a place of enhanced experience, to its characterization as emotional, mysterious, metaphysical, and poetic. Probably the site's and, indirectly, the project's most striking quality, he proposes, is its timelessness. This timelessness suggests an isolation from the present.

What is more interesting than the orientalist residues in his presentation of Sharaan, however, is the realization that 'the scenography of contemporary architecture' is operating with qualities that were formerly associated with 'the Orient'. In other words, the architectural discourse on affect is self-orientalizing. It is self-orientalizing in contemporary architecture's positioning as the 'other' of the modern(ist) architecture, but not in the sense of denigrating itself. It is clearly not operating within a hierarchical order, and clearly not measuring itself against a developmental standard to justify exploitation. This time the otherness is set to celebrate, and to indulge in its differences without an excuse: its curves, patterns, surface qualities, its promise to offer a rich experience inside, enhanced by all the senses. Even though the scenography of contemporary architecture is not about 'the Orient' per se – however 'Orient' might be imagined – its qualities are as 'Oriental' as it gets.

Sharaan, too, as an impressive spot in this scenography, moves away from the rational, Cartesian, and the critical, toward the sensual, organic, and instinctual; no matter how calculated it actually is. So if we recall the words of Spencer, Sharaan is

> the friction-free space supposed to liberate the subject from the strictures of both modernism and modernity, to reunite it with nature, to liberate its nomadic, social and creative dispositions, to re-enchant its sensory experience of the world, to conjoin it with a technology itself now operating in accord with the very laws of the material universe, with emergence, self-organization and complexity.[32]

Sharaan in this sense is a stellar example of the global scenography of contemporary architecture, located within the geography of Islam. Compared to the many other flashy 'starchitecture' projects out there, Sharaan is the ultimate 'friction-free space', where the building completely disappears into its surrounding nature. It is a great contextual response to a site that is naturally and culturally significant. Its organic character, curved lines, its relatively introverted space organization, its almost hidden structural system, the patterns that dominate the interior spaces, the way the natural light is filtered through its surfaces, are all qualities that were once stereotypically associated with Islamic architecture. And yet, as Douglas Spencer shows us, these are the qualities of global contemporary architecture. And in this scenography there is no differentiation based on forced – even colonialist – categories like 'Islamic architecture', but a continuation of the contemporary scenography of global architecture. This is the state of celebrated architecture in any neo-liberal economy. This is the best that money can buy.

Notes

1. Nezar AlSayyad, 'From Modernism to Globalisation: The Middle East in Context', in *Architecture and Politics in the Twentieth Century*, ed. Sandy Isenstadt and Kishwar Rizwi (Seattle: University of Washington Press, 2008), 263.
2. AlSayyad, talking about urbanism in Middle Eastern cities, states that 'globalization has made the issues of identity and representation in urbanism very cumbersome and has cast doubt on urbanism's ability to fully represent the peoples, nations and cultures within which it exists.' Ibid., 263–64. I believe that the same can be said about architecture.
3. Amale Andraos, 'Problematizing a Regional Context: Representation in Arab and Gulf Cities', in *The New Arab Urban: Gulf Cities of Wealth, Ambition, and Distress*, ed. Harvey Molotch and Davide Ponzini (New York: New York University Press, 2019), 61.
4. Ibid.
5. I am using the term 'brandscapes' in the way that Anna Klingman uses it in Anna Klingman, *Brandscapes: Architecture in the Experience Economy* (Cambridge, MA: MIT Press, 2010).
6. While there is no clear date for the start of construction for the last two projects, their proposals attracted a lot of attention as they hit the architectural media.
7. Quoting Atelier Jean Nouvel regarding its Louvre Abu Dhabi Project. Atelier Jean Nouvel, 'Louvre Abu Dhabi', accessed February 13, 2021, http://www.jeannouvel.com/en/projects/louvre-abou-dhabi-3.
8. Douglas Spencer, *The Architecture of Neoliberalism: How Contemporary Architecture Became an Instrument of Control and Compliance* (New York: Bloomsbury, 2016), 1.
9. According to Spencer, the proponents of both this contemporary architecture and of neoliberalism share a 'hatred of hierarchical planning', and an enthusiasm for 'spontaneous ordering and self-organization', with their theory and practice feeding from the systems theory and cybernetics. And he underlines 'what they share, most of all' is 'a conception of the nature of the human subject, of its relations with the world around it, and of how it should be governed'. Ibid.
10. It is possible to trace the foundations of affect theory to Spinoza. After Spinoza, Deleuze is probably the most cited figure in relation to its development. Donovan Schaefer describes affect theory as follows: 'Affect theory is an approach to history, politics, culture, and all other aspects of embodied life that emphasizes the role of nonlinguistic and non- or paracognitive forces. As a method, affect theory asks what bodies do – what they want, where they go, what they think, how they decide – and especially how bodies are impelled by forces other than language and reason. It is, therefore, also a theory of power.' Donovan O. Schaefer, *The Evolution of Affect Theory* (Cambridge: Cambridge University Press, 2019), 1. Additionally, essays in *The Affect Theory Reader* are very helpful in understanding the areas that influenced, and are influenced by, affect theory. See Melissa Gregg and Gregory J. Seigworth, eds, *The Affect Theory Reader* (Durham, NC: Duke University Press, 2010).
11. Spencer, *The Architecture of Neoliberalism*, 140.
12. Ibid., 142.
13. Farshid Moussavi, *The Function of Form* (New York: Actar/Harvard University Graduate School of Design, 2009).

14 Spencer, *The Architecture of Neoliberalism*, 142.
15 Ibid., 159.
16 For example, see Philip Stevens, 'Jean Nouvel to Sculpt Saudi Arabian Landscape to Create Subterranean Resort and Hotel', *Designboom*, October 27, 2020, https://www.designboom.com/architecture/jean-nouvel-sharaan-saudi-arabia-subterranean-resort-hotel-10-27-2020/. Although the video was uploaded on YouTube by *Dezeen* on October 26, 2020, the news was broadcasted on October 27. See Tom Ravenscroft, 'Jean Nouvel Reveals Cave Hotel in Saudi Arabia's AlUla Desert,' *Dezeen*, October 27, 2020, https://www.dezeen.com/2020/10/27/sharaan-jean-nouvel-alula-desert-saudi-arabia/.
17 Afalula, 'Interview Jean Nouvel – Resort Sharaan Project', YouTube, October 28, 2020, https://youtu.be/-i3uZkhckFc.
18 French Agency for AlUla Development Press Kit (2019), accessed May 27, 2021, https://www.afalula.com/wp-content/uploads/2019/10/AFALULA_DOSSIER_DE_PRESSE_EN_10_2019.pdf.
19 Reuters gave the news of the plan's announcement with the headline: 'Saudis Await Prince's Vision of Future with Hope and Concern' in its 'Banks' section. The story reads: 'Saudi Arabians are anticipating with hope, doubt and worry the release this week of a government plan to liberate the kingdom from its reliance on oil, which could solve deep-rooted problems but bring economic pain.' Marwa Rashad, 'Saudis Await Prince's Vision of Future with Hope and Concern', *Reuters*, April 24, 2016, https://www.reuters.com/article/us-saudi-plan-idUSKCN0XL0B2.
20 'Message from HRH Prince Mohammed bin Salman bin Abdulaziz al-Saud', Saudi Vision 2030, accessed January 10, 2021, https://vision2030.gov.sa/en/vision/crown-message.
21 Economic benefits include 'enhancing the tourism economy by bringing in tourists keen to experience the cultural and natural heritage of AlUla'. Royal Commission for AlUla, 'Sharaan Resort Fact Sheet', accessed January 10, 2021, https://www.rcu.gov.sa/en/fact-sheets/sharaan-resort/.
22 Andraos, 'Problematizing a Regional Context', 63.
23 Ibid.
24 Spencer, *The Architecture of Neoliberalism*, 10.
25 Emotion and affect are two words that are entangled together. Affect theorists that follow a Deleuzian path prefer to draw a clear line between affect as 'a precognitive sensory experience' preceding emotion, and emotion as a culturally loaded, more conscious process; while others seem to be 'less committed to the differentiation between affect and emotion'. Schaefer, *The Evolution of Affect Theory*, 7–8.
26 Nigel Thrift, 'Understanding the Material Practices of Glamour', in Gregg and Seigworth, *The Affect Theory Reader*, loc. 3902–3905 of 5490, Kindle edition.
27 Ibid.
28 Akari Nakai Kidd borrows the term 'sticky' from Sarah Ahmed's discussion of 'happy objects'. According to Ahmed, 'Affect is what sticks, or what sustains or preserves the connection between ideas, values, and objects.' See also Sara Ahmed, 'Happy Objects', in Gregg and Seigworth, *The Affect Theory Reader*, loc. 396–397 of 5490, Kindle edition. Kidd adopts the terminology to discuss how '"stickiness of affect" operates through architectural image-making practices'. See

also Akari Nakai Kidd, 'The Stickiness of Affect in architectural Practice: The Image-making Practice of Reiser + Umemoto, RUR Architecture DPC', *ARQ* 22.2 (2018): 127–38.
29 Thrift discusses glamorous personas as existing 'in the realm of mediated imagination, as stimuli promoting further exploration, stirring up the proverbial itch of urges, desires, and identifications that we can't help but scratch'. Nigel Thrift, 'Understanding the Material Practices of Glamour', in Gregg and Seigworth, *The Affect Theory Reader,* loc. 4100–4101 of 5490, Kindle edition.
30 Jan Dalley, 'Jean Nouvel: Architecture Is an Art', *Financial Times,* December 27, 2019, https://www.ft.com/content/8d825fe0-2247-11ea-92da-f0c92e957a96.
31 Ibid.
32 Spencer, *The Architecture of Neoliberalism,* 1.

Chapter 23

The 'Islamic-Modern' Project in this Age of Uncertainty

Vikramaditya Prakash

The invitation to first write this essay for the *International Journal of Islamic Architecture* arrived at a moment of significant uncertainty, not just around our climate-defined planet's future, our political and economic futures, but also more immediately around the very viabilities of our daily lives. Coronavirus was, and is, reshaping the very fabric of global societies in a way that is expected to have long-lasting effects. But then again, the fact that we have all but forgotten the so-called 'Spanish Flu' of 1918, that in one year single-handedly killed more people than the devastation of World War I did, while popular films on the War are still being made, speaks to the cultural amnesia that accompanies traumatic events such as pandemics. When a problem is so gargantuan and so insurmountable – an existential risk, as some say – then it seems to serve us best to simply push it out of consciousness. What can we do about it anyway?

Eurocentrism, our response, which is to say both in the west and the non-west, to the deeply embedded global malaise that privilege must necessarily flow to the west, may be a cultural pandemic of the same kind. It is a kind of collective, shared amnesia. What can we really do about it anyway? Beyond setting up a few courses in diversity and 'global' topics, it is probably unrealistic to try to think about it more broadly, more systemicly. Meanwhile, right-wing nationalism of many a colour and hue are regaining traction across the world at a level not seen since the end of World War II, income inequality has reached absurd levels, and the president of the United States feels free to assassinate Iranian leaders at will, and when US Customs agents think nothing of dismantling a reliquary musical instrument as valuable as a Stradivarius in search of who knows what – drugs, alcohol, a stowaway devil? At this time, in these circumstances, the editors ask for a piece that interrogates the term 'Islamic architecture'. They are interested, the November 2019 invitation letter continues, in 'different ways of engaging the Islamic world through the study of colonialism, postcolonialism, modernism, globalization, &c., and not "Islamic" material in the traditional sense'.

Personally speaking, this is a precipitously positioned request for me to respond to. As a non-Islamic specialist historian (who nevertheless purports to speak 'for' the non-west and the 'global'), and as an architect who is only indirectly connected to the Islamic world via my country of origin, this query asks of me to step into the fray in an area outside my stated disciplinary comprehension, outside my comfort zone. There are established canons, both academic and non-, around this question – as for instance in well-endowed Aga Khan programs for Islamic Architecture at MIT and Harvard. I have no claims to such intelligences. Nonetheless, one of the key contentions of the Global Architectural History Teaching Collaborative (GAHTC),[1] of which I am with Mark Jarzombek a founding board member, and a frequent contributor and user, is that equity, or the demand for equity, in the global representation of architecture requires non-specialists to take on the risky task of learning and teaching non-specialist materials, particularly of underrepresented content. The purpose of the GAHTC is to support such tasks, but ultimately it is the faculty member taking on learning and teaching who has to step outside his/her/their comfort zone and take on the work of seeing and engaging the unfamiliar. Our contention is that unfamiliarity, like un-specialization, should not be used as an alibi to side-step the critical task of representing the under-represented. This is no doubt a challenging task, full of risks, with not minor chances of failure or mistakes. But my academic training in postcolonial thinking teaches me that it is precisely when I encounter my own incomprehension that the potential for the disciplinary voice of the Other to become accessible to me opens up. If I insist on sitting within the comfort of my own disciplinary comprehensions then I am likely to be blind to, and usually work to silence, the Other.

For the task at hand, I have chosen the strategy of using reflective autobiography to construct a narrative of reinterpretations, a history of sorts, of paths taken and those not. I propose to use the question: How did I encounter the question of the Islamic-modern in my career and life as a thread to try and at least untangle the knot of my own personal amnesia. The aspiration of my narrative is to use biography not as a pretext to position the present as the culmination of a teleology – although that temptation is not one that I will be entirely successful in totally avoiding – but to try and critically rethink events from my past. 'Critical thinking', I am well aware, can easily become a moniker, a catchall, for the unstated non-obvious, another ruse deployed by amnesia. Even as I understand this risk, I am not sure I have a better definition for it. My gambit is that a certain criticality, if not prescient hindsight, that comes available to oneself after a sufficiently long trudge of experience will help illuminate some of the blindnesses and oversights, even as it might obscure others, something like a flashlight in the dark.

Bio-graph

It was through the Aga Khan Awards in Architecture that I was introduced, as a young student of architecture in the early 1980s, to the obvious but to me somewhat counter-intuitive question of what a modern, contemporary Islamic architecture might be. My architectural education until that point had been typically postcolonial, which is to say rigorously colonial combined with the orthodoxically modernist. The complete history of human architecture could be divided into (mostly and most complexly) Western, Islamic, Other Minor Traditions (most particularly Indian) and of which culminated, most importantly, in the modern. Modern architecture was modern, precisely because it was not Islamic, or Hindu, or Christian, or any other such 'limiting', traditional identitarian conceit. Chandigarh was my hometown, and the very rationale for the city – 'unfettered by the traditions of the past'– was constructed around the narrative of a modernism that was putatively free of any identitarian baggage.[2]

Unlike history or religious identity, nationalism, at least for those of us in postcolonial nation-states like India, could quite happily be married to modernism. Indeed, the question of what an appropriately hyphenated 'modern-Indian' architecture could/should be, was the question of our times. The 1980s were postmodern times. With the critiques of modernism high-handedness the new orthodoxy, the quest was on for an appropriately hyphenated alternative to global/universalist modernism. Historical and cultural formalism seemed to be the answer. Typologies from historical architecture were measured, drawn, and debated endlessly, old building manuals and architectural codices from the eighth, twelfth, and sixteenth centuries were studied endlessly (in search of alternatives to those of the great Vitruvius and Alberti?) and many an esoteric reader of ancient Indian philosophical origin was dusted off from the library shelves to be caricatured and exoticized, alternately. But no one, not one self-respecting architect or architectural historian in my orbit, offered to assemble a Hindu-Modern architecture or to revive the old 'Indo-Saracenic' architecture for India's secularist credentials. Secularism remained unquestionable, at least in the upper echelons of urban culture that commanded and controlled the debates of architecture in India, at that time. The possibility of a modern Islamic architecture, like that of a modern Hindu or Buddhist one was one we had neither considered, nor was one we sought to broach, considering it well beyond the pale of modernism, a heresy of sorts.

Until, that is, the arrival of the Aga Khan Awards early in the 1980s. With established modernist architectural luminaries like Charles Correa, Balkrishna Doshi, and Hassan Fathy at its helm, the Aga Khan Awards sought to invest the question of an Islamic architecture with a determinedly modernist affect. The Islamic modern was a project, we were made to relearn, whose provenance lay in the many modernizers of the Nehruvian ilk such as Ataturk and of course the Aga Khan.

The first Aga Khan Award to come India's way, when I was still an undergraduate student there, was a fancy five-star hotel, a stone's throw from the Taj Mahal. Awarded in 1980, the Mughal Sheraton was a brick building with internal courtyards, loosely referencing the *charbagh* courts of the Taj and the other Indian Mughal tombs [Figure 23.1]. What made it Islamic *modern* architecture? It was certainly not a reimagining of Islamic formal typologies, or Islamic intellectual or philosophical content. Rather, it seemed that what was distinctive about it was its turn to modernist spatiality via abstraction. In the end, it seemed to me that the project was most creditable for the subtlety and quietude with which it deferred to the grand Islamic monument it was designed to serve. Was that a way to think the Islamic modern?

A second Aga Khan Award for architecture in India went to the Entrepreneurial Development Institute of India, a little outside Ahmedabad in Western India. It was also made out of brick with expressive concrete lintels. The formal vocabulary of this building was even less obviously Islamic in reference, looking more like colonial Indo-Saracenic. In plan, this structure was a versioning of Louis Kahn's IIM complex in Ahmedabad, loosely merged with Islamic palace complexes, like Sarkhej, built in the fifteenth century during the reign of Sultan Ahmed Shah, just on the outskirts of Ahmedabad. The loose formal reference to Sarkhej was enough, it seems, to consider this structure a paragon of the Islamic-modern.

Four more Aga Khan awards have been awarded to Indian projects, but I have picked the two that intersected with my autobiography to note that for those of us learning architecture in postcolonial India, the one that had yet to join the neoliberal empirization of the world. Islam,

Islamic Architecture Today and Tomorrow

Figure 23.1: Exterior views of the Mughal Sheraton Hotel. Located in in Agra, India, it was designed by ARCOP Design Group/Ramesh Khosla, Ranjit Sabikhi, Ajoy Choudhury, and Ray Affleck (1976). Source: Aga Khan Trust for Culture/ Christopher Little (photographer, top) and Justin FitzHugh (photographer, bottom).

just like Hinduism, in the secular public of the Indian nation-state, was set up to succeed only as a transformative concept, yoked to a progressive social vision, and not one that was only aesthetic, modernized through the ubiquitous, supposedly universal, trope of abstraction.

In 1985 my best friend and I undertook a motorcycle *bharat-darshan yatra*, a discovery-of-India voyage in the Nehruvian mould, organized around some of the 'greatest works' of history of the architecture of north-western India. We experienced Mughal architecture, from Humayun's Tomb in Delhi, to its late derivatives in the architecture and urbanism of eighteenth-century century Jaipur. After long nights of debate and discussion, over endless Gold Flake cigarettes and Golden Eagle lagers, we discussed the merits of Akbar's palace city of Fatehpur Sikri versus Shah Jahan's magnificent Rauza-i-Munnavara (the Taj Mahal). While unquestionably resplendent, there was no way to modernize the Taj, we concluded. But Akbar's Fatehpur Sikri, with its *Ibadat Khana* or Worship-Meeting House, where Akbar, 500 years ago, had called a multi-faith conference to discuss global theology, we reasoned somewhat exaggeratedly, embodied an ideal of modernity that was ahead of its time even today. Sikri's *Diwan-i-Khas*, the Hall of Special Audience, with its single column in the middle attached to the corners by bridges so that Akbar could actively draw on questions of law from various religious/philosophical frameworks, was for us *the* most modern of buildings in India that, for the conceptual and programmatic rigor of its design, was justifiably unique in the world. This was the vision of the Islamic modern that we, at least in the South Asian/ Indian context, imputed as the telos of Islamic architecture in the postcolonial world – a telos of intellectual possibility, not just of form. It was an expansive expectation, that seemed latent and available as a non-Eurocentric rebuttal to the prosaic formalism of western postmodernism that was in vogue at that time in the 1980s. Modern architecture of the rest of the Islamic world was gravely under-published at that time, and almost completely unavailable to us in India. Under the circumstances, we boldly imagined South Asia, with its recent history of grand modernist projects such as those in Dhaka, Islamabad, Chandigarh, and Ahmedabad, as the potential site of such a re-imagination of the Islamic-modern. This was the argument that I ambitiously made in my 'Statement of Intent' that enabled me to study, with full fellowship, the history of architecture and urban development at Cornell University, starting in 1986.

In 1988, on one of my many long trips back home from grad school in the United States, I took a layover in Paris, and went to see Jean Nouvel's Arab World Institute [Figure 23.2]. It was *the* new thing then. With its clever, sophisticated, and very expensive merging of the summer screen, a common element of a lot of desert architecture, with the Steampunk (not yet a cultural reference then) aesthetics of the shutter of an analogue camera, the Arab World Institute was represented to us coming from the Third World as the apotheosis of the Islamic-modern as cultured by the high western aesthetic. It was difficult not to see it as yet another orientalist (by then I was reading Edward Said!) fetishization and drastic oversimplification of the idea of the '*monde arabe*'.

In graduate school, Edward Said's *Orientalism*, and then the subsequent trenchant critiques of Eurocentrism that were launched by the series of post-structuralist scholars like Homi Bhabha and Gayatri Spivak, established the intellectual framework that I espouse to this day. Postcolonial theory framed the very complex problematic that was the quest for a

Figure 23.2: The façade of Jean Nouvel's Institut du monde arabe (Arab World Institute) in Paris, France (1987). Source: Daniel E. Coslett.

non-Eurocentric modernism for me. Given that modernity, modernism, and the Enlightenment itself were Euro-located constructs that were deeply entangled with the colonial project, and given the 'tug' – what Spivak called what you 'cannot-not' (versus 'want-to') do – that postcolonial subjects like myself inevitably feel towards this west as the site of the modern, forced me to reconcile with the idea that all projects of the modern have to reckon with their thrall to the 'West'. The question of what non-Eurocentric (Indian/Islamic/tropical, etc.) modernism might be was clearly not just the task of 'asserting our voice' against the hegemonic epistemologies of the west, but of 'working-though' our thrall to the Euro-modern. Working-through versus acting-out, both Euro-modernist bourgeois psychoanalytic concepts, became touch points for young scholars like me, for whom 'working-through' involved the very hard and painstaking work of first realizing that my-'self', my identity as a representative of the non-west and its architecture was already pre-contaminated by the Eurocentric. Simply asserting that the Indian in Indian architecture was known first and foremost as that which was not of the west, was simply acting out, uncritically repeating the fake distinctions between 'the West and the Rest'.

There can be little doubt that the deliberate and premeditated destruction of Babri Masjid by the Hindu nationalist *kar sevaks* (service workers) signalled the end of the Nehruvian modernist, secularist ethos in India. Like the destruction of the Twin Towers in Manhattan to follow, it was this very spectacular and emotionally charged destruction of a work of architecture that sounded the alarm in the public imagination that a new social order was in formation.

I remember that day well. There was no internet, and so the news travelled slowly via state-controlled radio and television, and then most apprehensible via print journalism. The picture of orange-scarfed *kar sevaks* perched triumphantly on top of the heavily weathered dome of Babri Masjid, moments before they forced its implosion, remains lodged indelibly in my imagination.

Retrospectively, perhaps just as frightening as the authorization of anti-Muslim violence that the destruction of Babri Masjid announced, was the un-ceremonial unmasking of the secularist hubris of Nehruvian India to which we had all subscribed. It was a wake-up call, a challenge to construct a new imagination for a post-postcolonial world. What we witnessed through the 1990s, in the shadow of the spectacular rise of the internet and economic globalization, was a shifting of the Cold War rivalry into a new imagined rivalry between the world of Islam, and the rest. (How the Hindu right wing, with its destruction of Babri Masjid came to play a prescient role in this theatre of cultural warfare, is a story that deserves to be told in another register.)

Since 9/11, architecture's response to the demonization of Islam has become a side preoccupation of mine. Again, not being a specialist on the topic, I have sought to engage the conversation around this question with multiple architects and scholars, using the instrument of my podcast 'ArchitectureTalk' as my forum.[3] Self-consciously designed as a cross-disciplinary platform, 'ArchitectureTalk' is intended to field the question of what architecture *is* and more importantly what it *could* be in the twenty-first century, in the face of the big questions of our times, such as climate change, globalization, xenophobia, artificial intelligence, transgender studies, queer theory, and thing theory. I am interested in the culturalist response to the looming crises of our time. In the twenty-first century, with the rise of sectarian fundamentalisms of every colour and hue – Christian, Islamic, Hindu, Buddhist, neo-Nazi, white supremacy, and so on – it has become clear that the old modernist project has failed to deliver, and even as the twin spectres of climate change and artificial intelligence are whipped up into a frenzy by their lord and master, global capitalism, a non-technologist answer to this era of anxiety and uncertainty that we find ourselves, I argue, has become more urgent than ever.

The looming question of the Islamic-modern, it seems to me, occupies a special place in this new firmament. It is no longer the question of parsing the question of Islam though the secularist exigencies and niceties of the nation-state, as in the India of my youth. Now it is the question of the very possibility of a cultural imaginary of our diverse world. As the topic of the Hashim Sarkis-curated 2020 Venice Architecture Biennale asks, 'how will we live together?' There is a very urgent need for us to re-construct a post-United Nations vision of the world, as a planet and as a society of multi-species beings, only one amongst which is the human, if we are to continue to believe that the coming generations will be able to ride out the uncertainties that beset us today. There are many questions that need to be parsed through this re-imagination. Ecological thinking, multi-species relatedness, queer theory-led rearticulation of gender and sexual identities, quantum entanglement, global historiography – to name a few – are some of the topics that I have taken an interest in on my podcast on architecture. It is clearly a work in progress.

A Post-humanist Cultural Imaginary

One of the best conversations I have had on 'ArchitectureTalk' was with Shima Mohajeri, author of the superb book *Architectures of Transversality: Paul Klee, Louis Kahn and the Persian Imagination*.[4] In her book, and in our conversation, Mohajeri grappled with the question of the Islamic-modern through the trope of 'transversality'. This is a term used mostly to describe complex graphic intersections. Transversality, as I understand from Mohajeri, is for her a moniker to signify a process of engagement that responds to multiple vectors and forces without singling out one or a few as dominant. As she argues, the quest for an 'Islamic-modern', which in her case concerns the metamorphosis of Iranian aesthetic and visual culture, is a process of dedicated unfolding, a constant and persistent remaking that does not have a known, or even intuited, predestination. Transversality, in other words, does not seek to merge or hybridize the western and Islamic, or the traditional and the modern, or any other such binary pre-knowns. Rather it operates in an agential manner in constant entanglement with the multiple contingent forces that it faces in the process of design and execution of an on-going project. It cuts into, and remakes, all its contingencies – local, non-local, universal, political, aesthetic – in a critical and self-critical manner.

So, for example, Mohajeri describes Paul Klee's famous *Twittering Machine* as an outcome of his earlier Nightingale paintings in which he translated fifteenth-century Persian miniatures into his own aesthetic through new readings of the very early twentieth-century modernist preoccupation with representation of time and space [Figure 23.3].[5] Unlike the Cubist device of faceting, by which the viewer was invited to enter into the more purportedly 'objective' representation of time and space (unlike the eye/I-centric vision offered by perspectival painting), Klee interpreted the Sufi-inspired miniature paintings as devices that sought to undo the very temporality of time as a linear construct – think Walter Benjamin's 'angel of history', which Klee also painted – and produced paintings that sought to 'annihilate' time altogether by collapsing the forever past (beginning of the world) into the present. If the present is also in a way the beginning of time (as we are now learning from astrophysics as we peer into deep space to beginning of time) then the past, present, and by implication the future are not 'objective' constructs that can be charted and graphed on paper, as the Cubist contention contends, but fluid parameters that can 'transversally' produce multiple, asynchronous possibilities of our engagement with time. That is how Mohajeri interprets Klee's famous *Twittering Machine* – an autonomous device, with a self-turning crank that unfolds time along many possible trajectories and simultaneities. From a modernist reading of Persian miniatures, in this sense, Klee's *Twittering Machine* models an agential way, which is to say, a way of working and thinking, that offers a dynamic way of thinking of the Islamic-modern, which is to say one that is not fixed or idealized.

In her second case study, Mohajeri turns to architecture. She looks at Louis Kahn's designs for the Abbas Abad or Tehran New Civic Center (1973–74) complex, a project that he was working on when he died unexpectedly in 1974.[6] In the Abbas Abad project, Kahn was invited by Farah Pahlavi to design a major government complex, quite like the one that he was then

The 'Islamic-Modern' Project in this Age of Uncertainty

Figure 23.3: Paul Klee's *Twittering Machine* (1922). Source: Artists Rights Society (ARS), New York.

designing in Dhaka for Pakistan, or like the one that Le Corbusier did for India in Chandigarh. Mohajeri describes how Kahn initially came into the project imagining a progressive, westernized vision as was supposedly championed by the project's clients, the Shah Reza Pahlavi and his wife Farah. Once on site, Kahn realized that the Shah's political vision was not quite what he had imagined, and that the interests of the couple were competitive and in tension. Furthermore, he quickly realized that though the central element of the public plaza was intended as a site for public protest, the protests on the street were effectively being silenced by the Shah. Finally, as he came to revise his project, done in collaboration with Kenzo Tange, Kahn changed the design from one that was clearly defined with well-defined public spaces and monumental structures, to one that was more ambiguous, open-ended, and uncertain in its spatial and formal description [Figure 23.4].

Mohajeri's point, in describing this metamorphosis in Kahn's project, as I understood it, was not to put up yet one more 'celebration' of the architect's mysterious design processes, or to evaluate the design against some preconceived aesthetic or cultural template – 'modernist' or 'Islamic' or 'Persian' or 'critical regionalist' – but to describe, index, and carefully annotate the innumerable mini accommodations and resistances that go into a complex and thoughtful design, which sees itself as somehow accountable to its many constituent stakeholders. Like the *Twittering Machine*, in the end the design is not a finished product nor a perfectly resolved solution, but an incomplete work indicative of and commensurate with the 'unfinished project of modernity' that was, and still is, Iran.

The Islamic-modern project, as Mohajeri describes it, is unfinished, not because it has not yet 'caught up' to some kind of a 'finished' project that is the west. The US White House of Donald Trump, with its neo-colonialist mindset, was ample evidence of that. Rather it is that modernity itself is a purposefully unfinished project, and in that register, the Islamic-modern, if done properly, must also in a fundamental way be indexed as such. The Islamic-modern, or the transversal in Mohajeri's words, is necessarily always a work in progress. Not because the Islamic world is behind, but because modernity as a project, at its very best, is always 'catching up'. Although transversality 'is invisible and in a sense unfinished', Mohajeri averred on my podcast, 'it is constantly in the state of resisting and concurring and making. It can assert itself at any time into reality and not stay in a utopian mode'.[7] That, I would argue, is the promise and possibility of the Islamic-modern.

Acknowledgement

I am grateful to Shima Mohajeri for her reading through this piece and offering constructive criticism in many registers.

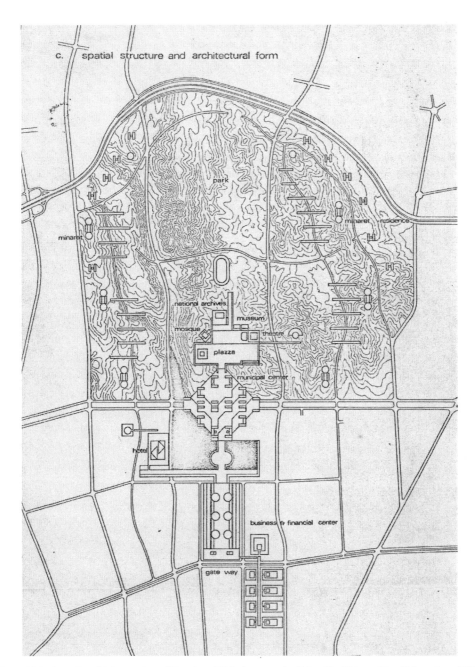

Figure 23.4: Arata Isozaki, integration of Tange's and Kahn's proposals, Abbas Abad Master Plan, Tehran, Iran (1974). Source: Louis I. Kahn Collection, University of Pennsylvania and Pennsylvania Historical and Museum Commission.

Notes

This chapter was previously published as Vikramāditya Prakāsh, 'The "Islamic-Modern" Project in this Age of Uncertainty', *International Journal of Islamic Architecture* 10.1 (2021): 269–80. The text has been updated for this publication.

1. 'Mission Statement', Global Architectural History Teaching Collaborative, accessed April 28, 2020, https://gahtc.org/pages/mission-statement.
2. India's partition in 1947 resulted in widespread communal violence between Muslims and non-Muslims, resulting in an estimated 1 million dead. Jawaharlal Nehru, the first prime minister of independent India, self-consciously asked that Chandigarh be built in a modernist idiom because he did not want the new city to have a communal identity, Hindu, Muslim, or otherwise. See Vikramaditya Prakash, *Chandigarh's Le Corbusier: The Struggle for Modernity in Postcolonial India* (Seattle: University of Washington Press, 2002).
3. 'About', ArchitectureTalk, accessed April 28, 2020, https://www.architecturetalk.org/about.
4. '37. Transversality: Klee, Kahn and the Persian Imagination with Shima Mohajeri', ArchitectureTalk, February 13, 2020, https://www.architecturetalk.org/home/37; Shima Mohajeri, *Architectures of Transversality: Paul Klee, Louis Kahn and the Persian Imagination* (New York: Routledge, 2018).
5. In her reading of the paper, Mohajeri commented: 'Klee became familiar with Persian miniatures within the context of Islamic art exhibitions in Berlin and Munich, and through his friendship with Kandinsky and Marc. I found a miniature with the twin motifs of the rose and the nightingale in the Munich Islamic art exhibition catalogue of 1910. Yet Klee's knowledge of the Persian Sufi culture is deeply influenced by Goethe's West-eastern Divan. In the tradition of Persian miniaturists, Klee's miniatures were visual translations of Goethe's poetic words'. Mohajeri quoted in '37. Transversality'.
6. See also Shima Mohajeri, 'Louis Kahn's Silent Space of Critique in Tehran, 1973–74', *Journal of the Society of Architectural Historians* 74.4 (2015): 485–504.
7. Mohajeri quoted in '37. Transversality'.

Part 8

Experience and Use

Chapter 24

The Tourist Gaze, Visiting Mosques, and the Folds of Architecture

Elif Kalaycıoğlu and Waleed Hazbun

By multiple measures, tourism is one of the largest economic sectors across the global economy.[1] With its roots in the practices of scientific exploration, the European Grand Tour, and different forms of religious pilgrimage, modern tourism expanded across the twentieth century with the growth of global transportation networks and capitalist consumerism.[2] Popular organized tourism first developed across North Europe and the United States, but states with Islamic heritage, such as those across the Mediterranean region, have long attracted global visitors to their pilgrimage locations, vibrant cities, sunny beaches, ancient ruins, and cultural heritage sites. Observing architecture has been central to the development of the tourist gaze or the 'visualisation of the travel experience'.[3] Tourist itineraries are often shaped by travel to view monuments and buildings that have been marked by travelogues, guidebooks, advertisements, and other media as culturally significant. Urban heritage and architecture, however, often have a contentious relationship with modern tourism. While programs for urban heritage preservation are frequently justified and financed by the anticipation of economic activity associated with tourism, tourism can also negatively impact urban spaces and the built environment. Mass tourism is often associated with the destruction, erosion, or commodification of urban architectural fabric that heritage preservationists seek to conserve as 'authentic'. As a result, organizations such as UNESCO's World Heritage Committee recognize that 'if undertaken responsibly, tourism can be a driver for preservation and conservation of cultural [...] heritage', but 'if unplanned or not properly managed, tourism can be socially, culturally and economically disruptive'.[4]

In considering how to responsibly plan tourism development, beyond seeking to limit the flows and negative impacts of mass tourism, we argue that scholars and practitioners of architecture, cultural heritage, and tourism must consider how alternative modes of tourism and sightseeing can serve as vehicles for imagining different ways to experience the city and its architectures, and thus sustain alternative modes for urban heritage development. We seek to build from Hasan-Uddin Khan's observation that while modern tourism tends to be 'embedded and viewed through western norms and standards', there are often multiple ways to experience and interpret place.[5] Drawing on historical and contemporary examples of visits to mosques in Cairo, Cordoba, Istanbul, and elsewhere, we highlight the pluralization of the tourist gaze through the rise of what can very loosely be referred to as 'Islamic tourism' as well as secular interest in forms of historical and contemporary Islamic architecture.[6] Using the example of mosques, but advancing an argument that applies to other forms of heritage such as souks, museums, monuments, and historic neighbourhoods, we explore how built environments can be experienced when a structure or monument reflects multiple meanings, uses, and histories that can be continually unfolded, and thus never settled. In doing so, we realize that the existence of different tourist practices and/or multiple meanings do not automatically result in pluralism, which values and seeks to preserve and create linkages among such diversity. Thus, we offer suggestions for how different forms of tourism can contribute to, rather than constrain, the pluralization of understandings and expressions of urban heritage and architecture.

Politics of Urban Preservation

Heritage preservation is intricately connected to politics and entails competition over whose version of the past, with its sanctioned narratives of triumph and belonging, will be maintained through material conservation. More specifically, the development and preservation of urban heritage is 'a reflection primarily of the values of whichever social group is ascendant at the time', as that group moulds the city in its image, conserving parts of it and opening other parts to redevelopment.[7] At the same time, conservation practices often lead to a tension concerning 'museumification'. In the name of preservation, these programs often reshape the built environment and the experience of urban spaces such that streetscapes can become urban heritage theme parks as local residents and their businesses are driven out by efforts to promote heritage authenticity.[8]

How does tourism intersect with these tensions of urban heritage preservation? First, increases in mass tourism flows result in renewed urgency for heritage preservation and protection. Second, tourism intersects with the domestic politics of determining what is to be preserved based on dominant constructions of the tourist gaze. What tourists will want to look at and how they understand what they see are often defined by existing knowledge and expectations. These expectations in turn influence decisions on what parts, or layers, of urban heritage to preserve and how to present it. For example, preservation and development efforts focused on *riad*s (urban courtyard homes) in Morocco and the medinas of Tunisia, which often draw on colonial nostalgia, are typically funded by foreign development agencies and cater to external investors and tourists.[9] Others, however, have argued more positively that the tourist gaze, with its demand for the unique, can lead to the preservation of plural layers of a place's past.[10] This dynamic has given rise to some optimism in relation to 'minority heritage', that is to say the heritage of non-ascendant ethnic, religious, or racial groups, which might otherwise go unprotected and unpreserved.

The Tourist Gaze and Modernity

In his classic 1976 text *The Tourist: A New Theory of the Leisure Class*, sociologist Dean MacCannell observes that 'the rhetoric of tourism is full of manifestations of the importance of the authenticity of the relationship between tourists and what they see'.[11] This notion of authenticity, however, is an ideological construction that has helped define how urban spaces and the built environment are viewed and understood by tourists. As such, the construction of authenticity, and thus the tourist gaze, is in many cases based on 'the ideological separation of the modern from the nonmodern world', often producing tourism development based on 'artificial preservation and reconstruction' of non-modern built environments.[12] Implicit in this early and incisive theorization of the tourist gaze is the figure of tourist as a middle-class traveller within or from industrialized western nations. As a result, much of heritage tourism across the Mediterranean Islamic region, a region with many layers of history, has been organized around a tourist gaze focused on familiar Greco-Roman features framed as authentic foundations of modern European (and Christian) heritage. Meanwhile, features of Islamic heritage are often presented as exotic and non-modern. Even in a majority-Muslim country like Jordan, a survey of roads and signage by landscape architect Erin Addison concludes that 'it is unavoidable that the impression forming in the tourist's mind is that of a landscape heavy with Christian history, and virtually void of Islamic remains.'[13]

Over time, however, mobilities and cultural practices have changed. The disposable income that makes tourism possible is available to a broader range of populations across geographies, along with the global infrastructures that make leisure travel possible. In parallel, tourism-studies scholars have come to recognize diverse constructions of the tourist gaze shaped by culture, class, gender, and other differences.[14] To date, much scholarly analyses of changing populations of tourists and transforming patterns and practices of tourism globally have focused on East Asia. Such works have demonstrated the rise of domestic and intra-regional tourism, and a parallel shift in the investors and the kinds of investment in infrastructure.[15] Moving beyond East Asia, Noel Scott and Jafar Jafari note that 'the Muslim market, both for religious and personal reasons, is of great importance', adding that the 'number of Muslim travellers is expected to increase'.[16] Others have begun to explore the qualitative changes implied by these shifts, contending that observant Muslims might look for different experiences, such as community links rather than a search for the 'exotic', as they take part in leisure tourism.[17] Such trends suggest new possibilities, as well as an analytical need, for (re)defining the tourist gaze.

Two Views of Al-Azhar

We suggest that this pluralizing tourist gaze can reveal alternative ways to experience urban places and the built environment and thus enable diverse ways to reconstruct the relations of modern tourism with urban heritage and architecture. In fact, such alternatives, while left at the peripheries, have long existed. One can turn to nineteenth-century Egypt to illustrate.

Cairo-based historian Michael Reimer offers an insightful contrast between how the French political journalist Gabriel Charmes (1850–86) and the Egyptian administrator and author Ali Pasha Mubarak (1823–93) viewed the al-Azhar Mosque at the centre of old

Cairo.[18] Although al-Azhar remains one of the most important religious and educational institutions in the Islamic world, Charmes was one of the few western travellers to Egypt in the nineteenth century to write about visiting it. While Egypt was an increasingly popular destination for European and American travellers during the nineteenth century, and would soon witness the expanded arrival of tourists, the emerging tourist gaze generally sought out Egypt's ancient monuments popularized by their depictions in the volumes of *Description de l'Égypte* (*Description of Egypt*).[19] Obscured by other buildings and lacking the remarkable features of more picturesque Cairene mosques, al-Azhar was not a tourist attraction legible to the western tourist gaze.

Charmes, however, recognized the importance of al-Azhar and declared the building a 'must-see' in Cairo. In his account, Charmes offers details about al-Ahzar's history and its system of Islamic education. Taking readers inside the complex, he offers a picturesque description of everyday life including fruit sellers, barbers, and school children reciting the Qur'an. Nevertheless, the depth and complexity of Charmes's view is limited. Remarking on Charmes's scenes of people of diverse races and dress, Reimer notes that the kaleidoscopic effect of his writing offers a motif recognizable to western readers in terms of the 'Orient's strangeness'.[20] These motifs are not unlike Bonfils's photographs of students at the mosque [Figure 24.1]. Timothy Mitchell reproduces such an image in *Colonising Egypt*, as he notes European descriptions of the scene as representing disorder and decay.[21] In fact, Charmes also depicted al-Azhar as an institution 'lacking an openness to new ideas of science and social progress'.[22] Al-Azhar thus becomes for Charmes a tourist site through which he can gaze at the contemporary Islamic world as a half-ruin, thereby relegating it to the past.

Charmes's contemporary, the Egyptian writer Ali Mubarak, by contrast, does not offer orientalist depictions of the historicized picturesque. Instead, he presents a rich, critical portrayal of al-Azhar. He views al-Azhar as a living centre of Islamic learning with a long history of change inhabited by a cosmopolitan body of scholars and students. An advocate for administrative and educational reform and modernization in Egypt, he observes that, like the rest of Egypt, al-Azhar is in transition; it is undergoing a period of much-needed, but not fully adequate, reform. By being able to relate to the specificities of al-Azhar as a contemporary, complex, and dynamic place, Ali Mubarak can critique the limits of reform within al-Azhar while remaining 'firmly convinced of the essential rationality of Islam'.[23]

Ali Mubarak's depictions of al-Azhar can be read along with efforts of others who produced nuanced visualizations. In contrast to the western tourist gaze reflected in Bonfils's photograph of al-Azhar noted above, historian of photography Michelle L. Woodward suggests the Istanbul-based studio of the Sébahs developed a style of photographic depiction, represented by what she terms 'community portraits', that 'reveals a negotiation between tourist desires for exotic images and local Ottoman self-conceptions as modern citizens, in the process subverting common European notions of a static and backwards Middle East' (see Figure 24.1).[24] These alternative gazes, however, remained peripheral and did not establish themselves as a basis for tourism that could compete with the rise of the modern tourist gaze defined by upper and middle classes in the western states.

The Tourist Gaze, Visiting Mosques, and the Folds of Architecture

Figure 24.1: Photographs of the al-Azhar Mosque courtyard, Cairo, 1867, by Maison Bonfils (top) and the interior of the Grand Mosque, Bursa (now Turkey), 1894, by Sébah and Joaillier (bottom). Sources: Prints and Photographs Division, Library of Congress, LC-DIG-ppmsca-04045 DLC (top) and Penn Museum, image no. 167009 (bottom).

Visiting Mosques and the Tourist Gaze

Conversely, the recent growth of diverse forms of Islamic tourism represents a revival of alternative pathways for tourism development and a pluralization of the tourist gaze. As noted above, this rise corresponds to Muslims becoming a major travel community.[25] At the same time, this movement is connected to efforts to articulate a critical project for pluralizing international tourism in the wake of 9/11.[26] Accordingly, practices of Islamic tourism have evolved over recent decades, including the commercialization of religious pilgrimage as well as leisure holidays conducted within the context of Halal religious guidelines. There is now even a well-developed subfield within tourism management studies that focuses on diverse forms of 'Islamic tourism' beyond the Hajj and specialized firms that offer 'Halal tourism', addressing the growing volumes and varieties of tourism across the Muslim world.[27]

Under the broad umbrella of 'Islamic tourism', visiting mosques is part of religious practice and ritual and contrasts to non-Muslims' tourist visits to the same sites as the exploration of an authentic Other. There are, however, alternative modes beyond this binary. An illustrative example is the practice of Sarah Khan, a journalist of Muslim South Asian origin who grew up in Jeddah, Saudi Arabia, where her family frequently performed the *umrah* pilgrimage at the Grand Mosque in Mecca. As a tourist and travel writer, however, she developed a habit of visiting mosques wherever she travels. She writes in *Condé Nast Traveler* that 'seeking out mosques is also a way for me to sightsee and unearth chapters in history across the diaspora that don't make it into the rote scripts of cookie-cutter city tours' [Figure 24.2].[28] She offers mosque tourism as a means to explore the differentiations across Islamic society, rather than as an opportunity to observe the 'Other':

> In Paris, I learned that the Grand [sic] Mosquée was a refuge for hundreds of Jews during World War II; in Cape Town's rainbow-bright Bo-Kaap district, I discovered that the city's historic Cape Malay Muslim community were the first to record the Afrikaans language in writing – and they did it using Arabic script. In Nashville's hipster 12 South enclave I found a mosque established with the help of Yusuf Islam (formerly Cat Stevens); on Mozambique's Ibo Island, not far from decaying buildings from the Portuguese colonial era, I prayed in a village mosque dating back to the 1300s.[29]

Khan's travels echo historic practices of travel in the Islamic world, most broadly popularized by the figure of Ibn Battuta, the itinerant scholar who travelled from his native Tangiers in Morocco to Mecca and later across Asia. Ibn Battuta's travelogue gives us a rich depiction of the social world of the fourteenth century in which Islam – in all its diverse forms – gave rise to a 'cosmopolitan social and cultural system that spanned the hemisphere'.[30] Literate Muslims like Ibn Battuta formed a cultural elite who travelled between urban centres within the frontiers of the Islamic world in an era when the vast, ethnically diverse Islamic world was politically fragmented but nevertheless sustained a highly cosmopolitan civilization integrated by flows of travel, trade, and communication. Such travel has been picked up by political theorists

The Tourist Gaze, Visiting Mosques, and the Folds of Architecture

Figure 24.2: Visitors in the garden of the courtyard of La Grande Mosquée de Paris, Paris. Source: Eric Parker (licensed under CC BY-NC 2.0).

like Roxanne Euben to suggest that the Arab-Islamic world 'offers a particularly rich counter-genealogy of cosmopolitanism'.[31] But as she notes, this cosmopolitanism was bound by the hierarchical relation in which Ibn Battuta and his contemporaries placed and narrated the centre, boundaries, and the outside of the Islamic world.

The Folds of Architecture

Where do these threads of plurality, hierarchy, and boundaries leave us in relation to today's pluralizing tourist flows? The complex histories and architectures of Hagia Sophia in Istanbul and 'La Mezquita' in Cordoba – both leading tourist destinations – illustrate how individual monuments can simultaneously represent diversity, pluralism, and tensions. Hagia Sophia, built as a Byzantine cathedral, was converted to a mosque in the fifteenth century under the Ottomans and subsequently transformed into a museum by Mustafa Kemal Atatürk in the early twentieth century. Most recently, in the summer of 2020, it was converted back into a mosque by Turkey's President Recep Tayyip Erdoğan. In contrast, La Mezquita was built as a mosque by the Umayyads (adapting a Visigothic church) and then converted to a place for Christian worship in the thirteenth century following the *Reconquista*. A cathedral was inserted into its centre a few centuries later.[32] As Hasan-Uddin Khan notes:

> In the Cordoba and Istanbul examples, the notion of restoring cultural heritage is a politically charged one, raising questions regarding which cultural layer is accorded privilege over another and why this is so. It also highlights the time dimension of old monuments that problematizes simple notions of the cultural component of architectural legacies.[33]

These are the tensions of urban heritage preservation with which we began, especially as they concern ascendant and minority communities. These tensions call for attention to what we refer to as the 'folds of architecture' and to the need for interpretive strategies that respond adequately to the multiplicity of folds, as well as to the plurality of gazes upon the histories that produced and that are embedded in such folds.

In discussing 'folds of architecture', we draw from French theorist Gilles Deleuze who refers to the baroque logic of 'the fold' in which the world is interpreted as a body of infinite folds and surfaces that twist and weave through compressed time and space.[34] While archaeologists and historians tend to work in a framework of linear time, an alternative is to experience a place as a palimpsest, composed of views and memories from multiple eras. Within architecture we can experience it where a building or monument reflects multiple meanings, uses, and histories that can be continually unfolded and never settled. Let us illustrate. When one visits a Greco-Roman ruin in the Mediterranean region, the viewer might imagine a civilization at the height of its power, wealth, and artistic creativity, but at the same time, the sight of decay might remind one of its decline. Moreover, the reuse of some blocks of stone in a nearby structure might reflect reappropriation by later civilizations or even the dwellings of a recent community.

Similarly, in his cultural history of the Mediterranean, Iain Chambers presents the region as the hybrid product of cultural and material flows that resist the Cartesian mapping of borders and linear notions of progress.[35] To do this, Chambers follows the baroque logic of 'the fold' according to which a portrayal 'acquires depth when it is bent and deviated by excluded rhythms and dislocating narratives'.[36] Thus, unlike the archaeological excavations and preservation efforts that tend to prioritize one layer or time period, such an approach attempts to map 'co-presences', wherein accumulated layers of history seem to fold on top each other and where there are no clear beginnings and ends.

Such visions might be more difficult for archaeologists, art historians, and historic preservationists limited by disciplinary conventions or concerns for material authenticity. However, tourists need not be limited by a single temporal frame, linear stories, or material authenticity. Rather, these multiple pictures produced by horizontal slices, collected at one place or several, can be assembled to express multi-vocal, non-linear stories. Such tourist practices would require a tourist gaze that is guided by understandings of complex histories and expectations of often-conflicting narratives.

In fact, if the creative interpretation of folds might present too fundamental of a challenge to disciplinary commitments, conservation theory has nevertheless moved towards recognition of plurality in new and more expansive ways. Heritage interpretation began with offering sterile visions of 'high history', which sought to move beyond conflict. A later turn to multicultural cosmopolitanism sought to resolve contentious and competing histories that often play out at the local level by inserting sites into a universal history. More recent interpretive turns have attempted to overcome these limitations by including social history and daily life activities, bringing attention to questions of class and gender, as well as making a renewed push for inclusiveness that brings in multiple perspectives on sites and encourages reflection.[37] Most promising here are interpretive practices that do not ignore or smooth out multiple and possibly competing attachments, but rather seek to foster important conversations about these conflicting perspectives by involving multiple stakeholders and incorporating their narratives in the site's interpretation.

From Plurality to Pluralism

The key importance of interpretation takes us back to the preservation of urban heritage as an endeavour that is strung between political projects driven by dominant social groups on the one hand, and catering to expectations of tourism on the other. We noted multiple tensions and contradictory pulls at work when it comes to the preservation of Islamic urban heritage. While often the expression of ascendant groups' heritage, these sites were preserved in ways that catered to a tourist gaze, resulting in their material preservation and narrative framing as exotic and non-modern. At the same time, they were overshadowed by the vestiges of ancient – and especially Greco-Roman civilizations – through which tourists could trace a Western-Christian heritage. A pluralization of the tourist and the tourist gaze, we suggested, can be conducive to changing some of these dynamics by diversifying the range of places that are of interest and shifting the narratives away from museumification. We have illustrated these possibilities for pluralization with reference to two travellers in nineteenth-century Egypt and a contemporary travel writer.

At the same time, the pluralization of the tourist gaze through the rise of Islamic tourism, which challenges the expectations of the traditional western tourist gaze, raises the question of what happens to minority heritage in places like Istanbul or Cordoba. In other words, what might happen to minority heritage, when the pluralized tourist gaze begins to correspond in new ways to the heritage of ascendant populations? The decision of Erdoğan to convert Hagia Sophia from a museum back into a functional mosque is entangled with a range of domestic and international political dynamics. Internationally, it corresponds to a turn away from the cosmopolitan multiculturalism that was at the heart of previous preservation efforts. Domestically, the move is part of a populist-national identity building project that is increasingly turning to cultural heritage and religious symbols, drawn from Turkey's Muslim-Ottoman heritage, to counteract the regime's diminishing popular support. At the same time, this change coincides with shifts in tourism patterns that have increasingly brought domestic and international tourists who view Istanbul as a living Muslim city and seek corresponding touristic attractions. This pattern stands in contrast to earlier legions of western tourists who were visiting a city that has long been fashioned through conservation in a manner that allowed them to view its 'Old City' from the comforts of a recognizable secular modernity.

While places of minority heritage, or layers of architecture that correspond to non-majority identifications – such as the frescoes in Hagia Sophia – might have originally been preserved to cater to the western gaze, they also point to the diversity of the population, historically and/or at present. Further, while we have focused on mosques as an example, neither urban heritage nor questions of plurality are exclusive to religious sites. They also concern the form and representation of urban heritage found in museums, souks, government buildings, and residential neighbourhoods. Issues around the preservation of urban heritage can entail the gentrification or otherwise opening up to redevelopment of historic neighbourhoods, including those that mark the urban heritage of minority populations.[38] Thus, questions of plurality mark broader political tensions of preserving and/or redeveloping urban neighbourhoods and medinas. Pluralism requires the preservation of the material products of this diversity, along with the range of meanings and identifications they represent. The alternative would entail the transition from one set of hegemonic gaze and corresponding conservation practices to another.

The concurrent shifts laid out above give rise to worries about the future preservation and interpretation of urban heritage in cities such as Istanbul.[39] These worries are compounded by the concrete actions taken by the Turkish authorities since Hagia Sophia's recent conversion, which suggest that its Byzantine-Christian 'folds' will not be given equal attention in the site's preservation and interpretation [Figure 24.3].[40] We have noted the ways in which a universal cosmopolitan interpretation can fall short of engaging with the multiplicity of relations to sites such as Hagia Sophia, which are not merely art historical, in the past, or easily reconciled.[41]

The Tourist Gaze, Visiting Mosques, and the Folds of Architecture

Figure 24.3: People gather to perform Friday prayer in Hagia Sophia, Istanbul, on July 24, 2020, for the first time in 86 years, after its recent conversion to a mosque. Source: Esra Bilgin/Anadolu Agency via Getty Images.

This recognition does not, however, obviate the need for pluralistic interpretations that take into account the various layers of architectural artefacts, as they attach to different periods but also to the multiplicity of groups, who have used or attached value to the same artefact over time. The shift away from the western-dominated gaze should, therefore, not result in a new hegemonic gaze, such as one that privileges Islamic heritage exclusively to the detriment of others. Rather, we advocate for a pluralism that recognizes value in a range of sites, and also sees in each site a range of values and cultural expressions. Such range includes the secular and the religious, but beyond that divide, it concerns the multiple meanings that have been attached to the same site by different communities over time. Take cases such as the Hagia Sophia or the Chora Church in Istanbul, having been long preserved as tourist attractions and each now (re)converted into mosques. Their preservation as museums may well have been linked to the western gaze, including its touristic incentives, and yet, they are also sites that hold meaning for communities such as Armenians, Jews, and Greek Orthodox Christians who have and continue to call Istanbul their home. The task of both tourism studies and urban heritage preservation then becomes learning how to move to a commitment to pluralism that can embrace the multiple attachments to a range of sites, in the past and present, as the grounds for interpretation and preservation amidst various political pulls to reduce such multiplicity.

Notes

1. World Tourism Organization, *International Tourism Highlights, 2020 Edition* (Madrid: UNWTO, 2021), 6, https://www.e-unwto.org/doi/epdf/10.18111/9789284422456.
2. For a general history of modern tourism, see Eric G. E. Zuelow, *A History of Modern Tourism* (New York: Palgrave, 2016).
3. John Urry, *The Tourist Gaze* (London: Sage, 1990), 4.
4. 'Convention Concerning the Protection of the Works Cultural and Natural Heritage' (2012), UNESCO World Heritage Committee, accessed May 25, 2021, https://whc.unesco.org/archive/2012/whc12-36com-5E-en.pdf.
5. Hasan-Uddin Khan, 'Consuming Culture: Tourism and Architecture', *International Journal of Islamic Architecture* 5.1 (2014): 6–7.
6. Khan refers to Islamic tourism as 'a framework for travel whereby Muslims can learn about other communities and can also share their faith: essentially an interpretation of pilgrimage that merges religious and leisure tourism.' Ibid., 6. See also Waleed Hazbun, *Beaches, Ruins, Resorts: The Politics of Tourism in the Arab World* (Minneapolis: University of Minnesota Press, 2008), 225–30.
7. John E. Tunbridge 'Whose Heritage to Conserve? Cross-Cultural Reflections on Political Dominance and Urban Heritage Conservation', in *The Heritage Reader*, ed. Graham Fairclough et al. (London: Routledge, 2008), 236.
8. Aylin Orbaşlı, 'Urban Heritage in the Middle East: Heritage, Tourism and the Shaping of New Identities', in *Routledge Handbook on Tourism in the Middle East and North Africa*, ed. Dallen J. Timothy (London: Routledge, 2018), 95–105. See also the chapter by Hossam Mahdy in the present volume.
9. Nancy Demerdash-Fatemi, 'The Road's Resurgence: Questioning the Historical Legacy and Neocolonial Currency of the Moroccan Courtyard House', in *Neocolonialism and Built Heritage: Echoes of Empire in Africa, Asia, and Europe*, ed. Daniel E. Coslett (New York: Routledge, 2020), 217–35; Daniel E. Coslett, 'Preservation and Tourism in Tunisia: On the Colonial Past in the Neocolonial Present', *Journal of North African Studies* 25.5 (2020): 727–57.
10. Arjun Appadurai et al., 'The Globalization of Archaeology and Heritage: A Discussion with Arjun Appadurai', in Fairclough et al., *The Heritage Reader*, 218.
11. Dean MacCannell, *The Tourist: A New Theory of the Leisure Class* (Berkeley: University of California Press, 2013 [1976]), 14.
12. Ibid.
13. Erin Addison, 'The Roads to Ruins: Accessing Islamic Heritage in Jordan', in *Marketing Heritage: Archaeology and the Consumption of the Past*, ed. Uzi Baram and Yorke Rowan (Lanham, MD: Alta Mira Press, 2004), 239.

14 See, for example, John Urry, *The Tourist Gaze 2.0* (London: Sage, 2002); John Urry and Jonas Larsen, *The Tourist Gaze 3.0* (London: Sage, 2011).
15 Tim Winter, 'Heritage Tourism: The Dawn of a New Era?', in *Heritage and Globalisation*, ed. Sophia Labadi and Colin Long (London: Routledge, 2010), 117–30.
16 Noel Scott and Jafar Jafari, eds, *Tourism in the Muslim World* (Bingley: Emerald, 2010), 10.
17 Hera Oktadiana et al., 'Travel Career Patterns: The Motivations of Indonesian and Malaysian Muslim Tourists', *Tourism Culture & Communication* 17.4 (2017): 231–48. See also Scott and Jafari, *Tourism in the Muslim World*.
18 Michael J. Reimer, 'Views of Al-Azhar in the Nineteenth Century: Gabriel Charmes and 'Ali Pasha Mubarak', in *Travellers in Egypt*, ed. Paul Starkey and Janet Starkey (London: I. B. Tauris, 1998), 267–79.
19 *Description de l'Égypte* (Paris: Impr. impériale, 1809–28).
20 Reimer, 'Views of Al-Azhar in the Nineteenth Century', 273.
21 Timothy Mitchell, *Colonising Egypt* (Berkeley: University of California Press, 1991), 80–81.
22 Reimer, 'Views of Al-Azhar in the Nineteenth Century', 276.
23 Ibid., 277.
24 See Michelle L. Woodward, 'Between Orientalist Clichés and Images of Modernization: Photographic Practice in the Late Ottoman Era', *History of Photography* 27.4 (2003): 363–64.
25 Oktadiana et al., 'Travel Career Patterns', 232.
26 Ala al-Hamarneh and Christian Steiner, 'Islamic Tourism: Rethinking the Strategies of Tourism Development in the Arab World after September 11, 2001', *Comparative Studies of South Asia, Africa and the Middle East* 24.1 (2004): 173–82.
27 Scott and Jafari, *Tourism in the Muslim World*.
28 Sarah Khan, 'Why I Visit a Mosque Wherever I Travel', *Condé Nast Traveler*, March 29, 2018, https://www.cntraveler.com/story/why-i-visit-a-mosque-wherever-i-travel.
29 Ibid.
30 Ross E. Dunn, 'International Migrations of Literate Muslims in the Later Middle Period: The Case of Ibn Battuta', in *Golden Roads: Migration, Pilgrimage and Travel in Mediaeval and Modern Islam*, ed. Ian Richard Netton (Chippenham: Curzon Press, 1993), 83. See also Roxanne Euben, *Journeys to the Other Shore: Muslim and Western Travelers in Search of Knowledge* (Princeton: Princeton University Press, 2006), 63–89.
31 Euben, *Journeys to the Other Shore*, 178.
32 For the structural changes that accompanied these successive conversions, see Patricia Blessing and Ali Yaycıoğlu, 'Church, Mosque, Museum? Reflections on Monuments in Turkey and Spain', *Middle East Report Online*, March 2, 2021, https://merip.org/2021/03/church-mosque-museum-reflections-on-monuments-in-turkey-and-spain/.
33 Hasan-Uddin Khan, 'Architectural Conservation as a Tool for Cultural Continuity: A Focus on the Religious Built Environment of Islam', *International Journal of Islamic Architecture* 2.2 (2013): 259.
34 Gilles Deleuze, *The Fold: Leibniz and the Baroque* (Minneapolis: University of Minnesota Press, 1992).
35 Iain Chambers, *Mediterranean Crossings: The Politics of an Interrupted Modernity* (Durham, NC: Duke University Press, 2008).

36 Ibid., 18.
37 See, for example, 'ICOMOS Charter for the Interpretation and Presentation of Cultural Heritage Sites' ('The Ename Charter') (2008), ICOMOS, accessed May 25, 2021, http://icip.icomos.org/downloads/ICOMOS_Interpretation_Charter_ENG_04_10_08.pdf; 'Interpretation of Sites of Memory' (2018), International Coalition of Sites of Memory, accessed June 6, 2021, http://whc.unesco.org/document/165700. For the landmark document that proposes a context-based approach to interpretation, see 'Nara Document on Authenticity' (1994), ICOMOS, accessed May 25, 2021, https://www.icomos.org/charters/nara-e.pdf.
38 Orbaşlı, 'Urban Heritage in the Middle East'.
39 While these worries find their starkest expression in religious buildings, they also extend to historic neighbourhoods. Two examples are the choice of Tarlabasi and Sulukule for 'urban transformation' projects. The former is a neighbourhood historically inhabited by the Greek orthodox minority. After their departure, most infamously after the September 6–7, 1955 pogroms, the neighbourhood was settled by internal migrants, including internally displaced Kurds. Sulukule has historically been a neighbourhood of the Roma minority. Both gentrification projects involved the displacement of populations and resulted in activist mobilization for the preservation of the urban fabric and the communities and histories associated with it.
40 Blessing and Yaycıoğlu, 'Church, Mosque, Museum?'.
41 Laurajane Smith's seminal work has dubbed expert-led heritage interpretation that focuses on tangible elements 'authorized heritage discourse'. There is an important way in which cosmopolitan universalism has become the authorized heritage discourse adopted by international institutions. Our concern, however, is not simply to move from the tangible to intangible, expert to community, but to point to the plurality that is inherent in the materiality, and reflective of the multiple meanings that heritage accumulates over time, often for more than one community. See Laurajane Smith, *Uses of Heritage* (New York: Routledge, 2006).

Chapter 25

Decolonizing the Conservation of Islamic Built Heritage in Egypt

Hossam Mahdy

The conservation of Islamic built heritage in Egypt today faces many serious challenges, such as aggressive development pressures, poor public awareness, the need for specialized capacity building, poor research quality, insufficient funding, and the absence of political will, among others. Though these limitations are certainly relevant, I would argue that the critical cause of all these challenges is the absence of a genuine philosophical and theoretical framework for conservation (or historic preservation, as it is called in some parts of the world). A technically excellent conservation project is often unsustainable due to inefficient management and the lack of sustained maintenance, but most importantly due to the underappreciation of the meaning and significance of historic built heritage and its role in the life of the city.

Although Egypt's cultural heritage offers historical roots and material evidence to support its national identity as a modern nation-state with a great past, Islamic built heritage is less convenient for this purpose than material from its iconic ancient period. Notwithstanding the significance of the country's Pharaonic heritage, this is likely because Egypt has been ruled by non-Egyptians throughout most of the Islamic period of its history.[1] The patrons of almost all premodern Islamic architecture in Egypt were not Egyptians. Moreover, early modern neo-Islamic architectures were usually created and patronized by Europeans, so other outsiders, whose attention was often trained on antiquities. Another reason for excluding Islamic built heritage from modern Egyptian national discourse has been that it is not exclusively Egyptian, as it is shared by many other modern Muslim-majority nation-states.[2]

Historic Islamic buildings are often enjoyed and celebrated by the Egyptian intelligentsia as a manifestation of high culture – not unlike high art genres such as classical music, opera, ballet, theatre, and fine arts – from an architectural rather than functional or religious perspective. On the other hand, local communities in historic quarters, while holding on to their traditional culture and arts, seem to be indifferent – if not hostile – toward Islamic built heritage and its conservation, despite their apparent commitment to, and high regard of, Islam as a religion. Most restoration projects include the appointment of guards, the installation of security cameras, and the construction of fences around historic mosques, *sabil*s (water fountains), and other Islamic buildings that were initially built and endowed as inclusive and inviting religious and charitable people-centred buildings. Such measures are meant to protect these historic Islamic buildings from vandalism and encroachments by local communities whose use of them might – according to the professional conservators' opinion – jeopardize the integrity of the building-as-object.

Gentrification and adaptive reuse for elitist cultural, leisure, and tourism-related functions seem to be the preferred approach for buildings chosen for preservation. The majority of historic Islamic buildings sit empty, either restored and open for visitation or ruined and neglected. Some mosques have escaped this fate because of the continued use of their original function by the local communities in their vicinities, or because of their high religious or associational values on a national level. Other historic mosques – those of more archaeological and architectural value and of less religious and symbolic significance – became mere tourist venues devoid of religious and social functions. On the other hand, historic Islamic buildings that are not listed as 'antiquities' are not protected by law, and, more often than not, they are damaged by uninformed repairs, unsympathetic adaptations, neglect, and slow decay, or they succumb to intentional demolition for a variety of reasons that are beyond the scope of this essay.[3]

The Colonial Roots of Today's Practices

What is Islamic built heritage? Why should it be conserved? For whom? And how? These are big questions that are often dismissed as useless longwinded talk. Egyptian conservators are often preoccupied with the technical and executive aspects of conservation without addressing their philosophical and theoretical frameworks. This is a continuation of practices from the British colonial era (ostensibly 1882–1956 under several different political arrangements), when European orientalists were the masterminds for the identification and conservation of what they called at the time 'Arab art'. They were connoisseurs and antiquarians whose interests were focused on the archaeological and aesthetic values of the Islamic built heritage.

Both the modernization and conservation in Cairo were masterminded and executed by Europeans or European-educated Egyptians. Efforts to modernize Egypt throughout the nineteenth century were planned and executed according to the European model of the modern nation-state that sought to demonstrate both modernity and historicity.[4] Grand projects endeavoured to transform Cairo into a modern city, a 'Paris on the Nile'.[5] Hundreds of historic Islamic buildings were destroyed to make way for new wide boulevards that were opened up in the old urban fabric of Cairo.[6] 'The Committee of Conservation for Monuments of Arab Art' was established in 1881 as a reaction to pressure from European connoisseurs of Arab art and architecture.[7] The majority of the Committee's members were Europeans and the language of its meetings and reports was French. The Committee identified, documented, inventoried, studied, and restored the aesthetic, stylistic, and archaeological aspects of Islamic historic buildings as single monuments in isolation from their urban and environmental contexts with disregard to their functions, religious dimensions, intangible aspects, and their social interests and associations. Accordingly, listed *sabils*, *kuttabs* (elementary schools for teaching the Qur'an, reading, and writing), *madrasas* (religious schools), *khanqahs* (convents for Sufis), and other Islamic buildings were divorced from their original meanings and functions. The restoration of a historic *sabil*, for example, included the discontinuation of the function of offering drinking water. The justification for that was that water could damage the historic fabric of the building. Notably, this argument was not considered in the conservation of historic fountains in Rome and all over Europe. These double standards were due to the dismissal of the Islamic meaning and function of *sabils* by European conservators. Furthermore, the Committee's restoration of a *sabil* contradicted and ignored its *waqf* (charitable endowments) arrangements and conditions, which are mandatory under Islamic sharia law. The label 'Arab' art and architecture, which was initially used to name museums, committees, and academic departments, reflects the European colonial disregard for the fact that Islamic historic buildings are the heritage of a living culture and faith, not mere archaeological relics of a dead culture.[8]

The conservation of Pharaonic heritage was also initiated, masterminded, and practiced by Europeans throughout the nineteenth and the first half of the twentieth century. However, unlike the Islamic heritage, it was celebrated as the cultural heritage that identified the country. Thus, the museum dedicated to Pharaonic artefacts in Tahrir Square was named the 'Egyptian Museum', as if the heritage of other periods was not Egyptian.[9] The Egyptian national movement in the early twentieth century adopted this attitude and used Pharaonic images and subjects to symbolize endeavours to establish an independent Egyptian nation-state, which was copying the European concept of the Renaissance as the revival of ancient civilizations – the Pharaonic in the case of Egypt – as the way to establish a modern nation-state. The same attitude was continued after independence and was manifested by Pharaonic-themed monuments and statues in public spaces, logos for governmental institutions such as ministries, banks, universities, public-sector companies, and other expressions of the state's sovereignty.[10] In other words, early modern heritage conservation endeavours sought to revive the heritage of a dead civilization (i.e., Ancient Egyptian heritage) while treating a living heritage (i.e., Islamic heritage) as if it belonged to a dead civilization. An explicit manifestation of this attitude is the statue of *Nahdet Masr* (The Renaissance of Egypt), which was created by Mahmoud Mukhtar and commissioned by the Egyptian national movement, led by the Wafd Party. Depicting a woman taking off her hijab beside a rising sphinx, it was erected in the square outside Cairo's main railway station in 1928 [Figure 25.1]. The statue was moved after independence to the square in front of Cairo University and its image adorned the 25-piaster banknote as a symbol of modern Egypt.

Today, the colonial legacy from the nineteenth and early twentieth centuries is not limited to Egyptians' attitudes toward conservation, but also includes the understanding (or rather lack thereof) of Islamic built heritage. This legacy has heavily influenced the laws that protect the heritage, the relevant governmental institutional structures and mandates, as well as academic and professional research, education, and training in the field, all of which continue to identify single monuments according to their material, archaeological, and aesthetic values in isolation from their contexts, and with disregard to their intangible social and religious dimensions. Local Muslim-majority communities are considered, as they were in colonial times, to be a great threat facing the protection of Islamic monuments. Communities' needs and interests are considered a completely separate issue and irrelevant to their Islamic built heritage.[11] Today, *sabils* are restored as monuments with no function, or given a function that is neither relevant to their original function nor to the needs of the local community, such as a

Islamic Architecture Today and Tomorrow

Figure 25.1: Mahmoud Mukhtar, *Nahdet Masr* (The Renaissance of Egypt), Cairo, 1928. Source: Hossam Mahdy.

specialized library, a museum, or a visitor centre, even when there is an obvious need for communal water infrastructure for the local community [Figure 25.2]. The English translation of the Arabic term *athar* as 'antiquities' – rather than 'archaeology' or 'heritage' – in the name of the Ministry of Tourism and Antiquities reflects the antiquarian roots and the nineteenth-century colonial logic that continue to prevail up to the present. Moreover, the fact that 'tourism' precedes 'antiquities' in the ministry's name reflects the continued presence of the western visitor as the main stakeholder and target audience of the conservation and management of Egyptian cultural heritage.

National bodies that are responsible for the conservation and management of heritage in other Middle Eastern countries, such as Lebanon (Directorate General of Antiquities), Syria (Directorate-General of Antiquities and Museums), Jordan (Ministry of Tourism and Antiquities), Palestine (Ministry of Tourism and Antiquities), Algeria (Ministry of Antiquities), and Libya (Department of Antiquities) carry on the European colonial legacy in their names, mandates, and policies, as being responsible for antiquities rather than heritage and living culture. The political system in each country is a major factor that determines formal attitudes toward the Islamic built heritage. For example, the enthusiastic secularization of Turkey under Mustafa Kemal Atatürk after World War I was reflected in adapting the Mosque of Hagia Sophia into a museum. Then, the enthusiastic Islamization of Turkey under Recep Tayyip Erdoğan during the first decades of the twenty-first century was reflected in restoring the building to its mosque function.[12] The Atatürk regime dealt with the Islamic dimension of the building as the heritage of a dead culture, whereas the Erdoğan regime dealt with the same building as the heritage of a living culture. Attitudes in Morocco reflect the continuation of the ruling system, for which the livelihood of the Islamic cultural heritage is an important pillar of the monarchy's legitimacy. Accordingly, Islamic built heritage there has been conserved and managed as a living heritage and has not suffered from the suppression of its intangible dimensions.

Premodern Practices

Attitudes toward the built heritage in premodern Egypt were categorically different from modern ones. They should be understood within the framework of Islamic worldviews and value systems, which were the main basis for thought and conduct in premodern Egypt. Notions such as history, utility, aesthetics, art, architecture, environment, sustainability, and others that are relevant to Egyptian cultural heritage today should be understood within the Islamic worldview.[13]

History is a continuum of ups and downs depending on ethical attitudes of communities and societies. Unlike the modern popular understanding of history, humanity from an Islamic point of view is not continuously progressing despite all technological and scientific advances. The conservation of Islamic built heritage was therefore not carried out in premodern times in isolation from the rest of the built environment. It was not considered the remains of a

Figure 25.2: Sabil-Kuttab Nafisa al-Bayda, Cairo. Constructed in mid-eighteenth century, it was restored and adapted as a bookshop in 1998 by the American Research Center in Egypt. At present it is locked up and is an example of a non-functional *sabil-kuttab* in Cairo. Source: Hossam Mahdy.

primitive or less advanced people but rather the living, changing setting for contemporary life. According to the Qur'an, the causes that allow a nation to flourish or perish are the same for all humans throughout history. Accordingly, many verses of the Qur'an instruct Muslims to travel and visit the remains of old civilizations and see how they perished because of their unethical attitudes despite their material advances.[14]

Utility and aesthetics are two faces of the same coin according to Islamic values. Indeed, beauty and goodness are one and the same, as expressed by the Arabic word *ihsan*. Accordingly, no separation is made between art and craft, or between architecture and the act of building. And thus, art does not exist for art's sake. Built heritage was conserved according to both sets of values, the aesthetic and the utilitarian. An artistically written and bound Qur'an was not conserved to be put in a glass box, but to be read. A grand mosque was not to be conserved as a monument, but as a place for active worship and other related functions. In premodern times, a building that lost its function or meaning was recycled to serve a new function and meaning, rather than maintained as a relic.

Architecture is an endeavour seeking to balance and integrate many aspects, such as protection from nature and integration with it, which is expressed in architectural elements such as courtyards, windcatchers, projecting upper floors, and lattice windows. A balance is also sought in observing individuals' privacy on the one hand, and on the other hand, cementing bonds between individuals within a community. This is expressed in the inviting open doors that at the same time keep the privacy of the interior by the design of a bent entrance. Another integration is sought by fulfilling the tangible requirements as well as the intangible ones. This is reached by integrating both utility and aesthetics as a manifestation of the Islamic concept of *ihsan*. Thus, most architectural elements and parts of a building fulfil both functional and aesthetic purposes. The conservation of old buildings in premodern Egypt observed the same principles, as the same approach was adopted for both the conservation of existing buildings and the construction of new ones.

Sustainability is central to Islamic belief and conduct. However, the motivation for observing sustainability and its span is essentially different from the idea's modern conception. According to Muslim beliefs, all good deeds are substantially better if they are sustainable as *sadaqah jareyah* (continuous charity), which should outlive its initiator and carry on through the end of life on earth, thus securing the individual reward in the hereafter. The span that the Islamic concept of sustainability covers is not a decade, a generation, or even a century, but up to the end of human existence on earth. As for the environmental aspect of sustainability, Muslims are instructed to both enjoy the natural environment and to assume responsibility for its wellbeing. According to the Qur'an, the earth is created for man and man is appointed by God as its guardian. Waste is discouraged, no matter the circumstances, and recycling is always encouraged. In the field of conservation, historic buildings that had lost their function and/or meaning were thus 'recycled' by giving them new functions and/or meanings, or if demolished, a building's components were used in new constructions. The al-Azhar Mosque is a good example [Figure 25.3]. Although it was built as a Shi'a university by the Fatimids, the Ayyubids who made every effort to erase the Shi'a impact on Egypt, did not demolish the building, but rehabilitated it as a Sunni university after a long period of preventing its use for prayers.

The institution of *waqf* is the mechanism that flourished in premodern times by Muslim communities to satisfy their needs, interests, and desires while observing their faith and shaping their lives according to the Islamic worldview and value systems. An individual who built a charitable institution, such as a mosque, a hospital, a *sabil*, or a *kuttab* would make it a *sadaqah jareyah* by allocating money for an investment that could have been made in farms, *suqs* (markets), *wakalas* (commercial buildings for wholesale trade), *rab*'s (multi-unit residential buildings), or *hammams* (baths). The revenue from the investment secured the sustainability of the charitable institution by securing its continued function, management, maintenance, and repairs. In many cases, a charitable institution attracted other patrons in later times to add further funds to add more investments, the revenue of which would go to maintaining the sustainability of the institution by devoting a new *waqf* for the institution, even if it was initially established by someone else.[15] In other words, the *waqf* system was the premodern vehicle *par excellence* for the sustainable conservation of functional built heritage in premodern Egypt and other Muslim-majority countries.

Figure 25.3: The al-Azhar Mosque, Cairo. Source: Hossam Mahdy.

Developments in International Thought and Practice

Attitudes and underlying philosophies of conservation practices in Egypt today are easily traced to nineteenth-century European thought and practice. Ironically, since that time, attitudes have changed dramatically in Europe and the whole world. The birth and development of the international conservation movement after World War II resulted in the foundation of the International Council of Monuments and Sites (ICOMOS) and the creation of its 1964 Venice Charter, as well as many charters and documents that followed and informed contemporary theories of conservation that set the standards for best practice.[16]

Conservation theory and practice has developed – and continues to evolve – since the adoption of the Venice Charter, in two main regards. The first concerns the identification, valorisation, and scope of built heritage, the second, the methodology and scope of activities for the conservation of that built heritage. Both developments strove to move away from the Eurocentric early beginnings of the field, in recognition of the richness and diversity of philosophies and practices from other cultures and regions of the world. Another aspect that influenced developments in conservation was the universal realization, acknowledgement, and acceptance that different aspects of built heritage and its conservation are culture specific. That they, therefore, may require different approaches, methodologies, and practices in different contexts is an understanding advanced in several charters and documents, notably the Nara Document on Authenticity (1994).[17]

The identification, valorisation, and scope of built heritage has moved from the archaeological and aesthetic values of single monuments to the less monumental and more inclusive notion of places of cultural significance according to a wide scope of values, including the social, spiritual, and functional. The types of accepted built heritage are no longer limited to monuments and archaeological sites, but are extended to include a wide range of other typologies such as vernacular buildings and industrial, modern, and water heritage. The scope of heritage has also expanded geographically to include historic cities and villages, cultural landscapes, cultural routes (such as the Silk Road linking China to Europe), underwater heritage, and transnational serial heritage sites. Also, synergistic and integrated approaches have been developed between different categories of heritage, such as the tangible with the intangible, the movable with the immovable, the cultural with the natural. The methodology and scope of activities for the conservation of the built heritage continue to move from the technical restoration of isolated monuments to the inclusive conservation management of sites within their contexts and with the proactive participation of communities and stakeholders. In recent years approaches and toolkits were developed to integrate the conservation of built heritage with sustainable development efforts. For example, the historic urban landscape approach was developed by UNESCO in 2011 to integrate the conservation of built heritage within the sustainable development of historic cities, as is explored in the Cairo case.

Toward Decolonization

Nineteenth-century attitudes toward the conservation of built heritage in Europe were logical consequences of the birth and development of a modern worldview during the Renaissance, the Enlightenment, and the Romantic era, which broke away from the traditional premodern worldview. The application of such attitudes in Egypt and other Muslim-majority countries at the time was mixed with orientalism, racism, colonialism, and other aspects of nineteenth-century European thought that were alien to the Muslim mind, such as archaeological research that was motivated by orientalist literature, Biblical studies, and Darwinism.

The Eurocentric approach to the conservation of built heritage was introduced to Egypt during the late nineteenth century with the assumption that no conservation philosophy or practice existed in the country before its encounter with Europe. Negative attitudes about local communities stemmed from outsiders' assumptions about Egyptians' supposed ignorance, racial inferiority, and vulgar religion, all the products of orientalist and colonialist nineteenth-century European attitudes. Egyptians who worked with early European conservators concentrated on the technical and practical aspects of conservation without any consistent attempt to challenge the theoretical and philosophical bases of their technical work. They did not mind the contradiction with the Islamic worldview, nor did they question the validity of the theoretical framework of their conservation practices pertaining to Islamic built heritage. Such acceptance continued after the independence of the country, which was not limited to the field of heritage conservation. A class of Egyptian elites who were educated in the European tradition and who had previously supported the colonial administration of the country carried on most, if not all, cultural, legal, and administrative attitudes that were established by Europeans during the colonial period.

Today, Egyptian conservation of Islamic architecture follows and respects religiously the notions, laws, administrative structures, academic research, and professional practices that were established by Europeans during the late nineteenth and early twentieth centuries. This remains the case, even after such attitudes have been almost totally challenged and dismissed in Europe and the west. Today, international organizations such as UNESCO and ICOMOS exercise pressure on the Egyptian government to move away from its colonial legacy, but without much success.[18]

It is my suggestion that decolonization of the conservation of Islamic built heritage in Egypt should begin with the study and validation of premodern and precolonial attitudes and practices, and their potential reconciliation with international developments in the field. As international best practices are moving toward attitudes that are not that far from premodern Islamic notions – such as respect for culture-specific approaches, an inclusive and integrated notion of built heritage that encompasses a wide scope of buildings, sensitivity and respect for the context of the heritage and all its stakeholders – the importance of good management and financial feasibility, and the integration of conservation and development in order to secure a sustainable environment, have all become critical.

Figure 25.4: The Ibn Tulun Mosque, Cairo. Source: Hossam Mahdy.

For example, the mosque of Ibn Tulun, which was built as the main Friday Mosque of Al-Qata'i' (the Tulunid capital of Egypt that preceded Fatimid Cairo) to accommodate a huge capacity, is currently conserved and managed as an archaeological resource and a tourism venue [Figure 25.4]. Any local who wishes to pray in the mosque must go through security screening, which includes an identification review, body search, and metal detection by Tourism Police, while busloads of foreign non-Muslim tourists are warmly welcomed, ushered in without security checks, and treated favourably. Consequently, the mosque has lost its meaning and function as an open spiritual and social hub for the local community. According to current international best practices, the mosque should be valorised, conserved, and managed in accordance with all its values, including religious, symbolic, social, and spiritual ones, which should not contradict with its touristic potential. The local community and stakeholders should be proactive in all decisions pertaining to the mosque. The conservation of the mosque should not mean it is to be treated like an isolated monument or museum piece. It should be integrated into urban conservation and sustainable development plans for its urban context. In other words, were international best practices applied in the conservation and management of the Ibn Tulun Mosque, the result would be an 'Islamically conserved' and fully functional building, which could include a tourism program that respects the religious and social values of the mosque in terms of visitation times and the interpretation of the building as a living and functioning mosque and not a mere aesthetically pleasing archaeological relic.

Conclusion

The lack of clear philosophy and rationale for the conservation of the built heritage is not limited to Egypt. Colonial attitudes that persisted in postcolonial contexts, thanks to national elites, can be observed with different intensities, details, and chronologies in all Muslim-majority countries, and particularly in the Middle East. However, the case of Egypt is perhaps an outlier since it is the first country in the region that experienced an encounter with modern Europeans with Napoleon's 1798 invasion of Egypt, and it is the home to an iconic and unique ancient culture. Other Middle Eastern countries were impacted by colonialism and do continue to carry on a colonial legacy in the field of heritage conservation, albeit in different ways that merit individual discussions. A number of factors influence attitudes, such as the ideology of the ruling regime and its position regarding Islam and secularization, the popularity of pre-Islamic heritage for mass tourism, and the attitudes of colonial administrations before independence. The robustness of the Middle Eastern sections at the British Museum, the Louvre, and other western imperial museums may be seen as an indicator of the scope and extent of European nineteenth-century colonial attitudes and practices, many of which remain relevant in Egypt and some in other Middle Eastern countries.

A rediscovery of Islamic notions that are relevant to the built heritage and its conservation would not only give professionals and academics a chance to develop culture-specific rationales and approaches to the conservation of the built heritage, but will also equip them with a common worldview, value system, and language that both the intelligentsia and traditional local communities could share. This would secure an effective participatory approach to the protection, conservation, and management of Islamic built heritage. However, this is not an easy task. As a break from the colonial legacy will require not only a change of mentality with firm self-confidence on the part of conservation professionals, but also – and more importantly – significant structural changes in legislation, institutional structures and mandates, and other deep-rooted pillars of the Egyptian establishment.

Notes

1. The early Islamic rulers and governing elite were from the Arabian Peninsula, the Abbasids and Tulunids were from Iraq, the Fatimids were from the Maghreb, the Ayyubids from Kurdistan, the Mamluks from Central Asia and Eastern Europe, the Ottomans from Turkey, and Muhammad Ali's dynasty from Albania. Gamal Abdel Nasser was announced in the 1950s to have been the first Egyptian ruler of Egypt since the ancient Egyptian era.
2. Ottoman architecture is found all over the lands that were once part of the Ottoman Empire. Mamluk buildings are found in Egypt, the Levant, and Hijaz. The same could be said about Islamic architecture from other Islamic periods such as the Ayyubid, Fatimid, and earlier ones.
3. See Hossam Mahdy, *Approaches to the Conservation of Islamic Cities: The Case of Cairo* (Sharjah: ICCROM-ATHAR, 2017), 67–76.

4   Mrinalini Rajagopalan, 'Preservation of Modernity: Competing Perspectives, Contested Histories and the Question of Authenticity', in *The Sage Handbook of Architectural Theory*, ed. C. Greig Crysler, Stephen Cairns, and Hilde Heynen (London: Sage, 2021), 308–13.
5   See Mercedes Volait, 'Making Cairo Modern (1870–1950): Multiple Models for a "European Style" Urbanism', in *Urbanism: Imported or Exported? Native Aspirations and Foreign Plans*, ed. Joe Nasr and Mercedes Volait (London: Wiley, 2003), 17–50; Mercedes Volait, 'Mediating and Domesticating Modernity in Egypt: Uncovering Some Forgotten Pages', *Docomomo Journal* 35 (2006): 30–35.
6   See Khaled Asfour, 'The Domestication of Knowledge: Cairo at the Turn of the Century', *Muqarnas* 10 (1993): 125–37.
7   Many articles were published in the British media that eventually led to the establishment of the Committee. See for example, 'The Preservation of Mediaeval Cairo', *The Architect & Contract Reporter*, March 6, 1896, 153.
8   See Wided Rihana Khadraoui, 'Arguing Semantics: What Exactly Is "Arab Art"?', Middle East Institute, October 3, 2017, https://www.mei.edu/publications/arguing-semantics-what-exactly-arab-art.
9   This elision is perpetuated in the new Grand Egyptian Museum at Giza (which, when it opens in 2022, will supersede the original Egyptian Museum), although Cairo's new National Museum of Egyptian Civilization does include artifacts from antiquity through the modern era.
10 See Donald Malcolm Reid, *Contesting Antiquity in Egypt: Archaeologies, Museums & the Struggle for Identities from World War I to Nasser* (Cairo: American University in Cairo Press, 2015), 1–6.
11 On the rationale and approach for the massive interventions completed in Cairo by the Ministry of Culture during the late 1990s, see Supreme Council of Antiquities, *Historic Cairo* (Ministry of Culture, 2002).
12 See also the contribution by Elif Kalaycioglu and Waleed Hazbun in the present volume.
13 See Hossam M. Mahdy, 'Attitudes Towards Architectural Conservation, the Case of Cairo' (Ph.D. diss., Glasgow University, 1992).
14 See, for example: 'How many populations have We destroyed, which were given to wrong-doing? They tumbled down on their roofs. And how many wells are lying idle and neglected, and castles lofty and well-built? Do they not travel through the land, so that their hearts (and minds) may thus learn wisdom and their ears may thus learn to hear? Truly it is not their eyes that are blind, but their hearts which are in their breasts' (Qur'an 22:45–46). See also Qur'an 12:109, 16:36, 27:69, 29:34–35, and 51:37.
15 There is a huge body of research on *waqf* and its role in urban and architectural management and conservation. See for example, Pascale Ghazaleh, ed., *Held in Trust: Waqf in the Islamic World* (Cairo: American University in Cairo Press, 2011); Sylvie Denoix, 'A Mamluk Institution for Urbanization: The Waqf', in *The Cairo Heritage: Essays in Honor of Laila Ali Ibrahim*, ed. Doris Behrens-Abouseif (Cairo: American University in Cairo Press, 2000), 191–202.
16 ICOMOS, 'International Charter for Conservation and Restoration of Monuments and Sites (The Venice Charter 1964)', accessed February 20, 2021, https://www.icomos.org/charters/venice_e.pdf. Other ICOMOS charters and doctrinal documents could be found at 'Chartres

et autres textes doctrinaux', International Council on Monuments and Sites, October 12, 2011, https://www.icomos.org/fr/ressources/chartes-et-normes.
17 'Nara Document on Authenticity' (1994), ICOMOS, accessed May 24, 2021, https://www.icomos.org/charters/nara-e.pdf.
18 See UNESCO reports and recommendations on the 'Historic Cairo' World Heritage Site at 'Historic Cairo', United Nations Educations, Scientific and Cultural Organization, accessed January 22, 2021, https://whc.unesco.org/en/list/89/documents/.

Chapter 26

(Dis)placement and Placemaking: Reconsidering Islamic Architecture through Refugee Agency

Kıvanç Kılınç and Bülent Batuman

It is important to rethink the boundaries of the field of Islamic architecture in light of the ongoing refugee crises and the forced displacement of populations, including those beyond traditionally conceived 'Islamic geographies'. Refugee crises are of course not new, but they are a recurrent phenomenon and are particularly acute today.[1] To date, the issue has remained largely neglected in the field of Islamic architecture. Islamic architecture, on the other hand, sounds 'historical' almost immediately, at least to the uncritical ear; its formation as a field was very closely linked to the designation of 'non-western', and mostly religious, architecture – of 'traditional' building stock and styles frozen in time.[2] Secondly, Islamic architecture implies a certain geography: that of Muslim-majority countries. Moreover, until recently, the field's focus was limited to the regions that had historically experienced Muslim rule, ignoring the peripheries of this geography. These two aspects defining Islamic architecture – its temporal and the geographical limits – comprise an ongoing debate.[3] This chapter argues that looking at the recent experience of displaced Muslim populations, from Palestine since 1948 and from Syria since 2011 – especially their resettlement in Europe – provides us with opportunities to think about Islamic architecture beyond these traditionally conceived temporal and geographical boundaries and to consider the agency of displaced persons.

Sheila S. Blair and Jonathan M. Bloom argue that scholarship on Islamic architecture has come to cover 'regions once considered peripheral, including west and east Africa, Southeast Asia, and China. Recent issues of the *International Journal of Islamic Architecture* have included articles on hitherto-unexplored places ranging from A (Albania) to Z (Zanzibar).'[4] Yet this geographical reconsideration is still conceived as an expansion into the hitherto marginalized places, whereas what we need is a further 'geographical jump' into non-Islamic (i.e., non-Muslim-majority) geographies.[5] Even if one ignores the historical Muslim populations of the Balkans, it is crucial to consider the fact that the twentieth and twenty-first centuries have witnessed constant migration to Europe, a significant portion of which comprised Muslim individuals, families, and communities.

The refugee experience highlights the already existing outcomes of migration that have so far been overlooked. An example here is the controversial Swiss referendum on banning minarets.[6] Hostility toward the minaret as the architectural signifier of Islam is hardly specific to Switzerland and has been observed in various European countries to varying degrees. Yet, the controversy over the minaret – and mosque architecture in general – in Europe is not considered as an agenda within the field of Islamic architecture, although ethnographic studies have scrutinized the mosque as a space of diasporic identity. The mosque of course is a key site for the reproduction of individual and collective identities for resettled Muslims, and the very architecture of the mosque – including the spatial practices it shelters – operates differently in a non-Muslim context.[7]

The increasing influence of religion and its impact on the urban realm have been examined during the past decade.[8] While this phenomenon has brought into question the legitimacy of secularism in urban life, it has also made it possible to think about the intrinsic secularism of urban theory that has overlooked the role of religiosity for a long time.[9] Along the same lines, consideration of the refugee condition allows us to think about the role of religion in the production of space, not in an essentialist way accepting religion as an inherent feature always already marking space, but as a historically contingent determinant. This is in fact most often the case in refugee experiences; one's survival within networks of aid and solidarity are often faith-based, and regardless of one's previous level of religiosity one practically partakes in religious socializations.[10] It is also important to note that the traumatic experience of dislocation may lead the refugee to turn to religion.[11] As much as it may trigger Islamophobia within host societies, the arrival of refugees can inspire negotiations with Islamic practices that may ease integration. Policymakers have only recently begun to accept the role of tradition and religious performances in providing aid for refugees.[12] Strikingly, shelter provision – production of refugee spaces by host institutions – is still oblivious to faith.[13]

As soon as one begins to think of the possibility of acknowledging religion when providing shelter for Muslim refugees, one steps into the territory of Islamic architecture.[14] Although this might sound like an overstatement, given the lack of concern afforded to religious practices in shaping refugee spaces, it is possible to see a shift through which the refugees' presence in host cities is recognized following a period of denial.[15] Let us consider the example of Berlin. Receiving approximately 80,000 refugees from Muslim-majority countries in 2014–15, the city enacted emergency measures.[16] The most spectacular of these measures was the transformation of the empty hangars of the historic inner-city Tempelhof airport (which was closed in 2008) into an emergency shelter in late 2015.[17] Following criticism regarding the inhumane conditions of the camps inside the hangars, the city administration introduced more substantial community shelters, which they called 'Tempohomes', to replace emergency shelters in 2016 [Figure 26.1].[18] Although they were an improvement in terms of living conditions, the Tempohomes – one of which was built on Tempelhof's former apron – were also criticized for strict control and monitoring, which frustrated inhabitants. Nevertheless, the short story of the successive refugee shelters at Tempelhof has two significant points that illustrate an important theme relevant to this discussion. To improve the conditions of the initial camp, the authorities organized one of the hangars as a large dining hall during Ramadan for the Muslim residents to collectively break their fast.[19] This example illustrates the role of faith in the organization of refugee space. The second point is the fact that the refugees penned several letters and petitions to the authorities during the move from the emergency shelter to the community shelter.[20] The involvement of the refugees in the shaping of their environment is important because the conception of space production for refugees as 'provision' serves the reproduction of a paternalistic relationship

Figure 26.1: Refugee shelter (Tempohome) on Alte Jakobstraße in Kreuzberg, Berlin (photographed July 29, 2021). Source: Sevim Burulday.

between the host institutions and the refugees.[21] And, in fact, refugees have been active in organizing to challenge the spatial politics of such top-down policies.[22]

Agency and Placemaking: Displacing the Conventions of the Field

As a term, 'displacement' has a negative connotation on two levels. It implies a negativity regarding the social experience itself because an act is assumed to be forced on the subject. Additionally, it strips away the capabilities of the subject to (re)place her- or himself, despite the fact that it is obviously absurd to think of ordinary people losing their social and spatial agency as soon as they are displaced due to an external catastrophe. Thus, every displacement is simultaneously one of (em)placement; the refugees continue to exist, albeit in a different space. Moreover, if one recognizes the inherent agency of the refugee, one then sees that every displacement is necessarily coupled with placemaking.

In the last couple of decades, a globally connected architectural community, including both practitioners and scholars, has challenged the corporate visions and the profit-based economy surrounding architectural production and the claims of professional autonomy by championing social missions and engaging with socio-economic problems in the urban structures and lives of ordinary people.[23] Such practices that acknowledge the significance of agency and the user's role in the reappropriation of spaces call into question the entire architectural establishment, redefining the role of the architect from hero-maker into one that extends the use of the profession for the public good and embraces participatory design principles. In these accounts, agency is usually placed alongside social engagement and activism.

We believe that agency is also a useful keyword that binds the refugee and Islamic architecture.[24] There is a compelling parallel between the figure of the refugee (regardless of one's faith) and the Islamic subject (of architecture). Not unlike how the 'Islamic' or 'Oriental' subject was denied agency in western literature and art, the refugees of today are denied agency in dominant representations.[25] They often appear as victims or recipients of aid at the mercy of their oppressors (i.e., those causing the displacement) and 'saviours' (e.g., hosts, politicians, NGOs, et al.). The contemporary formulation of the displaced as a potential threat to the established norms of the 'civilized' world and lifestyles is not remarkably different from the misrepresentation of the 'Oriental' subject as a passive onlooker, or a wild, unruly resident of an overcrowded medina with its irregular maze of streets and culs-de-sac, starkly contrasted with the 'rationally planned' colonial city and the image of its idealized western settler. In his ground-breaking work, Edward Said most aptly described the absurdity of such orientalist imaginations:

> So there develops a kind of image of the timeless Orient, as if the Orient, unlike the West, doesn't develop, it stays the same. And that's one of the problems with Orientalism. It creates an image outside of history, of something that is placid and still and eternal, which is simply contradicted by the fact of history. In one sense it's a creation of you might say, an ideal Other for Europe.[26]

Yet both subjects, one historical but written as if 'outside of history', and the other contemporary but silenced and sidelined, defy these depictions. In both emergency camp settlements and traditional city centres, refugees actively intervene in spaces and create places with meaning through reorganizing the structures they inhabit. They name and reimagine the spaces around them and develop strategies to overcome systematic exclusionary practices.[27] In their introduction to the *Refugees as City-Makers* edited collection, Mona Fawaz and her colleagues argue that prevalent representations of the displaced populations in the media and by most international organizations emphasize their passivity and their vulnerability against external forces.[28] In these narratives, 'refugees endure their reality; they rarely participate in its making'.[29] In response, the authors suggest repositioning 'the study of forced population displacements through the lens of individual and collective agency and the transformative roles that individuals tagged as refugees play as home-makers, city navigators, urban producers, or political subjects'.[30] To this end, the authors argue, 'there is a need to acknowledge the transformative impact refugees have on the very substance of "urban life"' [Figure 26.2].[31]

We believe that emphasizing the agency of the displaced populations and their role as space-makers would not only help extend the perimeter of discussions around the refugee crises and displacement, but would also open up new possibilities for the field of Islamic architecture to reconsider both its scope and reach. In 'Reorienting Perspectives', Jelena Bogdanović argues that

Figure 26.2: An apartment building in Ayn-el-Mreisseh, Beirut, inhabited by refugees and migrant workers (2019). Source: Kıvanç Kılınç.

the space of 'Oriental' or 'Islamic architecture' [has] lost geographic and cultural specificity. Defined in opposition to 'Western' space, 'Oriental' and 'Islamic' space has floated over time from the Middle East to Bosnia and Herzegovina and from Japan and to Chicago.[32]

Yet, does this more extensive list include places where Islamic communities have not (yet) settled or had a significant existence in the past? Is this where we would stop using 'Islamic architecture' as a conceptual framework to make sense of the contemporary built environment and its histories? Or, to the contrary, can we see this as an opportunity to scrutinize the contemporary role of religion in the production of space?

As contemporary scholars have argued, the increased mobility of images, data, news, people, objects, and technologies has eroded the divides between regions, nation-states, cities, and neighbourhoods, challenging 'the fixed boundaries and enclosed spaces that have characterized civilization over the last ten thousand years'.[33] According to Thomas Fisher, 'The rapid response of entrepreneurs in Europe to the needs of its 1 million refugees, selling food, shelter, and transportation services to people in need of such things' have created a 'demand-on economy' that is not limited to upper and middle class groups.[34] Such exchanges then become the catalyst of change in politics and material culture. Like anywhere else on earth, in places where Islam is a marker of identity, the ways in which diverse communities find visual expression in the built form are in constant flux.[35] When we take into consideration that there were

'232 million migrants moving around the planet in search of a better life' in 2015 alone, this picture becomes even clearer.[36]

Yet, especially with the Syrian Civil War and the refugee crisis, the European Union and its member states have strengthened their borders and limited the number of refugees that can cross them.[37] Refugee-receiving centres and 'temporary' camps built adjacent to state boundaries offer overcrowded and poorly maintained facilities. Such spaces often appear in the news with grim stories of mistreatment and abuse of human rights while refugees continued to attempt to illegally cross these borders by sea, river, and land, at times at the cost of their lives.

Concluding Thoughts: Islamic Architecture as a Critical Perspective in the Study of Place and Placemaking

Since 'place-making' is now more of a traveling practice than a settled experience, we can no longer define or understand 'Islamic architecture' – or any such (initially) geography- or religion-bound field of scholarship – as a fixed entity and deny it the contemporaneity it already possesses. The question is less about what types of buildings, geographies, or timelines Islamic architecture does or should include and exclude. Rather, it concerns the politics of positionality: How does Islamic architecture as a field of scholarship and practice creatively inhabit its discursive space today? What can we make out of the 'traditional' use of the term and the potential that lies in its reappropriation?

We would like to suggest that by intentionally 'decolonizing' its own institutional building blocks, the field of Islamic architecture could offer a lens that connects to other scholarly frameworks, such as postcolonial urban studies and the growing body of literature on the Global South, and therefore position itself as more of a critical perspective than a list that needs expanding. The main proposition here is that understanding refugees as active place-makers would not only allow us to further expand this line of inquiry, pushing the boundaries of the field to include the everyday spaces beyond the monumental,[38] but also provide a fresh theoretical lens in the study of place and placemaking in geographies of Islam and beyond.

Acknowledgement

We would like to thank the editors of this volume for their constructive criticism, valuable comments, and feedback.

Notes

1 According to the United Nations High Commissioner for Refugees (the UN Refugee Agency), the number of forcibly displaced people has doubled between 2010 and 2020. The list of origin

countries of refugees is led by Syria, Venezuela, Afghanistan, and South Sudan. See United Nations High Commissioner for Refugees (UNHCR), 'Global Trends in Forced Displacement – 2020, Copenhagen: UNHCR, 2021' accessed July 22, 2021, https://www.unhcr.org/60b638e37/unhcr-global-trends-2020.

2. For a broader discussion on the subject, see Patricia Blessing, Heather L. Ferguson, and Kıvanç Kılınç, 'Islamic Architecture in Print: Reflections on Ten Years of *IJIA*', *International Journal of Islamic Architecture* 10.1 (2021): 13.

3. For instance, Blair and Bloom see an 'expansion of the field' in both aspects in recent years. Nasser Rabbat discusses the temporal boundaries in terms of continuities and ruptures, arguing that there are analogous breaks perceived between the pre-Islamic and Islamic architectures and that of the historical and the contemporary in Muslim societies. See Sheila S. Blair and Jonathan M. Bloom, 'The Study of Islamic Architecture: Reflections on an Expanding Field', *International Journal of Islamic Architecture* 10.1 (2021): 57–73 (reproduced in this volume) and Nasser Rabbat, 'What Is Islamic Architecture Anyway?', *Journal of Art Historiography* 6 (2012): 1–15, https://arthistoriography.files.wordpress.com/2012/05/rabbat1.pdf.

4. Blair and Bloom, 'The Study of Islamic Architecture', 61.

5. See the chapter by Caroline 'Olivia' Wolf in the present volume for this type of work on Islamic architecture in the Americas.

6. See, for instance, Nick Cumming-Bruce and Steven Erlanger, 'Swiss Ban Building of Minarets on Mosques', *New York Times*, November 29, 2009, https://www.nytimes.com/2009/11/30/world/europe/30swiss.html.

7. For a comparative analysis of two mosques and the spatial practices of the respective communities in Berlin and London, see Elisabeth Becker, 'Reconstructing the Muslim Self in Diaspora: Socio-Spatial Practices in Urban European Mosques', *International Journal of Islamic Architecture* 8.2 (2019): 389–414.

8. Bülent Batuman, ed., *Cities and Islamisms: On the Politics and Production of the Built Environment* (New York: Routledge, 2021).

9. Helmuth Berking, Silke Steets, and Jochen Schwenk, eds, *Religious Pluralism and the City: Inquiries into Postsecular Urbanism* (London: Bloomsbury Academic, 2018); Jochen Becker et al., eds, *Global Prayers: Contemporary Manifestations of the Religious in the City* (Zurich: Lars Müller, 2014); Irene Becci, Marian Bruchardt, and Jose Casanova, eds, *Topographies of Faith: Religion in Urban Spaces* (Leiden: Brill, 2013); David Garbin and Anna Strhan, eds, *Religion and the Global City* (London: Bloomsbury, 2017).

10. For a case study on Syrian refugees in Turkey, see Ulaş Sunata and Salih Tosun, 'Assessing the Civil Society's Role in Refugee Integration in Turkey: NGO-R as a New Typology', *Journal of Refugee Studies* 32.4 (2019): 683–703.

11. Anna Elia and Valentina Fedele, '"Islam Is a Place Inside Myself": Material and Immaterial Re-Positioning of Religion in the Living Experience of Unaccompanied Muslim Minors in Italy', *International Journal of Islamic Architecture* 10.2 (2021): 441–64.

12. UNHCR, *Partnership Note on Faith-based Organizations, Local Faith Communities and Faith Leaders* (Geneva: UNHCR, 2014), https://www.unhcr.org/en-us/protection/hcdialogue%20/539ef28b9/partnership-note-faith-based-organizations-local-faith-communities-faith.html.

13 A recent collection focusing specifically on refugee shelters across Europe and their architecture, for instance, has no discussion of religion. This suggests that neither the cases discussed nor the authors themselves consider the role of religion in the production of these spaces. See Tom Scott-Smith and Mark E. Breeze, eds, *Structures of Protection?: Rethinking Refugee Shelter* (New York: Berghahn, 2020).

14 Here we use 'Islamic architecture' in the broadest sense possible, in a way similar to how Hasan Uddin-Khan has defined the term: as a civilizational cultural expression and practice 'encompassing the secular and religious'. Hasan-Uddin Khan, 'Editorial: Towards a New Paradigm for the Architecture and Arts of Islam', *International Journal of Islamic Architecture* 1.1 (2012): 6.

15 We will discuss this issue at a greater length in a forthcoming publication. See Bülent Batuman and Kıvanç Kılınç, eds, *The Urban Refugee: Space, Displacement, and the New Urban Condition* (Intellect, forthcoming).

16 Most of the refugees were from Syria, Albania, Kosovo, Iraq and Afghanistan. See Sabrina Juran and P. Niclas Broer, 'A Profile of Germany's Refugee Populations', *Population and Development Review* 43.1 (2017): 149–57.

17 Irit Katz et al., 'The Bubble, the Airport, and the Jungle: Europe's Urban Migrant Camps', in *Camps Revisited: Multifaceted Spatialities of a Modern Political Technology*, ed. Irit Katz, Diana Martin, and Claudio Minca (London: Rowman & Littlfeld, 2018), 61–82; Toby Parsloe, 'From Emergency Shelter to Community Shelter: Berlin's Tempelhof Refugee Camp', in Scott-Smith and Breeze, *Structures of Protection?*, 275–86.

18 LAF, 'Tempohomes FAQ', accessed July 8, 2021, https://www.berlin.de/laf/wohnen/allgemeine-informationen/tempohomes-faq.

19 Parsloe, 'From Emergency Shelter to Community Shelter', 279.

20 Give Something Back to Berlin, 'Petition from Tempelhof Refugee Shelter Residents Regarding the Container Village' (2017), accessed July 8, 2021, http://gsbtb.org/2017/04/06/petition-fromtempelhof-refugee-shelter-residents-on-the-container-village/.

21 Ayham Dalal et al., 'Planning the Ideal Refugee Camp? A Critical Interrogation of Recent Planning Innovations in Jordan and Germany', *Urban Planning* 3.4 (2018): 64–78.

22 Fazila Bhimji, 'Visibilities and the Politics of Space: Refugee Activism in Berlin', *Journal of Immigrant & Refugee Studies* 14.4 (2016): 432–50.

23 For the concept of spatial agency in architecture, see Bryan Bell and Katie Wakeford, eds, *Expanding Architecture: Design as Activism* (New York: Metropolis, 2008); Nishat Awan, Tatjana Schneider, and Jeremy Till, *Spatial Agency: Other Ways of Doing Architecture* (London: Routledge, 2011).

24 For two recent works that consider spatial agency within the context of the broader Middle East, see Sibel Bozdoğan, 'A Case for Spatial Agency and Social Engagement in the Middle East', *International Journal of Islamic Architecture* 4.1 (2015): 31–35; İpek Türeli, '"Small" Architectures: Walking and Camping in Middle Eastern Cities', *International Journal of Islamic Architecture* 2.1 (2013): 5–38.

25 See Mona Fawaz et al., eds, *Refugees as City-Makers* (Beirut: Social Justice and City Program at the Issam Fares Institute for Public Policy and International Affairs, American University of Beirut, 2018).

26. Sut Jhally, 'Edward Said on "Orientalism"', interview with Edward Said, *Media Education Foundation* (2005), accessed July 21, 2021, https://www.mediaed.org/transcripts/Edward-Said-On-Orientalism-Transcript.pdf, 4.
27. For a documentary film on the everyday life of a Syrian refugee camp in northern Iraq, see *Refugee Republic* (Dirk Jan Visser, Jan Rothuizen, Martijn van Tol, 2014), http://refugeerepublic.submarinechannel.com/. See also the essays published in Bülent Batuman, ed., 'Dis-placed', special issue, *International Journal of Islamic Architecture* 10.2 (2021).
28. Fawaz et al., 4–9.
29. Ibid., 4.
30. Ibid.
31. Ibid., 5.
32. Jelena Bogdanović, 'Reorienting Perspectives: Why I do Not Teach a Course Titled "Islamic Architecture"', *International Journal of Islamic Architecture* 10.1 (2021): 115. This essay is reproduced in the present volume.
33. Thomas Fisher, 'What We Can Learn from Refugees', in *The Routledge Companion to Architecture and Social Engagement*, ed. Farhan Karim (New York: Routledge, 2018), 403.
34. Ibid.
35. See Christiane Gruber, ed., 'Islamic Architecture on the Move', special issue, *International Journal of Islamic Architecture* 3.2 (2014).
36. Fisher, 'What We Can Learn from Refugees', 399.
37. See, for example, Kim Rygiel, Feyzi Baban, and Suzan Ilcan, 'The Syrian Refugee Crisis: The EU-Turkey "Deal" and Temporary Protection', *Global Social Policy* 16.3 (2016): 315–20; Piro Rexhepi, 'Arab Others at European Borders: Racializing Religion and Refugees Along the Balkan Route', *Ethnic and Racial Studies* 41.12 (2018): 2215–34.
38. It is only recently that scholars of Islamic architecture have begun looking into the 'invisible geographies', such as informal squatter settlements inside Muslim-majority cities. See, for example, Abidin Kusno, 'Invisible Geographies in the Study of Islamic Architecture', *International Journal of Islamic Architecture* 5.1 (2016): 29–35. This essay is reproduced in the present volume.

Part 9

Practice and Profession

Chapter 27

'Islamic Architecture' and the Profession

Nasser Rabbat

The term 'Islamic architecture' typically evokes domed and sumptuously decorated monuments, preferably with minarets and lots of arches. Reductive and exotic, these images are nonetheless quite popular both in the west and in the Islamic world. Even the specialized literature on Islamic architecture, erudite and extensive as it is, still falls for a similar, though less fantastic, kind of historicism. Most surveys of Islamic architecture begin with the Dome of the Rock in Jerusalem, built in 692, and end with the Taj Mahal in Agra, completed in 1654, as the first and last instances of an architectural tradition comprised mostly of mosques, shrines, palaces, and castles, with its best creative days behind it. So pervasive was this restrictive historical construct that Islamic architecture had a very hard time making the transition into the modern world of design. Even today, with many architects around the world using the vocabulary of Islamic architecture in their design – mainly in response to passionate requests from their clients – the notion of 'Islamic architecture' sits uneasily within both the practice of design and the field of architectural history, where its name, scope, and claim to specificity are constantly questioned and, in a few cases, reconceptualised, or simply rejected.

Why is it so? How has Islamic architecture as a historical category and a body of knowledge interacted with the practice of design? And is the uncertainty with which architectural historians treat the notion of a contemporary Islamic architecture related to the expediency and frivolity with which many architects respond to requests of incorporating 'Islamic architecture' into their design? Here, I will try to chart a few venues for tackling these questions, which are of course interrelated. I hope that my brief historical analysis of the relationship between Islamic architecture and the profession will stir some critical reactions, reactions that will push this politicized and ideologized debate out of the realm of polemics and facile solutions and into the broadest scholarly and professional context.

The ambiguity about Islamic architecture goes back to the turn of the nineteenth century when the term was first coined as an alternative to other, more archaic terms, such as Mohammedan, Moorish, or Saracenic architecture. Before that date, Islamic architecture was simply the architecture of the land of Islam, and it would be difficult to imagine premodern Islamic designers fretting about its representativeness. It was their architecture, encapsulating their history, structural and material knowledge, aesthetic sensibilities, and understanding of the constraints of their environment. It was, to them, architecture *tout court*. But when the first European architects and draftsmen arrived in the 'Orient' in the wake of the first European military interventions, they had a difficult time understanding, situating, and naming the architecture they encountered. Because of its apparent strangeness, they had to differentiate it from the architecture they knew, while at the same time they had no choice but to define it using concepts borrowed from that same familiar architecture, which was per force classical and European. Thus, 'Islamic architecture', from the moment of its inception as a category, was simultaneously and paradoxically hitched to the conceptual contours of another, well-studied architectural history, and resolutely separated from its established chronological, cultural, and conceptual structure. Constructed against a stratified and linear western architectural historiography with its roots in ancient Greece and its triumphal telos in modern, industrial Europe, Islamic architecture was, over time, confined to the timeframe of medieval architecture, with no roots in the classical past and no connection to the present. This has remained the case until very recently with the majority of the architectural historical surveys taught to architectural students in the west squeezing the entirety of Islamic architecture, regardless of the actual dates of its examples, between late Medieval and Renaissance architecture. Such is the case, for instance, with the very popular book of Spiro Kostof, *A History of Architecture*, first published in 1985, wherein he pairs Cairo and Florence together in the late Middle Ages and Istanbul and Venice in the Renaissance.

That notion of interruption, or more precisely of withering away in the premodern period, was one of the main reasons for which Islamic architecture entered the world of modern design primarily through the revivalist portal. European architects active in the major Islamic cities, such as Istanbul, Cairo, Delhi, and Tehran, at the height of the colonial age devised numerous revivalist styles that borrowed motifs from the varied repertoires of the past and blended them with eclectic western stylistic modes. Thus, we see neo-Islamic, neo-Mamluk, Indo-Saracenic, neo-Moorish, and other 'neo' styles dominating the civic architecture of the late nineteenth and early twentieth centuries in the majority of Islamic countries that fell under colonial rule. But the identity confusion caused by mixed terminology and stylistic dependency on western categories amplified the historical discontinuity, so that the 'neo' styles, many of which were sincerely meant as national styles for modern times, never managed to bridge the gap with the historical periods to which they formally referred. Instead, a sense of alienation pervaded their examples, which, though innovative and aesthetically elegant, were treated as formalist exercises and kept outside the sanctioned narrative of architecture in both the Islamic world and the world at large.

The postmodern solution to the conundrum of authenticity and continuity was to revert to selective copying from venerated historical models unmediated by stylistic reinterpretation. This suited the mood of the time in many Islamic countries, several of which had belatedly gained their independence from colonial rule and were eager to establish a visual identity with solid roots in the past. The available academic presentation of 'Islamic architecture', consisting essentially of catalogues of grand monuments, offered a streamlined package of images for contemporary architects looking for recognizable historical anchors to their designs. They 'sampled' celebrated historical models, chief among them the Alhambra and imperial Ottoman mosques, to compose variations on these archetypes cherished by a new class of wealthy and culturally traditionalist patrons. Consequently, most of the 'Islamic architecture' of the 1970s and 1980s, and sometime even later decades, was postmodern in

Figure 27.1: The Museum of Islamic Art, Doha, by I. M. Pei, 2008, seen from the entrance bridge. Source: Nasser Rabbat.

spirit and appearance, even when it was cloaked in environmental or technological rhetorical arguments [Figure 27.1].

Thus, notwithstanding the brief rationalist attempts to learn from 'Islamic architecture' throughout the twentieth century, the two major moments of engagement with its legacy, the revivalist and the postmodern, were essentially formalist and historicist. Instead of challenging the effects of the Eurocentric art-historical paradigm of cultural autonomy, these more recent examples reinforced the prevalent view of Islamic architecture as ornamental, historicist, and insular, even though they never managed to extend its timeline or enlarge its canonical referents. They floated without an acknowledged genealogy, having been absorbed neither into the history of Islamic architecture, whose academic purview stopped at the end of the eighteenth century, nor in modern architectural discourse, because they were dubbed derivative and latecomers. The failure of the profession to fully historicize 'Islamic architecture', while at the same time modernizing it, made the late-twentieth-century efforts to define it more broadly and to uncover in it universal architectural values a more onerous task. Not only was a revision of the ways through which historical Islamic architecture was presented and interpreted necessary, but so too was a re-education of the design professionals to wean them from the facile appropriation of forms and ornamental patterns as a convenient means to incorporate 'Islamic architecture' into their design. Several corrective approaches have been tried, mostly in academe and by a number of research-oriented practices in countries like Egypt, Turkey, the Soviet Union, and Iran. None has been totally successful in breaking out of the particularism trap, although in their sum they have at least created a true dialogue on Islamic architecture with an active global audience and many salient concerns and propositions.

At least two of these approaches contribute more consciously to the question of the relationship of Islamic architecture to the design discourse today. The first is the architectural enterprise of the Aga Khan, which began in the mid-1970s with an international award programme, the Aga Khan Award for Architecture (AKAA), and is still unfolding today with many more institutional forays into all aspects of architecture from academe to urban and landscape conservation and a whole array of developmental projects. The AKAA, wide-ranging and long term as an initiative, is rather pragmatic in determining its intellectual trajectory. Over more than 40 years and 14 triannual cycles, it has striven to project itself as inclusive of all geographies and all genres of architecture and as intentionally evolving to reflect the changing conditions of architecture in the Islamic world as well as, and perhaps more importantly, the shifting theorization of architecture worldwide, but especially in the west. In fact, a cursory review of the more than one hundred projects it has rewarded thus far reveals both a sensitivity to criticism and a desire for inclusion in the global architectural discourse coupled with a steady move toward the recognition of a more humanistic and more environmentally responsive architecture.

The second endeavour is more introspective but also intellectually introverted. It can be called 'fundamentalist' in the sense that its proponents seek to find in the Islamic intellectual heritage a framework for the understanding of Islamic architecture and to extend that understanding to the practice of design today. This approach arose in the 1970s and 1980s through two distinct venues. The first aimed to recover a conceptual basis for architecture in the specialized literature of *fiqh* (jurisprudence), a vast and thoroughly deductive body of knowledge that covers all aspects of Islamic social life. Its main proponents are academics from Saudi Arabia, Egypt, Iraq, and Iran who had studied in western universities and felt challenged by the absence of Islamic-based theories in their curricula, even when the subject of study was Islamic. The second derived its interpretive basis from the enormous repertory of mystical Sufi writing and saw art and architecture as symbolic manifestations of a transcendental Islam. Sometimes called the 'Perennial School', it has attracted mostly western artists, spiritualists, theorists, and art historians (but also a few prominent Muslims) who were looking for ways to counter the materialism they saw as invading modern art and modern life in general. Both discourses based their argument on the inability of western theories to explain Islamic architecture, thus rejecting the western theories' claim of universal applicability. But instead of falling back on the cultural autonomy paradigm of the colonial period, they emphasized instead a more radical belief in epistemological independence grounded in a long history of Islamic learning, both in the applied and the reflective domains.

The two approaches of the AKAA and the 'fundamentalists', the one accepting of the universality and pertinence of western theory and the other insisting on epistemological rupture, represent two poles in the debate on the role of Islamic architecture in the design profession today. They are not, however, autonomously constructed within the field of architecture. Each embodies a major current in an older, much deeper, and almost existential intellectual debate that started when the Islamic world awoke to the reality of the modern age with the arrival of European colonial powers on its shores at the end of the eighteenth and beginning of the nineteenth centuries. Recognizing that the Islamic world lost the civilizational competition to modern Europe, the two sides of the debate differed on how to redress the imbalance. One side insisted on the adoption of western modernity, wholesale or selectively, as the surest road to parity with the west. The other proclaimed the solution in a return to the authentic Islamic ways and a refusal of western modernity. The debate waxed and waned, but never died down – it is in fact at its sharpest stance in decades in these first decades of the twenty-first century. Can the debate on Islamic architecture contribute insight to that larger one?

Note

This chapter was previously published as Nasser Rabbat, '"Islamic Architecture" and the Profession', *International Journal of Islamic Architecture* 3.1 (2014): 37–40. Updates, where appropriate, have been made to the present version.

Chapter 28

A Trinity of Values in Architecture for Muslim Societies

Rasem Badran

I take issue with the term 'Islamic architecture', which might seem strange since my work has come to exemplify what is generally considered to be 'contemporary Islamic architecture'. What I strive for – and how I would define my work – is *architecture for Muslim societies* – architecture that responds to the social habits, values, and understandings that tie Muslims together as a distinctive group of people. I aim for intimate spaces that draw their forms from historical context and examples, from the human scale, and from the careful study of human interactions. Rather than deploying decorative elements that superficially mark buildings as 'Islamic' in appearance, I advocate for the design of buildings that serve the needs of people and reflect the diverse cultural heritage of the Islamic world. In the essay that follows I articulate my perspectives on the inadequacy of todays 'Islamic architecture', architecture for Muslim societies, and my own approach to design using a few examples of projects from Saudi Arabia and Iraq.

The term 'Islamic architecture' is problematic for me for two reasons. Firstly, Islam is evolutionary, and it has been adapted to different societies across the world, as well as across time. Thus, as Vikramāditya Prakāsh once questioned: 'Is the singular term "Islamic" robust enough to completely, or even adequately, capture the diversity and the width of the work it seeks to represent?'[1] Unfortunately, I do not think so, and I find this to be a significant shortcoming. Secondly, the constant (and, in my view, inappropriate) use of the term 'Islamic architecture' has come to drown its definition in misleading associations. Many design elements are now strongly associated explicitly with Islamic architecture, such as the dome and the arch, despite having originally been incorporated into public buildings for the sake of function. They were used for resolving structural and acoustic challenges rather than to reflect particular religious ideas. Of course, architecture in Muslim societies also incorporated Islamic arts, which are, as we know, non-figurative. It relies on geometric shapes inspired by cosmology and mathematics. Today, by contrast, Islamic architecture is often associated with façade treatments that display disfigured *mashrabiya* or structurally unnecessary arches, domes, and ornamentation, as if abstracted 'Islamic' structural and decorative features were the primary means for representing and uniting Muslims.

Architecture for Muslim Societies

Islam is a timeless religion, and its principles offer guidelines for privacy, relations to public and private spaces, and how to promote ethics, respect, and harmony. As such it organizes society and relationships between all social groups. These essential principles relate to the habitual interaction between all members of society and they materialize through architecture as a by-product. They should be reflected in society and in its architectural and urban expression through more than abstracted formal design elements. As architects, we must ensure that these values – called for by Islam – are materialized in the micro and macro scales of cities. Architecture in Muslim societies is not only about a building or the shapes on its exterior, but it is also about the urbanity, and the fabric of the city and its function. It is the dialogue between people and the harmony of their interrelation. It should be a bridge between traditional urban expressions so as to feel familiar and relevant, yet it should respond to the physical and spiritual needs of its users today. Architecture for Muslim societies should, therefore, value the human experience, while encouraging connectivity and responding to the geographical and cultural contexts. These three points are dependent on one another and form the trinity of fundamentals for positive, useful architecture for Muslim societies.

I have reached these conclusions from my own personal development and from years of practice in Muslim-majority contexts. Born in Jerusalem, I was raised in the house of an artist – the late Jamal Badran – who was an expert in Islamic crafts, ornamental arts, and calligraphy. I grew up in a vibrant and culturally rich home on the outskirts of Jerusalem, and spent my days examining the meaning of harmony by observing his decorative artwork and understanding geometry, scale, and ratio by studying his calligraphy. My father inspired me to appreciate art, and he encouraged me to draw freely, nurturing in me a keen understanding of Arab-Islamic tradition. Compounding the influences of my father were a childhood and young adulthood spent moving between several traditionally Arab-Islamic cities, including Jerusalem, Ramallah, and Damascus. My immediate environments, which were ever changing, enriched my creativity and instilled a series of dynamic images of people and places in my mind. Even today, memories from my earlier years drive my design approach and understanding of spaces and places, and their relation to human behaviour. Later, my life and career took me to Jordan, the Gulf coast countries, North Africa, and Muslim-majority countries elsewhere, including Malaysia.

Many scholars and architects have misinterpreted the purpose of 'Islamic architecture' by neglecting the importance of the human experience. Today, it seems the only focus is abstracting superficial design elements for the exterior of a building, which results in the undervaluing of the story and experience of that building's interior.[2] I consider this to be the main problem challenging architecture for Muslim societies – the over-abstraction of elements, which arrives at nothing but meaningless design and a lost spiritual journey. Rarely do I see arches and geometric shapes used correctly; they are too often decorative. The arch, utilized across civilizations from the Greeks to the Romans, used to provide structural support. Now, such features are taken for granted and used just to mark a building as Islamic architecture, but their superficiality reduces the spiritual meaning of a space and distracts from the purpose of the building.[3] Symbolism has replaced meaning.

Were we to look to mosques that were built centuries ago, such as Cairo's al-Sultan Hassan Mosque, we can learn what true building design for a Muslim society looks like. Take for example the entrance, which is perhaps its most special feature. We call it *al majaz*. It is a place that prepares you for the transmission into a private, spiritual space. It inspires and comforts visitors as they move from a public area where they are distracted with daily life and chaotic forces, such as noise and negativity, to an intimate, tranquil area that welcomes religious ceremony and contemplation.

To value humans and nurture their ritual imagination and state of meditation, it is essential to understand the difference between architecture for Muslim societies and 'contemporary architecture'. Contemporary architecture often does not respect the human scale, and presents humans in a powerless way, as if their value in society does not exist. However, Islam – which has had a long and great impression on architecture – calls for an architecture and urbanism that inspires each individual to sense their own presence in society, which is not meant to be built according to different social classes.[4] In fact, in the Islamic city, the public zone is without social distinctions – and the experience of the public zone differs from that of the private zone.

The public zone is the open space where people can meet and create a larger family. These meeting points include small plazas, marketplaces, and mosque premises. This is where people gather and get to know one another, creating micro social networks. These spaces break down social barriers, such as economic status and ethnic division, allowing people to connect and interact. The public zone is for the rich and the poor, the cultured, and the uncultured. People come here to feel that they are living under the umbrella of Islam. The private zone is the intimate, private home, where the traditional family unit resides, lives, and sleeps. The private zone is what gives users the full ownership and freedom to create their own atmosphere.

Throughout my career, I have completed a number of mosque designs, including the Baghdad State Mosque (1982). When you examine the design, you will find that its strength lies in its not being designed solely as a mosque. It was designed as a fuller, functional city. I tried to transform the meaning of 'mosque' and enlarge it to incorporate the social context, because mosques have always been part of the urban fabric. They were never isolated or seen as monumental objects – they were modest and approachable. Thus, what I proposed was not just a temple. My design for the Baghdad State Mosque was humble, human. I stretched it out and allowed it to interrelate with the city; I resolved the solids and voids and respected the existing site.

The workplace, house, school, and sacred space are meant to function as one network in Muslim society. They are not separate entities that turn their backs to one another, and this is influenced by Islam's values – that we live within an interrelated sense of daily activities. In mosques, you will find a madrasa, because you do not only go to the mosque to pray – it is a part of your life, even outside of the five daily prayer times. So we combine the spiritual value with the materialistic needs and physical demands – this to me is architecture for Muslim society. It is the balance between the tangible and intangible, physical space and practice.

The projects that I have designed are based on a methodological approach in defining architecture as a continuous dialogue between contemporary needs and historical, inherited cultural values. They are also place-specific in response to environmental conditions, and reflect modern reinterpretations of the past to serve the future.

Islamic Architecture Today and Tomorrow

Figure 28.1: Justice Palace and Grand Mosque, Riyadh, Saudi Arabia (1985–1992). A revitalizing presence in the city centre, the project was awarded the Agha Khan Award in Architecture in 1995. Source: Rasem Badran/Dar Al-Omran.

In 1985 I worked on the design for the Grand Mosque and Justice Palace of Riyadh, which would later win an Aga Khan Award [Figures 28.1 and 28.2]. The main concept of the project was to revitalize Riyadh's old city centre based on its historic, urban, and architectural heritage by developing the existing streets and introducing landscaped plazas and pathways that link the different spaces together. The contemporary reinterpretation of local traditions continues in the interior design through spatial organization, details, colours, and materials, but more importantly, we applied building techniques that were used in the past, and that can be seen in older parts of Saudi Arabia, such as precast and pre-production. So while the scale has changed, the technique remains the same because it is logical. Hassan Fathy used this method in his urban development of Qurna and for a palace in southern Egypt.

Both of these projects in Riyadh use the same approach when it comes to the value of place – public spaces were scattered throughout the sections based on the existing programme of the projects and the types of facilities they have on-site. An important aspect in the design process was also having the right amount of public spaces to ensure the user's journey is enjoyable and distinguishable from the experience of the private zones. We also distributed special educational spaces. Together, the different parts created a micro city that contains several important services for the community, from spiritual to educational

A Trinity of Values in Architecture for Muslim Societies

Figure 28.2: Interior of the Grand Mosque, Riyadh, Saudi Arabia (1985–1992). A revitalizing presence in the city centre, the project was awarded the Agha Khan Award in Architecture in 1995. Source: Rasem Badran/Dar Al-Omran.

and recreational. Perhaps its most significant space is the plaza, which invites community members to spend their day there with their family and friends. It is the heart of the city and the spirit of the mosque.

The incorporation of plazas, courtyards, and pathways is a key example of how connectivity enriches the human experience in Muslim societies. Such spaces serve as tunnels that buffer external pressures and noise from outside areas. They also serve as a backdrop to universal divinity, as the colour of plants, the air, and other natural elements change during the day and across seasons, further re-establishing connections between the visitor and the earth, merging with the spiritual connection with the beyond.

This crucial element is most evident in Riyadh's Al Bujairi Development, which we completed in 2016 [Figures 28.3 and 28.4]. Facing the historical Mud City, a UNESCO World Heritage site,[5] the development contains entertainment facilities and is submerged partially underground, allowing its roof to transform into a plaza that is 200 metres in length. Appearing to bow toward the Mud City, this plaza invites the community to enjoy it and does not disturb the context. It maintains harmony with the existing Al Turaif area, which has become a living museum. The funny thing is that the plaza covering Al Bujeiri has become an iconic

Figure 28.3: Bujairi Quarter, Diriyah, Saudi Arabia (2000–2015). This development takes the special culture, form, climate, context, and agricultural nature of the site into consideration. Source: Rasem Badran/Dar Al-Omran.

feature, and not through its monumentality, but rather, through its modesty and its respect for the existing fabric.

How do I arrive at these results? Ahead of each project, I always visit the site and reflect on the life that existed, exists, and will exist. When I worked in Riyadh, I visited old buildings and simple neighbourhoods that really impressed me with their modesty, nature, and humanity. Upon returning to Jordan, where I was based, I would pull influences from what I saw and felt. I began to communicate the impact of the images I stored in my mind and combine them with what I imagined. From studying the Mud City, I learned the scale of the indoor and outdoor spaces, the proportions of the private living space and the courtyard.

Conclusion

In the west, the golden ratio has long been the rule to end all rules, and arches and openings have often been determined by it. I do not think the old masters, like Sultan Hassan, used such universalist ideas. To great effect, the great architects of Muslim civilizations defined length and width by intuition and spiritual feeling. They determined, by eye, how to reach *mizan*, or

A Trinity of Values in Architecture for Muslim Societies

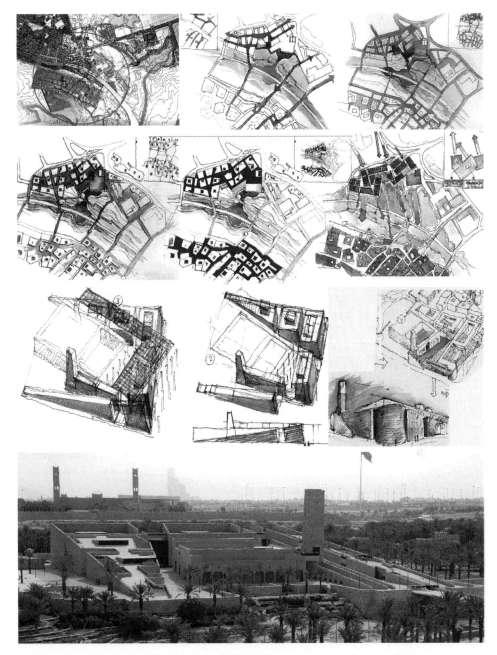

Figure 28.4: Bujairi Quarter, Diriyah, Saudi Arabia (2000–2015). Source: Rasem Badran/Dar Al-Omran.

Islamic Architecture Today and Tomorrow

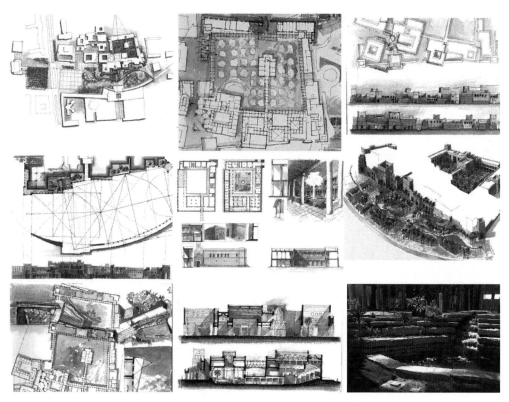

Figure 28.5: King Abdul Aziz Historical Center, Riyadh, Saudi Arabia (1996–1999). This project was in part inspired by the architectural heritage of Najd. Source: Rasem Badran/Dar Al-Omran.

balance, so that when one looks at something, one feels harmony. This intuition appears to have been forgotten by many architects who depend instead on visual tropes and decorations intended to represent Islam and Muslim people.

Visual harmony, and therefore inner harmony, was significant for the old masters. Sometimes, they would put models inside to examine the proportion of domes and openings, so they could see if they felt relaxed in a space and assess its suitability to the human scale. I use the same approach in my work. For example, in the Grand Mosque of Riyadh, the distance between the columns was determined by my own experience and feeling (see Figure 28.2). I have learned the art of proportions through cumulative observations of nature and its elements; for example, the layout and proportions of fields of palm trees inspired this structural system. Studying the inherited architecture found in our region – whether located in old Jerusalem, Cairo, Damascus, or Istanbul – has also been helpful. Another contributing factor was of course the artistic upbringing that helped me to learn the proportions, rules, and guidelines of Arabic calligraphy. My contributions therefore emerged from combining lessons from the past with the revolutionary/industrialized/engineered modern movements and techniques of

Figure 28.6: King Abdul Aziz Historical Center, Riyadh, Saudi Arabia (1996–1999). Rasem Badran/Dar Al-Omran.

today. The architecture that I design is thus a hybrid of modernity and traditions [Figures 28.5 and 28.6].

As an architect, based on my practice and observation of different Islamic cities and buildings, I have come to the understanding that architecture for Muslim societies should not be dependent on the static replication of shapes and formal elements. Rather, it should be a revival of the values of Islam, which I view to be ethics, respect, and harmony. Islam has had great influence on how to envision architecture, promoting equality between people and respecting the privacy and personal needs of individuals. Far more important than horseshoe arches and painted tiles, Islam emphasizes the value of each individual in his or her community and creates a sense of belonging and interaction, organizing different aspects of life and breaking the barriers between different social classes. This, perhaps, is the closest definition of Islamic architecture that I can accept.

Acknowledgements

The author thanks Rima Alsammarae and the Badran Design Studio for their assistance with this essay.

Notes

This chapter was previously published as Rasem Badran, 'A Trinity of Values in Architecture for Muslim Societies', *International Journal of Islamic Architecture* 10.1 (2021): 247–56. The text has been updated for this publication.

1. Vikramāditya Prakāsh, 'The "Islamic" from a Global Historiographical Perspective', *International Journal of Islamic Architecture* 6.1 (2017): 19.
2. Jenine Kotob, 'Why Islamic Architecture in the United States is Failing American Muslims', *ArchDaily*, July 21, 2016, https://www.archdaily.com/791724/why-islamic-architecture-in-the-united-states-is-failing-american-muslims.
3. Ibid.
4. Spahic Omer, 'The Qur'an and Sunnah as the Foundation of Islamic Architecture', *IslamiCity*, November 9, 2011, https://www.islamicity.org/4551/the-quran-and-sunnah-as-the-foundation-of-islamic-architecture/.
5. Rawan Radwan, 'Al-Turaif: How Saudi Arabia is Bolstering Future Tourism by Reviving Past Treasures', *Arab News*, December 11, 2018, https://www.arabnews.com/node/1418806/saudi-arabia.

Chapter 29

Relevance, Tradition, and Practice in Islamic Architecture

Kamil Khan Mumtaz

In an age obsessed with novelty and innovation, the practice of 'Islamic architecture' raises several questions, not least of which are those concerning Islamic architecture's definition as a distinctive field and its relevance to our time. Less inclined to use the 'Islamic' label, I prefer to describe my work as 'traditional', in the sense of being determined by pre-industrial modes of production and a metaphysical worldview shared by all wisdom traditions. In my own context, this worldview is informed predominantly, but not exclusively, by Islam.

Our time has been called the 'Age of Man', the Anthropocene, because the most significant changes in the geosphere in this epoch are caused by human activity. Human activities are responsible for global changes at rates that are far in excess of the limits of the planet's bio-capacity, and are pushing one indicator after another past the tipping point, the point of no return. This essay argues that pre-industrial building practices allow us to build what we need without exceeding the planet's bio-capacity, while the narratives of pre-modern civilizations provide the guide maps for returning to the normative state, in harmony and balance with nature. The wisdom embedded in these narratives is communicated in art and architecture through symbols, metaphors, similes, and images that have meaning and relevance in each local culture, reflecting its history and geography. Thus for the Muslim architect in the twenty-first century, critical engagement with the theory and practice of Islamic architecture is not only timely and meaningful, but in the context of the present global ecological crisis, it is the need of the hour. My own quest for a contemporary and appropriate architecture for Pakistan, an architecture that is responsive to climate, economy, and materials, yet rooted in the indigenous culture, has been a journey from modernity to tradition.

Modernity to Tradition: A Personal Journey

On completion of my high school studies I was faced with a choice between pursuing a career as a nuclear physicist or as an artist painter. My father and my housemaster both suggested that I could combine both interests in the field of architecture. As no professional courses in architecture were available in Pakistan then, I followed my friend Habib Fida Ali to the Architectural Association School of Architecture (AA) in London in 1957.

The mid-twentieth century was the heyday of Modernism, and the AA was at the cutting edge. The appeal of Modernism lay in its rationalism, universalism, and Humanist philosophy, and the promise of modern science and technology to deliver a material paradise, a new world of plenty for all mankind, based on the principles of justice, equity, freedom, and the 'brotherhood of Man': liberty, equality, and fraternity. A central theme of the Modernist project was the idea of 'development' or 'evolution' as a relentless natural process, the ascent of Man being the very destiny of humanity. In this construct of history, the 'west' was seen as 'modern and developed' and the east as 'backward and under-developed'.

Like so many others of my generation, schooled in the theories of the modern movement, our aesthetic was ruled by scientific logic, and our design methods sought to emulate the efficient systems of the machine age. Again, like so many of us from the Third World, I was also concerned with the problems of underdevelopment. The enormity of the tasks faced by our societies called for innovative solutions. We believed our role was to develop an architecture based on technologies that were appropriate to the climates and economics of our own region. But I was clear that the machine aesthetic of the International Style was patently irrelevant to industrially primitive economies. Steel and glass façades, standardized modular components, rectangular grids, and precision engineering, were not only made possible, but were also demanded by the industrial modes of production and climatic conditions of Europe and North America. But the natural materials, artisanal modes of construction, and tropical climates of most newly independent nations called for radically different forms of building.

In the early 1960s, I began to experiment with the geometry of forms derived from simple basic units. Then at Kumasi in Ghana, I had an opportunity to work with Buckminster Fuller and Keith Critchlow, and each of them had a very strong influence on my own work. Returning to Pakistan in 1996, I began to experiment with the possibilities of applying these geometries to low-cost housing systems, temporary exhibition structures, and even sculpture.

At the same time I was critical of the aberrations of the International Style, which reduced the modern movement to a set of clichés and symbols of westernization and modernity. I therefore deliberately sought to cultivate a form of expression that would not be derivative of western forms, but would rather be based on available local materials, appropriate technologies, and the demands of our specific climates. I was convinced that my buildings were thus necessarily regional, and if my brick vaults were rejected by the community for whom they were designed, I put this down to peasant suspicion of anything new, and not to my own failure to recognize the functional advantages of a flat roof as useable floor space in our climate.

In the late 1960s and 1970s, as a political activist, I was making posters and other illustrations for peasant and labour organizations. In doing so I became increasingly aware that my work in this field was in some respects inadequate. I realized that effective visual communication involved culture-specific graphic conventions, symbols, and colour pallets. I desperately needed to learn something from our native popular art. Miniature paintings, art on trucks and motor rickshaws, bazaar posters of religious festivals with iconic symbols, and hagiographic portraits of local saints and shrines were an endless source of fascination and wonder. Clearly, these art forms shared something very powerful in common, but I was not sure quite what it was.

At the time, in 1977, when I was working on the competition design for the Data Durbar Mosque in Lahore, I knew nothing about our traditional attitudes towards architecture. As a modernist, I had abandoned religion to the 'rubbish heap of history'. But working for hours on end, day after day, on the drawings had been a deeply satisfying experience for me. It had put me in a contemplative frame of mind, and as I searched the Qur'an for an appropriate text for an inscription, I began to realize that this was no ordinary document. It filled me with a strange feeling of wonderment. But I left it at that.

Then in 1980 some architecture students who had been assigned to study current trends among the architects practising in Lahore came to interview me. 'Do you work in the western or the indigenous style?', they asked. I was amused by their naiveté. 'Why don't you go and look at some of my buildings, and then you tell me', I replied. So they did, and they came back beaming. It was clear they had seen the light. 'Yes sir', they said. 'It's quite clear. You design in the western style'. I was shattered. Obviously something other than form and function immediately identified a building in the popular mind as either 'indigenous' or 'western'. In that moment I realized that buildings communicate on a level of which I had been totally unaware.

Then, at about the same time, I received a letter from the Aga Khan inviting me to join the steering committee of the Award for Islamic Architecture. I was overwhelmed. 'What do I know about Islamic architecture?', I thought. I decided to educate myself. The first book I read was Nader Ardalan and Laleh Bakhtiar's *Sense of Unity: The Sufi Tradition in Persian Architecture* (1973).[1] It was a revelation. Next, I read Laleh Bakhtiar's *Sufi*.[2] I was converted. An aspect of my mind and my heart had been touched that I never knew existed. I was prompted to re-examine the cultural expressions of other societies, and in the process began to realize that monumental architecture and higher forms of art in all cultures have always been used to convey abstract ideas. But more significant was the realization that ideas about man and his relationship to the cosmos are essentially the same in all pre-modern cultures: all of them find their origins in a single source to which everything must ultimately return, and all of them believe that beyond the apparent physical reality is a metaphysical reality, that truth exists within man and around him, that man has both an animal temporal self and a higher potential self, that man's purpose in this life is to attain a knowledge of the truth, and that ultimate knowledge lies in becoming one with the object of one's quest.

My first opportunity to apply these insights to my own work was in the design for a khanqah for Shaikh Fadlullah Haeri. When I was contacted by the Shaikh's representatives, I was convinced this was providential. I put my heart and soul into the design. When I eventually met the Shaikh he was effusively warm and friendly, and said 'Kamil Khan, where have you been? We have been waiting for you'. But when the drawings were presented to him he was silent. When I pressed him for his comments he said 'Kamil Khan, we are not looking for great architecture, where people come and say "ooh" and "ah!" We do not want them to become aware of the building, we want them to become aware of themselves'. I was humbled. I had been given my first lesson in the traditional role and function of art and architecture, and a lesson on the attitude the architect needs to adopt in his work.

I had already understood that geometry and proportional sub-division comprised an essential method of design. But understanding is one thing and doing is quite another. Despite having a sense of what I wanted to do, I found that my hand refused to obey my mind. In fact the really big barrier was my own education and training as an architect. The compulsion to be innovative, to be creative, to be original, the imperative to be 'expressive of our time', had always stopped me short of 'imitation' and 'copying'. In the last analysis, it was the ego that simply refused to let go, to surrender. Eventually, I was able to cross this barrier under the guidance of a spiritual master, Shaykh Abu Bakr Siraj-ed-din.

When I discussed my internal/professional conflict with Sheikh Abu Bakr, he said 'But whatever you do will be of our time', and asked what was the reality of 'our times?' I thought of science, the high tech industry, urbanization, and what has followed in its wake – weapons of mass destruction, the alienation of the individual, the disintegration of society, the corruption of values, the degradation of the environment, etc. He agreed that these were the aberrations of our times. 'But the writings of Guenon, Coomeraswamy and Schuon are also "of our times". It is a question of which "reality" you choose to reflect in your work', he said.[3]

The writings of these masters of metaphysics and spirituality helped me to understand the nature of 'our times' and the timeless nature of the 'real'. The study and analysis of the built work of the master-builders helped me understand how this timeless reality was reflected in traditional art and architecture. In my own practice I have been able to explore the possibilities of experiencing structure, form, light, and space, using familiar materials, patterns, and surface decoration as the grounds for contemplation, which help the viewer to become aware of a reality beyond the immediate materiality of a brick wall, a marble floor, or a wooden screen. I have learned to work within the framework of a discipline of symmetries, proportions, and rhythms that reflect both the cosmic order and perfect balance underlying the apparent chaos of the universe. I have been able to evoke the delights of discovering the hidden paradise with internal patios and fountains. I have learned much, and continue to learn, from the wisdom and skill of our master craftsmen.

My introduction to the traditional architectural vocabulary and practice occurred during several meetings with Mistree Haji Ghulam Hussain in 1982, at a mosque he was building in Dina, and at his residence in Rawalpindi. In my practice we have had longer associations with other masters, including Ustad Saif-ur-Rahman (beginning with his work for me on the frescos for my Dar-ul-Hikmat in 1994); master mason Ishaq, contractor Arshad, and fresco painter Ustad Rafaqat (three brothers); the *thoba* (stucco plaster) artist Ustad Jaffar; the *kashigars* (ceramists) Siddique of Nasarpur, Jani Soomro of Hala, and Alla Diwayo of Multan; *chitrai* (beaten metal) master Maulvi Yaqoob and his younger brother Hafeez. We have been fortunate and learned a great deal from collaborations with these talented craftsmen.

The last *ustad* who could build brick 'flat domes' was Ustad 'Ilm Deen. He had retired when I met him at one of our sites. It was not anything he said, but his smile and the twinkle in his eyes that told me that he approved of what we were doing. The last *leekhai* (drafting) master was Haji Abdul Aziz, who taught us much of what we have learnt of the language and grammar of geometry and design and who formally adopted my son, Taimoor, as his *shagird* (student). Among the other young men we have seen blossoming into masters in their own right are

Azmat Naqqash, Baqi the *thoba* and mirror work artist, and Boota, the brick mason. We are optimistic for the future of traditional craftsmanship.

But the future of traditional craftsmanship will depend on the continuation of patronage by a discerning clientele, guidance and leadership by competent designers and architects, and rigorous scholarship, including documentation, research and analysis, conducted by our academic institutions. With the passing away of the older generations of hereditary craftsmen, many skills and knowledge have been lost. Some of these we have had to struggle to re-discover, through documentation and analysis of surviving monuments, through trial and error in our own projects, testing materials in laboratories, experimenting on site, and searching for widely scattered documents in private collections and on the internet. Most of our work has been in central Punjab, where fired clay bricks and lime mortar were found to be the materials of choice for construction of foundations, bearing walls, arches, and roofs. This led to the revival of 'lost' techniques of flat and ribbed domes, and *muqarnas*, built without Portland cement, reinforcing steel, or shuttering.

Two projects that illustrate the participatory nature of our work are a mosque, located about 350 kilometres west of Lahore, and two tombs located in Lahore. The clients for both of these projects came to us because they wanted strictly traditional buildings based on specific historic structures. I had reached a point in my own understanding of traditional design theory where I could accept these demands as perfectly normal, indeed necessary to the design process.

The site of the mosque, known locally as 'Pak Wigah', or 'sacred field', is a pilgrimage site where a waking vision of the Prophet was witnessed by hundreds of Sufis in 1739 [Figure 29.1]. The client, Dr. Sahibzada Mohammad Farakh Hafeez, was an eye surgeon and a shaykh of a Sufi *tariqa*,[4] who traced his ancestry back to the saint who had presided over the historic gathering. The design had called for extensive carving, and the client spared no effort to find two parties of skilled masons. But since the output of both was slow and of poor quality, they were sent packing. And then a miracle happened.

> A hundred stone carvers materialized out of nowhere to take up the work. Twice a week, they appear after dark and work through the night. At the break of dawn, the work stops, they say their morning prayers in congregation, and disperse. Washed and changed, they step into the day as ordinary teachers, lawyers, paramedics, shopkeepers, and go about their daily routines.[5]

None of them had worked with masons' tools before. Without previous training in art or calligraphy, the client himself became an accomplished designer and draftsman.

> He started one day to compose the required texts in an entirely new script, perfectly balanced and proportionate, clearly the result of pure inspiration. Among the new workforce are several teenagers, who were sent to work on the project by their parents to keep them out of trouble. These good-for-nothing dropouts have blossomed into fine, and utterly devoted craftsmen.[6]

Islamic Architecture Today and Tomorrow

Figure 29.1: Pak Wigah Mosque, Kiranwala Sayidan, near Mandi Bahauddin, Gujrat. Here in the interior of the main prayer hall one finds carved marble details of floral patterns and calligraphy designed by the client Dr. Farrukh Hafeez and executed by local community volunteers. Source: Hast-o-Neest Institute of Traditional Studies and Arts, Lahore.

We have experienced the transformative nature of these buildings, in ourselves, in our clients, builders, craftsmen, and ordinary visitors. Whether 'due to the architecture, the performance of religious rites, or the presence and association of these places with holy relics and pious persons, there is no doubt that these spaces make us aware of the presence of the Divine'.[7]

Crucial to these projects has been the unreserved support of the builders, not only in the form of time, manpower, and materials, but equally, with their professional knowledge of material sciences and structural engineering.

The clients for the tombs, two young engineers, Rizwan Qadeer and Shahid Niaz, who run a construction firm, belonged to the inner circle of a remarkable saintly person, Hafiz Mohammad Iqbal,[8] who died in 2001, and his equally remarkable master, Baba Hasan Din,[9] who died in 1968 at the age of 106 [Figures 29.2 and 29.3]. The two engineers approached us to design the tombs some twenty years ago. They fully embraced our design philosophy and approach and responded with enthusiasm to find imaginative solutions to many technical challenges including the revival of *pichi kari* (precious stone inlay), *aina kari* (mirror work), brick flat domes, and the uniquely Lahori *kashi* (glazed tile mosaic).

Figure 29.2: Tomb of Baba Hassan Deen and Hafiz Iqbal, Gujjarpura, near the Tomb of Madhu Lal Hussain and the Shalamar Garden, Lahore. The courtyard, dome, and recessed panels are to receive Lahori *kashi* (glazed tile mosaics). Source: Hast-o-Neest Institute of Traditional Studies and Arts, Lahore.

Figure 29.3: Tomb of Baba Hassan Deen and Hafiz Iqbal. Gujjarpura, near the Tomb of Madhu Lal Hussain and the Shalamar Garden, Lahore. Seen here is the courtyard wall with recessed panels and lime *thoba* (plaster relief) designs. Source: Hast-o-Neest Institute of Traditional Studies and Arts, Lahore.

The intimate relation of the architecture of the Sufi shrine to Islamic spirituality illustrates the profound connection between the traditional arts and crafts and the metaphysical and idealist worldview common to all traditional societies. Two essential components of the traditional design method are proportioning and the use of 'ideal forms'.[10] Every traditional building type has a predetermined essential typology, a prototype, a generic or 'ideal' form, but a single form may be 'manifested' in an infinite variety of scales, proportions, and details of construction and decorations. This diversity is due to the specific materials, topology of the site, user requirements, climate, and other conditions.[11]

Lessons Learned and the Future of Islamic Architecture

The work of the designer begins with copying from a pre-existing model. Traditionally the term 'art' is applied to making or doing anything that meets the dual criteria of utility and beauty. Now beauty is traditionally understood as a quality of the Divine. In the traditional cosmology, all creation is a manifestation of the Divine. In the creative process, the attributes and qualities of the Divine are reflected first as archetypes on the plane of the Spirit or the ideal plane, then as pure forms on the imaginal plane, and finally as natural and man-made objects and acts on the earthly plane. However, some objects and acts are more 'transparent', that is, the ideal forms are more readily recognized in them than in others that are more 'opaque'. Indeed every earthly object, artifice, or act takes on a symbolic meaning to the extent that it reflects its heavenly archetype.[12]

Within this framework the artist or craftsman cannot presume to be 'original' or to 'create' beauty. He can only aspire to reflect it in his work. Every artist or craftsman acquires his art or craft skill from a recognized master, who traces the source of his art through a chain of masters, to a divinely inspired source. But these sources claim only to have been the vehicles or recipients of these gifts from the Divine Spirit. This is why the great classical forms in every traditional art and craft are held in such veneration and esteem. They are used by professionals as exemplars, points of reference, guiding frameworks, or grounds for their own work.

The 'ideal' forms can be read as a language of symbols whose meanings may be implicit, as in architectonic elements or geometric patterns, or explicit as in the case of iconographic sculpture and painting but, in Islamic art and architecture, more often in calligraphy [Figures 29.4 and 29.5]. However, 'copying', and working from prescribed models involves intelligent interpretation, adaptation, and application of critical judgment and discernment at every step of the way. There always comes a point when the craftsman has to exercise his imagination. As our *ustad* Haji Abdul Aziz would say, 'It is a question of *hawa*. This is a subtle quality. It cannot be defined. You have to let your eye and your heart guide you'. Location, the size and shape of the site, adjoining properties, public road access, user profiles, related functional requirements, available materials, local climate, etc., are only some of the factors that call for numerous modifications, adaptations, and design decisions. The clients play the major role in the selection of the texts and their locations. But the whole design process is a close collaboration between architect, client, and craftsmen.

We are convinced that the present global crises – environmental degradation, mass extinction of species, economic disparities, and social disintegration – are largely the result of the pursuit of the modern economic development paradigm that measures progress in terms of material wealth. In its post-modernist phase, driven by consumerism, this juggernaut has crossed many sustainable limits, and now threatens to destroy our very humanity and life as we know it on our planet. In the wasteland ahead are the scattered remains of our civilization. Architecture in the Islamic world can choose to build on the traditions that have defined our humanity and sustained our environment for millennia, or ignore them and join the race to the bottom.

Figure 29.4: Sally Town Mosque, Harbanspura Road, Lahore. Seen here is the prayer hall with *naqqashi* (fresco), *ghalibkari* (ribbed dome form-work in lime plaster), and calligraphy. Source: Hast-o-Neest Institute of Traditional Studies and Arts, Lahore.

Figure 29.5: Sally Town Mosque, Harbanspura Road, Lahore. Seen here is the *mihrab* (prayer niche) with *naqqashi* (fresco), *ghalibkari* (ribbed dome form-work in lime plaster), and calligraphy. Source: Hast-o-Neest Institute of Traditional Studies and Arts, Lahore.

Notes

This chapter was previously published as Kamil Khan Mumtaz, 'Relevance, Tradition, and Practice in Islamic Architecture: A Personal Journey', *International Journal of Islamic Architecture* 10.1 (2021): 257–67.

1. Nader Ardalan and Laleh Bakhtiar, *Sense of Unity: The Sufi Tradition in Persian Architecture* (Chicago: University of Chicago Press, 1973).
2. Laleh Bakhtiar, *Sufi: Expressions of the Mystic Quest* (London: Thames and Hudson, 1976).
3. Kamil Khan Mumtaz, 'Art and the Real, Alam-e-Khayal', Martin Lings Memorial Lecture, Lahore, December 18, 2008.
4. In this case the Naushahi order or Sufi 'way'.
5. Kamil Khan Mumtaz, 'Architecture of Sufi Shrines', in *Sacred Spaces: A Journey with the Sufis of the Indus*, ed. Samina Qureshi (Cambridge, MA: Peabody Museum Press, 2009), 60.
6. Ibid., 60–61.
7. Ibid., 61.

8   Iqbal left a promising academic career – he had three MA degrees and a teaching position at the Government College, Lahore – to spend the rest of his life in relative seclusion.
9   Baba Hasan Din was a Sufi of the Awwal Qadir order. Named Alfred Victor by his British father and French mother, he was a mechanical engineer for British Railways before he left England, under the guidance of the eleventh-century saint Ali Hajveri. He spent 40 years in the forests of Kenya before he settled in Lahore.
10 M. S. Bulatov, *Geometricheskaya garmonizaciya v arhitekture Srednej Azii IX–XV vv.* (Moscow: Nauka, 1978); W. E. Begley and Z. A. Desai, *Taj Mahal: The Illumined Tomb* (Cambridge, MA: Aga Khan Program for Islamic Architecture, Harvard University, and Massachusetts Institute of Technology, 1989); and Archie G. Walls, *Geometry and Architecture in Islamic Jerusalem* (Essex: Scorpion Publishing, 1990).
11 Mumtaz, 'Architecture of Sufi Shrines', 43–44.
12 See Martin Lings, *Collected Poems* (Cambridge: Archetype, 2002), 8, where he maintains that true artistic creativity requires an action of the Spirit. In the Greek tradition this function was called Apollo the god of light and the muses were then further aspects of the same function. In this context it is truer to say that Apollo is not the god of light, but the light of God.

Chapter 30

Architectural Competitions: Creating Dialogues and Promoting Excellence

Hasan-Uddin Khan

Architectural competitions have long been a method of selecting architects for major commissions as a counterpoint to direct commissions. Competitions are significant for the architectural profession because they have 'been used to generate a pool of designs for specific projects, as well as more hypothetical ideas'.[1] Further,

> they are a way to quickly collate different perspectives and concepts that just could not be conceived by a single firm or architect. Add to that the sense of public input and community collaboration that they can create, and it's clear to see why architecture competitions have been used to create some of the world's greatest architectural structures.[2]

Architectural competitions are often used to validate a client's process or to cast a wide net for potential design options. The permutations and types of competitions are multitudinous. There are national and international, urban design and architecture competitions, interior design competitions, those that recognize a person for his or her impact and body of work, those for built work, and those for ideas. Some are open for anyone to enter, and there are many that invite only a small group of participants. The list goes on and on.

Here, my focus is on international architectural competitions that elicit more than just a building in their attempts to extend the conversation about architecture. I have found that both built and unbuilt work produces a world of possibilities, ideas, and solutions, contributing to the legacy of built (realized) projects. In the Islamic world, very little material has been created that reflects on the lessons of proposed and selected solutions, as few organizations produce publications or web sites or maintain critical or self-reflective archives. However, this situation has begun to change with the activities of organizations such as the Aga Khan Award for Architecture (AKAA), the series of competitions by Al Fozan for mosques, and the publications of one-off competitions such as the 2019 one for the new Kuwait Foundation for the Advancement of Science (KFAS) headquarters.

In this chapter I reflect on over four decades of personal experience in architectural competitions, in some cases as the clients' representative and in others as a jury member. The approach is selective and anecdotal, but it raises relevant and compelling questions related to the selection of projects and thoughts about the state of, and roles played by, architecture competitions, especially in the Islamic world.[3]

Types of Competitions

In the modern era, the Royal Institute of British Architects drafted a set of architectural competition rules in 1839, and a set of formal regulations was produced in 1872. The German Regulations were introduced in 1867. In the same period in the Netherlands, an association for the advancement of architecture started organizing conceptual competitions with the aim of stimulating architects' creativity.[4]

Following World War II, Europe, and France in particular, saw architecture competitions as an ideal method for supporting innovation in architecture and reinvigorating previously occupied or damaged territories. Architecture was identified as a matter of public interest and laws were put in place to regulate and encourage more architecture competitions.[5] In the past fifty years or so, design competitions in France, Germany, and some other European countries are compulsory for all public buildings exceeding a certain cost.[6] In France, for example, the Centre Pompidou – a central part of Paris's architectural heritage – is the result of an architecture competition concluded in 1971. Held at the behest of a president anxious for an architectural legacy, it was won by the then-less prominent team of Rogers and Piano, whose intervention revived a shabby quarter of Paris and rehabilitated the city's reputation as a convivial home of the avant-garde.[7] The now-iconic Parc de la Villette was also an outcome of an architecture competition; inspired by the deconstructionist philosopher Jacques Derrida, Bernard Tschumi won the competition in 1983.[8]

There are many different forms of architectural competitions, 'each with its own set of specifications for the desired result and guidelines controlling who will be allowed to participate'. More specifically, two main types are more commonly adopted across the world: project competitions and ideas competitions. The focus of the former is on 'creating designs for a project or building that is planned for construction', whereas the latter dwells on 'creative concepts, out of the box thinking, and the use of architecture as means for creative thinking and discussion'.[9]

While architectural competitions go back centuries, a more recent type recognizes selected built works or an individual designer for his or her design oeuvre. Often this process entails a set of nominations and documentation stating the merits of the projects or people. This kind of recognition started in 1977 with the AKAA in honour of contemporary work for Muslim communities and societies.

Adding to varieties of competition types, one might also consider the methods of the competitive process: open competitions (international, national, or regional), limited or restricted competitions, and selected/invited competitions, including single-stage or two-stage competitions, depending on the scale and complexity of the project and competition structure. It can be argued that anonymous procedures support greater objectivity during the evaluation and award-granting deliberations. On the other hand, cooperative procedures in which the authors are invited to make in-person presentations to the jury in order to explain their design strategies and allow focused discussion can yield results that better answer the clients' needs. Different procedures may be adapted to different situations. However, general rules accepted by most international competitions follow the International Union of Architects (UIA) guidelines.[10]

It is interesting to note that architectural competitions have grown considerably in popularity and importance with the modernization of the field. For example, the competition for the White House in Washington, DC, in 1792 (won by James Hoban) elicited just nine entries (and many fewer practicing architects), whereas in 1989, the Bibliotheca Alexandrina in Alexandria, Egypt received over 1000 entries of which 523 entries from 44 nations were eligible [Figure 30.1].[11] The elaborate competition brief by the client, the Egyptian Ministry of Education, was developed by a diverse team of administrators, politicians, librarians, architects, and engineers. UNESCO, through the United Nations Development Programme (UNDP), provided the funds to run the competition and the prize money – $60,000, $35,000 and $25,000 for the first, second, and third prizes respectively. Competition prize money has increased substantially in recent years. The winning design, judged by an international jury, came from the Norwegian firm Snøhetta and was completed some twelve years later in 2001.[12]

The Players

There are essentially four groups of people in the architectural competition process: the clients (or commissioning bodies), the organizers (usually acting on behalf of the sponsors/clients), project architect(s), and juries. These are supplemented by a number of other people, including the users, technical experts, and budget controllers.

At first glance these roles appear straightforward, but upon reflection they are seen to be more complicated. There are usually multiple stakeholders: the organizers and awarding authorities, researchers, and data analysers, regulators who ensure the fairness of the process, and professional competition organizers who often conduct briefing workshops. The latter are appointed by the sponsoring client who usually does not understand the subtleties of the process. There are exceptions where the sponsor sets up their own organization to do this. Thus, Jean-Pierre Chupin, a professor of architecture in Montreal, in reference to the Canadian experience with such competitions, notes 'that one might postulate that there are several clients – the ones who launch and end the competition, and in a sociological model replacing the sponsor with that of the user. They are not synonymous entities.'[13]

Competition guidelines define roles, responsibilities, processes, and procedures as well as provide guidance on possible competition types, eligibility criteria, jury composition, participation conditions, payments, prizes, publication of results, and other aspects. The rules of each competition are defined by the organizer based on discussions with the client or sponsor of the project. However, a majority of international competitions in Muslim-majority countries are conducted under the auspices of the UIA, because clients look to this organization for validation and guidance. The UIA, as part of UNESCO, provides guidelines for the relevant national or regional architecture organization and is perhaps the most important national player in the competition field.[14] The UIA principles and regulations for competitions were

Islamic Architecture Today and Tomorrow

Figure 30.1: The Bibliotheca Alexandrina, Alexandria, by Snøhetta (2001). The international competition was organized by UNESCO in 1989 and was won by this Norwegian architectural office, which was selected from among 523 entries. It was inaugurated in 2002. Source: Hasan-Uddin Khan.

revised in 2014 and ratified in 2017, some sixty years after they had first been adopted. The reasons for revision were explained in *Resolution 22*:

> This was in response to growing demands for competitions for increasingly complex projects that not only include buildings but also city development, planning and urban regeneration [...] set against the challenges of sustainability and climate change. There is a strong call for more creative solutions that will enhance the quality of life for the communities where the projects are located, as well as for their users.[15]

The statement directly addressed competitions, noting that:

> A competition provides the best solution for a concrete task, selected from among several entries by the jury, with a majority of professionals. The rules on architectural competitions are characterized by the principle of anonymity, transparency, equal treatment, and non-discrimination. They are thus the best weapons against corruption. They protect intellectual property and copyright for the competitors and promote creativity. The rules benefit both the promoter and the competitors. In consequence, it is the best way to achieve high value projects and to commission the architect/ winner. Through architectural competitions, society benefits from solutions with cultural value that contribute to a sustainable future.[16]

Some UIA-controlled competitions have included the Georges Pompidou Centre, Paris; the Indira Gandhi Centre, New Delhi; and perhaps the most publicized of them all, the Sydney Opera House in Australia. There is a growing need for professionals who organize competitions as they increase in number, as does the amount of prize money offered. Statistics indicate that over 2000 such competitions occur annually.[17] Private organizations, such as Bee Breeders out of Singapore and [phase eins] from Berlin, specialize in running international competitions for clients based in different countries.

The second group involved in the architectural competition process is the design team. Teams might consist of architects and other specialists that help formulate designs at their various stages. Landscape architects, site and structural engineers, acoustic engineers, and sociologists all play significant roles depending on the scope and nature of the project. Often the users are brought into the process to help formulate the design, a participatory role that has gained increasing prominence. The team of designers in smaller architectural practices is usually formed for a particular competition and disbands after the competition ends.

Oftentimes, the client might suggest that the entrants demonstrate competence in some aspect of design such as landscape design or energy efficient design, and the ability to keep to a given budget.[18] Larger commission competitions often are held in two stages, the first being a conceptual design based on the client's brief that narrows the field of architects, followed by a second stage for a more detailed proposal based on which a winner or winners are selected.

The winning design and the runners-up are usually chosen by an independent panel of design professionals and stakeholders, such as government and local representatives. This procedure is often used to generate new ideas for building design, stimulate public debate, generate publicity for the project, and to allow emerging designers the opportunity to gain exposure. Furthermore, architectural competitions are often used to award commissions for public buildings: in some countries the rules for tendering public-building contracts stipulate some form of mandatory open architectural competition.

It is worth noting that winning first prize in a competition does not guarantee that the project will actually be constructed as designed, if at all. The commissioning body often has the right to veto the winning design, and both requirements and finances may change, thwarting the original intent. The 2002 New York City World Trade Center site design competition is an example of a highly publicized competition where only the basic elements of the winning design (in this case by Daniel Libeskind) appeared in the finished project. An interesting earlier case is the competition for the mausoleum of Pakistan's founder, Muhammad Ali Jinnah. In 1957, it was decided to hold an international competition under the auspices of the UIA for this important symbolic project. The international jury of 7 members judged 57 entries and selected the entry by the British team of Raglin Squire & Partners with William Whitfiedd and the Pakistani architect M. A. Mirza, who designed a modernist hyperbolic paraboloid tent-like structure and gardens. However, the winning design was rejected by Jinnah's sister, Fatima Jinnah, who campaigned bitterly against the winning proposal. At an impasse, a few years later, President Ayub Khan decided to leave the decision to Fatima Jinnah who selected Yahya C. Merchant, an Indian architect and friend of Jinnah from Mumbai, ending up with a more conventional design based on historical Indian models [Figure 30.2]. The mausoleum was completed in 1970, 23 years after Jinnah's death. The decision-making course is sometimes subverted.

Notes on Three Architectural Competitions

I have been fortunate to have participated in numerous architecture competitions over the years in the roles of organizer and jury member as noted in the sections of each competition. The following competitions, in which I participated, illustrate some of the different types of architecture competitions. The first was a 'competition' that was more about creating a discourse about the built environment than an actual buildable project design. The second was an open competition for a project master plan and buildings. In the third example, the focus was on the design of a complex of buildings and landscapes, leading to the design of two of them.

The most significant global competition is probably the Aga Khan Award for Architecture (AKAA), due to the thoroughness of its program, process, and thinking, all of which is carefully considered and has affected the discourse of architecture worldwide. Strictly speaking, it is not a competition as we understand it because the projects considered for the award can vary greatly, and include buildings, urban plans, landscapes, and other environmental revitalization projects. They do not compete against each other but are selected for their intrinsic values that the jury considers significant and thus award-worthy. The jury also decides how to distribute the pool of prize money, which is almost always done unevenly.

Figure 30.2: The mausoleum or *mazaar* of Pakistan's founder, Qaid-e-Azam by Yahya Merchant. Source: Wikimedia Commons/Ghazala Shah.

Figure 30.3: The very first Steering Committee of the Aga Khan Award for Architecture, which developed the award program in 1977–1980. Seated left to right: Hassan Fathy, The Aga Khan, and Renata Holod. Standing left to right: Hasan-Uddin Khan, William Porter, Doğan Kuban, Hugh Casson, Oleg Grabar, Gar Campbell, Nader Ardalan, and Charles Correa. Source: Aga Khan Award for Architecture/Christopher Little.

Very little meaningful discourse about the contemporary architecture of Islam occurred until 1977 when the AKAA was founded by His Highness the Aga Khan [Figure 30.3]. Rather than privilege any particular style as an 'Islamic Architecture', he sought to explore and identify buildings that capture what one might term the pluralistic 'Spirit of Islam'. The scope of AKAA activities has included not only the awards given every three years but also the conferences, publications, exhibitions, films, documentation projects, as well as educational programs held all over the world that bring together architects, clients, planners, scholars, and educators. As the architectural historian Sibel Bozdoğan wrote in 1992:

By refusing to be exclusive or doctrinaire, the AKAA has effectively installed itself within the architectural culture at large. It is not a small achievement to do this without collapsing back to what Edward Said sees as a postcolonial 'obsession with the West frequently accompanied by a politics of blame'.[19]

The AKAA process is perhaps the most rigorous of any such endeavour. The Steering Committee of the Award articulates the approaches to, and a philosophy of, architecture embodied in the competition, while it is the independent Master Jury that selects winners from a wide range of candidates, nominated from around the globe. An on-site Review Team travels to each shortlisted project and verifies its qualities. The AKAA office in Geneva coordinates this whole process, effectively playing the role of organizer, as there is no 'client' as such.

The initial Steering Committee that oversees the enterprise's expected five project awards for the total prize money of $500,000, now at $1 million. However, for the first awards, the Master Jury unexpectedly selected fifteen projects in recognition of a wide range of concerns. Other juries have varied the number of projects recognized in any one cycle from five to eleven.[20]

One of the unique features of the AKAA is that it recognizes all the people responsible for a winning project, including the designers, the clients, and every group involved in the success of the project. In the 2017–19 cycle, the nine-person jury shortlisted twenty projects, and six winning projects were awarded in September 2019 at the ceremony held in Kazan, Republic of Tatarstan, in the Russian Federation. The 2020–22 cycle has commenced but it is unclear how the process will be affected by the COVID-19 crisis. However, it is expected that an on-site ceremony will eventually be held.

The AKAA is now the most important forum for the dissemination of ideas and building designs in Muslim societies, in addition to contributing to the development of architectural ideas in the international arena.

The second architectural competition is the triannual series of the Abdullatif Al Fozan Award for Mosque Architecture based in Al Khobar, Saudi Arabia. The award, established in 2011, focuses on one building type – categorized into three groups: central mosques, Jumaa mosques, and local mosques – with the aim of not only giving out prize money of 2 million SAR but also creating an archive of mosque architecture and a publication program, holding seminars and promoting research on the mosque. In addition to the building awards, Lifetime Awards (which are similar to the AKAA Chairman's Award) are also conferred to individuals.

The first award cycle (2012–14) covered only mosques in Saudi Arabia, the second (2014–16) expanded to the Gulf States.[21] In April 2016, after a review of 122 mosques, the jury selected three building winners and two Lifetime Awards.[22] A year later, under the patronage of Prince Sultan bin Salman and Prince Khaled Alfaisal, the awards ceremony took a place in Jeddah. The third cycle (2017–19) accepted nominations from all Muslim countries. A shortlist of ten projects was selected, but the award ceremony was delayed due to COVID-19 and held online [Figure 30.4]. However, the fourth cycle (2020–23), is now underway. It is notable just how much this award is based on the AKAA processes, ideas of judgement, and program of meetings and publications.

Figure 30.4: The Sancaklar Mosque, near Istanbul, by Emre Arolat Architecture (2012) – a shortlisted project for the third cycle of the Al Fozan Award. Source: Emre Arolat Architecture.

I have chosen the Kuwait Foundation for the Advancement of Science (KFAS) competition as a third case study here because it was one of the most carefully conducted and thorough exercises in which I have participated. For more than forty years, KFAS has played a catalytic role in advancing and promoting science, technology, and innovation throughout Kuwait. Having outgrown the capacity of its current headquarters in Kuwait, KFAS made plans for a long-term expansion and in 2018 commissioned [phase eins], a Germany-based firm, to organize and manage an international design competition for the construction of new headquarters and convention centre, two buildings with a net utilization area of 11,000 square metres each, including a master plan on the waterfront site of sixty hectares.[23]

The very detailed document of 62 pages covered all aspects of the competition, the brief for which

> called for the designers to utilize their expertise in urban planning and architecture to ensure that innovation and creativity will play a vital role in the designs submitted for the buildings and surrounding area, embodying the characteristics of the Foundation's mission and vision, along with showcasing a highly attractive and efficient work environment.[24]

The competition was organized as a restricted, international, two-stage project competition in agreement with the UIA. However, within the framework of the regulations, in both stages an on-site colloquium with the participants and an online forum was included. Out of 106 applicants, some 60 participants were selected by [phase eins] for this task. The competition itself was a year-long process. Submissions were reviewed by an international professional jury, also selected by [phase eins] in consultation with the client.[25]

During stage one of the competition the jury chose ten proposals from among the proposals. The jury offered recommendations for further design development to those ten during stage two, from August to November 2018. A total of $530,000 was allocated for prizes and honoraria. As compensation for the expenses incurred by the entrants, $400,000 was divided in equal parts among the ten competitors who advanced to the second stage. In addition, $130,000 was awarded as prizes in stage two, with the following distribution: first prize $50,000, second prize $35,000, third prize $25,000, and fourth prize $20,000. Competitors from the first round were reimbursed for the accommodation expenses incurred for two people attending the stage one colloquium. Furthermore, competitors of stage two were additionally reimbursed for the travel and accommodation expenses incurred from attending the stage two colloquium. Organizers' fees and expenses and those of all the jury members further added to the competition budget. The process was indeed an expensive one.

At each stage of the competition, based on the jury reports, the organizers gave detailed feedback to each of the competitors. The ten shortlisted project winners were able to visit the site, ask questions of the organizers, and discuss their projects with them. At no stage did the jury get to meet or know the identity of the entrants. The jury only learned of the actual names of the winner and the three commended projects after first informing the client, then the winners, just before the results were made public. In March 2019, the design by the Swiss-German firm, Topotek 1, was awarded the first-place prize [Figure 30.5]. A year later, the organizers, along with the client, produced an award book of over 350 pages that included all 106 entrants.[26]

Why Enter Competitions?

Some of the points made below, which I endorse, have been taken in part from the website of Bee Breeders, a private firm that organizes international architectural competitions. They are included here as a reminder about the necessity of entering competitions, even if there is little chance of winning.[27] Most architectural offices will enter competitions as a way of exercising their creativity, to get beyond what they can normally do in the actual practice that comprises a firm's everyday work. This creative freedom is important for all architects regardless of what stage of career development they are in.

Competitions provide the opportunity to experiment with new tools and new concepts in design, and to build a firm's portfolio. As juries often give feedback on the submitted project, especially if one makes it to the shortlist or is asked to participate in a limited/invited competition, they can be productive learning experiences.

When taking part in an architecture competition, the more creative and 'out of the box' thinking, the better. This applies whether a final project is planned for construction – as is the case in project competitions – or whether the project is used as a means of starting a discussion or raising awareness – as in ideas competitions.

Figure 30.5: A rendering of the 2019 winning entry design for the KFAS Headquarters and Conference Center in Kuwait by the Swiss-German firm Topotek 1. Source: [phase eins].

In open competitions, as all submissions are assessed anonymously, the jury and the client will be looking for creativity and originality above all else. Once the winning designs are selected, collaboration between the designers, clients, and other industry professionals can begin to further develop the design. On occasion, competitions can be a platform for turning designs into projects planned for construction.[28]

Whether designs are ever actualized as real-life structures or not, architecture competitions are a way to earn recognition. Large-scale international media and publications such as CNN, Sky News, *ArchDaily*, and *Dezeen* have all published winning designs, and sometimes the competition clients themselves will publish shortlisted projects as a record.

Although the frequency of holding both national and international competitions in Muslim societies is on the rise, they are often badly run and are not always fairly judged. Results can be tampered with, leading to acrimony and loss of confidence in the process. This seems to occur in both rich and poor countries, but often happens with the approval of those in power, which is why architectural groups often ask for UIA involvement and oversight to ensure fairness and transparency. Despite setbacks, more societies of the Islamic world have come to accept that architectural competitions are a better way of proceeding to realize projects.

Postscript

The eminent Australian architect and academic Michael Keniger, of Bond University's Abedian School of Architecture, noted that 'as architecture competitions almost seem to have become the default process for selecting architects and designs for every project, their proliferation risks devaluing the real merits of a fair and well-ordered competitions process.'[29] Keniger added:

> And yet today, our enthusiasm wanes. Competitions are no longer reserved for high-profile projects and have rather become the default process for selecting architects and designs for virtually any form and scale of project, public or private. Various competition formats are now almost-ubiquitous elements of common procurement processes, their value in driving forward new ideas diminished as clients and public bodies mix and match their preferred options across designs, design teams and contract types. The resulting loss of coherence dilutes the value of the competition process and diminishes the quality of the compelling architectural ambitions. As architectural services are divided and truncated by the increasing use of novation there is a risk that commitment to high-quality design outcomes will continue to be eroded, leading to even less time for design development or for the oversight of project delivery. Practical experience for many students and graduate architects is increasingly dominated by the preparation and rendering of documents for competition presentations. Broader involvement with projects is curtailed and site-based engagement during construction is often minimized, furthering a waning of skill within the profession.[30]

However, it is not all negative. Perhaps the best way to sum up this brief reflection on architectural competitions is to recall the words of the critic Talbot F. Hamlin, who in 1938 wrote that

> competitions lead inevitably to experimentation in Design, and the effect of the experimentation will be seen not only in the building finally erected but even more in the education they give to juries, to architects, to clients and to the public.[31]

Archives of design submissions for these competitions can become databases that researchers can use to build new theoretical knowledge that contributes to the architectural discipline as a whole. As Keniger has also suggested, 'Focused research into the consequences of the broadened use of subsidiary design competition selection and appointment processes would seem to be timely.'[32]

Notes

This chapter was previously published as Hasan-Uddin Khan, 'Architectural Competitions: Creating Dialogues and Promoting Excellence?', *International Journal of Islamic Architecture* 9.1 (2020): 5–18. Updates, where appropriate, have been made to the present version.

1. 'A Brief History of Architecture Competitions', Bee Breeders: Architecture Competition Organizers, accessed November 5, 2019, https://beebreeders.com/a-brief-history-of-architecture-competitions. There are, of course, competitions for most things, from product design to

fashion, to from literature to art, to name just a few. Recent scholarship has addressed the role played by architectural competitions in the development of global modernism. See, for example, Jorge Mejía Hernández and Cathelijne Nuijsink, eds, 'The Architecture Competition as Contact Zone: Towards a Historiography of Cross-Cultural Exchanges', special issue, *Footprint* 14.1 (2020); Tom Avermaete and Cathelijne Nuijsink, 'An Architecture Culture of "Contact Zones": Prospects for an Alternative Historiography of Modernism', in *Rethinking Global Modernism: Architectural Historiography and the Postcolonial*, ed. Vikramaditya Prakash, Maristella Casciato, and Daniel E. Coslett (New York: Routledge, 2022), 103–19.
2. 'A Brief History of Architecture Competitions'.
3. 'Historically, architectural competitions were less common in Asia, with only a few significant structures known to be products of competitions. It is possible that a number of stone building models dating to the eighth century found in Mahabalipuram, India, originated from architecture competitions.' See 'A Brief History of Architecture Competitions'. In many cases the names of the builders or architects are hard to discern. There are of course exceptions, such as the sixteenth-century architect and engineer Mimar Sinan, renowned for his work across the Ottoman Empire. Unfortunately, there is little record of competitions in South and Southeast Asia before the nineteenth century, and the monuments there are often attributed to the commissioning patron, often the sultan.
4. Cees De Jong and Erik Mattie, *Architectural Competitions 1792–1949* (Cologne: Taschen, 1997).
5. Jacques Cabanieu, 'Competitions and Architectural Excellence', *Places Journal* 9.2 (1994): 40–41.
6. 'Architectural Design Competition', Wikipedia, last modified October 2, 2019, https://en.wikipedia.org/wiki/Architectural_design_competition.
7. As a student at the Architectural Association, I was first exposed to architectural competitions by Renzo Piano and Richard Rogers who were my studio teachers and were working on their own entry for the Pompidou competition. They set it as our studio project.
8. 'A Brief History of Architecture Competitions'.
9. Bee Breeders homepage, accessed November 5, 2019, https://beebreeders.com/.
10. See International Union of Architects, International Competitions Commission, 'Guidelines: UIA Competition Guide for Design Competitions in Architecture and Related Fields', Adopted by the 130th Council in Seoul, March 2017, amendments adopted by the 131st Council in Kuala Lumpur, July 2017, https://www.uiaarchitectes.org/webApi/uploads/ressourcefile/32/uiacompetitionguide.pdf.
11. Ismail Serageldin, *A Landmark Building: Reflections on the Architecture of the Bibliothecha Alexandrina* (Alexandria: Bibliotheca Alexandrina, 2006). Also, for a detailed account of the competition, see Mohsen Zahran, *The New Bibliotheca Alexandrina: Reflections on a Journey of Achievements* (Alexandria: Bibliotheca Alexandrina, 2007).
12. The international jury, chaired by John Carl Warneke from the United States, consisted of seven professional architects including Charles Correa from India, Fumihiko Maki of Japan, and Francoise Lombard from France as the UIA representative. There were also three librarians, several project advisors from Egypt, and a slew of other helpers.
13. Jean-Pierre Chupin, 'What is a "Client" in a Theoretical Model of the Competition Phenomena?', in *Architectural Competitions and the Production of Culture, Quality and Knowledge*, ed. Jean Paul Chaupin et al. (Montreal: Potential Architecture, 2015), 182.

14 The UIA was founded in Lausanne, Switzerland, in June 1948. From the 27 delegations present at the founding assembly, the UIA has grown to encompass the key professional organizations of architects in 124 countries and territories, and now represents more than 1,300,000 architects worldwide. See International Union of Architects homepage, accessed June 8, 2021, https://www.uia-architectes.org/webApi/en/.
15 Competition guidelines define roles, responsibilities, processes, and procedures, and they provide guidance on possible competition types, eligibility criteria, jury composition, participation conditions, payments, prizes, publication of results, and other aspects. See *UIA Competition Guide for Design Competitions for Architecture and Related Fields* (Paris: UIA-UNESCO, 2017), 3, https://www.uia-architectes.org/webApi/uploads/ressourcefile/32/uiacompetitionguide.pdf.
16 Ibid.
17 The figures vary greatly and are based on those by UNESCO and national architectural bodies (such as the AIA, RIBA, etc.). I use these numbers only as indicators, as they may not be fully accurate or up to date in 2021. See also De Jong and Mattie, *Architectural Competitions*.
18 This last item is often changed as the client and architectural jury discuss the design in relation to the prepared brief.
19 Sibel Bozdogan, 'The Aga Khan Award for Architecture: A Philosophy of Reconciliation', *Journal of Architectural Education* 45.3 (1992): 182–88.
20 The AKAA is well documented in its own publications and website. See Archnet homepage, accessed June 8, 2021, www.archnet.org.
21 I was a member of the jury for the first two cycles.
22 See Mashary Al Naim and Waleed Al Sayyed, *Minarets of the Arabian Gulf* (London: Lonard, 2017).
23 Founded in 1998, [phase eins] is a competition organizing and management firm with twenty years of experience as competition manager with more than 200 competitions in four continents, and headed by two architects, Benjamin Hossbach and Christian Lehmhaus. Staffed by a team of architects and other professionals, the company specializes in 'phase one' of architecture and urban planning projects. Their services cover management consultancy for preparing project fundamentals, fine-tuning project design, and selecting optimal partners for subsequent stages of planning. See [phase eins] homepage, accessed May 17, 2021, https://www.phase1.de/.
24 See *Competition Brief and Regulation* (Kuwait: KFAS with [phase eins], 2018), 62.
25 The final five international jury members were Markus Allmann (architect, Germany), Nezar AlSayyad (professor, United States), jury chair Hasan-Uddin Khan (professor and architect, United States), Mark Mack (professor and architect, United States), and Luca Molinari (professor and architect, Italy). There were also general jurors in addition to H. E. Abdlatif Yousef Al-Hamad (chairman of the Board of Directors and Director General of the Arab Fund for Economic and Social Development, Kuwait City), Ahmed Almanfouhi (Director General of Kuwait Municipality, Salmiya, Kuwait, Member HSCDC), and Sabah Abi Hanna (architect, Beirut).

26 *International Competition for the KFAS Headquarters and Conference Center in Kuwait: The Process, Entries and Winners* (Kuwait: KFAS with [phase eins], 2019), 346.
27 'Why You Should Enter Architecture Competitions!', Bee Breeders, Architecture Competition Organizers, accessed November 5, 2019, https://beebreeders.com/why-competitions.
28 Some years ago, a student of mine produced a somewhat outrageous and bold design for his thesis project. Upon applying for a job, he was fortunate to find that the firm was looking for a new idea on which to base a project in China and used his project to build it. This is, of course an unusual circumstance, but even if he did not get to build his design, he attracted the attention of the firm by standing out amongst the applicants.
29 Michael Keniger, 'Regaining a Competitive Edge', ARCHITECTUREAU, July 24, 2019, accessed November 5, 2019, https://architectureau.com/articles/regaining-a-competitive-edge/.
30 Ibid.
31 Talbot Hamlin, 'Competitions', *Pencil Points* (1938): 565, quoted in Hélène Lipstadt, 'In the Shadow of the Tribune Tower', in *The Experimental Tradition: Essays on Competitions in Architecture*, ed. Hélène Lipstadt (New York: Princeton Architectural Press, 1989), 79.
32 Ibid.

Contributor Biographies

Samer Akkach, FAHA, is a professor of architectural history and theory and founding director of the Centre for Asian and Middle Eastern Architecture (CAMEA) at the University of Adelaide. His expertise is in Islamic art and architecture, mysticism, and intellectual history. His interdisciplinary research interests extend to the socio-urban and cultural history of the Levant and the history of Islamic science in the early modern period. His publications include *Cosmology and Architecture* (SUNY, 2005), *Islam and the Enlightenment* (Oneworld, 2007), *Letters of a Sufi Scholar* (Brill, 2010), *Intimate Invocations* (Brill, 2012), *Damascene Diaries* (Bissan, 2015), *Istanbul Observatory* (ACRPS, 2017), *'Ilm: Science, Religion, and Art in Islam* (ed.) (AUP, 2019), and *Naẓar: Vision, Belief, and Perception in Islamic Cultures* (Brill, 2022).

Rasem Badran is an architect based in Jordan. His approach emphasizes dialogue between contemporary needs and inherited cultural values. Badran founded his design firm, Dar Al-Omran, in 1981. In 1995 he received the Aga Khan Award for Architecture for his work on the Grand Mosque and Justice Palace of Riyadh and the Redevelopment of Riyadh's Old City Centre. Badran has received the Abdullatif Al Fozan Award for Lifetime Achievement in Mosque Architecture (2016), the Nile Award for 'The Most Creative Arab Personality' (2019), and the Tamayouz Lifetime Achievement Award (2019) for his outstanding contributions to the built environments of the Near East and North Africa.

Bülent Batuman is an associate professor of architecture at Bilkent University in Ankara. He studied at the Middle East Technical University and received his Ph.D. in history and theory of art and architecture from Binghamton University–the State University of New York. His recent work focuses on the relationship between Islamism and the built environment. He is the author of *New Islamist Architecture and Urbanism: Negotiating Nation and Islam through Built Environment in Turkey* (Routledge, 2018) and editor of *Cities and Islamisms: On the Politics and Production of the Built Environment* (Routledge, 2021).

Sheila S. Blair retired in 2018 as the Norma Jean Calderwood University Professor of Islamic and Asian Art at Boston College and in 2019 as the Hamad bin Khalifa Endowed Chair of Islamic Art at Virginia Commonwealth University, positions she shared with her husband and co-author, Jonathan Bloom. The author of books on subjects ranging from a shrine in

Iran to Islamic inscriptions and calligraphy, she continues to work on the arts of the Mongol period across Eurasia.

Patricia Blessing is an assistant professor in the Department of Art & Archaeology at Princeton University. Her first book, *Rebuilding Anatolia after the Mongol Conquest: Islamic Architecture in the Lands of Rūm, 1240–1330* (Ashgate, 2014) investigates the relationship between patronage, politics, and architectural style after the integration of the region into the Mongol Empire. Her work has been supported by the Samuel H. Kress Foundation, the International Center of Medieval Art, the Society of Architectural Historians, the Barakat Trust, and the Gerda Henkel Foundation.

Jonathan M. Bloom retired in 2018 as the Norma Jean Calderwood University Professor of Islamic and Asian Art at Boston College and in 2019 as the Hamad bin Khalifa Endowed Chair of Islamic Art at Virginia Commonwealth University, positions he shared with his wife and co-author, Sheila Blair. The author of books on subjects ranging from the minaret to the history of paper in the Islamic lands, he has most recently published *Architecture of the Islamic West: North Africa and the Iberian Peninsula* (Yale University Press, 2020).

Jelena Bogdanović is an associate professor at Vanderbilt University and specializes in cross-cultural and religious themes in architecture of the Balkans and Mediterranean. She is author of *The Framing of Sacred Space: The Canopy and the Byzantine Church* (Oxford University Press, 2017), editor of *Icons of Space: Advances in Hierotopy* (Routledge, 2021) and *Perceptions of the Body and Sacred Space in Late Antiquity and Byzantium* (Routledge, 2018), co-editor with Jessica Joyce Christie and Eulogio Guzmán of *Political Landscapes of Capital Cities* (University Press of Colorado, 2016) and with Lilien Filipovitch Robinson and Igor Marjanović of *On the Very Edge: Modernism and Modernity in the Arts and Architecture of Interwar Serbia (1918–1941)* (Leuven University Press, 2014).

Sheila R. Canby, Curator Emerita at the Metropolitan Museum of Art, was Curator in Charge of the Department of Islamic Art at that institution from 2009 to 2019. From 1991 to 2009 she curated Islamic collections at the British Museum. She also worked for the Museum of Fine Arts, Boston, Philadelphia Museum of Art, Los Angeles County Museum of Art and Brooklyn Museum. Her publications include *The Seljuqs and Their Successors* (Edinburgh University Press, 2020), *The Shahnama of Shah Tahmasp* (Yale University Press, 2011 and 2014), *Shah ʿAbbas: The Remaking of Iran* (British Museum Press, 2009), *Hunt for Paradise: Court Arts of Safavid Iran, 1501–76* (Skira, 2003), *The Golden Age of Persian Art, 1501–1722* (Abrams, 1999), and *Persian Painting* (Thames and Hudson, 1993).

Jorge Correia holds a design degree and a Ph.D. in architecture from the School of Architecture at the University of Porto, Portugal. Correia is an associate professor in architectural and urban history at the School of Architecture, Art and Design, University of Minho. He is also director of the Landscape, Heritage and Territory Lab (Lab2PT) and president of the European Architectural History Network (EAHN). His main research interests are devoted to the study of architectural and urban aspects of the European colonial sphere from the fifteenth through nineteenth centuries and the cultural challenges of heritage, as well as traditional Islamic cities and their representation.

Daniel E. Coslett is a scholar of colonial and postcolonial architecture and urbanism whose work focuses on intersections of architecture, preservation, archaeology, and tourism. He received a Ph.D. in the history and theory of built environments from the University of Washington, and an MA in the subject from Cornell University. Coslett teaches art and architectural history at Western Washington University and the University of Washington. His edited volume entitled *Neocolonialism and Built Heritage: Echoes of Empire in Africa, Asia, and Europe* (Routledge) was published in 2020 and his co-edited volume *Rethinking Global Modernism: Architectural Historiography and the Postcolonial* (Routledge, with Vikramaditya Prakash and with Maristella Casciato) was published in 2022. He is an associate editor at the *International Journal of Islamic Architecture*.

Rami F. Daher is an associate professor of architecture at the German Jordanian University in Jordan and principal architect at TURATH: Architecture and Urban Design Consultants (1999–present). He co-edited, with Irene Maffi, *The Politics and Practices of Cultural Heritage in the Middle East: Positioning the Material Culture in Contemporary Societies* (I. B. Tauris, 2014) and, with Myriam Ababsa, *Cities, Urban Practices, and Nation Buildings in Jordan* (IFPO, 2011). He also edited *Tourism in the Middle East: Continuity, Change and Transformation* (Channel View Publications, 2007). Daher's ongoing work investigates the politics and dynamics of public place-making; levels of place understanding and their effects on interventions within historic settings; neoliberal urban transformations; and cultural heritage definition, conservation, adaptive reuse, and management.

Mohammad Gharipour is a professor of architecture and chair of the Department of Graduate Built Environment Studies at Morgan State University in Baltimore, Maryland. He obtained his master's degree in architecture from the University of Tehran and his Ph.D. in architecture from the Georgia Institute of Technology. He has published twelve books, including *Persian Gardens and Pavilions: Reflections in Poetry, Arts and History* (I. B. Tauris, 2013), *Synagogues of the Islamic World* (Edinburgh University Press, 2017), *Gardens of Renaissance Europe and the Islamic Empires* (Pennsylvania State University Press, 2017), *Architectural Dynamics in Pre-Revolutionary Iran* (Intellect, 2019), and *Architecture and Health: The History of Spaces of Healing and Care in the Pre-Modern Era* (Bloomsbury, 2021). Gharipour is the director and founding editor of the *International Journal of Islamic Architecture* and the Second Vice President of the Society of Architectural Historians.

Waleed Hazbun is the Richard L. Chambers Professor of Middle Eastern Studies in the Department of Political Science at the University of Alabama. He previously taught at the American University of Beirut. He is the author of *Beaches, Ruins, Resorts: The Politics of Tourism in the Arab World* (University of Minnesota Press, 2008) and serves on the editorial committee of the *Journal of Tourism History*. His ongoing research explores the global politics of airports, aviation, and air travel in the Middle East.

Elif Kalaycıoğlu is an assistant professor in the Department of Political Science at the University of Alabama. She has published articles and book chapters on global cultural politics, with a focus on UNESCO's world heritage regime. Her ongoing research explores how questions of cultural diversity and cultural recognition impact global politics and how existing institutions attempt to govern this diversity.

Hasan-Uddin Khan is an architect and writer who was editor-in-chief of the international journal *Mimar: Architecture in Development* and from 2012 to 2020 served as Academic Editor of the *International Journal of Islamic Architecture*. Khan helped set up the Aga Khan Award for Architecture in 1977 and coordinated His Highness the Aga Khan's worldwide architectural activities between 1984 and 1994. He has been a Visiting Professor at MIT and Berkeley and joined Roger Williams University in 1999 as Distinguished Professor of Architecture and Historic Preservation. He is now Distinguished Professor Emeritus. He lectures widely and is the editor/author of nine books and over sixty published articles.

Kıvanç Kılınç is an associate professor of architecture at Kadir Has University (KHAS) in Istanbul. He received his Ph.D. in the history and theory of art and architecture (2010) from Binghamton University–the State University of New York and a master's degree (2002) from the Middle East Technical University. His current research focuses on transnational connections and their consequences, which shaped contemporary social housing practices in the Middle East. He is the co-editor of *Social Housing in the Middle East: Architecture, Urban Development, and Transnational Modernity* (Indiana University Press, 2019) and currently serves as an editor of the *International Journal of Islamic Architecture*.

Lorenz Korn is professor of Islamic art and archaeology at the University of Bamberg. His research focuses on architecture, architectural decoration, and urbanism in the central Islamic lands between the tenth and sixteenth centuries. He has done numerous field surveys and completed archaeological work in Iran and Uzbekistan. His publications include *Ayyubidische Architektur in Ägypten und Syrien* (Heidelberger Orientverlag, 2004) and *Islamic Art in Oman* (with A. al-Salimi and Heinz Gaube, Mazoon, 2008) as well as recent articles on the German Fountain in Istanbul, relics of the Prophet Muhammad, and various aspects of the architecture of Iran and Central Asia.

Abidin Kusno is a professor in the Faculty of Environmental and Urban Change at York University, Toronto where he also serves as director of York Centre for Asian Research. Kusno has published *Behind the Postcolonial: Architecture, Urban Space and Political Cultures in Indonesia* (Routledge, 2000), *Appearances of Memory: Mnemonic Practices of Architecture and Urbanism in Indonesia* (Duke University Press, 2010), and most recently, *After the New Order: Space, Politics and Jakarta* (University of Hawai'i Press, 2013).

Hossam Mahdy, Ph.D., is an Egyptian and British conservation architect. He is an international consultant and researcher on the conservation of the built heritage. His professional experience is in the conservation of Islamic built heritage, earthen vernacular buildings, and World Heritage nominations. His academic work focuses on Islamic views on conservation of cultural heritage, Arabic terminology of conservation for the built heritage, and culture-specific philosophy and theory for the conservation of cultural heritage in the Arab region. Mahdy is the President of ICOMOS Committee on Vernacular Architecture (CIAV).

Brian L. McLaren, Ph.D., is an associate professor in the Department of Architecture at the University of Washington. His scholarship has concentrated on the tension between architecture and politics in Italy during the Fascist ventennio, with recent attention to the intersection of modern architecture, empire, and racial politics. He is currently working on a book-length research project that examines the conflicted nature of mobility in Italian Africa, which greatly expands upon his earlier research on architecture and tourism in Libya.

Leslee Katrina Michelsen is the Curator of Collections and Exhibitions at the Shangri La Museum of Islamic Art, Culture & Design in Honolulu, Hawai'i. Previously, Michelsen was the Head Curator of the Museum of Islamic Art (Qatar) from 2011 to 2015, and Consulting Curator for UNESCO Afghanistan from 2015 to 2016. She earned a Ph.D. in Islamic art history from the University of Pennsylvania (2011) and writes on topics ranging from medieval architecture to multi-sensory learning. Upcoming projects include co-curated exhibitions with contemporary artists Slavs & Tatars, Diana Al-Hadid, Lazo Studios, Kamran Samimi, and Maimouna Guerresi, as well as a pan-Pacific exhibition on scent.

Nancy Micklewright (Ph.D., University of Pennsylvania) was until the summer of 2021 an Andrew W. Mellon Fellow in the Department of Islamic Art at the Metropolitan Museum of Art, New York. She was head of public and scholarly engagement at the Smithsonian's Freer and Sackler Galleries until 2019. From 2010 to 2019 Micklewright was editor-in-chief of the scholarly journal *Ars Orientalis*. Previously she had been senior program officer at the Getty Foundation, after having taught the history of Islamic art and architecture and the history of photography at the University of Victoria, British Columbia, and the University of Michigan. She is currently working on a book entitled *Dressing for the Camera: Fashion and Photography in the Late Ottoman Empire*, an examination of visual culture and identity formation in the late

Ottoman period. Her edited volume *Mohamed Zakariya, the Life and Times of a 21st-Century Calligrapher* (Fons Vitae) will appear in 2022.

Kamil Khan Mumtaz studied at Architectural Association School of Architecture (1957–63). In London he worked with Quine and Newberry (1960–61) and Architects' Co-Partnership (1963–64). He taught at KNUST, Kumasi, in Ghana (1963–66) and was Head of the Department of Architecture at National College of Arts, Lahore, from 1966 to 1977. Mumtaz was a member of the Aga Khan Award for Architecture steering committee (1981–84). He established the partnership, BKM, in 1975, and has been in independent practice since 1984. He is the author of *Architecture in Pakistan* (Concept Media, 1985) and *Modernity and Tradition* (Oxford University Press, 1999). The Government of Pakistan awarded him Tamgha-i-Imtiaz in 1993 and Sitara-e-Imtiaz in 2019.

Alona Nitzan-Shiftan is an architect, architectural historian, and theorist. She is an associate professor at the Technion, where she heads the Arenson Built Heritage Research Center. She received her Ph.D. from MIT, and her work on the politics of architecture and heritage, on architectural modernism in Israel and the United States, and on critical historiography was sponsored by CASVA, Getty/UCLA, and the Universities of Michigan (Frankel Institute) and Chicago. Her award-winning book *Seizing Jerusalem: The Architectures of Unilateral Unification* was published in 2017 by the University of Minnesota Press. She is currently preparing the Israeli volume of Reaktion Books' Modern Architectures in History series.

Bernard O'Kane is a professor of Islamic art and architecture at the American University in Cairo, where he has been teaching since 1980. He has also been a visiting professor at Harvard University and the University of California at Berkeley. He is the author of seven books, the most recent being *Mosques: The 100 Most Iconic Islamic Houses of Worship* (Assouline, 2019).

Vikramaditya Prakash is a professor of architecture at the University of Washington in Seattle. He works on modernism, postcoloniality, global history, and fashion and architecture. His books include *Chandigarh's Le Corbusier: The Struggle for Modernity in Postcolonial India* (University of Washington Press, 2002), *A Global History of Architecture* (Wiley, 2007, 2011, 2017, with Francis D. K. Ching and Mark Jarzombek), *Colonial Modernities: Building, Dwelling and Architecture in British India and Ceylon* (Routledge, 2007, edited with Peter Scriver), *The Architecture of Shivdatt Sharma* (Mapin, 2012), *Chandigarh: An Architectural Guide* (Altrim Publishers, 2015), and *One Continuous Line: Art, Architecture and Urbanism of Aditya Prakash* (Mapin, 2021). His co-edited volume *Rethinking Global Modernism: Architectural Historiography and the Postcolonial* (Routledge, with Maristella Casciato and Daniel E. Coslett) was published in 2022.

Nasser Rabbat is the Aga Khan Professor and Director of the Aga Khan Program for Islamic Architecture at the Massachusetts Institute of Technology. He is the author of many books and articles, most recently *The Architecture of the Dead Cities: Toward a New Interpretation of the History of Syria* (Hamad bin Khalifa University Press, 2018); *Criticism as Commitment: Viewpoints on History, Arabism, and Revolution* (Riad Alrayyes Publisher, 2015) both in Arabic; and as co-editor with Pamela Karimi, *The Destruction of Cultural Heritage: From Napoléon to ISIS* (Aggregate Architectural History Collaborative, 2016). His book on the Mamluk historian al-Maqrizi will be published in 2022. He is currently working on a book on the cultural history of Syria and another on Mamluk Cairo.

D. Fairchild Ruggles is professor and the Debra L. Mitchell Chair in landscape architecture at the University of Illinois, Urbana-Champaign. She is the art and architecture field editor for the *Encyclopaedia of Islam*, and is the author of two award-winning books on Islamic landscape history – *Gardens, Landscape, and Vision in the Palaces of Islamic Spain* (Penn State University Press, 2000) and *Islamic Gardens and Landscapes* (University of Pennsylvania Press, 2008) – as well as eleven other authored, edited, and co-edited volumes on Islamic art, cultural heritage, landscape history and theory, and the arts patronage of women in the Islamic world and South Asia.

Ashraf M. Salama is a professor of architecture and Director of Research at the University of Strathclyde's Department of Architecture. Having authored and co-edited fourteen books and published over 170 articles and chapters in the international refereed press, Salama is the recipient of the 2017 UIA Jean Tschumi Prize for Excellence in Architectural Education and Criticism. His books include *Demystifying Doha* (Ashgate, 2013); *Architecture Beyond Criticism* (Routledge, 2014); *Spatial Design Education* (Routledge, 2015); *Building Migrant Cities in the Gulf* (Bloomsbury, 2018); *Architectural Excellence in Islamic Societies* (Routledge, 2020); and *Transformative Pedagogy in Architecture and Urbanism* (Routledge, 2009/2021). He is currently completing the *Routledge Companion to Architectural Pedagogies of the Global South*. He established, and is currently leading, the Cluster for Research in Architecture and Urbanism of Cities in the Global South (CRAUCGS).

Sharon C. Smith earned her Ph.D. from the Department of History and Theory of Art and Architecture at Binghamton University. Currently, Smith serves as Curator, Middle East and Africa, and Associate Academic at Arizona State University. Smith served as the founding Program Head for the Aga Khan Documentation Center at MIT and as Co-Director and PI of Archnet, a globally accessible, intellectual resource focused on architecture, urbanism, environmental and landscape design, visual culture, and conservation issues within the Muslim world. Smith has lectured widely on issues of documentation, digitization, and the dissemination of knowledge, as well as on visual and material culture in the Early Modern Mediterranean.

Imran bin Tajudeen is a senior lecturer at the National University of Singapore. He researches architectural encounters in maritime Southeast Asia across the longue durée, studying its historical mosque forms in transregional interactions and translations across the vernacular and Indic architecture. He also examines the vernacular city and its contemporary representational and heritage tropes. He has published work in the *Journal of the Society for Asian Humanities, ABE Journal, Traditional Dwellings and Settlements Review, Journal18*, and *A Companion to Islamic Art and Architecture* (Wiley-Blackwell, 2017). He is co-editor of *Southeast Asia's Modern Architecture* (NUS Press, 2019). He was postdoctoral fellow at MIT's Aga Khan Program (2009–10) and the IIAS in Leiden (2010–11). He is now working on a monograph on Southeast Asia's Islamic architecture.

Nancy Um is a professor of art history and associate dean at Binghamton University. Her research explores the Islamic world from the perspective of the coast, with a focus on material, visual, and built culture on the Arabian Peninsula and around the rims of the Red Sea and the Indian Ocean. She is the author of *The Merchant Houses of Mocha: Trade and Architecture in an Indian Ocean Port* (University of Washington Press, 2009) and *Shipped But Not Sold: Material Culture and the Social Protocols of Trade during Yemen's Age of Coffee* (University of Hawai'i Press, 2017).

Dell Upton is distinguished research professor in the Department of Art History at the University of California, Los Angeles. He previously taught at the University of California, Berkeley, and the University of Virginia. His most recent publications are *American Architecture: A Thematic History* (Oxford University Press, 2019) and *What Can and Can't Be Said: Race, Uplift, and Monument Building in the Contemporary South* (Yale University Press, 2015).

Caroline 'Olivia' M. Wolf is an assistant professor of art history at Loyola University Chicago. Her teaching and research take a global perspective, with areas of specialization in Latin American as well as Islamic art and architecture, and an emphasis on the diasporic and transregional visual intersections of these traditions across the Global South. Her work has been supported by a Fulbright-Hays DDRA fellowship and the Society of Architectural Historians.

Şebnem Yücel researches the representation of places, buildings, and histories and concentrates on the process of modernization in non-western contexts. She received her BArch (1993) from Middle East Technical University, Turkey, her MScArch (1998) from the University of Cincinnati, and a Ph.D. (2003) from Arizona State University. Some of her publications include 'Minority Heterotopias: The Cortijos of Izmir', in *ARQ: Architectural Research Quarterly* (2016); 'Regional/Modern and the Rest', in *Architecture, Culture, Interpretation* (Paideia, 2015); and 'Identity Calling: Turkish Architecture and the West', in *Architecture, Ethics and the Personhood of Place* (University Press of New England, 2007). She is currently teaching at MEF University in Istanbul.

Index

Note: Page numbers in italics refer to figures.

A

Abbas Abad project (Tehran), 348, 350, *351*
Abdali real estate development (Amman), 314–15, *315*, 318, 319, 322n6
Abdullatif Al Focan Award for Mosque Architecture, 445, *446*
Abedian School of Architecture (Bond University), 448
Abhaya, *263*
Abrahamic Family House, 328
Abraj al-Bait (Mecca), 34, *35*
Abu Dhabi
    Saadiyat Island, 328
    Abu Dhabi Performing Arts Center, 328
    Guggenheim Abu Dhabi, 328
    Zayed National Museum, 328
Access to Middle East and Islamic Resources (AMIR), 192
Ackerman, Phyllis, *298*
Acre, UNESCO declaration in, 81
Addison, Erin, 359
Adjaye Associates, 328
Advancement of Science (KFAS) headquarters (Kuwait), 437
affect theory, 328, 335n10
Affleck, Ray, *344*
Afghanistan, 14, 16, 34
Africa, 17, 424
    see also North Africa

Aga Khan, 343, 406, 425, 444, *444*
Aga Khan Award for Architecture (AKAA), 17, 19, 32, 34, 46, 207, 342, 406–7, 414, 425, 437, 438, 442
    first steering committee, *444*
    founding of, 444–45
    for Indian projects, 343
Aga Khan Documentation Center (AKDC), 191–92, 198–99
Aga Khan Museum (Toronto), 17, 266, 269n2
Aga Khan Program for Islamic Architecture (Harvard), 46
Aga Khan Program for Islamic Architecture (MIT), 21, 46, 197–98, 341
Aga Khan Trust for Culture, 47, 53n11, 191–92, *344*
Agra
    Mughal Sheraton Hotel, 343, *344*
    Mahtab Bagh, 63
    gardens, 62
    see also Taj Mahal
Ahmed Shah, 343
Ahmedabad, India, 343, 345
Akkasah, 185
Al Bujairi Development (Riyadh), 415–16, *416*, *417*
Al Fozan, 437
al-Asaad, Khaled, 194
al-Azhar Mosque (Cairo), 359–60, *361*, 379–80, *380*
Aleppo, 22, 34

Alfaisal, Khaled, 445
Algeria, 16, 34, 377
  see also Algiers
Algiers, 45–46
Alhambra, 14, 16, 404
  adaptations of, 98
  'Alhambrology', 16
  Court of the Lions, 65
  Court of the Myrtles, 65
  gardens, 65–66
  as landscape, 65–67
Alhambras: Arquitectura NeoArabe en Latinoamerica (ed. Guzman and Viñuales), 100
Alhambrology, 16
Al-Hijr (Madâin Sâllih), 330
Ali, Habib Fida, 423
Al-Ibrahim Mosque (Caracas), 103
alleyways, 71–74, 75, 76
al-Maqrizi, 59
Almohad mosques, 16
Al-Rashid Mosque (Fort Edmonton, Canada), 103
Al-Saud, Mohammed Bin Salman Bin Abdulaziz, 330
AlSayyad, Nezar, 46
Al-Sultan Hassan Mosque (Cairo), 412
AlUla, 330–31, 333–34
alun-alun towns, 146
Amador de los Rios, José, 96
American mudejar, 96, 97–98
Amman
  Abdali real estate development, 313–15, *315*, 318, 319, 322n6
  Gulf investments in, 314–15
  neoliberal developments in, *317*
Anatolia, 180–81
  Buruciye Medrese, 180
  Çifte Minareli Medrese, 180, 185
  Gök Medrese, 183, *183*
  Islamic architecture in, 16
Andalucia (Amman), 315
Andrew W. Mellon Foundation, 275, 281, 292

Anthropocene Age, 423
anthropology, 5
Appreciative Inquiry (AI), 227–28, 229–30
Aqaba, Jordan, 313
  ASEZA (Aqaba Special Economic Zone Authority), 318
aqueducts, 60
Arab cities, *252*
  mega-projects, 313–14
  neoliberal urban transformation in, 313–21
  uneven geographies in, 313–21
  see also Islamic city/cities
'Arab Villages', 83
Arab World Institute (Institute du monde arabe), 345, *346*
archaeology, 5
  contemporary approach to, 22
  Dutch colonial, 154
  in Iran (rock-cut ruins), *21*
  in Spain, 16
Architectural Association School of Architecture (AA), 423
architectural competitions, 437–49
  Abdullatif Al Focan Award for Mosque Architecture, 445
  Kuwait Foundation for the Advancement of Science (KFAS), 445–46, *448*
  participants, 439–42
  reasons for entering, 447–48
  types of, 438–39
  see also Aga Khan Award for Architecture (AKAA)
architectural details
  African influence, 96
  aina kari (mirror work), 428
  arabesque ornaments, 103
  arches, 403, 411
  artesonado ceilings, 96, *97*
  brick flat domes, 428
  calligraphy, *268*, 418, 427, *428*, 431, *432*, *433*
  ceramic tiles, 51
  chitrai (beaten metal), 426

Index

Corinthian columns, 117
domes, *301*, *302*, *304*, 411, 427
frescoes, 426, *432*, *433*
horseshoe arches, 98, 100
interior murals, 100
Ionic columns, 117
kashi (glazed tile mosaic), 428, *429*
keel arch windows, 105
lion as decorative element, 151
mashrabiya, 239, *239*, 411
masonry details, *302*
*merlon*s, 117, 118, *119–20*
minarets, 100, 105, *215*, 403
mirror work, 427
muqarnas, 105
onion domes, 98, 100
pichi kari (precious stone inlay), 428
plaster relief (*thoba*), *430*
polychrome accents, 98, 100
polylobe windows, 103
polylobed arches, 105
ribbed domes, *432*, *433*
rooftop crenelations, 103, 105
Spanish influence, 96
stone roundels, *152*
triple-arch typology, 315
architectural documentation
  of the Middle East, 197–99
  need for, 200
  and preservation, 198
  and sustainability, 198
  see also digital humanities
architectural education, 223–24
  Abedian School of Architecture (Bond University), 448
  Aga Khan Program for Islamic Architecture (Harvard), 46
  Aga Khan Program for Islamic Architecture (MIT), 21, 46, 197–98, 341
  Appreciative Inquiry (AI) in, 227–30
  Architectural Association School of Architecture (AA; London), 423
  decolonized, 229–30

Ecole des Beaux-Arts (Paris), 223
European Architectural History Network (EAHN), 86, 281
experiential learning in, 228–29
Global Architectural History Teaching Collaborative (GAHTC), 31, 280, 341–42
inherited models of, *225*
and Inquiry-based learning (IBL), 228
in the Middle East, 224, 226–29
National Architectural Accreditation Board (NAAB), 31, 212
role of museums, 235–42
textbooks, 13, 288, 291–93, 296, 298–302
traditional pedagogy, 226–27
western models of, 224, 226
Architectural Education in the Islamic World (Evin), 231n7
Architectural Histories, 281, 292
architectural historiography, 134, 136–37
architectural history
  digital publication of, 273, 275, 277–82
  digital resources for, 192–94
  documentation of, 191
  global, 95, 117
  illustration of, 287–302
  in Israel, 81–89
  study of, 209
architectural materials
  fired bricks, 427
  marble, 63
architecture
  academic viewpoint, 223
  as art form, 273
  Ayyubid, 17, 379–80
  Buddhist, 277, *278*
  Byzantine, 178, 209, 364
  civil engineer viewpoint, 223
  Classical, 119
  craftsman-builder viewpoint, 223
  Deccan, 14
  Fatimid, 379
  folds of, 364–65
  Gothic Revival, 100

463

Hindu-Modern, 343
Hispano-Moorish, 98
'ideal' forms of, 431
in India, 342–43, 345–48, 350
Indo-Saracenic, 343, 404
International style, 83, 424
layers of, 366
Lebanese, 315
local expressions of, 83
Mahgrib, 46
Mamluk, 17
Moorish Revival, 98, 100
mudejar, 95–96
Mughal, 14, 345
of museums, 254–56
for Muslim societies, 411–19
Neo-Andalusian, 98
Neo-Arab, 98, 100, 107
neo-Islamic, 404
neo-Mamluk, 100, 103, 105, 404
neo-Moorish, 98, 404
neo-Mudéjar, 98
Palestinian, 81–89
and photography, 273
Qajar, 17
religious, 212
revivalist styles, 404
Seljuq, 299
social scientist viewpoint, 223
Spanish, 97–98
starchitecture, 3, 328
Sultanate, 14
Uighur, 34
Umayyad, 364
western, 31, 34
see also architectural competitions; architectural details; architectural documentation; architectural education; architectural historiography; architectural history; architectural materials; Islamic architecture; Ottoman architecture; traditional architecture
Architecture of the Islamic West (Bloom), 16

'ArchitectureTalk,' 347–48, 350
Architectures of Transversality: Paul Klee, Louis Kahn and the Persian Imagination (Mohajeri), 348
Archnet, 21, 191–92, *193*, *194*, 199, 279
Archnet-IJAR: International Journal of Architectural Research, 32
ARCOP Design Group, *344*
Ardalan, Nader, *301*, 425, *444*
Ars Islamica (Smith), *297*
Ars Orientalis (*AO*), 275, 277, 281, 292
Art Bulletin, 13
art history, 4, 5, 38–39n7
artesonado ceilings, 96, *97*
Artstor, 21
ASEZA (Aqaba Special Economic Zone Authority), 318
Asian Studies, 154
Atatürk, Mustafa Kemal, 343, 364, 377
Auburn Gallipoli Mosque (Sydney), *134*
Australia
    Auburn Gallipoli Mosque (Sydney), *134*
    Australia Islamic Centre and Mosque (Newport, Victoria), *135*
    Sydney Opera House, 441
Australia Islamic Centre and Mosque (Newport, Victoria), *135*
authenticity, 359, 381, 404
Avermaete, Tom, 47
Aykaç, Pınar, 185
Ayyubid architecture, 17, 379–80
Aziz, Haji Abdul, 426, 431

B

Babri Masjid, 346–47
Badran, Jamal, 412
Baghdad State Mosque, 413
Bai'tul Islam Mosque (Toronto), 102, 103
Baker, Bill, *211*
Bakhtiar, Laleh, *301*, 425
Ballon, Hilary, 273, 275
Bangladesh. *See* Dhaka
Baqi (*thoba* and mirror work artist), 427

Bargellini, Clara, 97
Barjeel Foundation, 266
Barsiyan, Great Mosque, *297*
Barthel, Pierre-Arnaud, 313
Bauhaus, 90n10, 223
Bayt Sidi Nunu (Mocha, Yemen), *164*
Bee Breeders, 441, 447
Beirut, 313
    Gulf investments in, 314
    neoliberal urban restructuring in, 315–16
    neoliberalism in, 319
    refugee housing in, *393*
Belting, Hans, 130–31
Benjamin, Walter, 348
Berlin, 390, *391*
Bhabha, Homi, 345
Bibliotheca Alexandrina (Alexandria), 439, *440*
Bilad al-Sham, 296
'Black Taj' myth, 63
Blair, Sheila, 4, 31, 127, 389
Block Museum, 267
Bloom, Jonathan, 4, 31, 127, 389
'Blue Mosque' of Tabriz, 291
Bogdanović, Jelena, 392–93
Bond, Sarah, 194, 196
Bonfils, Felix, *274*
Boota (brick mason), 427
Bosnia-Herzegovina
    destruction of sites in, 198
    Šerefudin White Mosque, 207, *208*, 209
Bozdoğan, Sibel, 444–45
brandscapes, 328
Brazil Mosque (São Paolo), 100, 102, 103, *104*, 105–7
Brey, Alexander, 281
British Art Studies, 281, 292
British Museum (London), 254, 266, 269n2, 384
built environments
    in the Islamic world/Middle East, 4, 59, 191

    non-modern, 359
    relationship to museums, 254–56
Burgoyne, Michael, 296
Burj Dubai. *See* Burj Khalifa (Dubai)
Burj Khalifa (Dubai), *33*, 39n19, 210, *211*
Bursa, Grand Mosque, *361*
Burujird, Great Mosque, 299, 300, *300*, *304*
Byzantine architecture, 178, 209, 364

C
Cairo, 22, *252*, 313, 404
    al-Azhar Mosque, 359–60, *361*, 379–80, *380*
    al-Maqrizi's survey of, 59
    Al-Sultan Hassan Mosque, 412
    architects in, 404
    conservation in, 374
    Dreamland, 313
    Egyptian Museum, 375
    Grand Egyptian Museum (Giza), 385n9
    Gulf investments in, 314
    Ibn Tulun mosque, 215, *215*, 383, *383*
    modernization in, 374
    Nahdet Masr (Mukhtar), 375, *376*
    plans of mosques, *290*
    Sabil-Kuttab Nafisa al-Bayda (Cairo), *378*
    Tahrir Square, 375
    view of canal with bridges, *290*
    view of houses, *252*
calligraphy, *268*, 418, 427, *428*, 431, *432*, *433*
Camasmie, Paulo, 105
Cambridge World History of Religious Architecture, 13
Campbell, Gar, *444*
Canada
    Aga Khan Museum (Toronto), 17, 266, 269n2
    Al-Rashid Mosque (Fort Edmonton, Canada), 103
    architectural competitions in, 439
    Bai'tul Islam Mosque (Toronto), 102
    mosques in, 103
    United States-Mexico-Canada Agreement (USMCA), 314
Canby, Sheila R., 266

Carr, E. H., 199
castles
　in Tripoli, 49
　see also palaces
Çelik, Zeynep, 32, 46, 48, 98
Central Asia, Islamic architecture in, 14, 16
Central Synagogue (New York City), 98, *99*
Centre Pompidou (Paris), 438
chadars, 64
chahar bagh, 60, 62, 67–68n5
chahar taq, 299
Chambers, Iain, 365
Chandigarh, 342, 345, 350
char-bagh courts, 343
charitable endowments (*waqf*), 375, 380
Charmes, Gabriel, 359–60
China
　destruction of Uighur heritage, 34
　Hongshuiquan Mosque (Qinghai, China), *19*
　Islamic architecture in, 17, *19*, 36
　Uighur architecture, 34
chini khana, 64
Choudhury, Ajoy, *344*
Chow, Rey, 209
Chupin, Jean-Pierre, 439
Çifte Minareli Medrese, 185
'civilizing mission', 334
clash of civilizations, 130
Classical architecture, 119
climate change, 60, 342, 347, 441
Cohen, Jean-Louis, 47–48
Colonial Modern: Aesthetics of the Past, Rebellions for the Future (Avermaete, Karakayali, and von Osten), 47
　and decolonization, 233–30
　digital, 195–96
　and heritage preservation, 330–31, 333–34, 377, 384
colonialism/colonialist perspective, 3, 16, 45–49, 51–52, 209–10, 249, 255, 293, 341, 346, 382
　'civilizing mission', 334

　and decolonization, 230–33
　digital, 195–96
　in Egypt, 375
　in Israel, 83
　in Latin America, 96
　in Libya, 48, 49, 51
　see also heritage preservation
Colonising Egypt (Mitchell), 46, 360
Comité de conservation des monuments de l'art arabe (Committee for the Conservation of Arab Art Monuments), 291, 374
Companion to Islamic Art and Architecture, A (ed. Flood and Necipoğlu), 34, 122
conservation. *See* heritage preservation
Córdoba
　historic centre, 19
　Great Mosque/'La Mezquita', 14, 364
　palaces, 16
Correa, Charles, 343, *444*
Coste, Pascal, 291, *292*
COVID-19 pandemic, 178, 184, 280–81, 341, 445
　and Islamic art museums, 241–42
Creswell, K. A. C., 20, 291, 293
Crinson, Mark, 46–47
Critchlow, Keith, 424
Cubism, 348
cultural heritage, 191, 194
cultural identity, 136
cultural relativity, 133
Cummings, Thomas, 96

D
Damascus, 313, *274*
Damascus Fountain (Bonfils), *274*
Danusari, Aryo, 75
Dark, Kenneth Rainsbury, *276*
Darwinism, 382
Darwish, Mahmoud, *268*, 269–70n10
Data Durbar Mosque (Lahore), 424
David Collection, 269n2
Deccan architecture, 14, 15
decolonization

Index

of architectural education, 229–30
of the conservation of Islamic built heritage, 382
Deconstructing the American Mosque: Space, Gender and Aesthetics (Kahera), 102–3
deconstructionism, 136, 438
Deen, Ustad 'Ilm, 426
Deleuze, Gilles, 364
Delhi
  architects in, 404
  Humayun's Tomb, 62, 345
  see also New Delhi
Demak Mosque (Indonesia), 149–50
Denkmäler Persischer Baukunst (Sarre), *294*
Denny, Walter B., 180, 183
Derrida, Jacques, 438
Description de l'Égypte (*Description of Egypt*), 288, *290*, 291, 360
Deutsche Bauzeitung (Jacobsthal), *295*
Dewey, John, 228
Dhaka, 345, 350
Dictionary of Art (ed. Turner), 13
Dieulafoy, Jane, 291
Diez, Ernst, 291, 296
digital humanities
  allure and challenges of, 197–99
  ethics in, 194–97
  outcomes of, 199–200
  role of, 192–94
Digital Library of the Middle East, 192
digital publishing, 273–79
  in education, 279–81
  opening access to, 281–82
digital resources, *193*
digitization, 192–94
Din, Baba Hasan, 428
Displaying the Orient: Architecture of Islam at Nineteenth Century World's Fairs (Çelik), 46
Diwayo, Alla, 426
Djurović, Vladimir, 17
Dodds, Jerrilynn D., 102
Doha

Museum of Islamic Art, 17, *20*, 215, 253, *253*, 265, 266, 269n2, *405*
National Museum of Qatar, 329
Pearl Island, 313
Dome of the Rock, 13, 14, 17, 119, 120–21, 403
  access to, 16–17
  Haram al-Sharif, 17
  interior view, *18*
  origins of, 121
domes, 411, 427, *432*
  brick flat, 428
Doshi, Balkrishna, 343
Doyle, Shelby, *213*
Dubai, 212, *251*, 313
  Burj Khalifa, *33*, 39n19, 210, *211*
  Gulf investments in, 314
  Sama Dubai, 319

E
Early, James, 97
East Asian studies, 209
Ecole des Beaux-Arts (Paris), 223
education. *See* architectural education
Edwards, Holly, 95, 98
Egypt, 46
  architecture in, 296
  Bibliotheca Alexandrina (Alexandria), 439, *440*
  chandeliers from, 105
  Egyptian Ministry of Education, 439
  Egyptian Museum, 375
  Giza pyramids, 241
  Grand Egyptian Museum (Giza), 385n9
  illustrations of, 288, *290*, 291
  Islamic architecture in, 17
  Islamic heritage conservation in, 373–84
  Ministry of Tourism and Antiquities, 377
  mosques in, *290*
  neoliberalism in, 314
  Pharaonic heritage in, 375
  photographs of, 296
  tourism in, 366
  see also Cairo

467

Empire, Architecture, and the City: French-Ottoman Encounters, 1830–1914 (Çelik), 48
Empire Building: Orientalism and Victorian Architecture (Crinson), 46–47
Emre Arolat Architecture, *446*
Entrepreneurial Development Institute of India, 343
environmental perspectives, 60, 62, 63–67
Erbil Citadel (Iraqi Kurdistan), 88
Erdmann, Kurt, 180, 183
Erdoğan, Recep Tayyip, 177, 364, 366, 377
ethics in digital humanities, 194–97
ethnocracy, 82
Euben, Roxanne, 364
Eurocentrism, 127, 129, 131–32, 210, 341, 345, 346, 405
  and conservation, 382
  see also Neo-Eurocentrism
European Architectural History Network (EAHN), 86, 281
European exceptionalism, 129
European Union, response to refugee crisis, 394
Ewert, Christian, 296

F
Fatehpur Sikri, 345
Fathy, Hassan, 343, 414, *444*
Fatimid architecture, 379
Fawaz, Mona, 392
Feener, R. Michael, 279, *280*
Feliciano, María Judith, 96
Fernbach, Henry, 98
Fez, studies of, 22
First International Symposium on Traditional Dwellings and Settlements, 46
Fisher, Thomas, 393
FitzHugh, Justin, *344*
Flandin, Eugène, 291
Flaubert, Gustave, 250
Fletcher, Banister, 13, 254
Flood, Finbarr Barry, 38, 122, 132
Florence, 404
Forehand, Leslie, 212, *213*
formalism, 59, 62, 343
Forms of Dominance: On the Architecture and Urbanism of the Colonial Enterprise (AlSayyad), 46
Fossati brothers, 293
Foster and Partners, 328
Foucault, Michel, 46
Freer/Sackler Gallery, 269n2
French Agency for AlUla, 330
Frishman, Martin, 103
Fuller, Buckminster, 424
fundamentalism, 347

G
Gaber, Tammy, 95, 103
Gabriel, Albert, 183
Galdieri, Eugenio, *302*
Garden Mansions, 85, *86*
gardeners, 66
gardens
  at the Alhambra, 65–66
  design, 14, 60
  in Kashmir, 64
  Mahtab Bagh (Agra), 63
  of the Taj Mahal, 60, 62–64
Gehry Partners, 328
gender studies, 34
Generalife Palace, 65, *66*
gentrification, 73, 180, 316, 366, 370n39, 374
Georges Pompidou Centre (Paris), 441
Geschichte der Baukunst (*History of Architecture*, 1856–73), 292
Gifford, Gloria Fraser, 97–98
Giralda tower, adaptations of, 98
Global Architectural History Teaching Collaborative (GAHTC), 31, 280, 341–42
Global History of Architecture, A (Ching, Jarzombek, and Prakash), 31, 133
globalism, 134, 341
globalization, 249–50, 255

see also World Economic Forum (WEF), World Trade Center; World Trade Organization (WTO)
Godard, André, 293, 298–99, *300*
Goddess of Love, The, 263
Goitein, S. D., 122
Goitia, Fernando Chueca, 96
Gök Medrese (Sivas, Turkey), 183, *183*
Google, 20, 21
Google Earth, 163–64, *165,* 275
Gothic cathedrals, 302, 364
Gothic Revival, 100
Grabar, Oleg, 22, 31, 38, 59, 121, 132, 296, 444
Gramsci, Antonio, 46
Granada
 Generalife Palace, 65, *66*
 see also Alhambra
gravestone art, 154
Grazda, Edward, 102
Great Divergence: China, Europe, and the Making of the Modern World Economy (Pomeranz), 130
Great (Friday) Mosque of Isfahan, 291, 296, 299
 details of, *302*
 north dome, *303*
Great Mosque of Córdoba, 14, 364
Green Land (Amman), 315
Grotefend, Georg Friedrich, 288
Grove Encyclopedia of Islamic Art and Architecture, 13
Gruber, Christiane, 281
Grünemberg, Konrad, 288
Guggenheim Abu Dhabi, 328
Gulf Cooperation Council, 314
Gunbad-i Qabus, *298*
Gurlitt, Cornelius, 293
Guzman, Rafael López, 100

H
Haeri, Shaikh Fadlullah, 425
Hafeez, Sahibzada Mohammad Farakh, 427

Hagia Sophia (Istanbul), 178, 364, 366–67, *367*
 images of, 293
 as museum, 377
Haider, Gulzar, 102
Hajjaj, Emad, *316*
Hakan Elevli Associates, *135*
Haram al-Sharif, 17
Harker, Christopher, 88
Harvey, David, 313
Hassan, Sultan, 416
Herbert, Gilbert, 84
heritage preservation
 colonial, 45–49, 51–52, 330–31, 333–34, 372–75, 377, 379–84
 and tourism, 230, 357–60, 362, 364, 368
 Venice Charter, 381
 see also UNESCO
hasht behesht, 62
heterotopias, 315
Hill, Derek, 296
Hillenbrand, Robert, 14, 21, 31, 34
Hinduism
 in India, 342–47
 in Indonesia, 151, 155
Hispano-Moorish architecture, 98
historians, role of, 81–89
Historians of Islamic Art Association (HIAA), 34, 36, 275
historic preservation. *See* heritage preservation
History of Architecture, A (Kostof), 404
History of Architecture on the Comparative Method, A (Fletcher), 254
Hoban, James, 439
Hobson, John, 129, 130, 131
Holod, Renata, 103
Holy Land, 291, 296
Hongshuiquan Mosque (Qinghai, China), *19*
housing for refugees, 87
Huff, Toby, 130–31
Hugo, Victor, 250
Humanism, 47, 59, 423

humanitarianism, 88
Humayun's Tomb (Delhi), 62, 345
Hume, David, 119–20
Hunt, Erin, *213*
Huntington, Samuel, 130
Hussain, Mistree Haji Ghulam, 426

I
Iberian Peninsula, 16
  see also Spain
Ibn al-Haytham, 130
Ibn al-Shatir, 130
Ibn Battuta, 362
Ibn Tulun Mosque (Cairo), 215, *215*, 383, *383*
ice-houses, 14, *15*
İmamoglu, Ekrem, 180, *182*
imperialism, 47
Index Islamicus, 20
India
  Ahmedabad, 343, 345
  architecture in, 342–43
  Babri Masjid, 346–47
  Chandigarh, 342, 345, 350
  Deccan architecture, 14, 15
  Entrepreneurial Development Institute of India, 343
  Fatehpur Sikri, 345
  Hall of Special Audience, 345
  Humayun's Tomb (Delhi), 345
  India Art Fair (2018), *263*
  Indira Ghandi Centre (New Delhi), 441
  Islamic architecture in, 14, 16, 46, 342–43, 345–48, 350
  Jaipur, 345
  Moghul, 100
  Mughal Sheraton Hotel, 343, *344*
  see also Agra; Delhi; Taj Mahal
Indira Gandhi Centre (New Delhi), 441
Indonesia
  Islamic architecture in, 71–77, 143–55
  Jakarta slums, 143
  Majelis Ulama Indonesia, 76
  see also Java (Indonesia)

Indonesian Council of Muslim Scholars, 76
Indo-Saracenic architecture, 343, 404
Inquiry-based learning (IBL), 228
Institut du monde arabe (Arab World Institute), 345, *346*
International Association for the Study of Traditional Environments (IASTE), 46
International Council of Monuments and Sites (ICOMOS), 381
International Journal of Islamic Architecture (IJIA), 4–5, 6, 17, 51, 249, 389
International Style, 83, 424
International Union of Architects (UIA), 439, 441, 442, 446, 448, 451n14
Iqbal, Hafiz Mohammad, 428
Iran
  Abbas Abad project, 348, 350, *351*
  archaeology in, *21*
  architecture in, 293, 296
  'Blue Mosque' of Tabriz, 291
  Great Mosque of Burujird, 300, *300*, *304*
  ice-house in, *15*
  images of, 291
  Islamic architecture in, 298–99
  Islamic monuments in, 293
  limited access to, 16, 34
  mausolea in, 293, *294–95*
  as Persia, 207
  photographs of, 296
  rugs from, 105
  Tehran New Civic Center, 348
  tomb tower at Rayy, 291
  see also Isfahan; Tehran, Iran
Iraq
  Baghdad State Mosque, 413
  destruction of sites in, 34, 241
  Erbil Citadel (Iraqi Kurdistan), 88
  limited access to, 16, 34
  Mosul monuments, 34, 279
  muqarnas dome (Imam Dur), 34
  war crimes in, 196
Irving, T. B., 97

Index

Isfahan
   Great (Friday) Mosque of Isfahan, 291, 296, 299, *302*, *303*
   Madrasa-i Shah Sultan Husayn, 291, *292*
   Masjid-i Shah, 291
   Safavid, 288, *289*
ISIS, destruction of architectural heritage by, 34, 241
Islam
   as civilization, 4
   demonization of, 347
   influence on architecture, 4
   information about in museums, 237–38
   as marker of identity, 393
   Salafi, 34
   in southeast Asia, 145, 151
   Sunni, 380
   values/principles of, 215–16, 379, 411–12, 419
   xenophobia toward, 88
   see also Muslim community
Islam and Image: Beyond Aniconism and Iconoclasm (Flood), 38
Islamic architecture
   access to, 165–67
   in Afghanistan, 14, 16, 34
   in the Americas, 95–107
   in Anatolia, 16
   anonymous vernacular, 14
   in Brazil, 100, 102, 103, *104*, 105–7
   and the built environment, 59
   in China, 17, *19*, 36
   chronology of, 17, 19
   in the colonial era, 47
   colonialism in, 45–49, 51–52
   contemporary, 5–6, 17, 47, 210, 212, 327–34, 403–7, 411, 423
   defining, 4–5
   destruction of architectural heritage, 34, 241
   diversity of, 3
   fieldwork in, 166–67
   as formal expression of Islam, 4
   fundamentalist approach to, 406–7
   geography of, 14, 16–17, 71–77
   Hagia Sophia, 377
   history of, 171
   illustration of, 287–302
   informal and neighborhood applications of, 143
   Islamic-modern, 343, 345, 347, 348, 350
   in Kurdistan, 88, 177
   local expressions of, 71–77
   methodology of study, 21
   modern, 343
   modern change in, 127
   in Morocco, 16, 313, 358
   in Pakistan, 16, 350, 242, 442, *443*
   periodization in, 127–37, 150–51
   in Persia, 207
      see also Iran
   postcolonialism in, 47
   re-envisioning, 4–5
   and refugee agency, 392–94
   religious uses of, 102, 212
   researching, 19–21
   revivalist styles, 405
   scholarly approaches to, 13
   secular uses of, 102
   in Sicily, 207
   in southeast Asia, 143–55, 154–55
   study of, 31–32, 167–68, 207–16
   and technology, 19–21
   in Thailand, *146*
   and tourism, 357–68
   transdisciplinary approach to, 4–5
   in Turkey, 177–85
   typology of, 14
   see also Australia; Beirut; Lebanon; Bosnia-Herzegovina; Cairo; Canada; Dubai; Egypt; India; Indonesia; Iran; Iraq; Israel; Turkey; Jordan; Libya; Pakistan; Palestine; Qatar; Syria; Tunisia; Turkey; United Arab Emirates; Yemen
Islamic Architecture (Hillenbrand), 14

Islamic art, 3, 4, 13, 134, 136–37
  access to, 165–67
  compared to western art, 127
  contemporary, 13
  curation of, 261–68
  dissertations related to, 168, *169–70*
  in Polynesia, 265
  relationship to architecture, 31
  and the role of museums, 235–42
  street art, 267
  study of, 31, 34, 167–68
  see also museums
Islamic Art: Past, Present, and Future (conference), 34
Islamic cemetery, *280*
Islamic Center (Washington, DC), 14, 105–7, *106*
Islamic city/cities, 22, 224, 250–51, 255
  see also Arab cities
Islamic civilization and culture, 127, 133
Islamic identity, 3
Islamic intellectual history, 131
Islamic Society of North America (Plainfield, Indiana), 102
Islamic Studies, 154
Islamic tourism. *See* tourism
Islamic-modern, 343, 345, 347, 348, 350
Islamophobia, 194
Isozaki, Arata, *351*
Israel
  Anis Srouji Family Villa, *85*
  architectural history in, 81–89
  Garden Mansions, 85, *86*
  Haifa, 85–86
  housing for refugees, 87
  Nazareth, *82*
  Tel Aviv, *84*
  Zionism, 83, 84
  see also Jerusalem; Palestine
Istanbul
  1559 panorama of, 275, *276*
  fieldwork in, 178
  Gezi Park protests, 177, 187n14
  Hagia Sophia, 178, 364, 366–67, *367*
  historic neighborhoods in, 370n39
  İstanbul Büyükşehir Belediyesi (IBB) Atatürk Kitaplığı, 180
  Kanal Istanbul project, 178
  Mahmud Pasha Hammam, 180, *181*
  mayoral election, 180, *182*
  pluralism in, 367
  revivalist styles in, 404
  Sancaklar Mosque, *446*
  Sarıyer area, *179*
  studies of, 22
  Topkapı Palace, 178
  urban preservation in, 366
Italy
  colonialism in Libya, 48–51
  Sicily, 207
  Venice, 404
  Venice Charter, 381

J
Jabal Omar Project, 313
Jacobsthal, Eduard, 293, *294–95*
Jafari, Jafar, 359
Jafet family, 100
Jaffar, Ustad, 426
Jahan, Shah, 63
Jaipur, 345
Jakarta slums, 143
Jarzombek, Mark, 88, 210, 341
Java (Indonesia)
  alun-alun towns, 146
  Kudus Mosque, *148*
  Mantingan mosque, *152*
  ruins of Taman Sari, *147*
Jerusalem, 296
  see also Dome of the Rock
Jinnah, Fatima, 442
Jinnah, Muhammad Ali, 442, *443*
Jomard, Edme François, *290*
Jones, Owen, 98, 105
Jordan
  Aqaba, 313, 318

Index

deregulation in, 319–20
heritage preservation in, 377
Mshatta Façade, 288
neoliberalism in, 314, 319, 319–20
tourism in, 359
see also Amman
Journal of the Society of Architectural Historians (JSAH), 31–32, 275, *276*, 281–82
JSAH Online, 275, 277
Justice Palace (Riyadh), 414, *414*

K

Kaempfer, Engelbert, 288, *289*
Kahera, Akel, 95, 102–3, 105–6
Kahn, Louis, 343, 348, 350, *351*
kampung areas, 71–74
Kampung Hulu mosque (Malaysia), *153*
Kanal Istanbul project, 178
Karakayali, Serhat, 47
Karz, Marion, 34
Keniger, Michael, 448–49
Keshani, Hussein, 292
KFAS Headquarters and Conference Center (Kuwait), *448*
Khalidi, Omar, 98, 102, 105
Khamseen: Islamic Art History Online, 281
Khan, Ayub, 442
Khan, Hasan-Uddin, 4, 103, 249–50, 357, 364
Khan, Sarah, 362
khanqahs, 374, 425
Khosla, Ramesh, *344*
Kidd, Akari Nakai, 333
King Abdul Aziz Historical Center (Riyadh), *418–19*
Klee, Paul, 348, *349*, 352n5
Kleiss, Wolfram, 296
Kolb, David, 228
Komanecky, Michael, 97
Konyalı, İbrahim Hakkı, 185
Kostof, Spiro, 404
Krecker, G., *294*
ksars, 14
Kuala Lumpur, 32, *33*, 39n19
Kubler, George, 97
Kudus Mosque (Java), *148*
Kugler, Franz, 292
Kumasi (Ghana), 424
Kuran, Aptullah, 185
Kurd, Nadia, 103
Kurdistan, 88, 177
Kusno, Abidin, 143
Kuthayr, Yusuf ibn, mausoleum of, 293, *295*
kuttabs, 374, 380
Sabil-Kuttab Nafisa al-Bayda (Cairo), *378*
Kuwait, Advancement of Science (KFAS) headquarters, 437
Kuwait Foundation for the Advancement of Science (KFAS), 437, 446–47, *448*

L

La Grande Mosquée (Paris), 362, *363*
'La Mezquita' (Córdoba), 364
Lahore, 427
landscape design, 5, 14
landscape history, 60, 62
landscapes
at the Alhambra, 65–66
at the Taj Mahal, 62–65
see also gardens
Latin America, 95–96
Latour, Bruno, 288
Lavin, Sylvia, 328
Le Corbusier, 45–46, 350
'Le Corbusier and Algiers' (McLeod), 45
'Le Corbusier, Orientalism, Colonialism' (Çelik), 46
Lebanon
Civil War, 315
heritage preservation in, 377
immigration from, 100
modernism in, 85
see also Beirut
Lefebvre, Henri, 313
Libeskind, Daniel, 442
Libya
ceramic artisanry in, 51

heritage preservation in, 377
Islamic architecture in, 16
Italian colonial, 48, 49
limited access to, 16, 34
see also Tripoli
Limo Kaum Mosque (Indonesia), *149*
Lin, Wei-cheng, *278*
literary culture, 22
Little, Christopher, *344*
Living Well (Hajjaj), *316*
Lombard, Denys, 148
Lorenz, Andrea, 103
Lorichs, Melchior, 275
Louvre Abu Dhabi, 14, 17, 269n2, 328, 329, 331, 333
Louvre (Paris), 253–54, 256, 269n2, 384

M
MacCannell, Dean, 358–59
Madâin Sâlih (Al-Hijr), 330
Madinat al-Zahra (Spain), 16
Madrasa-i Shah Sultan Husayn, 291, *292*
*madrasa*s, 374, 413
Maghrib. *See* North Africa
Mahjoub, Abu, *316*
Mahmud Pasha Hammam, 180, *181*
Mahtab Bagh (Agra), 63, *64*
Majelis Ulama Indonesia (MUI), 76
majolica tiles, 49
Maki, Fumihiko, 17
Malaysia
  Kampung Hulu Mosque, *153*
  Kuala Lumpur, 32, *33*, 39n19
  Museum of Islamic Art, 266
Maldives Heritage Survey, 279, *280*
Mamluk architecture, 17
Manama, 313
Mannan, Rami, 215
Mantingan Mosque (Indonesia), *152*
Marçais, Georges, 16
mashrabiya, 212, *213*, 239, *239*, 411
Mashrabiya 2.0, 212, *213*

Masjid-i Shah, 291
Massumi, Brian L., 328–29
Mathaf, 266
Mausoleum of Öljeitü in Sultaniya, 291
Mawared, 318, 319
Maydan (Isfahan), *289*
McLeod, Mary, 45–46
Mecca
  Abraj al-Bait, 34, *35*
  geographical orientation to, 75
  Grand Mosque, 362
  Jabal Omar Project, 313
  Meccan haram, 34
Medinah Temple (Chicago), 100
*medina*s, in Tunisia, 358
mega-projects, 313–14
Melis, Melkiorre, 49, 51
MENA (Middle East and North Africa) region, 256, 264–65
  see also Middle East; North Africa
Menéndes y Pelayo, Marcelino, 96
Merchant, Yahya C., 442, *443*
Meromi, Eylon, *87*
Metropolitan Museum of Art (New York), 235–37, 238, 240, 253–54, 256, 266, 269n2
  bowl with Arabic inscriptions, *238*
  fellowships offered by, 240
  mashrabiya screens, *239*
  public programs and outreach in, 240
  response to COVID-19 pandemic, 241–42
Michelson, Leslee, 280
Middle East
  architectural education in, 224, 226–29
  cities in, 250
  destruction of architecture in, 34, 191
  documentation of, 197–98
  information about in museums, 237
  limitations on travel in, 16
  museums in, 252–56
  restoration policies in, 34
  theft of cultural objects in, 191

474

see also MENA (Middle East and North Africa) region
Middle East Materials Project (MEMP), 192
Middle Eastern studies, 209
Mimar: Architecture in Development (journal), 46
minarets, 100, 105, *215*, 403
　banning of, 389
　in Jam, 16
Mirza, M. A., 442
Mitchell, Timothy, 46, 360
mobility, 249–50
Modern Architecture and the End of Empire (Crinson), 47
modernism/Modernism, 47, 341, 423–25
　Arab, 81, 85
　and Eurocentrism, 210
　global/universalist, 343
　Islamic-Modern, 342–50
　in Lebanon, 85
　non-Eurocentric, 346
　Palestinian, 85
modernity, 48, 346, 419
　colonial, 47–48
　and Eurocentrism, 127
　and the tourist gaze, 358–59
　western, 407
Monuments modernes de la Perse mesurés, dessinés et décrits(Modern Monuments of Persia Measured, Drawn and Described), *292*
'Monuments of Mosul in Danger,' 279
Moore, Kathryn, 103
Moorish Revivalism, 98, 100
Morocco
　Islamic architecture in, 16
　preservation in, 358
　religious architecture in, 16
　riads, 358
　see also Rabat
Mosque, The: History, Architectural Development and Regional Diversity (Frishman and Khan), 103

Mosque and the Modern World, The: Architects, Patrons and Designers since the 1950s (Holod and Khan), 103
Mosque of Ahmad al-Karamanli (Tripoli), 49, *50*
Mosque of al-Shadhili (Mocha, Yemen), *164*
mosquée kiosque, 299, *300*
mosques, 379–80
　Abu Dhabi Sheikh Zayed mosque, 39–40n20
　African-American, 102
　al-Azhar Mosque (Cairo), 359–60, *361*, *380*
　Al-Ibrahim mosque (Caracas), 103
　Almohad, 16
　Al-Rashid Mosque (Fort Edmonton, Canada), 103
　Al-Sultan Hassan Mosque, 412
　Arolat, Emre, 39–40n20
　Auburn Gallipoli Mosque (Sydney, Australia), *134*
　Australia Islamic Centre and Mosque (Newport, Victoria), *135*
　Baghdad State Mosque, 413
　Bai'tul Islam Mosque (Toronto), 102, 103
　'Blue Mosque' of Tabriz, 291
　Brazil mosque (São Paolo), 100, 102, 103, *104*, 105–7
　in China, 17, *19*, 36
　community-built, 143
　competitions for, 437, 445
　contemporary design, 34
　Data Durbar Mosque (Lahore), 424
　Demak Mosque (Indonesia), 149–50
　in Egypt, *290*, 374
　in the European diaspora, 36
　Fanar mosque, *215*
　gender-separated areas in, 34, 103
　Grand Mosque of Bursa, 360
　Grand Mosque (Riyadh), 414, *414–15*, 418
　Great (Friday) Mosque of Isfahan, 291, 296, 299, *302*, *303*
　Great Mosque at Barsiyan, *297*
　Great Mosque of Burujird, 299, 300, *300*, *304*

475

Great Mosque of Córdoba, 14, 364
Great Mosque of Granada, 41n35
in the Gulf States, 445
Hagia Sophia (Istanbul), 178, 364, *367*, *377*, *466–67*
Hongshuiquan mosque, *19*
Ibn Tulun mosque, 215, *215*, 383, *383*
in Indonesia, 152–53
Islamic Center (Washington, DC), 14, 105–7, *106*
Kampung Hulu (Malaysia), *153*
Kudus Mosque (Indonesia), *148*
La Grande Mosquée (Paris), 362, *363*
Limo Kaum Mosque (Indonesia), *149*
Mantingan Mosque (Indonesia), *152*
Monuments modernes de la Perse mesurés, dessinés et décrits(Modern Monuments of Persia Measured, Drawn and Described), 291
Mosque of Ahmad al-Karamanli (Tripoli), 49
Mosque of al-Shadhili (Mocha, Yemen), *164*
Nuri Great Mosque, 40n26
Ottoman, 293, 404
Pak Wigah Mosque (Gujirat, Pakistan), 427, *428*
Quwwat al-Islam Mosque, 14, 17
as representative, 3
Sally Town Mosque (Lahore), *432–33*
Sancaklar Mosque (Istanbul), 39–40n20, *446*
in Saudi Arabia, 445
Šerefudin White Mosque, 207, *208*, 209
in southeast Asia, 144
as space of diasporic identity, 389–90
Süleymaniye Mosque, 178
at Telok Manok (Thailand), *146*
as tourist attractions, 362, 364
in Turkey, 177
types of, 445
Üç Şerefeli Mosque (Edirne), *37*
in the United States and Canada, 95, 103
Mosul monuments (Iraq), 34, 279
Moussavi, Farchid, 328

Moynihan, Elizabeth, 63
Mshatta Façade, 288
Mubarak, Ali Pasha, 359–60
Muchal Indian architecture, 14
mudejar architecture
  American, 95
  in Latin America, 96
  neo-, 98
  in Spanish missions, 95
mudejarismo, 96–97
Mughal architecture, 345
Mughal Sheraton Hotel, 343, *344*
Mukhtar, Mahmoud, 375, *376*
Mulder, Stephennie, 280
Mu'mina Khatun mausoleum, 293, *294–95*
Mumtaz, Taimoor, 426
Mumtaz Mahal, 63
Muqaddas, Muhammad, *304*
muqarnas, 427
Muqarnas (journal), 34
muqarnas dome (Imam Dur), 34
Murcutt, Glenn, *135*
museums
  addressing the audiences of, 236–40
  architecture of, 254–56
  Block Museum, 267
  bowl with Arabic inscriptions, *238*
  educational goals of, 235
  Egyptian Museum, 375
  Grand Egyptian Museum (Giza), 385n9
  Guggenheim Abu Dhabi, 328
  Louvre Abu Dhabi, 14, 17, 269n2, 328, 329, 331, 333
  Louvre (Paris), 253–54, 256, 269n2, 384
  in the Middle East, 252–56
  Museé du Louvre. *See* Louvre Paris
  Museum fur Islamisches Kunst, 269n2
  Museum of Fine Arts (Boston), 235
  Museum of Islamic Art (Berlin), 266
  Museum of Islamic Art (Cairo), 266
  Museum of Islamic Art (Doha), 17, *20*, 215, 253, *253*, 265, 266, 269n2, *405*
  Museum of Islamic Art (Malaysia), 266

Museum of Modern Art (MoMA), 267
National Museum of Qatar (Doha), 329
  online offerings, 242
  public programs and outreach in, 240
  response to COVID-19 pandemic, 241–42
  role of, 256
  Shangri La Museum of Islamic Art, Culture & Design (Honolulu), *262*, *268*, 269–70n10
  training offered by, 240–41
  Victoria and Albert Museum, 269n2
  Zayed National Museum (Abu Dhabi), 328
  see also Metropolitan Museum of Art (New York)
mushollas, 71–74, *72*, 143
  histories of, 74–75
  moving geography of, 75–76
  plan for building, *73*
Muslim community
  African-American, 106
  Afro-Latino, 106–7
  architecture for, 411–19
  Muslim diaspora, 102
  Muslim identity, 106
  see also Islam
Muslim Mutual Aid Society (São Paolo), 100
Muslim School of Arts and Crafts (Tripoli), 49
Muslim travel ban, 167
My People (Shehab), *268*, 269–70n10

N
Nahdet Masr (Mukhtar), 375, *376*
Nakhchivan (Azerbaijan), 293, *294–95*
Naqqash, Azmat, 427
Nara Document on Authenticity, 381
National Architectural Accreditation Board (NAAB), 31, 212
National Endowment for the Humanities (NEH), 275
National Museum of Qatar (Doha), 329
National Organisation for the Preservation of Historical Monuments of Iran (IsMEO), *303*
Navai, Kambiz, 299

Near Eastern studies, 209
Necipoğlu, Gülru, 31, 122, 132
Neo-Andalusian architecture, 98
Neo-Arab architecture, 98, 100, 107
neo-colonialism, 255, 350
Neo-Eurocentrism
  and cultural relativity, 132–34
  and the historiography of science and art, 130–32
  and thresholds of change, 128–30
  see also Eurocentrism
neo-Islamic architecture, 404
neoliberalism, 313–14
  and Islamic architecture, 328
  and urban restructuring, 314–18
Neo-Mamluk architecture, 100, 103, 105, 404
Neo-Moorish architecture, 98, 404
Neo-mudéjar architecture, 98
Nerval, Gérard de, 250
Neumeier, Emily, 280
New Delhi
  Indira Gandhi Centre, 441
  see also Delhi
New York Masjid: The Mosques of New York (Dodds and Grazda), 102
Niaz, Shahid, 428
Niebuhr, Carsten, 288
Nineteenth-Century Art Worldwide, 281, 292
North Africa
  architecture of, 20, 46
  colonial history in, 52n1
  Islamic architecture in, 16, 46
  urbanism in, 17
  see also Algeria; Egypt; Libya; MENA (Middle East and North Africa) region; Morocco; Tunisia
North America
  Spanish architecture in, 97–98
  see also Canada; United States
North American Free Trade Agreement (NAFTA), 314
Nouvel, Jean, 17, 328, 329–30, 331, *332*, 333–34, 345, *346*

O

O'Kane, Bernard, 95, 180
Opa Locka, Florida, 98
Oppositions (journal), 45
Oriental studies, 209
orientalism. *See* orientalist perspective
Orientalism (Said), 4, 38, 42n47, 46, 47, 209, 345
orientalist perspective, 3, 4, 38, 42n47, 45–47, 88, 209, 212, 214, 249–50, 293, 345, 382
    on contemporary architecture, 333–34
    in domestic architecture, 98
    in North America, 95, 98, 100, 106
Ottoman architecture, 17, 48, 100, 103
    in Acre, 81
    Baroque, 17
    mosques, 293, 404
    tomb complex of the Muradiye (Bursa), 40n29
    in Turkey, 178
Ottoman Empire, 184
Oxford Centre for Islamic Studies, 279

P

Pagoda SkethUp (Zhou), 277, *278*
Pahlavi, Farah, 348, 350
Pahlavi, Shah Reza, 350
Pak Wigah Mosque (Gujirat), 427, *428*
Pakistan, 423, 424, 442
    Data Durbar mosque (Lahore), 424
    Dhaka, 350
    Islamabad, 345
    limited access to, 16
    mausoleum of Muhammad Ali Jinnah, 442, *443*
    Pak Wigah Mosque (Gujirat), 427, *428*
    Sally Town Mosque (Lahore), 432
    Tombs of Baba Hassan Deen and Hafiz Iqbal, *429*, *430*
palaces
    Fatehpur Sikri, 345
    Generalife Palace, 65, *66*
    in Madinat al-Zahra, 16
    of Pasha 'Abd al-Kari, 60, *61*
    at Qasr al-Hayr al-Sharqi, 22
    Sarkhej, 343
    Topkapı Palace, 178
    in the western Mediterranean, 16
    see also castles
Palacete Rosa (São Paolo, Brazil), 100, *101*
Palestine, 316, 318
    heritage preservation in, 377
    immigration from, 100
    limited access to, 16
    war crimes in, 196
Palestinians, architecture of, 81–89
Palmyra arch (Syria), 193–95, *195*, *196*
Parc de la Villette (Paris), 438
Paris
    Arab World Institute (Institut du monde arabe), 345, *346*
    Ecole des Beaux-Arts (Paris), 223
    Georges Pompidou Centre, 441
    La Grande Mosquée, 362, *363*
    Louvre, 253–54, 256, 269n2, 384
Parker, Eric, *363*
Pasha 'Abd al-Kari, 60, *61*
Pei, I. M., 17, *20*, *215*, *405*
Pelican History of Art, 14
Perret, August, 85
Persia. *See* Iran
Persian miniatures, 348
Petronas Towers (Kuala Lumpur), 32, *33*, 39n19
[phase eins], 446
photography
    of architecture, 273
    Damascus Fountain (Bonfils), *274*
    digital, 273, 275, 277
    digital archives, 279
    historical, 180, 183–84, *185*, 360
    of Islamic architecture, 296, 298
    of Istanbul, 275, *276*
Piaget, Jean, 228
placemaking, 75, 76, 105, 391, 394
Places Journal, 281–82

Planographia (Kaempfer), 288
Plateresque style, 97
podcast. *See* 'ArchitectureTalk'
Pomeranz, Kenneth, 130
Pompidou Centre (Paris), 441
Pope, Arthur Upham, 293, 296, 298–99, *298*
postcolonialism, 46, 47, 226, 341, 345–46
postmodernism, 136, 343, 404–5, 431
poststructuralism, 210, 345
Prakash, Vikramaditya, 411
Pyla, Panayiota, 86
pyramids (Giza), 241

Q
Qadeer, Rizwan, 428
Qajar architecture, 17
qanats, 60
Qasba (Rabat), *23*
Qasimi, Kambiz Hajji, 299
Qasr al-Hayr al-Sharqi, 22
Qatar, 215–16
  National Museum of Qatar (Doha), 329
  see also Doha
Quirarte, Jacinto, 97
Qur'an
  and *chahar bagh* design, 60
  on conservation and waste, 379
  four rivers of paradise, 67–68n5
  instructions to travel and learn, 379
Quwwat al-Islam Mosque, 14, 17

R
Rabat, 313
  Bou Regreg River Development, 313
  Gulf investments in, 314
  Qasba, *23*
  studies of, 22
Rabbat, Nasser, 4
racism, 382
Rafaqat, Arshad, 426
Rafaqat, Ishaq, 426

Rafaqat, Ustad, 426
Raglin Squire & Partners, 442
Rauza-i-Munnavara. *See* Taj Mahal
Rawabi (West Bank), 316
Raymond, André, 22
refugees
  agency of, 389–94
  in Berlin, 390
  and displacement, 391–94
  housing for, *87*
  religion and, 390
Refugees as City-Makers, 392
Reimer, Michael, 359
Religious Architecture of Islam, The (ed. Moore and Khan), 103
restorations
  in Libya, 49, *50*
  in Turkey, 34, *37*
  in Uzbekistan, 34, *36*
Revivalist styles, 95
riads, in Morocco, 358
Riedlmayer, András, 197–98, *199*
Risvi, Kishwar, 103
Riyadh
  Al Bujairi Development, 415–16, *416*, *417*
  Grand Mosque, 414, *414–15*, 418
  Justice Palace, 414, *414*
  King Abdul Aziz Historical Center, *418–19*
Roberts, David, 291
Rodney, Seph, 267
Rogers and Piano, 438
Rossi, Mario, 105
Rouhi, Leyla, 96
Rousseau, Jean-Jacques, 133
Royal Commission for AlUla, 330
Royal Institute of British Architects, 438
ruination of ruins, 197
Ruskin, John, 292

S
Saadiyat Island (Abu Dhabi), 328
Sabikhi, Ranjit, *344*
Sabil-Kuttab Nafisa al-Bayda (Cairo), *378*

sabils, 374–75, 380
   Sabil-Kuttab Nafisa al-Bayda (Cairo), *378*
Safavids, 17, 288, *289*
SAHARA, 21, 279
Said, Edward, 4, 38, 42n47, 46, 47, 52n2, 88, 209, 250, 345
Saif-ur-Rahman, Ustad, 426
Saladin, Henri, 291
Salam al-Din Chisti tomb (Fatehpur-Sikri), 63
Saliba, George, 131
Sally Town Mosque (Lahore), *432–33*
Salman, Prince Sultan bin, 445
Salzenberg, Wilhelm, 293
Sama Dubai, 319
Samat, Anne, *263*
Sancaklar Mosque (Istanbul), *446*
Sanctuary of Bel at Palmyra (Tadmor, Syria), 117, 118–21, *118–21*
Sarkis, Hashim, 347
Sarre, Friedrich, 293, *294*, 296
Saudi Arabia
   Abdullatif Al Focan Award for Mosque Architecture, 445
   Al-Hijr (Madâin Sâllih), 330
   'Saudi Vision 2030', 330
   Sharaan Resort, 329–34, *332*
   see also AlUla; Mecca; Riyadh
Schinkel, Karl Friedrich, 292
Scholars at Risk Network, 167
Schroeder, Eric, 293, 299
Schwerda, Mira Xenia, 281
Scott, Joan Wallach, 122
Scott, Noel, 359
secularism, 343, 390
Seggerman, Alex Dika, 280
Seljuq architecture, 299
Semper, Gottfried, 98
Sense of Unity, The: The Sufi Tradition in Persian Architecture (Ardalan and Bakhtiar), 425, *301*
Senske, Nick, *213*
Šerefudin White Mosque, 207, 209

Serpuş Han (Karaköy), 180
Sewell, William H. Jr., 122
Shah Jahan, 345
Shah-i Zinda (Samarqand), 34, *36*
Shanghai Expo 2010, 328
Shangri La Museum of Islamic Art, Culture & Design (Honolulu), *262*, *268*, 269–70n10
Sharaan Resort (Saudi Arabia), 329–34, *332*
   see also Nouvel, Jean
sharia law, 375
Shaw, Wendy, 4
Shehab, Bahia, *268*, 269–70n10
Sheren, Ila Nicole, 96
Shriner Temples, 95, 100
   Medinah Temple (Chicago), 100
   Tripoli Temple (Milwaukee), 100
Sicily, Islamic architecture in, 207
Siddique of Nasarpur (*kashigar*), 426
Silk Road, 381
Sir Banister Fletcher's Global History of Architecture, 13
Siraj-ed-din, Shaykh Abu Bakr, 426
Siroux, Maxime, 293, 299, *300*, 304
Smart History, 280
Smith, Adrian, *211*
Smith, Myron B., 296, *297*
Snøhetta, 439, *440*
social history, 59–60
social justice, 197–98
Société Libanaise de Développement et de Reconstruction (Solidere), 315, 318
Society of Architectural Historians (SAH), 21, 275
   see also Journal of the Society of Architectural Historians (JSAH)
sociology, 5
Soomro, Jani, 426
Southeast Asia, Islamic architecture in, 17
Spain
   Great Mosque of Granada, 41n35
   Islamic architecture in, 14, 16, 207

Index

Madinat al-Zahra, 16
  see also Alhambra; Córdoba; Granada
Spanish architecture, in North America, 97–98
Spanish missions, 95, 97
Spencer, Douglas, 328–29, 334
Spivak, Gayatri, 345, 346
Spuybroek, Lars, 328
Srouji, Anis, 85, *85*
starchitects/starchitecture, 3, 328
State Historic and Cultural Park 'Ancient Merv,' 19
Steinhardt, Nancy, 17
Stones of Venice (Ruskin), 292
Sufi (Bakhtiar), 425
Süleymaniye Mosque (Istanbul), 178, *208*
Sultanate architecture, 14
Suq al Mushir (Tripoli), Artisanal Quarter, 49, *51*
Survey of Persian Art (Pope), 293, 296, *298*, 299
sustainability, 171, 198–99, 212, 226, 314, 318, 377, 379–80, 441
Sydney Opera House, 441
synagogues
  Central Synagogue (New York City), 98, *99*
  Moorish Revivalism in, 98
Syria
  destruction of sites in, 197, *198*, 241
  heritage preservation in, 377
  immigration from, 100
  limited access to, 16, 34
  Palmyra arch, 193–95, *195*, *196*
  refugees from, 394
  war crimes in, 196
  war in, 193–94, *198*
  see also Aleppo; Sanctuary of Bel at Palmyra (Tadmor, Syria)

T
Tabbaa, Yasser, 197
Tabet, Antoine, 85
Tahrir Square (Cairo), 375

Taj Mahal, 14, *61*, 343, 345, 403
  'Black Taj' myth, 63
  garden of, 60, 62–63
  as landscape, 62–65, 66–67
Taman Sari ruins (Indonesia), *147*
Taner, Melis, 281
Tange, Kenzo, 350, *351*
Tariqa Alawiya Youth Movement, 75–76
teaching. See architectural education
Tehran
  Abbas Abad project, 348, 350, *351*
  architects in, 404
  New Civic Center, 348
  research in, 167
Tehran New Civic Center, 348
Tel Aviv Municipality, *84*
Temple of Artemis (Gerasa), 120
Temple of Bel. See Sanctuary of Bel at Palmyra (Tadmor, Syria)
temples
  Greco-Roman, 117
  Temple of Artemis (Gerasa), 120
  Temple of Bel. See Sanctuary of Bel at Palmyra (Tadmor, Syria)
Tempohomes, 390, *391*
Tequitqui style, 97
Terasse, Henri, 16
Terra Foundation, 292
terrorism, 237
  September 11, 2001, attack, 3, 13, 88, 346–47, 362
  see also ISIS
Thailand, Telok Manok Mosque, *146*
Thatcher, Margaret, 314
Third World, 314, 319, 345, 424
3D Mekanlar, 280
Thrift, Nigel, 331, 333
Tomb of Humayun, 62–63, 345
Tomb of Itmad al-Dawla, 63
tombs
  of Baba Hassan Deen and Hafiz Iqbal (Lahore), 428, *429–30*, 430
  Indian Mughal, 343

in Jakarta, 76
Javanese, 154
in Lahore, 427
mausoleum of Muhammad Ali Jinnah, 442, *443*
mausoleum of Mu'mina Khatun, 293, *294–95*
mausoleum of Yusuf ibn Kuthayr, 293, *295*
of Salam al-Din Chisti (Fatehpur-Sikri), 63
Shah-i Zinda (Samarqand), 34, *36*
tomb complex of the Muradiye (Bursa), 40n29
Tomb of Humayun, 62–63, 345
Tomb of Itmad al-Dawla, 63
Wali Songo mausolea, 151
see also Taj Mahal
Topçu Kışlası (Istanbul), 177
Topkapı Palace (Istanbul), 178
Topotek 1, 446, *448*
tourism, 327–334, 357–68
 at the Alhambra, 16
 AlUla, 330, 331
 in Egypt, 366
 Halal, 362
 Islamic, 357, 362, 366
 In Jordan, 359
 and mosques, 362, 364, 383
 riads, in Morocco, 358
 and urban preservation, 358
 see also tourist gaze
Tourist, The: A New Theory of the Leisure Class (MacCannell), 358–59
tourist gaze
 and modernity, 358–59
 at mosques, 362, 364
 pluralization of, 365–66
Toussaint, Manuel, 96
traditional architecture
 and architectural education, 224, 226, 229
 design principles of, 223, 226
 geographical frameworks of, 107
 Islamic, 3, 4, 14, 17, 76, 95, 103, 250, 252, 254, 341, 373, 389, 392
 Lebanese, 315

modernization of, 215, 255, 348, 412
preservation of, 47, 51–52, 384
and site assessment, 62
timelessness of, 426–27
transhumanism, 136
Transnational Mosque Architecture and Historical Memory in the Contemporary Middle East, The (Risvi), 103
transversality, 348
Treasures of Islam: Artistic Glories of the Muslim World (O'Kane), 32
Tripoli
 Artisanal Quarter at the Suq al Mushir, 49, *51*
 Mosque of Ahmad al-Karamanli, 49, *50*
 Muslim School of Arts and Crafts, 49
Tripoli Temple (Milwaukee), 100
Troelenberg, Eva, 288
Trouillot, Michel-Rolph, 82, 86, 87, 88
Trump, Donald, 167
Tschumi, Bernard, 438
Tuncer, Orhan Cezmi, 183
Tunis, 185
 Al Baraka, 318
 Gulf investments in, 314
 Société de Promotion du Lac de Tunis, 318
Tunisia, 313
 majolica tiles from, 49
 *medina*s, in 358
 neoliberalism in, 314
 preservation in, 358
 religious architecture in, 16
 studies of, 22
 see also Tunis
Turkey
 architectural history in, 177–85
 architecture in, 296
 archives in, 184–85
 Atatürk Kültür Merkezi, 177
 Grand Mosque of Bursa, 360
 Muslim-Ottoman heritage in, 366
 restorations in, 34
 secularization in, 377
 tiles from, 105

Topçu Kışlası, 177
see also Istanbul
Twittering Machine (Klee), 348, *349*, 350

U
UAE Pavilion, 328
Üç Şerefeli Mosque (Edirne), 37
Ugljen, Zlatko, 207
Uighur architecture, 34
Um, Nancy, 177
Umayyad architecture, 364
UNESCO, 19, 81, 357, 381, 439, *440*
    UNESCO World Heritage cities, 163
    UNESCO World Heritage Committee, 357
    UNESCO World Heritage Sites, 19, 330, 415
    see also heritage preservation
United Arab Emirates. *See* Abu Dhabi; Dubai
United Nations Development Programme (UNDP), 439
United States
    Islamic Center (Washington, DC), 14, 105–7, *106*
    mosques in, 95, 102–3, 105
    Shriner temples, 100
    Spanish mission architecture in, 97
    United States-Mexico-Canada Agreement (USMCA), 314
    White House, 350, 439
United States-Mexico-Canada Agreement (USMCA), 314
urban planning, 5, 47
urban preservation, 358
urban studies, 250
urban theory, secularism of, 390
urbanism, 413
    in North Africa, 17
    scholarly study of, 47
    studies of, 22
Uzbekistan, restorations in, 34

V
van Meeuwen Rene, *276*
Varada, *263*

Venice, 404
Venice Architecture Biennale, 347
Venice Charter, 381
Verdeil, Eric, 320
Victoria and Albert Museum, 269n2
Viñuales, Rodrigo Gutiérrez, 100
Viollet, Henry, 296
'Virtual Islamic Art History Seminar,' 281
virtual reality (VR), 163–64
Vkhutemas, 224
von Osten, Marion, 47

W
Wadi al-Qura, 330
Wali Songo mausolea, 151
waqf (charitable endowments), 375, 380
Watenpaugh, Heghnar, 34
water
    at the Alhambra, 65
    canals, 65
    fountains, 65
    pools, 64
    reservoirs, 65
    at the Taj Mahal, 63–65, 68n19
    water gardens, *147*
    water towers, 64, 68n10
Westbrook, Nigel, *276*
Westermann, Mariët, 273, 275
western architecture, 31, 34
    see also modernity
Whitfiedd, William, 442
Wikipedia, 280
Wilber, Donald, 293
wind-towers, 14
women
    as artisans, 98
    in mosques, 34
    Zaha Hadid Associates, 328
Woodward, Michelle L., 360
World Economic Forum (WEF), 314
World Trade Center (New York City), 346, 442
    see also terrorism
World Trade Organization (WTO), 314

Y
Yaqoob, Hafeez, 426
Yaqoob, Maulvi, 426
Yemen, 163–64, 166
    limited access to, 16, 34
    Mocha, 163, *164–65*
    Sanaa, 163
    war crimes in, 196
Yiftachel, Oren, 82

Z
Zaera-Polo, Alejandro, 328
Zaha Hadid Associates, 328
Zayed National Museum (Abu Dhabi), 328
Zhou, Zhenru, *278*
Zionism, 83, 84